Georg Knepler's critical study explores Mozart's life and works from many new perspectives, providing fresh insights into his music and the tempestuous times through which he lived. In what is more than just a biography, Professor Knepler takes a semiotic approach, explaining in readily accessible language the immediacy and universal appeal of Mozart's music. Based on a close reading of the family correspondence and a detailed look at Mozart's entire musical output, the book sheds new light on Mozart's creative psyche, his political leanings, his relation to the thoughts and currents of the Enlightenment, and the underlying basis of his musical expression. This is a book which raises important questions about Mozart the man, Mozart the towering genius, and the universal validity of his creations.

For John

WOLFGANG AMADÉ MOZART

Wolfgang Amadé Mozart. Oil painting by Barbara Krafft, Salzburg, 1819.
Though painted three decades after Mozart's death using likenesses supplied by his
sister (see MGG, IX, col. 738, no. 13), this painting is held to be one of the most
life-like and artistically valuable of all Mozart portraits.

Wolfgang Amadé Mozart

GEORG KNEPLER

Translated by

J. Bradford Robinson

PUBLISHED BY THE PRESS SYNDICATE OF THE UNIVERSITY OF CAMBRIDGE
The Pitt Building, Trumpington Street, Cambridge CB2 2RU, United Kingdom

CAMBRIDGE UNIVERSITY PRESS
The Edinburgh Building, Cambridge CB2 2RU, United Kingdom
40 West 20th Street, New York NY 10011–4211, USA
10 Stamford Road, Oakleigh, Melbourne 3166, Australia

Originally published in German as *Wolfgang Amadé Mozart: Annäherungen*
by Henschel Verlag, Berlin 1991 and © Henschel Verlag GmbH, Berlin 1991

First published in English by Cambridge University Press 1994 as
Wolfgang Amadé Mozart
English translation © Cambridge University Press 1994
Reprinted 1994, 1995
First paperback edition 1997

Printed in the United Kingdom at the University Press, Cambridge

Typeset in Sabon

A catalogue record for this book is available from the British Library

Library of Congress cataloguing in publication data
Knepler, Georg,
[Wolfgang Amadé Mozart. English]
Wolfgang Amadé Mozart/Georg Knepler: translated by J. Bradford Robinson
        p.   cm.
'Originally published in German . . . by Henschel Verlag, Berlin 1991' – T.p. verso
Includes bibliographical references and index.
ISBN 0 521 41972 7 (hardback)
I. Mozart, Wolfgang Amadeus, 1756–1791 – Criticism and interpretation.
II. Title.
ML410.M9K713   1994   780'.92–DC20   92–46591 CIP MN

ISBN 0 521 41972 7 hardback
ISBN 0 521 58823 5 paperback

Contents

Contents

Illustrations

Foreword

Looking back at the Mozart celebrations of 1991, it would be pointless to jeer at the excess and the commercialism; rather, we should be grateful for the many new publications and the performances of lesser-known – and, indeed, unknown – works. Now is perhaps a good time to take stock of the vast Mozart literature and to consider the future of Mozart studies. As work continues on watermarks, minor personalities of the time and obscure byways, as the music of lesser contemporary composers becomes available for study, and since we now have the opportunity to hear recorded performances of everything Mozart wrote, the need for a fresh overview becomes even greater. Biographies, picture books, studies of the operas and symphonies, books on the classical style and compendia proliferate, but there has been no attempt by a scholarly musician to impose his view on the whole extraordinary phenomenon. This is not to imply that we require from any one mind completeness of coverage, either of the historical background, the biography or the works, even if that were feasible.

The value and significance of the achievement of Jahn, Abert and Einstein have never been in doubt, although it is probably true that only the last of these has been at all widely read or consulted by an English readership. New scholarship, far-reaching developments in performance practice, and profound changes in the role and significance of all music in a rapidly developing and confusing (and confused) society, make a unified statement by a scholar of stature necessary and desirable. It is a tall order, one from which Mozart experts understandably shrink.

Georg Knepler's book on Mozart was published in Berlin in 1991. Having known him for over thirty years, it was obvious to me that he was supremely qualified to write the sort of book I have described. In his long life he has distinguished himself as a performer – as opera répétiteur and accompanist (at one stage to Karl Kraus!) – as a pedagogue – at the East Berlin Hochschule and Humboldt University – as a researcher – as chief editor of the journal *Beiträge zur Musikwissenschaft* – and as scholar and author in his two-volume

Musikgeschichte des 19. Jahrhunderts, the *Geschichte als Weg zum Musikverständnis*, the *Gedanken über Musik* and countless articles and essays on a wide diversity of subjects. Vast knowledge, experience and profound musicality, governed by an intellect of the highest order, are a sure foundation for the achieving of such a task.

A knowledge of the subtitle of the German edition, *Annäherungen* ('approaches'), and a glance at the chapter headings might lead one to expect a collection of rather freely related articles of disparate content. This is emphatically not the case. Knepler's book is constructed in a most intelligent, even cunning, way and possesses a logic and unity worthy of the finest compositions of its subject. These approaches – historical, biographical, analytical – have been organized into a seamless continuity which makes for compulsive reading.

Although to say that within the book there is a thesis might suggest an academic dryness which is quite absent from it, at its heart there is a standpoint about music which is fundamental to Knepler's thinking, and which stems from his Marxist convictions. A clue to this is given by the title of Chapter 20, where the approach is to demonstrate the close thematic relationships between the works which are instrumental and those involving texts and to draw some conclusions. With some daring, Knepler puts interpretations upon such thematic correspondences and apparent self-quotation and invites us to listen to the so-called abstract arguments of sonata, quartet and symphony in a different way. In my opinion, his insights are not only illuminating and convincing, but also frequently inspired.

The other case which Knepler argues with scholarly conviction and some passion is that Mozart was not the anti-intellectual innocent some writers have suggested, even less the buffoon we have seen in the cinema, lacking all interest in ideas, social problems and politics. Rather that, in spite of an extraordinary childhood and a hectically active professional life, he possessed a modest library and read, discussed and reflected.

Since this book's appearance in Germany, Europe has been politically and ideologically transformed. It is, for me, all the more moving when Knepler transgresses scholarly good conduct, discards the mask of the dispassionate academic and, in his concluding chapter, speaks as a person. The placing of himself as man and musician in an historic context, which, like Mozart's, is one of revolutionary turbulence, makes his rejection of attitudes, some past, many persisting, especially eloquent and emphasizes the wisdom and humanity of his summing up.

David Blake
Professor of Music
University of York

Preface

On countless occasions throughout his life Mozart signed his name 'Wolfgang Amadé Mozart'. The number of times he wrote 'Wolfgang Amadeus' amounts to a grand total of three, and then always in a spirit of tomfoolery, as in the following example: 'Wolfgang et Amadeus Mozartich, Augspurg den 25 octobrich 1700 Siebenzigich'. Admittedly the question of whether we should choose the French or Latin form of Mozart's second Christian name is hardly critical. After all, he was baptized under neither of the two, but rather under the Greek form 'Theophilus', and every now and then we even encounter the German form 'Gottlieb'. But the fact that posterity has settled with such unanimity for 'Amadeus' is symptomatic of the scant attention paid, then and now, to an extremely rich corpus of source material.

In other words, the way I chose to write Mozart's name in the title of this book is revealing of my method. My working principle was to investigate the many hundreds of pages of his letters and the many thousands of pages of his scores – all of them, even in their most seemingly insignificant aspects, expressive of an incomparable mind – and to read them as closely as possible for their overt and tacit opinions. Today, fortunately, this approach is no longer a rarity. Researchers and performers alike are increasingly in agreement that what Mozart put down on manuscript or writing paper is still far from completely understood.

But Mozart's written legacy has had a difficult time making headway. Mountains of interpretations and judgements, many of them distorted by misconceptions nearly two centuries old, as well as myriad performances of his music, translations of his writings and productions of his operas – all now weigh ponderously upon his œuvre. It is time once again to excavate that œuvre.

It would be foolish to believe that creative achievements of the magnitude we are dealing with here could be illuminated in their entirety. It is and will always remain inconceivable that this wealth of superb music could proceed from a single brain within the shockingly short time span of less than three decades, music that seems at times irreconcilable with itself, so various are its shades and hues. After all, we are equally at a loss to explain how Shakespeare, within a single year, was able to create both *Macbeth* and *The Tempest*.

But our inability to account for the genesis of such larger-than-life achievements of the human mind – how could we when even much simpler mental processes remain beyond our grasp! – should not be taken to mean that the products of this mind are themselves inexplicable. Mozart's music is, to be sure, inexhaustible in its plenitude, always summoning forth new explanations, displaying new facets and vistas. We never seem to come to the bottom of it. But these properties are quite different from obscurity, inaccessibility and enigma. Mozart himself sought and offered closeness: he was happy and proud to find people who seemed to love and understand his music. A genius is a human being like the rest of us, only more so. We have no cause to act as though his music were fundamentally unintelligible.

Even so, we will not advance far in our attempt to approach this music if we separate Mozart the composer from Mozart the thinker. This book proceeds on the assumption that Mozart was a keen observer, a critical judge and an accurate reader. He knew how to form his own opinions of events; as a Freemason he tried actively to intervene where he thought help was needed; and he learnt to think in the philosophical categories of the Enlightenment. This Mozart cannot be kept apart from Mozart the composer. We must therefore direct our attention not only to the way he responded musically to events in his surroundings, but also to the way he subordinated his life to his creative impulses, for example in his radical and seemingly irrational move to Vienna in 1781.

An approach of this sort cannot be done justice in a book that concentrates entirely on music. Analyses of individual pieces or groups of works, no matter how fruitful, will not add up to reveal what Mozart's inspiration responded to. Nor will they uncover the processes that link an initial stimulus, the composer's creative and developmental faculties, the writing down of a musical text, its performance by musicians, and its reception by listeners of many different types.

Conversely, there is no way that a book that focuses largely or even exclusively on biography can revitalize our sense of Mozart the musician. True, interdisciplinary methods of research and presentation are indispensable, as the present book hopes to demonstrate. But the essence of music cannot be subsumed in history or cultural history, nor in a general theory of art. To speak about Mozart is to speak about music. Our central task, then, is to probe this music in search of its intrinsic laws, however entangled they may be with other techniques or modes of behaviour.

Mozart's achievement was not without its assumptions and postulates. A vast panoply of events, experiences and encounters took part in it. To approach it, then, we must constantly start out from new angles and perspectives. Readers of this book are asked to give themselves over to its premisses, which will lead them now into the events of Mozart's life, now into an analysis of a musical problem, now into a glance at general history and the intellectual ambience in which Mozart did his composing. In the end, however, the focus will fall more and more clearly on what, in the final analysis, is the only thing that matters: Mozart's music.

There is one thing which this book cannot offer, and that is completeness. To say more or less inconsequential things about the bulk of Mozart's works, or even about every one of them, is a path I have deliberately rejected. Instead, I have adopted the course of using selected examples to explain what, to my mind, most needs to be said.

There has been no need for footnotes and commentary. All references to sources have been incorporated in the text in the form of keywords and abbreviations that can easily be followed up with the aid of the bibliography. Only one particular kind of reference, and that the most frequent, deserves special mention here: dates in parentheses always refer to the Mozart family correspondence.

Acknowledgements

It is impossible for me to itemize all the countless suggestions, remarks, criticisms and other acts of assistance I have received over the years. I can only ask my colleagues and friends to believe me when I say that my thanks are not less profound if I list their names in alphabetical order, than if I vainly attempted to describe their assistance or to arrange their names in order of importance for the writing of this book.

None the less, I would like to single out a few persons for special mention. One of the richest and most stimulating minds it has been my good fortune to encounter was responsible for much encouragement in my study of Mozart: Harry Goldschmidt (1910-86). My friends Hanns-Werner Heister and Gerhard Scheit read large sections of my typescript, adding many valuable annotations which I have painstakingly attempted to take into account. Renate Lerche, reader at the publishing house of Henschel, struck a rare and admirable balance of empathy and critical detachment, of meticulousness and conciliation.

In their different ways, these people and the following were involved in giving my book its final form: Philippe A. Autexier, Evelyn Bartlitz, Manfred Bierwisch, David Blake, Kurt Blaukopf, Ursula Bönisch, Miroslav Cerny, Friedrich Dieckmann, Ludwig Finscher, Martin Fontius, Wolfgang Goldhan, Peter Gülke, Florita and Axel Hesse, Hans-Gunter Hoke, Nicholas Jacobs, Jaroslav Jiránek, Christian Kaden, Reiner Kluge, Manfred Kossok, Rita and Günter Lembke, Rosmarie and Konrad Mann, Angela Mingardi, Walter Pass, Luigi Pestalozza, Pierluigi Petrobelli, Inge and Samuel M. Rapoport, Adelbert Schussner, Heinrich Scheel, Katharine Thomson.

Georg Knepler
Berlin-Grünau, May, 1990

Abbreviations and sigla occurring in the text and bibliography

BA   *Goethe: Berliner Ausgabe in 22 Bänden und einem Supplementband* (Berlin, GDR, 1965–78).

Briefe   *Mozart: Briefe und Aufzeichnungen, Gesamtausgabe*, ed. International Mozarteum Foundation in Salzburg, compiled and annotated by Wilhelm A. Bauer and Otto Erich Deutsch, I-IV (Kassel, 1962/3); V-VI: *Kommentare*, ed. Joseph Heinz Eibl (Kassel, 1971); VII: *Register*, ed. Joseph Heinz Eibl (Kassel, 1975).

BzMw   *Beiträge zur Musikwissenschaft* (Berlin, GDR, 1959–93).

Encyclo-pédie   *Encyclopédie ou Dictionnaire raisonné des sciences, des arts et des métiers*, ed. Denis Diderot and Jean Baptiste le Rond d'Alembert (Paris, 1751–72) (seventeen volumes of text and eleven of illustrations).

GDR   German Democratic Republic.

MGG   *Die Musik in Geschichte und Gegenwart: Allgemeine Enzyklopädie der Musik*, ed. Friedrich Blume (Kassel and Basle, 1949–79).

NMA   *Wolfgang Amadeus Mozart: Neue Ausgabe sämtlicher Werke* (Kassel, 1955–91). The Roman numeral indicates the series, the first Arabic numeral the group of works, and the next one the volume number.

Translator's note

Quotations from the letters of the Mozart family generally follow the well-known English translation by Emily Anderson (Macmillan: London, Melbourne and Toronto, 2nd edn, 1966. © Executors of the late Miss Emily Anderson, 1966), adapted wherever necessary by the author and translator. Many passages not included in Anderson's edition appear here in English for the first time. The loss of Mozart's idiomatic and often revealing German orthography is, it is hoped, compensated for by a gain in intelligibility for readers who are not thoroughly conversant in German. Wherever applicable, German-language quotations are given in English translations – likewise adapted as necessary – from O. E. Deutsch, *Mozart: A Documentary Biography* (Stanford University Press, Stanford 1965. © 1965, 1966 A. & C. Black Ltd).

Chapter 1
Outline of a remarkable life

On 27 January 1756 Anna Maria Mozart gave birth to the seventh offspring of her marriage with Leopold Mozart, a violinist and chamber musician in the service of the Prince-Archbishop of Salzburg. The child, a boy, was baptized one day later under the name of Joannes Chrysostomos Wolfgangus Theophilus. Five of their previous children had died in childhood. Only 'Wolfgangerl', as he was soon called, and his sister Maria Anna or 'Nannerl', four-and-a-half years older than he, were to survive.

When Mozart's father began to give music lessons to his highly gifted daughter at about the age of eight it soon transpired that Wolfgangerl had even more extraordinary musical abilities than she, and before long he had overtaken her. He was not quite six years old when his father decided to display the talents of his two prodigies at the court of the Prince Elector in Munich. From 1762 to 1779 the Mozarts undertook many lengthy journeys, including one lasting more than three years. Some of these involved the entire family – father, mother, daughter and son. Others were taken without the mother, and still others involved father and son alone. They travelled to the mighty courts of Vienna, Paris and London, to the principal centres of music in Italy, and to a multitude of minor courts, aristocratic palaces and bourgeois houses. They also held concerts in public. The children often performed for hours on end, sometimes two and even three times on a single day.

In the meantime Mozart's father had become deputy Kapellmeister in Salzburg. But much to his dismay and disappointment he was never to advance beyond this position. Wolfgang, with his remarkable talents, was meant to obtain a higher income and a more liberal and secure appointment, one less troubled by humiliations and setbacks, not only for his own benefit but also for the good of the family. To be sure, by 1769, at the age of thirteen, he had become concert master at the Salzburg court of the Prince-Archbishop, though without stipend; and in 1772 he was appointed *maestro di capella* of Salzburg cathedral with a modest salary that was later even tripled. But, understandably, this was hardly deemed sufficient, the less so as Leopold, a competent and intelligent musician, also hoped to escape from Salzburg. Nor were these hopes far-fetched: in 1756, the year of Mozart's birth, he published *Versuch einer gründlichen Violinschule*, a highly regarded treatise on the violin that underwent several reissues and was translated into French and Dutch.

By the time he was about fifteen Mozart was too old to be a child prodigy, yet too young to be a serious applicant for a position. By then Nannerl had grown to become a thoroughly competent pianist and piano teacher in Salzburg, earning the lifelong respect of her brother. Hence, the main object of the third Italian tour undertaken by Mozart *père* and *fils* in 1772–3, as well as the journeys to Vienna in 1773 and Munich in 1774–5, was primarily to obtain a *scrittura* – an opera commission – and only secondarily to give concerts. Their stays in Salzburg began increasingly to seem like interruptions in their journeys and preparations for future ones. Mozart's first lengthy tenure in Salzburg, from March 1775 to September 1777, may have been a result of the more stringent regulations following the installation of the new Prince-Archbishop Colloredo.

When Mozart reached the age of twenty-two, however, it seemed that the time had come for a fundamental change. Notice was given on the position in Salzburg, and Mozart, this time accompanied only by his mother, left on 23 September 1777 to try his luck elsewhere, first at the courts of Munich and Mannheim. When a position failed to materialize at either court he extended the journey, after some hesitation, to include Paris. Here, however, he met with one failure after another, despite the sound advice and letters of recommendation of his father. Of course Mozart performed with success both privately and in public; and of course a number of his compositions were successfully premièred. But his primary goal, an opera commission, never came about. He turned down a by no means unfavourable appointment as organist in Versailles despite the admonitions of his father to give it serious consideration. And he suffered a grievous blow. In summer 1778 his mother fell ill and died within two weeks.

Various circumstances now forced Mozart to leave Paris although several opportunities had seemingly arisen in the meantime. A renewed attempt to settle in Mannheim failed, and he suffered a bitter disappointment when the first great love of his life, Aloysia Weber, a highly gifted soprano, rejected him. Thereafter he had no choice but to admit defeat and return to the employ of the Prince-Archbishop in Salzburg, from whom his father had obtained a promise to reinstate him as court and cathedral organist with a modest salary. It was now mid-January of 1779.

By this time Mozart had become a masterly composer. He had written thirteen operas and other works for the stage, sixteen Mass settings, a large number of church compositions and many symphonies, divertimenti, string quartets, piano pieces and songs.

It was clear not only to Mozart himself but also to his father and sister that he would not remain in Salzburg. Curiously, the immediate occasion for this overdue change came from his employer Colloredo, who had journeyed to Vienna together with his court in order to attend the coronation of Joseph II. He now summoned Mozart to Vienna to complete his musical retinue. To Mozart, Vienna had long seemed an advantageous place to be. It was particularly so now that Joseph had become sole occupant of the throne following the death of his mother Maria Theresia in November 1780, for Mozart was in sympathy with Joseph's plans of reform. Determined to remain in Vienna, Mozart provoked a breach with the Archbishop. From this point on, from March 1781 until his death almost eleven years later, Vienna remained Mozart's permanent place of residence.

The first few years boded well. Mozart married Konstanze Weber, the sister of Aloysia, though much to the apprehension of his father and sister, who thought the Weber family beneath their station. From this union issued six children, of whom, however, only two survived to adulthood. The series of triumphs in Vienna began in March 1782 with the first performance of *Die Entführung aus dem Serail*, which had been commissioned by the Emperor. In the years that followed Mozart was brilliantly successful as a composer, a virtuoso pianist and improviser, and as a piano teacher. But a permanent position with a regular income continued to elude him. Not until 1787 was he given the title of composer to the royal-imperial chamber. This obligated him to write dance music for court balls and brought him an annual income of 800 gulden. Gluck, Mozart's predecessor in this honorific title, had received 2,000 gulden.

In 1784 Mozart joined a Viennese masonic lodge. At that time the goals of the Freemasons were to overcome the privileges of absolutist society and to display mutual respect and assistance for all men. That Mozart took these goals seriously is evidenced by the men he associated with in his lodge and, above all, by the compositions of his final years.

By the time he was fifteen, most of Mozart's works revealed a mastery of musical craftsmanship, a balanced application of the various elements of musical language, and originality of invention. They made it abundantly clear that this young lad was moving on from the astonishing achievements of a child prodigy to become a composer of genius. But it was not until the 1780s, when Mozart learnt to adopt topical and highly provocative subjects for his stage works and to bring his vocal and instrumental music into fruitful interplay, that he reached the pinnacle of his century and became its outstanding composer.

For this Mozart had to pay dearly. There can be little doubt that a number of his aristocratic patrons dropped him after he had taken up the cause of the third estate in *Le nozze di Figaro*, premièred in Vienna on 1 May 1786. And in 1788 – a year in which Emperor Joseph set out on a new campaign against the Turks, many noble families fled the capital, the theatre and concert life declined and Konstanze fell ill – Mozart found himself in disastrous straits.

During this same period his fame began to increase outside Vienna. Mozart's music, particularly his late works, assumed a special role in Prague, Mannheim and Mainz, where it accompanied the emergence of a bourgeois-democratic intellectual culture and a revolt against the privileges of the nobility. Wherever the theatre and the concert hall became forums of bourgeois public life (in the sense demanded by Friedrich Schiller), Mozart was played, esteemed and loved. Thus, his brief journeys to Prague in 1786, 1787 and 1791, and to the Rhineland in 1790 with a short stay in Mainz, were moments of light in a world that seemed to be darkening about him. Vienna, too, offered him one of these moments. On 30 September 1791 Mozart, for the first time, appeared with a major stage work before an audience not made up primarily of the aristocracy and the grand bourgeoisie when *Die Zauberflöte* was given in a suburban Viennese theatre. Its success was instantaneous and lasting, but it came a mere nine weeks before his death. There is something comforting in the thought that he took pleasure not only in the raucous applause and cries for encores, but also in what he called 'the silent applause' that greeted this work and cheered the final days of his life.

Nothing reliable is known about the cause of Mozart's death. According to Landon (1988, pp. 178f.), he probably died of a streptococcal infection acquired on 18 November 1791 during his attendance at a meeting at the masonic lodge, compounded by kidney failure, bloodlettings, cerebral haemorrhaging, and finally bronchial and pulmonary pneumonia. Nor can we completely discount Mozart's own suspicion that he had been poisoned, though if so, we have no way of knowing who the murderer might have been. Mozart died shortly after midnight on 5 December 1791.

Chapter 2

From child prodigy to genius

Mozart's musicality as a child was obviously unique. True, the fact that at the age of three he explored the keyboard for thirds and took delight in their euphony can hardly be called extraordinary. But the same cannot be said of the dozen little piano pieces he learnt to play within a year when his father started giving him lessons at the age of four. He was not yet five when he mastered two longer pieces, each within the space of half an hour. And it was at the age of five that he composed small pieces, meaning in this case that he invented them at the keyboard. (He was still unable to write them down; that was his father's task.) Not long thereafter he played the second part of a trio on a small violin without having received any instruction, and he was seven-and-a-half when it was discovered that he could play the organ, including the pedals, once again without any previous instruction. From his sixth year he also learnt to write down his own compositions – his first attempts are said to have been made when he was five – and at the age of eight he was given a notebook of his own which he proceeded to fill with astonishingly varied and imaginative pieces, some of them quite long. It was obvious that extraordinary things were going on in the boy's mind.

Looking a little more closely, we can see that Mozart's abilities were made up of several components. He had an astonishingly good ear; he could apparently detect eighth-tone discrepancies in pitch. His musical memory was phenomenal; thousands of pieces must have been stored in his brain, all of them complete. Still more astonishing was his ability to improvise; even as a boy he could elaborate given themes into fugues at the keyboard without preparation. The technical prowess he displayed on the piano, organ and violin was apparently limitless.

Now, if need be, we can quantify the components of musical talent. They can be measured with greater or lesser accuracy and compared with the accomplishments of other people. In fact, this has already been done in countless publications in music psychology (a general discussion of musical talent can be found in Helga de la Motte 1985, pp. 257–401). But there is little that we can conclude from these studies. For one thing, not all components of musical talent are measurable: there is no way, for example, of holding a yardstick to the imagination with which the eight-year-old Mozart wrote down his ideas. For another, even the rarest aptitude for music will lead nowhere unless it goes hand in hand with other aptitudes and meets favourable conditions; it is certainly not sufficient in itself to turn every talent into a genius. Superior musical abilities have even been observed here and there in people with mental disorders (one such case is recounted by de la Motte 1985, pp. 334f.).

We must, then, beware of the tacit assumption that Mozart was predestined to genius from his childhood. In this case genius would be equatable with the possession of an abnormally bounteous gift of musical abilities. Physiologists claim that what we receive from nature are predispositions; whether and how these predispositions develop is a question of circumstance. Ordinary observations confirm this view. Not all child prodigies with astonishing talents have grown up to become major composers, and, conversely, not all major composers started their careers as stupendous prodigies. Indeed, musical prodigies are more likely to become highly esteemed virtuoso instrumentalists when they come of age. Moreover, prodigies in other fields such as mathematics, chess or, recently, cybernetics, can accomplish remarkable things without necessarily having remarkable careers later. They have one thing in common: their brains are organized in such a way that they can produce extraordinary achievements within a special, circumscribed area through an interplay of mental faculties – gifts of observation, wealth of invention, shrewdness of deduction and powers of memory. This interplay, at our present stage of knowledge, is largely obscure and opaque. For the psychology of human creativity it is a crucial question – and one which, so far as I know, has yet to be researched – to discover whether, and if so in what way, experiences from the world outside this special field impinge on the mind of the prodigy. This question, while perhaps extraneous in the case of chess, is critical for achievements in the arts.

Fortunately, in the case of Mozart, we have a rich body of observations at our disposal. There exists, for example, an astute and telling account of his early childhood by his sister Nannerl, who observed her giant of a little brother lovingly and apparently without envy from early childhood. Following his death she had this to say of him (Deutsch 1965, p. 493):

> Mozart's over-rich imagination was so lively and so vivid, even in childhood, at a time when it still lies dormant in ordinary men, and perfected that which it had once taken hold of, to such an

extent, that one cannot imagine anything more extraordinary and in some respects more moving than its enthusiastic creations; which, because the little man still knew so little of the real world, were as far removed from it as the heavens themselves. Just one illustration: As the journeys which we used to make (he and I, his sister) took him to different lands, he would think out a kingdom for himself as we travelled from one place to another, and this he called the Kingdom of Back [*Rücken*] – why by this name, I can no longer recall. This kingdom and its inhabitants were endowed with everything that could make of them good and happy children. He was the King of this land – and this notion became so rooted within him, and he carried it so far, that our servant, who could draw a little, had to make a chart of it, and he would dictate the names of the cities, market-towns and villages to him.

Similar juvenile fantasies by the English writers Charlotte and Emily Brontë (1816–55 and 1818–48) deserve to be mentioned in this connection as their father's accounts help us to understand how childhood fantasies gradually begin to merge with impressions from the real world. When the two girls were, respectively, seven and nine years old they began to write stories together with their eight-year-old brother Branwell, and later with the youngest sister Anne. The children were given twelve tin soldiers, which they promptly supplied with names and put through fantastic adventures. These adventures gradually began to take in reports and events recounted to them by their father from books and newspapers, thereby turning the children into avid readers. The final upshot was a series of interlocking novels covering thousands of pages, a sort of trial run for the works of genius that Charlotte and Emily were to produce in their adulthood.

Mozart, of course, did not become a novelist – the distinction is worth noting because music and the novel bear completely different relations to reality. And as we are dealing with a region which is virtually uncharted, but all the more hotly contested, we would be well advised to pay close attention not only to those experiences and impressions under which Mozart's talent evolved, but also to the additional predispositions that took part in this evolution. A bent toward universality is, after all, often one ingredient of genius – witness Michelangelo, da Vinci and Goethe.

Nannerl's account of the 'Kingdom of Back' explicitly states that this was just one instance of the boy's teeming fantasy. The same account informs us that Mozart had learnt fencing before the age of twelve, that he was specially adept at imitating card tricks at sight, and that the work of draughtsmen, painters and engravers captured his fancy to such an extent that he asked for samples of their work, which he then carefully preserved. The variety of his talents and his openness in all directions is also stressed in an account by Schachtner, a writer and musician who was a close friend of the Mozart family (Deutsch 1965, pp. 452ff.): Mozart in his childhood had

> a fiery disposition, [and] any object was enough to arouse his interest... Whatever he was given to learn occupied him so completely that he put all else, even music, to one side... When he was doing sums, the table, chairs, walls, even the floor were covered with chalked figures.

Mozart never lost his interest in numbers. There exists a 'page of musical sketches on which he had begun to figure out the sum which the chess player would have received from the King, in the famous Oriental story', writes Einstein (1946, p. 36), referring to the legendary Persian sage who asked for a grain of corn on the first square of the chess board and double the amount on each successive square. Nannerl likewise remarked (April 1792) that as a youngster her brother had 'the desire to master whatever he saw, and he had great dexterity in drawing and calculations'. Even later in life, she continues in the same source, 'his brain was always occupied with music and *with other branches of knowledge* as well' (italics mine). This same view is endorsed by his father (23 February 1778): 'In all branches of knowledge you have always grasped everything with the greatest of ease.' Nor should we overlook a later account which has fallen victim to the widespread low opinion of Konstanze Mozart. On 28 August 1799, for a projected biography of Mozart, she sent 'missives' to Breitkopf & Härtel in Leipzig, adding the remarkable comment that there was much to be learnt from them 'about the traits of his character: his educational attainments, his exceeding tenderness toward myself, the goodness of his nature, his forms of recreation, his love of arithmetic and algebra (as demonstrated by several books [n.b.!]), his whimsy, which at times could be almost Shakespearean, as Herr Rochlitz once remarked of his musical whimsy, and of which I will send examples'.

There is, of course, no shortage of evidence for Mozart's gifts and aptitude for the theatre. We need not attach undue importance to his appearance at the age of five in a student production at Salzburg University, in a comedy with music, as one of the *salii* or 'leapers' (probably meaning dancers). But it is surely remarkable that during his Vienna years he should have written a (fragmentary) sketch for a farce and another for a comedy in the style of the Viennese 'Hans-Wurst' theatre (*Briefe* IV, pp. 167–73). Neither of them is devoid of interest, and the latter is theatrically very effective. Doubtless equally effective on stage, though not in a sense that we usually associate with Mozart, was his appearance as Harlequin. In the carnival season of

1783, when Mozart was twenty-seven, he performed a half-hour pantomime during the interval of a ball, a pantomime which he himself had invented and set to music (*Briefe* III, p. 259, and *NMA* II/6/2, pp. 120ff.). Its five characters embodied traditional figures from the *commedia dell'arte*: Aloysia Weber, formerly Mozart's beloved and now his sister-in-law, played Colombine; her husband, the actor and painter Joseph Lange, took the part of Pierrot; two others played Pantalon and the Doctor. Mozart reserved the part of Harlequin for himself. At his first entrance, cleverly postponed until No. 7 of an estimated two dozen musical numbers, he 'peeps out of the wardrobe'. Later, disguised as a Turk, he fights his brother-in-law Pierrot for the hand of Colombine-Aloysia, losing both the battle and his life, only to be resurrected later. The first half of No. 14 is surely a parody of a funeral march for the death of Harlequin; the second half, containing a *maggiore* variant of his entrance music, doubtless accompanied the resurrection of Harlequin–Mozart. In sum, this is a stage work which, we can see, abounded in irony and deeper meaning. The same might also be said of Mozart's appearance at a masked ball disguised as an Indian philosopher (in the eighteenth century the word 'philosopher' had a special meaning, with Enlightenment overtones) distributing handbills with scathing comments on the aristocracy.

We had best view Mozart's theatrical gifts, too, in their various components and in their evolution. Their basic component is probably to be found in Mozart's physical agility – his fondness for bodily motion and dance steps, for gesture and mime. At the age of seventeen, in a letter from Leopold to his wife (Vienna, 8 September 1773), Mozart added the following brief postscript: 'Wolfgangerl has no time to write, for he has nothing to do. He is walking up and down the room like a dog with fleas.' Konstanze's youngest sister Sophie Haibl, herself an astute and sensitive observer – she left a moving account of Mozart's last days (Deutsch 1965, pp. 524–7) and Mozart apparently had a high opinion of her – describes this side of Mozart's personality as follows (Deutsch 1965, p. 537):

> Even when he was washing his hands in the morning, he walked up and down in the room, never standing still, tapped one heel against the other the while and was always deep in thought... Also, his feet and hands were always in motion, he was always playing with something, be it his hat, pockets, watch-fob, tables, chairs, as if they were a clavier.

This picture agrees with a note which Mozart sent his sister from Milan at the age of fifteen (31 August 1771): 'My only amusement is to communicate [by sign language] with the deaf and dumb, for I can do that to perfection.'

A gift for the theatre, of course, does not reside solely in special talents. It also takes recourse to a large extent in ordinary human capabilities. Those who have no knowledge of human nature, who cannot observe and project themselves into other people, who have no understanding of human psychology, will never amount to anything in the theatre. The acuity of Mozart's observations even as a child, and the sometimes uncanny sensitivity with which he reacted to other people (in both a positive and negative sense), are part of his genius.

Yet we must not overlook another, darker side of Mozart's personality, one which has been pointed out and emphasized by Jean Massin (*Komponisten*, pp. 211–14). Massin, who in 1954, with Brigitte Massin, published one of the central books on Mozart (hitherto sadly neglected in German and Anglo-American scholarship), directs our attention to Mozart's manner of 'constantly questioning the real identity of people, and perhaps of himself'. Writing from Paris on 29 May 1778, Mozart relates that he is doing 'tolerably well' and continues, 'but I often can't make any sense of things – I am neither hot nor cold – and don't find much pleasure in anything.' Even one of his last letters, written to Konstanze in Baden on 7 July 1791, betrays a similar mood. Admittedly he connects this mood with the forced separation from his wife and contrasts it with his memory of 'how merry and childish we were together at Baden'. But one is forced to agree with Massin that outbursts of this sort give us a glimpse into the depths of Mozart's psyche. The passage reads as follows: 'I can't describe what I have been feeling – a kind of emptiness that just hurts, a kind of longing that is never satisfied and thus never ceases but persists and even increases from day to day.'

Mozart's gifts, perhaps even mania, for the theatre would never have come to full fruition had he concentrated on musical craftsmanship alone, no matter how intense that concentration. This inherently plausible claim can even be documented in several instances. In 1765, when Mozart was nine years old, his family was paid a visit in their London lodgings by the English savant Daines Barrington, who later set down his impressions in writing (Deutsch 1965, pp. 95–100). At Barrington's request Mozart improvised an aria of love and an aria of rage or anger at the keyboard. The latter was based on the Italian word *perfido*, part of the stock-in-trade of Italian opera seria that would even play a role in *Don Giovanni*. During his aria of rage Wolfgang 'worked himself up to such a pitch, that he beat his harpsichord like a person possessed, rising sometimes in his chair' (p. 98). We can well imagine what this sounded like. First of all, Barrington's circumspect report does not hide the fact that the music remained well within the bounds of convention, that though above average it was by no means 'amazingly capital'. We also possess an opera aria of Mozart's – indeed, his earliest surviving aria of all – which the boy wrote down during the same year in London (K21). And Barrington was right. The astonishing thing is that a nine-year-old could create, much less improvise, such a well-rounded and professional opera aria at all, despite its occasional infelicities. But it is neither outstanding nor the least bit unconventional. What the boy set to music was apparently not inspired by his own observations of reality. His relation to the emotions presented in these pieces – their 'affects', to use the language of the time – was much the same as the King of Back's to his kingdom. The boy's unique gifts and impressionability overlapped with an underdeveloped awareness of the world. His music drew, as it must, on received conventions, which of course had themselves arisen from observations of reality. It would not be far-fetched to assume that what jolted the boy from his chair during his improvisation was a juvenile imitation of stage histrionics.

Now, it so happens that we have evidence from Mozart's own pen, both musical and epistolary, on the way he transformed anger into music during his maturity. The piece in question is Osmin's famous rage aria 'Solche hergelaufne Laffen', No. 3 from *Die Entführung*. As we shall see later, this aria would not have come to be as we know it if it were not for experiences of a quite non-musical sort.

Stage histrionics were part and parcel of Mozart's education. In the course of his life he must have visited the theatre hundreds of times – in Salzburg, in the countries on his tours, in Vienna. And he probably attended as many tragedies, comedies and farces as operas. In Chapter 10 we shall see how, at the time Mozart arrived in Vienna, the city's theatrical life was undergoing profound changes that influenced the new spirit of the age which he encountered there. A letter of summer 1781 discloses that Vienna's actors left a lasting impression on him. One of the contemporary giants of the stage, Friedrich Ludwig Schröder (1744–1816), had just begun his tenure at Vienna's Burgtheater a few months previously.

Mozart's genius, then, is not simply the sum total of his musical gifts. Another gift, but one which is not always combined with musical aptitude, is what Schachtner (Deutsch 1965, p. 452) referred to as the boy's 'fiery disposition': his boundless inquisitiveness. It was nurtured during Mozart's early years of travel, which his father shrewdly organized into educational journeys offering opportunities for instruction. Mozart himself was fully aware of this. Writing from Paris on 11 September 1778, he exclaims:

> I assure you that people who do not travel (I mean those who cultivate the arts and learning) are indeed miserable creatures; and I protest that unless the Archbishop allows me to travel

every second year, I can't possibly accept the engagement. A fellow of mediocre talent will remain a mediocrity, whether he travels or not; but one of superior talent (which without impiety I cannot deny that I possess) will go to seed, if he always remains in the same place.

In his most impressionable years Mozart saw, with open eyes and ears, how people of the most various sorts behaved: both well and ill; in everyday surroundings, in places of work and as depicted on stage; in theatres, at fairs and at public executions; at court, in the palaces of the nobility and in the manors of the bourgeoisie; in church and in the masonic lodge. And he did so at a time when his contemporaries were performing deeds that men are only capable of performing when centuries-old historical developments come to fruition.

It is only in these contexts, then, that we can understand Mozart's concept of music, a concept which he himself put into words in an unexpected location.

Chapter 3
'Expressing convictions and thoughts ... in notes'

On 8 November 1777 Mozart wrote a letter to his father from Mannheim in honour of his fifty-eighth birthday. At that time Mozart himself was almost twenty-two and had already taken the decisive steps on his path to inimitability. It was left to a physicist, Gunthard Born, in an important and amiable book on Mozart (we will have more to say about this book later), to point out the underlying significance of these well-known and oft-quoted lines (G. Born 1985, p. 12). Mozart's letter reads as follows:

> Dearest Papa!
> I cannot write in verse; I am no poet. I cannot arrange the parts of speech so artfully as to produce effects of light and shade; I am no painter. Not even by signs and gestures can I express my convictions and thoughts; I am no dancer. But I can do so in notes; I am a musician. So tomorrow at Cannabich's I shall play on the clavier a whole congratulatory composition in honour both of your name day and your birthday.

The most striking thing about Mozart's birthday greeting is his choice of words to indicate what he knows himself capable of expressing in notes. It would have been in keeping with the style of the times, particularly for a birthday greeting, if he had written about emotions and 'affects', about feelings and sensations. But no, he speaks of convictions and thoughts.

The word 'convictions' – *Gesinnungen* – can be found elsewhere in Mozart's writings. Remonstrating with his father (30 January 1782) when the latter accused Konstanze of having a 'poor set of convictions' [*schlechte Gesinnungsart*], Mozart countered that he could not possibly love her if she 'maintained such convictions' [*Gesinnungen*]. In the language of the eighteenth century this word, and its related form *gesinnt sein* (to be convinced of or disposed toward), were nothing unusual. Indeed, they probably occurred more frequently than in our own century, with more or less the same meaning, except that greater emphasis was laid on the object of those convictions. At roughly the same time that Mozart wrote his letter, Lessing, in a preface to *Nathan der Weise*, could confess that 'Nathan's conviction against all positive religion has long been my own.' We must be forceful, claimed Moses Mendelssohn in 1789 (1978, p. 91), if 'our convictions are to be noble, our actions reasonable and our lives usefully employed'. Goethe, among many other examples, wrote that a certain person 'was not disposed to give way'. Schiller remarked that the prince knew 'how I am disposed toward him'. And when C. F. D. Schubart published his auto-biography in 1791 it bore the title *Schubarts Leben und Gesinnungen*.

Mozart's letter is carefully phrased even down to its punctuation, with its fourfold alternation of semicolon and full stop. Even the words 'not even' are significant, for what Mozart called 'signs and gestures' – *Deuten* and *Pantomime* – was apparently his second greatest talent. Yet not even they were sufficient to express his convictions and thoughts. Granted that Mozart, as always when dealing with his father, was trying to put himself in a favourable light, we still have every cause to take the lines of his letter literally.

To do so, however, is to concede that Mozart, unlike many of his present-day interpreters, related his music to non-musical reality. At the very most the word 'thoughts', if taken by itself, might refer to music alone, for Mozart also used the word to mean musical ideas. But convictions can only refer to a complex of meanings adumbrated by terms such as 'attitudes', 'persuasions', 'beliefs' – even 'values'.

Proof that Mozart meant to use the word in this sense comes once again from an unexpected quarter. If there was any one person among Mozart's contemporaries who was able to understand him fully, this person was not Salieri, as the film *Amadeus*, with all its cinemato-graphic panache, would have us believe, but Haydn. And when Haydn learnt of Mozart's death he wrote the following lines in January 1792 to Michael Puchberg, a Freemason and a friend of both composers:

> For a long time I was beside myself at the thought of his death, and could not believe that Providence would dispatch such an irreplaceable man to the other world so hastily. I only regret that he was not able beforehand to convince the benighted English of that which I have been preaching them day after day.

Since neither Haydn nor Mozart ever 'preached' with means other than music, Haydn's remarks and Mozart's congratulations to his father amount to the same thing: that music is capable of expressing convictions and thoughts both explicitly and compellingly.

For the remainder of this book, then, I will no longer argue *whether* this is so, but demonstrate *how* Mozart went about it. This demonstration will take place on several levels. First, bearing in mind Goethe's dictum of 1790 (from his play *Torquato Tasso*):

> Es bildet ein Talent sich in der Stille,
> Sich ein Charakter in dem Strom der Welt.
>
> (Talent is formed in isolation,
> Character in the torrent of the world.)

we shall consider in what ways Mozart was exposed to the torrents of his time. We will then retrace these encounters – which took place often enough amidst stormy conflicts and crises – in Mozart's 'convictions'. Finally, we shall link them to his musical creations: his melodic structures and key schemes, the variety of his forms, his techniques of development and variation, his handling of instruments, and so on. This approach imposes upon us the necessity of alternating our chapters between biography, history and music.

Chapter 4

Mozart's reading habits

Not just the film makers who gave us *Amadeus*, but many of Mozart's biographers as well, consider it unthinkable that Mozart should have kept himself informed by reading. Even Hildesheimer (1977, p. 203) claims that we can 'scarcely imagine' Mozart as a reader, except perhaps of plays or musical scores. This claim is groundless. First of all, we have Konstanze's testimony that Mozart was 'fond of reading' and that she herself, at the age of sixty-six, owned and frequently perused nine volumes by one of his favourite authors. This information was supplied to Mary Novello, who had arrived on the continent in 1829 with her husband, the London musician and publisher Vincent Novello, in search of reminiscences of Mozart. Mary Novello's comment on Konstanze's disclosures is most intriguing: 'Being a forbidden fruit in the Austrian states she did not name it – I suspect some of the French revolutionary works' (Novello 1829, p. 95). Her suspicion was not unfounded. Mary Novello well knew that Mozart was intimately acquainted with at least one play by a proto-revolutionary French author. She might also have discovered further clues about his reading habits among the forty-one items in the catalogue of Mozart's library drawn up after his death. Roughly half of the titles are collections of poetry, plays and anecdotes. Apart from seven volumes of C. F. Cramer's *Magazin der Musik*, which contain well-informed reviews of several of his works, only two of the forty-one titles deal with music. Among the others are a volume of history and another of philosophy, three treatises on topics from the natural sciences, one book on the personality and deeds of Joseph II, the collected works of Frederick II of Prussia, and writings by seven figures of the Enlightenment – Moses Mendelssohn, Joseph von Sonnenfels, Salomon Gessner, Aloys Blumauer, Adolph Freiherr von Knigge, Johann Pezzl and Joachim Heinrich Campe – of whom two, it should be noted, were Jewish. We have no reason to assume that Mozart left all these books unread. Even as a young man in Salzburg it was his habit, as we know from his own account (20 December 1777), to 'take a book out of my pocket and read'. Hildesheimer (1977, p.

138) looks askance at this passage, surmising that Mozart wanted to present a stolid and well-behaved pose to his father. That may be true; there were aspects of his visit to Mannheim which he wanted to keep secret from his father. Yet the passage at least shows that Mozart occasionally did take a book out of his pocket and read while still in Salzburg; he was clever enough to choose, as evidence of his good behaviour, a fact which his father could not dispute. The picture of Mozart as a non-reader is also incompatible with the thought that he read advertisements of newly published books. Yet we know well that he did, for in 1787 he subscribed to a weekly periodical on leisure reading for children, and in 1788 to Gottlieb Leon's poetry and Anton Stein's Austrian and Turkish war songs (Deutsch 1965, pp. 285 and 309).

Even the widely held view that Mozart could not have been interested in newspapers is also contradicted by his own evidence. In a lengthy passage from his letter of 20 July 1778, written during the War of Bavarian Succession (1778–9), he states that he 'had not read anything about it in the newspapers'. Indeed, this passage is so revealing of Mozart's habits of newspaper reading and his reactions to events unrelated to his music that I cannot resist quoting it in full (key words such as 'Emperor', 'Archduke' or names of persons appear in the original in the family's secret cipher):

> Well, what are you hearing about the war? For the last three days I have been dreadfully sad and depressed. True, it doesn't really concern me, but I am so sensitive that I immediately feel interested in any matter. I hear that the Emperor has been defeated. First of all, it was reported that the King of Prussia had surprised him, or rather that he had surprised the troops commanded by the Archduke Maximilian; that 2,000 had fallen on the Austrian side; that fortunately the Emperor had come to his assistance with 40,000 men, but had been forced to retreat. Secondly, it was said that the King had attacked the Emperor and completely surrounded him, and that if General Laudon had not come to his rescue with 1,800 cuirassiers he would have been taken prisoner; that 1,600 cuirassiers had been killed and Laudon himself shot dead... Today, however, I was told that the Emperor had invaded Saxony with 40,000 men; but I don't know whether this is true. A nice scrawl this, isn't it?... A propos, I saw in the papers that in a skirmish between the Saxons and Croats a Saxon captain of grenadiers, Hopfgarten by name, had lost his life and was deeply mourned. Can this be our good, kind Baron Hopfgarten, whom we knew in Paris with Herr von Bose? I should be very sorry if it were, although indeed I would much rather that he died such a glorious death, than a shameful one – in Paris in bed, for instance, as most young men do in this place.

Nor is this passage unique in Mozart's letters. Writing in Paris to his friend Abbé Bullinger on 7 August 1778, he describes what he has 'read in the papers', and it is highly interesting to follow his report and commentary. 'The King of Prussia' – meaning of course Frederick II in his war against Emperor Joseph for the possession of Bavaria – 'is rather alarmed'. The Prussians, he explains, have been belaboured by Croats and two regiments of cuirassiers and put into a dire predicament. He then notes that Frederick has been set upon by 'Bohemian peasants'. And his remark that 'the French have forced the English to retreat' gives evidence that Mozart even followed events in far-away America, for it refers to the French troops fighting the English on the side of the thirteen renegade American colonies.

Having established that Mozart was an avid reader of newspapers, we have the right to jump ahead in our story and examine, from the standpoint of his thirst for information, his brief but highly remarkable stay in Mainz during October of 1790, the penultimate year of his life. First he took lodgings in Schustergasse 45 in a humble inn later known as the Arnsberger Hof but then called the 'Caffé Noble'. As a Mainz historian explains (Gottron 1952, p. 47), Mozart

> must have chosen this inn deliberately since it stood opposite the ... 'Casino zum Gutenberg' (Mainz's first Gutenberg monument was located in the garden). It also contains the rooms of the reading society, which Krebel's travel guide of 1792 referred to as one of the best equipped in Germany. 'Their common rooms are open from 9 o'clock in the morning until 10 in the evening.' This, of course, must have been very agreeable to Mozart.

Thus Gottron. Just how agreeable this must have been to Mozart can only be truly appreciated if we recall that on 25 January 1790 the chief of police in Vienna issued an edict subjecting all newspapers in the country to censorship (Wangermann 1959, pp. 48f.). If the Viennese had previously been well informed about events in France such as the Storming of the Bastille and the Declaration of Human Rights – events that surely must have interested the composer of *Figaro* – all connections were cut off with the proclamation of this edict. Mainz, on the other hand, lay beyond the pale of Viennese censorship. Its reading societies were made up of men (women were excluded) of a social fabric similar to that of Mozart's circles in Vienna. Mozart went freely in and out of the Mainz court, where he gave a concert. If he needed an introduction at all it could have been obtained from the intendant of the court theatre, Friedrich Carl von Dalberg, a longstanding acquaintance of Mozart's and a member of the Mainz reading society since 1781. Things were congenial in the society's premises, where 'tea, chocolate, coffee, milk of almond, lemonade and punch' were served (Prüsener 1972, p. 207). We have no cause to doubt that Mozart found his way across the street to learn, from the newspapers on display, in which direction the current affairs of his day were heading.

The points of intersection between this sort of interest and musical works of art are many and varied. To understand them we will now direct our attention to some purely technical aspects of music.

Chapter 5
Making things significant

I shall now draw on a concept formulated by Harry Goldschmidt. Any musical entity, no matter how unassuming or bland, no matter how many thousands of times it may have occurred, can be isolated and emphasized by particular musical or even non-musical techniques and made significant. In short, it can be 'signified'. This entity may be a short melodic figure, a rhythmic tag, an instrumental timbre, under certain circumstances even a single note; or it may be a more complex musical event. And the techniques available for its signification range from frequent repetition, whether varied or not, to an association with words, images or stage action. The object of this undertaking may be to give the entity a function within the larger musical design – i.e. to treat it as a syntactical unit – or, beyond that, to give it a semantic meaning.

Now, although musical signs are related to linguistic signs, at the very least because both are transmitted through the auditory canal, there are many differences between the two. Musical signs are not nearly as generally or immediately intelligible as are linguistic signs (within a linguistic community). In compensation, musical events, whether they have the character of a sign or operate beneath the semiotic level, have a far greater proportion of modes of impact which are biologically predetermined and thus cross the bounds of linguistic communities. We will later take up other differences between these two semiotic systems. But what most interests us at the moment is the fact that only in very few cases do musical signs attain that degree of constancy and long-lasting validity that is one of the bases of linguistic communities. Most musical signs must, if I may be allowed an unpoetic metaphor, be freshly prepared like a cooked meal if they are to be palatable, that is to say, intelligible. And here a crucial role is played by that process of signification which is the topic of this chapter, and which I would now like to exemplify using two extracts from Mozart's music.

Betulia liberata is an oratorio which Mozart wrote at the age of fifteen to a shoddy text by Metastasio. It is not one of his more miraculous efforts. But its overture, in D minor, is a movement of breadth and grandeur. It is based on a well-worn motif that enters *forte* on the tonic note before proceeding twice to the third degree of the scale and back again to the tonic:

Example 1

I will not recount in detail the many ways that this leap of a third is repeated, shifted to other degrees of the scale, inverted, transposed to other keys, extended from minor to major, or otherwise varied, nor how often this takes place. Suffice it to say that by the time we reach bar 16 we can count some three dozen such events, including simultaneous variants, and this in a piece totalling 172 bars. We can easily follow this process in the score (*NMA* I/4/2) or even more compellingly in performance. Obviously, the insignificant third is being signified. This occurs most strikingly in the final five bars of the overture, where the violins play the third motif twice *piano*, unaccompanied, followed by seemingly conventional *forte* closing chords which, however, contain the complete motif in the bass:

Example 2

Whether the young composer was motivated, consciously or unconsciously, by an association with his church music of the same period is a moot point. Psychologically, the association could hardly have been avoided.

The second example is taken from the rich storehouse which Gunthard Born presents in his aforementioned book on Mozart's musical language. Here he demonstrates, to my mind correctly and convincingly, that Mozart's music uses hundreds of traditional figures as musical signs, a fact which Mozart scholars have tended to underplay or fully to ignore. In one passage of his book (1985, pp. 188f.) Born examines a descending figure of the sort that Hugo Riemann would have called 'scaly' (*schuppenförmig*), in which the first note of a descending figure elides with the last note of its predecessor. Born finds an instance of this figure (p. 189) in a scene from *Le nozze di Figaro*. The Count, having informed the bystanders that he recently discovered Cherubino hiding under a table, now demonstrates how he did this using a 'piece of cloth which happens to be lying on the chair ready to hand'. Mozart, Born continues (p. 190), 'depicts in detail the drawing back of the all-concealing cloth... Once it has slipped a bit (slurred minims) the Count grasps it with both hands (two crotchets) and, after reaching forward (rest), pulls it back a bit further (slurred minims).'

What Born has overlooked is that the theme he quotes is, in a manner of speaking, the main theme of the piece, No. 7, where it occurs no fewer than four times. The first and final occurrences (in the tonic) and the second (in the subdominant) all belong to Basilio, whereas only the third occurrence in G minor (the only one quoted by Born) is given to the Count. And the three versions sung by Basilio have nothing to do with the piece of cloth: in bars 16ff. Basilio remarks that he must have arrived at an inopportune moment; in bars 85ff. he claims that his words about the Page were merely conjecture; and in bars 175ff. he scornfully repeats those same words, which have proved to be more than conjecture after all. Since the four versions differ only in their pitch level (ignored in the example below), Born's interpretation fails to stand up:

Example 3

More convincing is another occurrence of this figure, which Born has called, in quotes, the *Enthüllungsmotiv* or 'disclosure motif' (p. 190). It comes from No. 13 (bars 177ff.) of *Don Giovanni*, the scene of the three maskers, who arrive at Giovanni's banquet with the intention of exposing him. Besides the highly visible masks (which we suspect will fall in due course) and the intentions of the three maskers (which are already clear to the audience), the decisive word is also pronounced: *scoprir*, to discover or disclose. This is sufficient to make the motif significant (see Example 4). Admittedly, here and everywhere else, it must be remembered that isolated 'passages' only receive significance within an overall musical context. Between the overture and the finale of *Don Giovanni* there are few numbers in which ascending and descending scalar motifs do not play a role of some sort.

Example 4

Less convincing, however, is another example of a descending scalar motif which, Born claims, likewise stands for 'disclosure'. This motif is one of the very few examples that he has taken from Mozart's untexted instrumental music. The famous *Eine kleine Nachtmusik* contains, as early as bar 12 of the first movement, a figure which seems similar in shape to those quoted above:

Example 5

But in no way is it made significant. The fact that there is, of course, no stage action or text is beside the point; we have already seen in *Betulia liberata* that Mozart has other methods of signification at his disposal. But he seems not to have applied them here. The descending figure appears on a mere three occasions, and is repeated only once; it plays no part in the development section; it is part of a larger phrase at its entrance; nor is it prominently featured within that phrase. In short, Born forgets that musical signs are not so constant and stable that they can be attached to such slender material.

Chapter 6

The major-minor opposition

The term 'major-minor opposition' refers to two different types of tonal design. We have cause to use it when a large-scale piece of music has a lengthy section (usually at least a third of the piece) in one mode and its remaining sections in the other, as in the following diagram:

Major – Minor – Major

or

Minor – Major – Minor

Alternatively, it refers to a large-scale piece beginning in one mode and ending in the other, thereby proceeding from major to minor or vice versa.

This term must be distinguished from 'major-minor duality'. By this we mean a view of music which, beginning in the seventeenth century, gradually took hold in European art music and 'achieved widespread currency in musical awareness around 1700' (Benary 1961, p. 107). During this process the number of the so-called 'ecclesiastical modes' was reduced to two – major and minor – which predominated in the eighteenth and nineteenth centuries and even today are inseparable from the most widespread music of our time. Peter Benary argues, convincingly, that the ecclesiastical modes survived longest in church hymns. (They figure in at least two of Mozart's masterpieces in the form of chorales: the Masonic Funeral Music of 1785 and the scene of the Men in Armour in *Die Zauberflöte*.) Were it not for their dependence on pre-existing hymn tunes, the choral and organ music of the time would have 'travelled the path to the major-minor duality much earlier, as was already the case in the other forms of instrumental music' (Benary, p. 39).

Mozart discovered the major-minor opposition during his childhood. The *da capo* arias of Italian opera seria occasionally followed the first of the two aforementioned designs. Mozart also became acquainted with it in the works of his predecessors and contemporaries – in Bach, Handel and Gluck. His gradual mastery of this technique is best illustrated in *Die Entführung aus dem Serail* (1782), *Le nozze di Figaro* (1786) and *Don Giovanni* (1787).

It goes without saying that Leopold Mozart discussed the minor mode in the boy's lessons. By the age of ten or eleven Mozart was thoroughly conversant with it, as can be seen especially in his so-called modulating preludes. These pieces, basically 'written-out' improvisations, had several functions in public performance: first, 'to explore the instrument (if unfamiliar) or to demonstrate its capabilities (if the performer's own)'; then, to act as a prelude to the main piece on the programme; and finally, if more than one piece was played, 'to modulate from one to the other (*interludieren*)' and to flaunt the player's musical prowess and training (Plath 1982, pp. xii and xiv). Mozart doubtless improvised countless pieces of this sort. That he occasionally wrote out one or another of them probably had to do with a desire on the part of his sister to bask in his glory by memorizing the written-out versions and playing them by heart. But being able to modulate between major and minor, or even to juxtapose the two modes, is quite a different thing from recognizing in their opposition the possibilities for an intelligible musical semantic.

One detail from Mozart's Mass settings provides insight into his way of handling the problem of major and minor. As is well known, the *Credo* contains two highly moving, adjacent sections of contrasting sentiment:

Et incarnatus est	And was incarnate
de Spiritu sancto	by the Holy Ghost,
ex Maria virgine	of the Virgin Mary;
et homo factus est.	and was made man.

and

Crucifixus etiam pro nobis	He was crucified also for us,
sub Pontio Pilato, passus	suffered under Pontius Pilate,
et sepultus est.	and was buried.

From the vantage point of Mozart's musical language of the 1780s, it was obvious how these two sections had to be set: the first in major, the second in minor. And this is exactly how they appear in the three Mass settings K257, K259 and K317 that Mozart wrote between the ages of eighteen and twenty-four. (The C minor Mass of 1783 is incomplete; its *Et incarnatus est* is in the major mode, and we can fairly well assume that the *Crucifixus*, had it been written, would have been in minor.)

But however obvious this formal design may seem in historical retrospect, it was in fact not obvious at all. A glance at the corresponding passages in Mozart's earlier Mass settings gives us a glimpse into the evolution of musical semantics. In his first Mass, K49, the twelve-year-old composer concludes both sections in the major. In his third setting, K65, written one year later, we find just the opposite of his later solution: the passage on the incarnation concludes in the minor, that on the crucifixion in the major. K337 is an ingenious special case: the *homo factus est* concludes in the minor, apparently because its final note and the word '*est*' elide with the *Crucifixus*, in the minor. On no fewer than ten occasions Mozart has the one or the other section – and on two occasions both – conclude with open octaves or fifths. This is an effective device. Those who regard major and minor sonorities as part of their musical lingua franca are left, as it were, floating in mid-air. It is an archaic device deriving from an era that had yet to decide in favour of the major-minor duality and the attribution of major to joy and minor to sorrow – with, of course, numerous qualifications and nuances.

Mozart seems to have first approached a major-minor opposition, in the sense outlined above, in his variations for piano, and then not until he was twenty-one. There exist four sets of variations, written between 1766 and 1774, in which all the variations are in the major mode. Not until his twelve variations on 'Je suis Lindor', K354, written in Paris in 1778, did Mozart introduce a practice which he then retained for his most mature sets of variations. One of the variations – but always only one, cleverly and artfully reserved for the final third of the set – is in the tonic minor. And with this change of mode the carefree merriment and brilliant virtuosity that largely pervade Mozart's piano variations merge with a touch of pensiveness, even melancholy.

A new quality of opposition, linked semantically to joy and sorrow, can be found in *Die Entführung* (1782). Here it stands out all the more in that the texts of the arias turn thematically on the antithetical concepts of joy and sorrow – *Freude* (*Wonne*) and *Schmerz* (*Kummer*, *Traurigkeit*). The paradigm of this musical association can be found at once in the overture and the first aria (No. 1), one of those pieces which Mozart claims was added to the libretto at his insistence (26 September 1781). The overture, marked *presto* and set in a pure C major, has a slow middle section in C minor, thereby presenting the most sharply defined type of major-minor opposition. Since the two main sections of the overture, taken together, amount to almost exactly two-thirds of its duration, and the middle section one-third, it anticipates the proportions taken up both musically and programmatically by joy and sorrow in this cheerful piece of theatre. But there is more to it than that. No sooner does the curtain rise than we discover that the central section of the overture was an instrumental anticipation in the minor mode of Belmonte's first aria. The lines 'Hier soll ich dich denn sehen, Konstanze!' and 'Schenk mir dafür nun Freuden' are sung to a major version of the melody we heard in the overture. Now we understand: the central section of the overture depicted the pain of separation, while Belmonte's first aria anticipates the reunion of the two lovers. 'Ich duldete der Leiden … allzuviel!' he sings, in the major, or 'I endured' (note the past tense) 'all too many sufferings!':

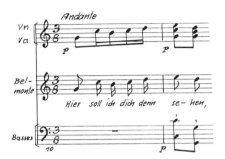

Example 6

This joy offsets the 'sufferings' which were, as Mozart put it in such cases, 'expressed' or 'enounced' in the minor mode in the overture:

Example 7

It could hardly be more naive, direct – or theatrically effective!

Later, in *Don Giovanni* and – in a single scene, but to telling effect – in *Figaro*, we shall show how magnificently Mozart used the major-minor opposition both to impart musical form and to create signs.

We will now attempt to relate Mozart's compositional techniques to his developing world-view, and this in turn to his experiences and growing political insight. In earlier writings on Mozart this approach would have seemed strangely out of place. But even Mozart's biographers refuse to stand still.

Chapter 7

Mozart in the eyes of posterity

It is becoming more and more evident that if we want to say something about Mozart's music we must also study the non-musical events of his day, the circumstances under which they took place, and the contradictory impressions they left in the minds of his contemporaries. In his book *Mozart in Wien* (1986) Volkmar Braunbehrens, a scholar born in 1941, has unearthed many highly revealing but previously disregarded facts about Mozart's everyday life. But not only that, he has also shown that these facts, taken together with an unprejudiced view of Mozart's creative process, lead to conclusions which were previously unknown in the Mozart literature. For example, Braunbehrens offers the following description of Mozart's intellectual position (1986, p. 259): although no 'explicitly political comments' by Mozart have survived, he was nonetheless an

> attentive and well-informed observer who, far from 'standing above it all' or being unconcerned with contemporary humanitarian issues, took a lively interest in political events and, in his operas, ventured closely and pointedly upon the pressing issues of his time. This presupposes that he was alert to social processes, committed in his observations, and detached in his judgement.

Gunthard Born, a scholar of the same generation (born in 1935), has arrived at similar conclusions. His book appeared in 1985. It falls into two parts, the second dealing with Mozart's musical language and the first, characteristically titled 'The Scene', deliberately renouncing the most stubborn of all Mozart clichés: namely, in Hildesheimer's words (1977, p. 23), that 'so far as we can tell the events of Mozart's day never reached the level of his awareness'. Born has assembled a large body of evidence, all of it drawn from available sources, that Mozart was indeed thoroughly aware of these events. Even Hildesheimer, though he reinforces the aforementioned Mozart myth, has deftly and elegantly demolished some of the hoariest white elephants of Mozart scholarship.

Another seemingly unshakeable prejudice used to be that Mozart's and Da Ponte's *Figaro* took the stuffing out of Beaumarchais's original, leaving behind nothing but a harmless comedy. This view was exploded as early as 1977 by Wolfgang Ruf. After closely comparing the play and the libretto Ruf came to the conclusion that the 'polarization of the classes' was even more 'sharply accentuated' in Da Ponte than in Beaumarchais (1977, p. 90), and that 'at least a major part of the libretto substantially retained the tendentiousness that underlies the original' (p. 84).

Recently Nicholas Till, in his *Mozart and the Enlightenment* (1992), has drawn on an impressive wealth of eighteenth-century literature, including the important but ever-neglected Johann Pezzl. In Till's narrative the thoughts, beliefs, actions and intellectual struggles of Mozart's contemporaries become vividly alive in their relevance to his work.

Yet this new direction in Mozart scholarship – and there are other examples of it not mentioned here – has not yet taken hold; far from it. The hollowest old saw still has a good chance of being considered the pinnacle of wisdom so long as it can appeal to well-established prejudices. And, of course, this is exactly what it does. It is worth examining one of these texts more closely. A widely known German publication has this to say about *Figaro*:

> Was Mozart's desire for this libretto a revolutionary pose? Can we find signs of revolt or even class struggle in his works? ... His letters are remarkably devoid of current topics or allusions. For the most part they are made up of reports on music, ideas about music, opinions on music theatre, experiences with music. Of course he followed the events of his time; he was, after all, a broad-minded man. But his true interests rarely went beyond music, and then never very far. None of his surviving utterances, none of his many letters has a single passage that either shows or suggests him to be the deliberate creator of a revolutionary opera. (Pahlen 1979, pp. 234f.)

Later I will have cause to take a closer look at the claim that Mozart's letters are 'remarkably devoid of current topics or allusions'. At the same time I will show that there is, indeed, more than 'a single passage' that identifies Mozart to be exactly what the author of these precious lines pretends he was not. The confusion he causes is all the more complete for being apparently heartfelt. Yet it resides in an inaccurate use of words, in what they mean and the values we attach to them. The author uses a number of expressions which have negative connotations for him and his prospective readers: 'class struggle', 'revolt', 'revolutionary'. To these we must add another which is not explicitly stated but always implied: 'politics'. Mozart, the author concedes, was broad-minded and followed the events of his day. But surely he was not revolutionary! And how can we even suspect him of striking a revolutionary pose! Surely he was worlds apart from class struggle and revolt! And heaven forfend that we should mention his name in connection with politics!

The Enlightenment philosophers of the eighteenth century fought against the imprecise use of words. Diderot, in one of his articles for the *Encyclopédie* (1755, p. 151), preached the following warnings into the wind: 'How many unforeseen difficulties crop up the moment one attempts to fix the meaning of the most common expressions!' and 'Every word must be defined'. Elsewhere he wrote: 'It may well be that you call vice what I call virtue, and virtue what I call vice.' The great *Encyclopédie*, which occupied the leading minds of the French Enlightenment for decades, is among other things a conscious attempt to enlist the struggle for clear definitions in the battle against the by then unbearable conditions of absolutism. Words such as 'nation', 'fatherland', 'property', 'natural right', 'philosophy' and many more, including 'revolution', were given fresh evaluations. This should give us pause for thought. When someone introduces latter-day concepts such as 'class struggle' into an assessment of Mozart's mental world without further comment, we should view it less as an aid to clarification than as a good cause to raise our eyebrows.

Instead, the task of Mozart scholarship is to investigate the way words have changed meaning – not least of all during Mozart's own lifetime – and the way new words have come into being. Take 'revolution', for instance. Diderot, who was older than Mozart by almost half a century, used the word rarely and judiciously. His translators and editors (Diderot 1961 and 1968) – correctly, I feel – sometimes render *révolution* as 'revolution' and sometimes as 'turnabout' (*Umwälzung*) – which is, after all, its literal meaning. Under the heading of 'encyclopedia', for instance, where Diderot discusses how far and how quickly progress in education would advance the human cause, he remarks: 'But these turnabouts [*révolutions*] are necessary; there have always been turnabouts and always will be.' This expresses a viewpoint that was then widely held among the bourgeoisie, unaware that the political, social, ideological and behavioural structures of absolutism were tough enough to make the application of violence necessary to overcome them.

During the final years of Mozart's life – Diderot had already died – the word *révolution* took on a concrete political meaning. From 1789 there appeared in Paris a newspaper entitled *Révolution de Paris*, and in the mouths of Marat, Desmoulins, Georg Forster and others who were born about the same time as Mozart, the word *révolution* acquired that meaning which it has retained ever since. 'I would like to see the proportion', wrote Georg Christoph Lichtenberg in 1797 (1975, p. 955), 'that expresses the number of times the word revolution was spoken and printed in the eight years from 1781 to 1789 as compared to the eight years from 1789 to 1797. Surely it cannot be less than 1:1,000,000.'

Mozart's stance toward the beginnings of the French Revolution, which he lived to experience, must be re-examined. It is untenable to maintain that he was as indifferent toward it as the ordinary citizen is toward comparable events today.

Finally, let us take the term 'politics'. Here are the words of a contemporary, only seven years younger than Mozart, who lamented as early as 1805 how quickly the concept and word had degenerated, despite the conscientious formulations and definitions of the Encyclopedists. Johann Gottfried Seume, in *Mein Sommer im Jahre 1805*, first defines what he is talking about, fully in keeping with the spirit of the Enlightenment: 'Something is political if it contributes, or is intended to contribute, to the common good: *quod bonum publicum promovet.*' He continues:

> This word has been greatly disfigured, confused and devalued. Or the speaker attempts, with something less than honesty, to enshroud it in a mist of his own making, so as to make it appear to the honest and upright burgher as a ghoulish object of terror. Sad to relate, the attempt usually succeeds.

We know how splendidly the attempt succeeds today, and that when many good people claim to be unpolitical they can mean one or more of three things: they are repelled by the filth usually associated with politics today; they are satisfied with their present situation in life and turn a blind eye to the disadvantaged; or they do not believe that these circumstances can be changed. But whatever the motives of the *soi-disant* unpolitical man, we have no cause to project bourgeois virtues of this sort onto Mozart.

For one thing can be concluded from our investigation of that verbal sleight-of-hand in the commentary to *Figaro* given above (and we might have taken any of a number of other texts – they are not in short supply): as helpless as they are in explaining the phenomenon of Mozart, they involuntarily reveal that the problems of Mozart's day are fundamentally similar to our own. Mozart's life fell into one of those eras in which humanity, whether consciously or not, went through a transition from one form of social organization to another. And we are doing the same today.

We need not spend time pointing out the differences between our age and the eighteenth century; they are self-evident. The points in common are less obvious, being rooted in the matter itself. But the more superficial the commentator, the more readily is he apt, like a modern-day Mime, to divulge his hidden motives. (Curious dialectics!) The *Figaro* commentary quoted above is followed by just this sort of disclosure. When Mozart gave notice to the Archbishop he expressed his anger to his employer and to Count Arco in no uncertain terms. 'But did he thereby question the existing order of society?' asks our author, to which he then supplies the answer: 'No! He merely sought satisfaction for himself.' How anxiously Mozart is shielded from any suspicion of having done something which, today, might cause him to be blacklisted or otherwise punished. Even in his own day such behaviour could have cost a man his life. We are dealing here with very big issues. Not only does the author betray his lack of interest in ideas that change society (we will gladly accept his limitations); not only is his Mozart tailored to the views of today's ordinary citizen, whose concerns are not likely to go far beyond 'satisfaction for himself'; nay, art itself is not allowed to derive greatness from an identification with the problems of humanity and its attempts to solve them. Mozart, in short, is not permitted to think differently from his commentator.

We have already hinted that the aforementioned *Figaro* commentary might have recourse to longstanding traditions. This claim shall now be substantiated. At the same time this should make it clear that the apology for bourgeois conditions at the end of our century tends to distort our picture of Mozart in a way that was unthinkable at its beginning. First, let us examine a book which is still important today, one which clings to humanitarian positions and is thoroughly researched as far as Mozart's biography and, especially, his musical development are concerned: Hermann Abert's *W. A. Mozart*. Abert's merits and strong points need not concern us here. The book was published from 1919 to 1921, and was thus written at least in part during the First World War and the post-war years, including the Russian Revolution and wars of intervention. Abert expressly acknowledges that 'at the end of his life Mozart was seized by that powerful movement of the intellect which, two years previously, had found its most manifest expression in the French Revolution' (Abert II, p. 767). But far from making this provocative idea the guiding theme of his book, Abert dilutes and even retracts it elsewhere. I am unable to determine whether he did this from indecision, a change of mind while writing his book, or from other motives of whatever sort. It seems logical to assume that in those troubled times not even Abert wished to venture too far toward a sympathy with revolutionary change. When, for example, he attempts to explain Mozart's overriding belief that rank and status do not matter as much as heart and reason, and that all men are in principle born equal, Abert remarks disparagingly that these represent occasional 'democratic effusions of the sort that the middle classes of the time were fond of spouting' (II, p. 13). Perhaps he noticed that he was on shaky ground, for he shores up his arguments with a failed attempt to distinguish Leopold's fondness for politics from Mozart's stance. Mozart, he claims, viewed his fellow men unpolitically and took them simply as they came: 'least of all did he question whether they were good or bad.' Did Abert never notice that Mozart's operatic characters are 'questioned' for exactly these qualities and treated accordingly in his music? But Mozart, Abert continues, was 'never a political man', as can be seen in the revealing fact 'that his letters do not spend so much as a single word on the most important political event he ever encountered, the French Revolution' (II, p. 12). This discovery, though true, does not prove what it is meant to prove. Strictly speaking, Mozart's letters do not contain a single word about Freemasonry, either, although Abert himself expatiates on the importance to Mozart of this movement and Mozart had three to four times as many years to react to it in his letters as to the French Revolution. For many years the Mozarts, whenever they were dealing with delicate matters in their correspondence, used a secret code and worried whether their letters might fall or had already fallen into the wrong hands. They knew very well what thoughts they could and could not commit to paper. Mozart was hardly likely to express his interest in, perhaps even his sympathy with, the French Revolution in an uncoded letter. (Incidentally, we will later encounter a coded reference on Mozart's part to the revolutionary changes in France.) And had not Abert himself, 400 pages earlier in his gigantic opus, pointed out that the allegedly non-political Mozart took up that revolutionary movement in *Die Zauberflöte*?

Another Mozart biography demonstrates that depth of research is perfectly compatible with intellectual poverty. Erich Schenk's *Mozart: sein Leben, seine Welt* was first published in 1955, translated into English in 1959 and reissued in a revised version in 1975. The picture that Schenk wishes to convey of Mozart and his world can best be discovered by comparing the length, vocabulary and evaluation of two groups of opinions: his opinions of Mozart's aristocratic patrons, and his opinions of Enlightenment figures. In the first category not even the least member of the *garde du corps* or the most minor deputy under-secretary is lacking. For one man of the cloth Schenk treats us to all seven of his titles, not failing to include the names of the villages of which he was 'lord and proprietor' (1975, p. 157). A lady before whom the Mozart children 'presumably' performed is introduced as 'Marie Louise de Rohan (born 1720), married to Gaston-Jean-Baptiste-Charles de Lorraine, Comte de Marson, and governess of the

legitimate children and grandchildren of the King (*Enfants de France*)'
(p. 104). Not even as a child did Mozart allow himself to be dazzled
by aristocrats; his biographer, it would seem, wishes to make amends
for this shortcoming. Conversely, Schenk exposes his weaknesses by
referring to the Encyclopedists as 'intellectuals and philosophizing
aesthetes such as Diderot, Rousseau, d'Alembert, d'Holbach and their
ilk'. Finally, as if to underscore his long and profitable experience with
those who were anything but revolutionary, he writes the barely
credible sentence: 'This world' – meaning Mozart's during his final
years – 'was beholden at that time to the revolutionary mentality and
was, accordingly, frivolous in its judgements' (p. 642).

Yet nothing in the Mozart literature can, of course, match the
impact and popularity of a film so brilliantly executed and so poorly
conceived as *Amadeus*. As Braunbehrens wittily observes, there is
justice in the fact that both the film and the play on which it is based
were given this title. As Mozart always called himself either Amadé or
Amadeo, the film 'proclaims to all and sundry that it will have no
points in common with Mozart's actual life' (p. 11). (See also Brigitte
Thurm in *Weimarer Beiträge* 12, 1987.) An even more acid exposé of
the film's underlying posture can be found in an essay on the ideology
of our time by Friedrich Dieckmann (*neue deutsche literatur* 11, 1986).
Having shown what gifted people must put up with today in other,
more dangerous fields – namely physics and engineering – Dieckmann
concludes that the film gives us Mozart 'as Hollywood wants to have
him: as a man incapable of action or even of coping with life, a man
who goes to rack and ruin rather than accept the aid of his betters.
This Mozart is the monopolists' dream incarnate of what they fondly
call "a major talent"' (p. 69).

Chapter 8

A turning point

No stage of Mozart's life is more amenable than the one about to be considered to the time-honoured methods of biography, when it was assumed that the omniscient biographer knew not only all the facts but the motives behind them as well.

The first journey that Mozart took without his father marked a turning point in his life. It lasted some sixteen months, from 23 September 1777 to January 1779, and brought about deep-seated and at times almost overwhelming convulsions. We are able to trace most of these convulsions because the letters of this period that passed to and fro between Mozart and Leopold, Leopold and his wife, and Mozart and his sister, are extraordinarily revealing in their level of detail. Taken together with letters to some other persons, they occupy no fewer than 540 pages of print. And there are other sources available as well.

At this stage of his life Mozart was motivated by several desires, goals and maxims. Probably his most urgent wish, and the one he was most aware of, was to grow up. This meant, above all, detaching himself inwardly and outwardly from his father, who had guided Mozart's life for a conspicuously long period of time as a teacher, mentor, impresario and, not least of all, as a role model. There is every indication that Mozart wanted to end this stage of his life as a natural by-product of his journey, so to speak, and not with a jolt. He travelled with his mother, a sort of trusty comrade with whom he was always able to have his own way. She was aware of this and accepted it with a certain resignation. As far as Mozart was concerned, this was to be a pleasant journey into manhood. On the very first day he wrote home good-naturedly, 'I am quite a second Papa', which is as much as saying that he no longer needed anyone's tutelage. The same passage continues, 'I see to everything', with the unstated presupposition that he was now perfectly capable of doing so.

The journey formed a watershed in the life of the Mozart family for the simple reason that, with his father's agreement, he had quit service at the court of the Prince-Archbishop, thereby burning his bridges to

Salzburg. Wolfgang never dreamt of returning there again, except perhaps to visit his parents. (In Vienna he acquired another reason for returning to Salzburg, namely, as he wrote on 13 June 1781, to give Count Arco a 'kick up the arse'. We will hear more of this later.) Mozart himself betrayed a desire to grow up when he wrote to his father on 11 September 1778 – at the lowest ebb of his estrangement from his fatherly protector Melchior Grimm – that 'Monsieur Grimm may be able to help *children*, but not grown-up people' (Mozart's emphasis).

Part of being a grown-up person is having a secure income. Mozart was only too aware of this. It was not his fault that his prospects of a court position in Mannheim and Munich, and even vague hopes of a position in Mainz, failed to materialize. The four-and-a-half months that Mozart spent in Mannheim with his mother gave him his very first opportunity to develop his own plans for the future. Mannheim had a superb orchestra, and it was by no means a bad idea to join forces with three of its best musicians – the flautist Johann Baptist Wendling, the oboist Friedrich Ramm and the bassoonist Georg Wenzel Ritter – and travel to Paris for the purpose of holding concerts there, with, of course, his own music. It had become virtually the pattern of Mozart's young life to travel with the intention of acquiring, in Leopold's priceless words of 11 May 1778, 'honour and money'. The present trip was not his first journey but his tenth. So even Mozart's father smiled benevolently upon this plan: Wendling was one of the best instrumentalists of his day; he had been to Paris several times already; and he belonged to Leopold's generation rather than Wolfgang's – probably no small factor in Leopold's thinking.

Such was the state of affairs when Mozart's newly discovered independence was revealed from a different angle: he fell seriously in love. The object of his affections was Aloysia Weber, a highly gifted seventeen-year-old soprano already well on the road to success. Part of being a mature and independent young man is to decide for oneself when and whom one wishes to marry. Leopold, who knew the ways of the world, was not averse in principle to a love affair. 'All young people must learn by playing the fool [*am Narrenseil laufen*]', he remarked on 3 September 1778. But we can well imagine his anxiety when Mozart told him, in a letter of 4 February 1778, that his plan to visit Paris with Wendling, Ramm and Ritter was to be scuttled in favour of a new plan, namely, to seek his fortune in Italy with Aloysia, her father and his eldest daughter Josepha. Would his father be so kind, he blandly asked, as to enquire of an Italian acquaintance how much a prima donna is paid in Verona. As if it were not already clear enough that this crazy scheme was destined to fail, Mozart added, in a tone that his father had never heard from him before, 'I think we shall go to Switzerland and perhaps also to Holland'.

Mozart had not passed his first test on the road to maturity with very high marks. In a lengthy letter (12 February), Leopold reproached his son for the hastiness of his actions. Mozart must have realized that this tongue-lashing was warranted in every word that exposed his Italian escapade, not to mention the Swiss and Dutch schemes, for what it was: ludicrous. Having read his father's violent protestations he even tried – not very convincingly, we have to admit – to present the plan as though he had only hit upon it for the sake of the Weber family and at their insistence (19 February). No matter, he would obey his father's will, which culminated in the phrase: 'Off with you to Paris!' Mozart probably did not feel half so secure in his role as an independent agent and decision-maker as he pretended. And the Weber family, far from having inspired the plan, were probably no more favourably disposed toward it than his father. In short, on 23 March 1778 Mozart arrived in Paris with his mother, who accompanied him likewise on Leopold's decree.

But Mozart's chances in Paris were not propitious, neither for his future livelihood (and thus his prospective marriage) nor for relations within the Mozart family. One thought seems never to have crossed Leopold's mind: that his son had grown up, however worrisome his gullibility and naivety, and that if he did not wish to anger and estrange Wolfgang he would have to stop patronizing him. Despite Leopold's desire to become a sort of paternal friend to his son, he slipped all too often and all too readily from the role of adviser into that of commander. Sometimes, perhaps for reasons more of diplomacy than conviction, he managed to strike the right tone. In his letter of 5 February, for example, he wrote: 'My dear Wolfgang, not only do I not distrust you in the very slightest degree; on the contrary, I place all my trust and confidence in your filial love.' Mozart's immediate response (14 February) was positive: 'I shall keep your fatherly letter among my most cherished belongings and shall always put it to good use.' But this harmony was not to last, on either side. The warnings and advice turned all too easily into the accusations which had already begun to appear in their correspondence and which were to intensify ominously in the months to come. Take, for example, Leopold's letter of 12 February. What in the world, he asks, has kept Mozart and his mother from seeking his advice and acting according to his will since he had, after all, a better practical grasp of things than they?

Where this practical grasp led can be gleaned from a close reading of his many instructions on how to behave in Paris, particularly those of 5 February. It is essential, he maintains, to obtain the favours of people of rank and quality; one must ever be at pains to enter their protection; on the other hand one should mistrust less well-placed people, nor is one under obligation to be honest with them. Mozart's father sent him a total of almost seventy names of Parisian dignitaries at his Mannheim address. Among them are a number of grand names which could not possibly have meant anything to Wolfgang: d'Alembert, Diderot, Voltaire, Madame d'Epinay. Most of the others are from the nobility, and Mozart is expressly urged to follow the example of his father, who made it his practice to 'obtain the acquaintance and seek the friendship only of people of position' (5 February). These are golden words and doubtless effective guides to behaviour. But whether Mozart kept them among his 'most cherished belongings' is doubtful; that he refused to follow them is notorious. On two occasions, on 10 December 1777 and again, years later, on 9 June 1786, he assured his father that he despised 'fawning' [*Kriecherei*]. On the first occasion his father replied, somewhat put out, that he felt the same way. But there was a difference, probably one of their respective generations. However unwillingly, Leopold had a consummate command of the conversational tone to be struck with persons of station and considered it perfectly natural to use it. To avoid doing Leopold an injustice we should recall that even greater men than he thought it expedient on occasion to adopt this tone from their repertoire of styles. We need only think of Goethe and Voltaire.

Wolfgang Amadé, on the other hand, knew nothing of this type of behaviour and had no desire to learn it. Significantly, it was Leopold who, in his own hand, wrote his son's petitions for dismissal and reinstatement. In Paris Wolfgang's task was to plod through the long list of addresses, hat in hand. He, however, had no such intention and quickly found plausible reasons for not doing so. To the end of his days Leopold probably believed whole-heartedly that his son would have achieved more in Paris, and elsewhere, if he had only followed instructions. The tragic thing about it is that Leopold, with his code of behaviour for Paris, was right. Albert Einstein (1946, pp. 55f.) describes vividly and amusingly how just a few years earlier Gluck had been able to take Paris by storm. He did so using all those devices sanctioned by Leopold, and known today as 'public relations'. Even eighteenth-century high society was susceptible to the early proto-types of these tricks. Mozart was unable and unwilling to play along.

Leopold also wanted his son to toe the line in his creative work. He outdid himself in admonitions to study the French taste, to imitate what was currently in favour and not to forget what was popular, to seek the advice of Melchior Grimm and the celebrated choreographer Jean Georges Noverre (1727–1810) and to follow their advice only. 'If you can only win applause and get a decent sum of money, let the devil take the rest' (20 April 1778); that was his philosophy. Mozart himself was not at all disinclined to pay due regard to the expectations of the persons for whom he wrote his music – and he wrote for all manner of people of many different countries and tastes. He accommodated these expectations, adhered to the traditions of the genres he cultivated, and paid very close attention to the demands and limitations of his singers and instrumentalists. But above and beyond this, he also had to do justice to further-reaching demands of his own. His lively mind tackled problems that could not be solved by accommodating other people's wishes. Although he must have sensed it, during his stay in Paris Mozart was not yet aware that his work had a non-musical, even non-aesthetic aspect, an aspect about which his father did not have the vaguest idea. We will have more to say about this aspect in due course.

Yet the most serious blow to the relations between father and son came later, when Mozart had to inform Leopold of his mother's death. He did this with as much grace and circumspection as he could muster. In the night of her death, holding vigil at her bedside, Mozart wrote three letters (3 July): one to his father and sister that only speaks of a very grave illness in order to prepare them for the worst; and another to a loyal friend of the family, Joseph Bullinger (1744–1810), asking him to relay the news of her death as gently as possible. The third letter, to Aloysia's father, is lost.

Leopold's reaction damaged his relations with his son beyond repair. There is no doubt that the death of his wife affected him profoundly, and that the growing debts imposed upon him by the unfortunate Paris journey were almost more than he could bear. It is also understandable that he expected his son to return to Salzburg as quickly as possible, to assume the organist's post that Leopold had by then requested and obtained for him from the Archbishop, and to help pay off the family's debts. But Leopold went one step further. First in vague insinuations, then with increasing insistence and clarity, he accused Wolfgang of being responsible for his mother's death. Mozart's guilt was twofold: had he not been so irresponsible he could have travelled to Paris alone, and his mother would have been safe in Salzburg. But since she had to chaperone him in Paris, the doctor should have been called sooner and more blood should have been let. If he, Leopold, had been present things would not have come to such a pass.

Mozart postponed his return home in part because of his prospective marriage; over half a year passed between the death of his mother and his arrival in Salzburg. This only made his father more reproachful and self-pitying. On 19 November 1778 he wrote: 'After having let your mother die so wretchedly in Paris I hope you will not add the hastening of your father's death to your conscience.' He should not even have thought such a thing, much less put it down in writing. Mozart's response, on 3 December, was as follows: 'My not having answered you sooner is the fault of no one but yourself, and of your first letter to me at Mannheim. Really I never could have believed – but peace! I will say no more about it. For it is all over now.'

This passage probably refers to more than the death of Mozart's mother. Just a couple of weeks earlier, on 22 November, Mozart had informed his father of his marriage plans in a manner which he himself called 'pretty oracular, wouldn't you say? It is obscure but still intelligible.' We should probably take the final words in their correspondence regarding the death of Maria Anna as 'oracular' in the same sense – that the days of Mozart's unalloyed filial love were 'all over now'. In any event, from this moment there was a note of bitterness in the dealings between Mozart and his father, a note which was never to disappear. In Leopold's case, the estrangement had very deep wellsprings. Years later, writing to a sincere lady friend of Mozart's (23 August 1782), he could still claim that 'both morally and physically I am the victim of his [Wolfgang's] misconduct'.

But to return to Paris. Mozart's original objectives – a position, money and 'honour' – were still far from fulfilled. True, there were commissions, performances and successes. Nor was his compositional output a mean achievement: eight choruses for a *Miserere* by Holzbauer, thirteen pieces for a ballet by Noverre entitled *Les Petits Riens*, a symphony, a *sinfonia concertante*, a concerto for flute and harp, three piano sonatas and another for violin and piano, three sets of variations and a capriccio for piano, an aria for Aloysia Weber, and a scena for a castrato. But his efforts had not paid off. Of the eight choruses only two had been performed, and hardly anyone was aware that they were by Mozart; even the pieces for Noverre's ballet, some of which are truly delightful, were performed more or less anonymously; and the *sinfonia concertante*, written for his Mannheim colleagues Wendling, Ramm and Ritter and the French horn virtuoso Punto, was apparently never performed at all. Only in the case of two symphonies, one composed in Paris, one brought with him, do Mozart's efforts seem to have been matched by the results: both were performed and acclaimed at the Concert Spirituel. But the projects on which Mozart set his greatest hopes – a planned large-scale French opera, a ballet-intermezzo for Noverre and a projected oratorio in French – came to nought.

At least one of the main reasons why Mozart made no headway in Paris is described by Mozart himself (1 May 1778). No sooner had he dutifully begun paying visits than he suffered a setback. In his first audience with a lady of society he was promised an invitation in one week's time. When it failed to arrive he appeared anyway, without an invitation. Here he was made to wait in an unheated room for half an hour before the lady finally appeared, and then for another hour (freezing from top to toe, he adds) before he resolved to play on a poor piano. No one paid any attention to him, and he had to perform to the 'chairs, tables and walls'. Characteristically for Mozart, no sooner had the lord of the manor finally arrived, sat down next to him and begun to listen attentively than the 'cold, headache and wretched instrument' were forgotten. But Mozart found precious few of this sort of interested and intelligent listener among the circles he frequented in Paris. He had arrived at an unfortunate moment. On 30 May of Mozart's year in Paris Voltaire died, and on 2 July, one day before his mother, Rousseau. Paris was deeply struck by the deaths of these men, whose popularity went far beyond anything then imaginable in the German-speaking countries. People had other cares than to worry about a young visitor. Those who knew Mozart at all recalled him as a boy of seven. This was confirmed to him 'in all seriousness' by Madame d'Epinay: 'They treat me here like a beginner' (31 July). Grimm may have viewed him in much the same light.

It thus came about that after moving into the Grimm-d'Epinay household Mozart seldom encountered interested and attentive listeners. While still a young man, Friedrich Melchior Grimm (1723–1807) had settled in Paris as the secretary and confidant of a German count, and soon entered the circle of the Encyclopedists. He was well acquainted with Holbach, d'Alembert and Helvétius and was for years the intimate friend of Diderot and Rousseau. In 1753 he began to issue his *Correspondance littéraire* in a limited number of handwritten copies. It was sent to influential people – among its subscribers were Frederick II and Catherine of Russia – and did much to disseminate the ideas of the French Enlightenment. The *Correspondance* contained announcements, book reviews and theatre notices and published a number of writings, including several by Diderot.

Madame d'Epinay, the authoress of many articles in the *Correspondance*, likewise stood at the centre of the French Enlightenment. The wife of a wealthy tax collector, she maintained friendships with Voltaire and Rousseau, decorating and bequeathing to the latter one of his favourite residences, the Eremitage. At the time that Mozart made her acquaintance she was living with Melchior Grimm. Admittedly, by this time the bonds of friendship between Voltaire and Madame d'Epinay, and between Rousseau and Grimm (and between many others), had loosened or torn where they had not turned into bitter enmity. But Grimm remained closely associated with Diderot to the end of his days. Mozart, then, spent almost three solid months living in a bastion of the French Enlightenment.

At first all went well. Mozart was in agreement with his father, mother and sister in considering Grimm the best and most trustworthy friend of the family. Indeed, Grimm had already proven his friendship during Maria Anna's illness. He and Madame d'Epinay wished to send for their physician immediately, little knowing that he would not be welcome as Mozart's mother preferred a German doctor. Following the disaster Mozart was taken without demur into the Grimm-d'Epinay household, where he received both lodging and board. On 9 July he reported to his father that he occupied 'a pretty little room'. Scarcely two months later there was 'nothing to recommend it except the view; it is just four bare walls' (11 September).

There were profound reasons for Mozart's change of mood, reasons which go beyond personal differences. Mozart may not have been entirely unjustified in finding Grimm miserly and small-minded, though he did offer to pay for the return journey to Salzburg. But it is difficult to see why Grimm should have had to turn his young guest so unceremoniously out of doors and insist on his departure. It is no small matter that even Leopold, who otherwise always took sides with Grimm, ultimately refused to concede his adulatory title of Baron. On 1 October he remarked testily, 'I am very much annoyed with Monsieur Grimm for the way he has hurried up your departure from Paris' – and this only a couple of weeks after Mozart had demoted Grimm to 'that upstart baron' (11 September). Perhaps part of the problem was the fifteen *louis d'or* that Mozart had borrowed from Grimm 'bit by bit' during his mother's illness. Perhaps there were political differences between the two, since Mozart hoped that 'the Prussians would get a good thrashing' in the War of the Bavarian Succession but added, 'I daren't say such a thing in this house' (31 July).

But the full significance of Mozart's encounter with Grimm cannot be understood on the levels we have considered up to now. He did not rush with flying colours to the Enlightenment camp. On the contrary. Only a few weeks previously he had mentioned the death of Voltaire in words that betray an apparently implacable hostility – 'That godless archrascal Voltaire has pegged out like a dog, like a beast' – and this in the same letter (3 July 1778) that attempted to inform his father and sister of his mother's death! The episode with Grimm, as we shall see, likewise ended in clear and gruff detachment.

This was, of course, not Mozart's first encounter with the Enlightenment. Later we shall have some things to say about his contacts with the Illuminati in Salzburg. In many respects even his own father was an Enlightenment figure; Mozart was raised in an atmosphere sympathetic to the Enlightenment. Typically, his father's comments on the death of Voltaire do not sound half as implacable as those of his son: 'So Voltaire is dead too, and he died as he lived: he might have done better for the sake of his posthumous reputation' (29 June 1778).

Mozart had to find and travel his own path, and the path he chose was not a smooth one. His encounter with Grimm cannot be reduced to a simple formula. Nor should we overlook its purely musical aspect, for this aspect is decisive.

'The picture that German musicology has given us of Grimm the music critic is more like a caricature than a sober, scholarly portrait.' Thus the words of Martin Fontius (1989, p. 47), an expert in Romance languages and philology. And Fontius is right. I will follow his discussion below, without of course attempting to do justice to his equally rightful demand that 'sooner or later a book entitled *The Aesthetic Ideas of Baron Grimm* will have to be written' (p. 49).

Our most grievous oversight has been to ignore Grimm's competence in questions of music. Grimm was, to be sure, not a trained musician; but he was an avid performer and even a composer, having acquired a technical understanding of music and having thought about it in close contact with the best minds of Europe. Rousseau (1770, p. 484) reports that his friendship with Grimm began in 1749 when they 'played music together the whole day long'. Grimm, then twenty-six years old, had just settled in Paris and established friendly contacts with Diderot and Helvétius. Three years later he wrote a brilliant and scathing satire on French opera, *Le Petit Prophète de Boehmisch-Broda* (1753). Two major articles for Diderot's *Encyclopédie* appeared in 1765: a purely technical discussion of *motif* in volume X, and the article '*Poème lyrique*' in volume XII. Until now musicologists have treated the latter as though it were a disquisition on some species of lyric poetry and of no further musical interest. In fact, it is a knowledgeable and highly critical discussion of the contemporary opera libretto – indeed, of operatic life as a whole – abounding in provocative opinions and recommendations (see Appendix, pp. 322–8). One might have learnt from the entry in Rousseau's *Dictionnaire de musique* that 'nowadays', meaning 1767, the word *lyrique* refers to the 'stale poetry of our operas'.

Let us now try to imagine Mozart's situation. At first, while his relations with Grimm were still intact and the little room in his house was still 'pretty', Mozart pricked up his ears whenever he heard Grimm proclaiming his well-founded and tightly argued opinions. He had good reason to take them seriously. Twice, on 11 and 28 May, Leopold had urged him to discuss the libretto of his projected French opera with Grimm. And Mozart did so: 'I also listened to the advice of

Baron Grimm and some other good friends' (3 July). Even though this advice involved a matter other than opera – namely, his rejection of an appointment as court organist in Versailles – there can be little room for doubt that Mozart also discussed the problems of opera librettos with Grimm. He had ample opportunity for discussion. In more than two months in the Grimm household he had, as he told his father on 11 September, 'not dined there more than fourteen times at the most'. It is not our purpose to keep count of his meals in Grimm's household. But his mother had already mentioned, on 12 June, that Wolfgang dined at Grimm's with Raff; and the remark about their joint condemnation of French music and his otherwise harmonious relations with Grimm (then still with his baronial title) dates from early April 1778. This is important, for it shows that there were many opportunities for the two to enter into conversation, and we can largely reconstruct how these conversations went.

Mozart's discussions with Grimm took place during a period of violent controversies in which Grimm was a leading participant. One of the main bones of contention was whether French opera had any chance whatsoever of surviving alongside Italian opera. This debate was triggered by the appearance in Paris of a company of Italian singers, who mounted Pergolesi's *La serva padrona* and other Italian comic operas before Mozart had even been born, namely, from 1752 to 1754. Progressively minded intellectuals and musicians, among them Diderot, Rousseau and Grimm, were enchanted by the freshness of these little masterpieces, by their musical invention and what was thought to be their naturalness. Indeed, so great was their enthusiasm that they felt called upon to proclaim that the French language was unsuitable for opera, and that the future of music as a whole lay in the hands of the Italians.

Rousseau responded to this event in two ways. First, as early as 1752, he was moved to compose *Le Devin du village*, a short comic opera to a French text that proved successful beyond all expectations. Then one year later he wrote his *Lettre sur la musique française*, which, though anonymous, was widely known to be his work. Here, in overstatements bordering on the grotesque, Rousseau takes French music to task. Analysing a famous number from Lully's *Armide* of 1686, he proves, not entirely without justification, that the verse is badly declaimed, that the work lacks both melody and a decent accompaniment, and that its harmonic progressions are not appropriate to the dramatic action. The entire letter, amounting to nearly fifty printed pages, culminates in the absurd discovery that 'the French do not and cannot have a music of their own' (1753, p. 95). This tirade must have been all the more provoking as Rousseau dared to stand up to the two giants of French opera, Lully and Rameau, with only a tiny comic opera – and in French. Today we can see that this little opera cannot have owed its enormous success to any outstanding musical qualities – it has none – but rather to its stance. Such things are by no means rare in music history. *Le Devin du village* shifted the emphasis to straightforward, singable melodies and away from allegorical figures and demigods to everyday human problems, even if these humans are shepherds who no longer strike us today as particularly human and natural. (Perhaps Mozart and Grimm discussed the interesting fact that in 1768, fifteen years after the appearance of Rousseau's opera, a twelve-year-old composer named Mozart set the same libretto in German translation as *Bastien und Bastienne*.)

Grimm too, as already mentioned, became and remained a confirmed believer in the superiority of Italian music and in the suitability of the Italian language for musical settings. As late as 1778 he wanted Mozart always to 'run off to see Piccinni' – 'his Piccinni' Mozart acidly added – 'and Caribaldi also, for they have a miserable opera buffa here now' (11 September). It seems that Grimm recommended Italian composers as models regardless of whether they wrote in Italian or French, for Piccinni had just produced a French opera in Paris. Mozart, intent on writing a French opera, could not possibly have guessed how important the possibilities of opera buffa would later become for him. And Rousseau, to add yet another twist, had just retracted his doubts about the musical potential of the French language. This revealed the impact of Gluck, who had arrived in Paris to engineer the triumph of his works in French: *Iphigénie en Aulide* and *Orphée* (both 1774), *Alceste* (1776) and *Armide* (1777). Feelings were ruffled, and music-lovers in the French capital fell into two camps. Niccolò Piccinni (1728–1800), a composer of no mean attainments, was touted as Gluck's rival by his adversaries, and these same differences of opinion were shared by the Encyclopedists. Gluck, with that sovereign generosity that was his hallmark, stood entirely above the fray during his stay in Paris. He paid a visit to Rousseau, expressed his high esteem, and not only sought his advice on the French versions of his own operas but also requested copies of Rousseau's own works. The latter immersed himself in Gluck's operas, found much in them to admire, and analysed several of their numbers with sensitivity and expertise. (A good account of this can be found in Gülke 1984a, pp. 180–211, and 1984b, pp. 158–68.) Grimm remained unimpressed.

Today, with the advantage of hindsight, we can see that the decisive question is not whether to choose between the Italian or the French language. When Gluck, just a few years later, spoke of the 'ridiculous distinction between national styles of music' and instead proposed a 'music common to all nations', he in fact ascended to a loftier plane than those still embroiled in the language issue. And Mozart, too, is supra-national.

Another hotly contested issue was equally wide of the mark: Rousseau and Rameau crossed swords over whether melody is the main ingredient of music or a product of the progressions of harmony. Jean-Philippe Rameau (1683–1764), equally important as a composer and music theorist, was closely allied with the Encyclopedists. He was a friend of Diderot; d'Alembert popularized the theories of this celebrated composer in a treatise published in 1752. Rameau's theories, however, are a story all their own. Part of his doctrine was that harmonic events can be derived from a small number of functions, which may be assumed by different chords. And this part of his theory is a penetrating insight, equally useful for the teaching and analysis of music, provided that it is only applied to music of a particular period in history.

But Rameau was no more willing to accept these restrictions than were, sad to relate, many later theorists. His doctrine was meant to follow from the laws of nature and to be valid for all eternity. It was also, we may safely assume, meant to give his compositions an aura of immutability and timelessness. No fewer than twenty-four books and articles appeared from Rameau's pen over a period of some forty years, mutually improving, modifying, and at times contradicting each other. Their purpose was to prove that harmonic events are grounded in the facts of arithmetic or, as he later surmised, in physics. The thought that laws of art are derivable from laws of nature must have been especially attractive to the Encyclopedists in their efforts to combat theocentric notions. As late as the 1750s Rameau was commissioned to write all the articles on music for the *Encyclopédie*. In the end he did not, probably because Diderot and Grimm had nagging doubts about the correctness of his theories.

These doubts were warranted. At least since 1863, the year in which the natural philosopher and physicist Hermann von Helmholtz (1821–94) published his *Lehre von den Tonempfindungen*, we have known 'that the construction of scales and harmonies is a product of artificial invention, and not, as generally claimed hitherto, directly given to us by the structure of nature or the natural activity of the ear' (in another passage Helmholtz says 'not simply residing in immutable laws of nature'). 'However,' he continues, 'the natural laws governing the activity of our ear have a large and influential role to play in this process. They are like building materials put to use by man's artistic urge' (1863, pp. 386 and 587). The point, for our purposes, is that Diderot's circles posited ideas of this sort one hundred years before Helmholtz. Admittedly they were not supported by experimental findings and apparently arose in ignorance of the experiments then being carried out (though only published later) by Mozart's exact contemporary Ernst Florens Friedrich Chladni, whose *Entdeckungen über die Theorie des Klanges* appeared in Leipzig in 1787. Chladni's 'acoustic figures', already famous in their day, prove that a very wide variety of vibrations must be taken into account in acoustics, and not merely the simple proportions of a vibrating string, as was generally believed until then. This discovery had far-reaching consequences for music theory.

In 1771 a small volume entitled *Leçons de clavecin et principes d'harmonie* was published in Paris. It was ascribed to a Monsieur Bemetzrieder, and we have no cause to doubt that its musical sections are in fact the work of Anton Bemetzrieder (b. 1743 or 1748, d. *c.* 1817), a musician highly esteemed and supported by Diderot. Yet, in the main, the book may be generally assumed to have been written by Diderot. Grimm, too, was in agreement with Bemetzrieder, as we know from a letter written by Diderot to his friend Charles Burney in which he warmly recommends the book. The significant passages for our purposes are those that attribute a musical role to taste, intuition, the whims of performers, even obscurity. Physics was not to be the final arbiter: the chromatic scale is a 'joint product of nature and art' (1771, p. 347). The book is written in the form of a dialogue between a philosopher, a teacher and his pupils, one of whom is a girl (Diderot's daughter), and is dominated by objections to Rameau's theories, which are even reviled as 'claptrap'. If Mozart had been one of the interlocutors it is obvious which position he would have taken. His pronouncement, quoted on p. 152, regarding the uselessness of old rules makes clear what he thought of immutable laws.

Another passage from the same book (p. 342) helps further to illuminate the background of Grimm's conversations with his young protégé. Diderot allows his 'teacher' to explain that 'the music of Cramer' – a composer mentioned earlier in the debate – 'is intended for a small minority, but the music I love is written for the multitude. And that must always be our goal: the instruction or entertainment of the multitude.' That, basically, was Grimm's line of thought.

In *Le Petit Prophète*, Grimm's brilliant satire of 1753, an insignificant dance musician named 'Waldstörchel', whose father came from the 'Judengass of the Old Town at Prague' and he himself from 'Boehmisch-Broda in Bohemia', hears a voice speaking to him in biblical inflections. Miraculously he is transported to Paris, where he of all people is instructed by The Voice to revitalize the Paris Opera. That preposterous hodge-podge of dances, ditties and psalmody that is called 'opera' must vanish, he is told. Instead of wretched caterwauling there must be singers; instead of a woodchopper at the head of the orchestra there must be musicians of taste who are alive to genius. The demons and shades, the fairies and genii and monsters *tutti quanti* must disappear from the stage, at which point The Voice will create a human being, breathe life and genius into him, and enjoin him to take command of the theatre known as the Académie de Musique.

In a completely different tone, but in the same spirit, Grimm criticizes Parisian operatic life in his great article on opera (see Appendix, pp. 322ff.). How can any rational listener, he asks, be captivated by those fairy-tale creatures that people the operatic stage? How can he enter into their minds and sympathize with their thoughts? French opera must take up the fates of real human beings, as has already been done in other lands. Otherwise music itself will be sapped of its true strength and degenerate into mere hackwork.

This article on opera was at least twelve years old when Grimm spoke with Mozart, and we cannot simply assume that he cast each and every one of his earlier opinions into the discussion. For since that time at least one major event had taken place: Gluck's arrival in Paris. The most important source of Grimm's views on music is, of course, the *Correspondance littéraire*, of which Grimm had been the editor since May 1753. But Grimm only retained this position until 15 February 1773. 'Thereafter, from 1775, the enterprise was entirely in the hands of the Zurich-born Jakob Heinrich Meister' (Fontius 1989, p. 48). Still, we cannot be far off the mark if we assume that the views on post-Gluckian opera expressed in an article in the *Correspondance* of April 1774 (volume 10, pp. 416–19) are identical to Grimm's own. This piece tells us that there are now three camps among opera-lovers. The adherents of early French opera are given the shortest shrift. They complain, we are told, that their genre has been scuttled without anything better to take its place. Rather than nodding off during the action [*durant la scène*] one now has to listen, and this despite the fact that there is nothing in it to warrant staying awake. Then come those who are fully committed to Italian opera, to Jommelli, Piccinni and Sacchini. They reproach Gluck for lacking melody, though without denying his understanding of the mysteries of harmony. The position of Gluck and the *Gluckistes* is presented with detached irony, but with that same respect that had marked earlier critiques of his works. This camp claims that Gluck has discovered the music most appropriate to the stage, a music that 'draws at the eternal wellsprings of harmony' (Gluck is thus equated with Rameau) 'and from our inmost feelings and sensations'. Then, after an allusion to Gluck's vision of a supranational music and a claim that he successfully adapted his music to the French language, there comes a 'grim' statement, in a dual sense of the word, alluding to Rousseau: 'This last-named party can boast of an illustrious convert' (p. 416).

The Encyclopedists' scepticism toward the state of opera cannot be reduced to conflicts over isolated issues. Whether they debated the suitability of one language or another, questioned the validity of eternal laws, dismissed or championed genres or subjects, the Encyclopedists had, for all their many differences of opinion, one point of common ground: to overcome the musical culture dominated by the aristocracy. D'Alembert (1759, p. 520) bears witness that they were well aware of this. Divining their goals with a keen political instinct, and slandering their true intentions as was their habit, the opponents of the Encyclopedists pictured them as 'a group ... which formed for the sole purpose of destroying religion, authority, morality and music in one fell swoop.'

When Mozart sat opposite the fifty-five-year-old Grimm he confronted a man who had well-founded opinions on the central events of this transitional era. Mozart, at twenty-two, had already done more for this transition than can be accomplished by the best of theories, and only a few years would pass before his music became virtually the quintessence of the age. But up to now he had followed this path without reflection. Only rarely had he offered criticism of his profession, and only rarely did he hear any – certainly not from his opportunistic father. It could hardly be otherwise that Grimm, with his seasoned opinions, and Mozart, with his quest for intellectual independence, should agree on many points. One of these we can point to with certainty: their low opinion of French music. 'Baron Grimm and I often give vent to our musical rage at the music here', reads Mozart's letter of 5 April 1778.

There was another point in which Mozart could, and apparently did, learn from Grimm's astute criticism. In Grimm's discussion of the opera libretto he shows himself to be what he himself called *un critique éclairé*, an enlightened critic. Not only is he concerned with the libretto as such, he also takes up the circumstances of its writing. Mozart had never heard such views before. Grimm was not one for half measures. In Athens, he assures us (p. 830), when Sophocles mounted a tragedy on stage he worked for fatherland, for religion, for the festivals of the Athenian republic, for the state. But today, when one of our most highly esteemed and best guarded poets, Metastasio in Vienna, has to deal with the state he does so in the form of the police, who find a thousand ways to harass him. Today's theatre, he continues, serves the pleasure of the idle, of that elite coterie known as *la bonne compagnie* – good society. At this point (p. 831) Grimm introduces *l'entrepreneur*, the opera impresario, the 'most unjust and absurd of all the poet's tyrants'. He has the impresario declare his credo in a lengthy passage of direct address covering eight points. First, the impresario proclaims, he has the least possible need for the services of the poet, still less the composer. His profession is to make money. To do so, everyone involved must do what the public expects and also, lest we forget, what the singers expect. From these axioms he derives all those senseless rules of opera seria which Mozart knew only too well. Whatever Grimm had to say to Mozart on this subject – and he had just as much if not more to say now in 1778 than he did earlier – it fell on fertile ground. When Mozart claims, as he did later from Vienna on 21 May 1785, that 'the directors of our theatre are too niggardly and too little patriotically-minded', he is thinking in exactly the same terms as Grimm. (Parenthetically, it is easy to see why a conservative historian such as Hermann Kretzschmar found little to praise in a thinker of Grimm's radicality. Kretzschmar made no minor contribution to the misrepresentation of Grimm by wrongly accusing his aesthetic of 'lacking any technical and historical basis' and declaring that one could 'toss it overboard without further ado' (1903, p. 214).)

In another area, one fundamental to Mozart's later work, Grimm also touched a nerve in the young composer. A central concept of Grimm's theory is *la rapidité*, meaning quick succession, brevity and conciseness of action and import. As this concept is rendered only approximately by the English term 'rapidity' I have left the word untranslated below. 'Just as *rapidité* is a quality inseparable from music and one of the principal causes of its marvellous effects' – thus Grimm's article on the libretto (pp. 826f.) – 'so must the course of the libretto likewise be *rapide*. Long and extraneous [*oisifs*] dialogues are nowhere more out of place than here.' Grimm must surely have expostulated to Mozart on the necessity of *rapidité*. Again and again we can observe that once a new discovery had ripened Mozart was quick to grasp it. Just how deeply the necessity of maximum conciseness and brevity in opera must have struck him can be seen first of all in his letters to his father from Munich regarding *Idomeneo*. And his father's reaction shows just how novel was this idea to the Mozart family's aesthetic. What could possibly be gained by deleting a few measures, he rejoined. But there was no stopping Mozart. In no fewer than fifteen passages from letters written between September 1780 and January 1781 he reveals an almost fanatical insistence on conciseness. Recitatives had to be shortened, arias and duets cut. He even uses the word 'unnecessary' [*unnötig*], recalling Grimm's 'extraneous' [*oisifs*], for excessively long dialogues (15 November 1780). The subterranean music is twice shortened, as are two other scenes. One insight with repercussions for Mozart's future develop-ment is that single-section arias can very well take the place of the customary bipartite or tripartite arias. In a characteristic example Mozart writes, in reference to an aria, that 'even if it had only one section it would do quite well, in fact I should almost prefer it' (5 December 1780). Nor does *rapidité* apply solely to the opera. In a letter of 11 September Mozart declares his intention to shorten his earlier symphonies and violin concertos, for 'in Germany we rather like length, but after all it is better to be short and good'.

Similarly, Grimm's discussion of the relation between poet and composer functioned as a catalyst for new insights and modes of behaviour on Mozart's part. Until now the Mozarts, both father and son, had not once thought to object to anything in the librettos Mozart was given to set. They were happy enough to be given one at all. But after his visit to Paris Mozart outdid himself in painstaking instructions to his librettist, beginning immediately with *Idomeneo* and continuing full throttle with *Die Entführung*. Mozart made the librettist his partner, but one subordinate to himself. Compare, for instance, the following two passages. The first is taken from Grimm's article on the libretto (p. 826) immediately preceding the quoted remarks on *rapidité*; the second is a famous passage from Mozart's letter of 13 October 1781.

> This internal economy of the musical theatre, residing firstly on verisimilitude of imitation and secondly on the nature of our sensory organs, must serve the opera librettist as his fundamental poetics. Indeed, it is essential that he subordinate himself to the musician in every point; the most he can claim is a secondary role. But he still has sufficient artistic means at his disposal to share the fame of his confrère. The manner in which he chooses to organize the subject matter, the structure and the pace of the entire drama – these are the work of the poet.

> In an opera the poetry must be altogether the obedient daughter of the music ... The best thing of all is when a good composer, one who understands the stage and is talented enough to make sound suggestions, meets an able poet, that true phoenix.

Thus, at least in musical matters, Mozart's meeting with Melchior Grimm would have been uncommonly productive had it not been for a conversation that must have taken place toward the end of July. This conversation caused Mozart completely to reverse his feelings toward his older friend. Grimm reported his side of the conversation in a letter to Leopold. This letter is now unfortunately lost, but as Leopold quotes long passages from it verbatim in a letter to his son (13 August), and as Mozart in turn reported the conversation in a letter to his father (31 July), it can be reconstructed. Wolfgang is 'too ingenuous' (*zu treuherzig*, Grimm's only German words in a letter otherwise written in French), too unwilling to act, too little concerned about the means for achieving success. He must go to work with greater cunning, enterprise and boldness. It would be better to have half his talent for a double portion of proper deportment.

Now, there was nothing Mozart needed less at this stage of his career than the all-too-familiar arguments of his father from the mouth of another paternalistic adviser. Mozart had already drawn up his plan of action, and it was not nearly as escapist as Grimm and his father apparently made it out to be. Mozart planned an opera for Paris while he was still in Mannheim. As he wrote on 7 February: 'My mind is set on writing operas, but they must be French rather than German, and Italian rather than either.' And on 28 February he tells of his resolve to concentrate on 'my favourite type of composition, namely, choruses'. They stand a chance of being performed in Paris, where choruses are highly valued because 'they are accustomed to Gluck's choruses here'. He then continues: 'Do rely on me. I shall do my very best to bring honour to the name of Mozart.' There follows a lengthy passage virtually entreating his father to have trust in him.

Mozart had come very close to realizing these plans in Paris; he seemed almost certain to receive a commission to write a French opera. There were two subjects under discussion. One was a libretto to be called *Alexandre et Roxane,* based on an idea by Noverre. Mozart mentions this libretto on 5 April and again on 3 July, at which time one act of the book had already been written. The second was a translation of Metastasio's *Demofoonte.* We can well imagine what Mozart had in mind if we think of the passage quoted above together with Mozart's next large-scale opera, *Idomeneo.* Mozart wanted nothing less than to challenge Gluck, for all his dutiful and apparently sincere respect, and to surpass him on his own terrain. It was to be a French grand opera with extended choral numbers for which Gluck was to be a springboard rather than an unattainable model. Gathering all his strength, the young genius was planning his leap to independence, to 'maturity', in the domain he had marked out as his home territory, opera. And at this very moment Grimm comes along and wishes he had half the talent and instead more of that form of behaviour that Mozart equated with 'antechambering' – bootlicking.

The problem was compounded by an obvious misunderstanding. 'He distrusts ... my talent', writes Mozart on 11 September, incidentally capitalizing the word 'my' [*Mein*], 'but I know that he distrusts the latter, for he himself once said to me that he did not believe I was capable of composing a French opera.' Whatever Grimm said, it probably derived from nothing but his unyielding scepticism toward French grand opera. We must also bear in mind that he had before him the young composer of *La finta giardiniera* and *Les Petits Riens*, not that of *Figaro.* He could not have known – indeed, there is no indication that he had the slightest inkling – that he was harbouring in his house a prophet who was about to bring forth miracles quite different from those of the little prophet of Boehmisch-Broda.

The disaster had taken place and ran its course. As important as many of Grimm's ideas were to Mozart's future aesthetic, his name disappears from the Mozart chronicle. In all likelihood Mozart forgot or repressed what he had heard at the home of the man who, in March, was still 'our dear friend Grimm', with whom he could still agree on musical matters in July, but whose household had become, by 11 September, 'boorish and stupid'. Grimm probably had given vent to one or another of his less promising ideas, for the harsh conclusion that Mozart drew from this interlude must have resulted from something more than personal antagonism. Perhaps Grimm advised his young house guest to distinguish between two types of declamation, the one calm and expressed in recitative, the other passionate and given to arias (Grimm, p. 825). Mozart's music, on the contrary, can take exactly the opposite tack. Perhaps he tried to convince him of the propriety of placing singers in the orchestra pit and letting dancers act on stage (pp. 835f.). Or perhaps he expressed his view, for they had not consulted with each other beforehand, that it was unnatural in a chorus or ensemble for the singers all to sing the same words to the same melody (p. 832). Finally, it is highly likely that Grimm, in his table conversation, struck a tone similar to that of his earlier article, when he set out to define what opera ought and ought not to be. Today we know where such ideas came from; Diderot had elaborated similar notions for the spoken theatre. Everything was meant to serve the goal of presenting to new audiences an incisive, topical, realistic spectacle on stage, including the musical stage. Even at that time this view cannot have been foreign to Mozart, but musically he was going in other directions. Listening to some of Grimm's views, he must have found himself gasping for breath.

We stand a good chance, then, of picturing Mozart's mood as he wrote to his friend Bullinger on 7 August. The subject of his letter is the music of the Salzburg court, the occasion of its writing the prospect of having again to work under those conditions. But the topic is a larger one: Mozart's thoughts rush beyond his immediate perspectives in Salzburg. He paints a bitter and sarcastic picture of everything that has been and continues to be done incorrectly in Salzburg. Instead of trying to find a capable conductor they are simply on the look-out for sopranos, who, Mozart jeers, will certainly never be in short supply, not even if the one should enter labour, the other land in prison, a third be whipped and a fourth decapitated. And even if they were, there would still be the castrati. One only needs to commission Metastasio in Vienna to write a few dozen librettos in which the primo uomo and the prima donna never meet. In this way the castrato could play the parts of both the lover and his mistress and the story would be even more interesting – for people would be able to admire that virtue of the lovers which is so absolute that they purposely avoid any occasion of speaking to one another in public. There is the opinion of a true patriot for you!

Though expressed in the negative, Mozart's letter outlines a complete aesthetic of opera. It lets us know that he intends to put his lovers and their conflicts on stage, and that they will expose their innermost feelings not only in arias but also in the plot. As we know, he carried out this conception to such an extent that he introduced new techniques into opera, techniques drawn from instrumental music. This idea was worlds apart from Grimm (though not from Diderot, who explicitly mentioned *bruits physicales* as a source of music). Even in purely musical terms there was more than enough kindling in Grimm's admonitions to inflame Mozart's imagination. We can see why the young composer now heard nothing in the words of his father's friend except those things that had until now kept him chained and fettered: namely, the rationalistic and pedantic side of his father's own views. In this light, we can understand that delightful passage in his letter to Bullinger in which Mozart lets off steam, a passage culminating in the following outburst: 'Do your utmost to help music find an arse, for that is what it needs most of all! It has a head now – indeed, that is just its misfortune!'

Most of Mozart's hopes for his journey to Mannheim, Munich and Paris had failed and much had been lost. His encounter with the intellectuals of the French Enlightenment had taken a curiously ambiguous course. Keeping them at arm's length, judging them one-sidedly, even showering them with invective, Mozart nevertheless learnt lessons from them which he could not have learnt elsewhere. And he did so without knowing it.

For changes in world-view during troubled times, this is nothing unusual. Such changes often travel convoluted paths.

Chapter 9

Taking stock of Salzburg

Salzburg was Mozart's place of residence for twenty-five years. But we can hardly call it his home: he was too outspoken and too consistent in his criticism not only of its court but about life there in general, its lack of 'entertainment', which for Mozart always meant stimuli, and the coarse manners of its townspeople. If we think Mozart's opinions one-sided we need only look at his father's, which were not much milder. Of course the Mozarts had carefree and pleasant moments in Salzburg in the company of family and friends or in target practice (*Pölzelschiessen*), a favourite Salzburg pastime in which the Mozarts often took part. Among their friends were Johann Andreas Schachtner (1731–95), a musician, writer and observant chronicler of many episodes from Mozart's childhood, and Franz Joseph Nepomuk Bullinger (1744–1810), a highly cultured, Jesuit-trained man much attached to the Mozarts, although after about 1781 he seems to have been closer to Leopold than to Wolfgang (Schmid 1953, p. 21). We will have more to say about other Salzburg friends in Chapter 11. Yet at no point did Mozart live whole-heartedly in Salzburg. Moreover, more than nine of these years were spent travelling. Subtracting the six years of his early childhood this amounts to roughly half of his entire Salzburg period.

In taking stock of Mozart's musical output of this period we must start with the fact that, as far as quantity is concerned, more than half of his music was written before he made Vienna his permanent residence (once again 'home' is not quite the right word). His opportunities to compose by no means suffered during his many years of travel; on the contrary, he received ever-new stimuli and employed the same methods of production as in Salzburg. Mozart wrote what the occasion or his patrons demanded of him. This was nothing unusual. Apart from occasional presents to friends, composers of the late eighteenth century, as is well known, wrote music for payment to satisfy the musical needs of the propertied and educated classes. We should keep in mind that the great majority of people satisfied those needs either by making music themselves or, in the towns, by some form of cheap commercial music. This state of affairs left an imprint on Mozart's development and on the evolution of music at the time: these people were potential listeners for music that stood at the pinnacle of its age. Mozart's self-imposed task of gaining the 'applause even of the ignorant' (13 October 1781) referred to these potential audiences. But until he moved to Vienna he had no way of reaching them.

In Salzburg and the lands Mozart visited it was understood that a composer would accommodate his talents to the wishes of his patrons, no matter how great his misgivings might be. These wishes merged with the predefined limits within which he had to ply his trade, limits set by a given location, occasion and performance tradition (which in turn varied according to region, nationality and social level) and by the capabilities of performers and the receptivity of listeners, even by the range of instruments and voices. Mozart seemed to find all this more of a challenge and incentive than an obstacle. Even in his very last works he brilliantly combined and unified his external circumstances with his inner sense of mission. Beethoven may have scoffed at the material conditions of music-making, as in his classic outburst that he cannot be expected to think of 'Schuppanzigh's wretched fiddle' when the spirit moves him. But such views were foreign to Mozart's age and to himself. This was doubtless related to the fact that Beethoven viewed the conditions under which he composed as rigid and unchangeable, as a force imposed from without, while Mozart felt called upon to work toward their improvement.

Accordingly, as Mozart grew older he became more and more dissatisfied. His discontent was directed mainly toward three inter-related factors. First, there was his boundless rage at musical conditions in Salzburg. He fumed at the 'coarse, slovenly and dissolute music at court' (9 July 1778) and concluded that 'we have always been utterly different *in every way* from court music' (24 March 1781). He sarcastically dismissed Metastasio's brand of opera (see pp. 53–4). Second, there was a steady increase of bitterness in Mozart's feelings toward the various princes who kept him waiting with vague and ultimately empty promises, merely costing him time and money. On 10 December 1777 he ended his conversation with the Hofmusikintendant in Mannheim as follows:

> Incidentally, I am very much obliged to you, Count, ... for having taken such an interest in me, and I beg you to thank the Elector [this last word is written in the Mozarts' secret code] on my behalf for his gracious though belated reply and to say that I can assure him that he would never have regretted it if he had taken me on.

Three months later (7 March 1778), having by then arrived in Paris, he was less orotund: 'The German princes are all skinflints.' Third, Mozart's disaffection gradually gave rise to a conviction that the intuitive development of his personal style required a goal and a direction. By the age of twenty-two Mozart had realized that stylistic renewal is a continuous and unending process. The greater his experience of the world the clearer this conviction became to him, and it continued to grow as he searched and groped over the years, even during his Vienna period.

Between 1881 and 1882 a series of no fewer than twenty articles appeared in the Leipzig *Allgemeine musikalische Zeitung*, all presenting a remarkable discussion of Mozart's juvenile operas. This discussion was occasioned by the publication of the relevant volumes in the 'old' Mozart *Gesamtausgabe*, which appeared in sixty-nine volumes between 1877 and 1905. The articles were the work of Friedrich Chrysander (1826–1901), who with extraordinary personal commitment edited the complete works of Handel in ninety-three volumes (1858–1901), the achievement of a superb scholar and an admirable man. His twenty-part review is in effect a debate with Otto Jahn, whose Mozart biography (1856–9) attributed high artistic value even to Mozart's early operas. Jahn's work, essentially a source study with a philosophical-aesthetic bias, was path-breaking for its time, but had the weakness of Jahn's limited understanding of music. It thus came about that he underestimated Mozart's forerunners, not knowing their music in any depth, and consequently overestimated Mozart's juvenile achievements, attributing to the boy a consistent and logical musical development. This conception doubtless resulted from his assumption, already exploded in Chapter 2, that Mozart's musical gifts, being unique, must perforce have grown organically to the pinnacle of compositional art. Chrysander counters this view by restoring three complexes of factors to their methodological rights. First, he rehabilitates Mozart's forerunners, particularly the Italian composers of opera and oratorio, so that 'they can again present themselves in decent society'. It not only does them injustice, Chrysander argues, but also misrepresents Mozart's achievement to imagine that the composers who preceded Mozart merely created conventions which the youthful genius was obliged to overcome. Second, Chrysander places the 'youthful, if not to say childlike works of the great Mozart' in proper perspective. (He is here referring to *Mitridate*, the opera seria Mozart had written before he had reached the age of fifteen.) Mozart, he claims, was simply not mature enough to master the psychological complexities of Metastasio's drama. Besides, he had been trained by his father in 'symphonistic instrumental music' rather than in the bel canto style. This one-sidedness left clear traces on the opera, much to its detriment. Finally, Chrysander polemicizes against Jahn's notion of Mozart's systematic and step-by-step evolution. 'Supposedly it did not manifest itself in leaps and explosions. But how else could it have developed?' he indignantly asks. 'What are *Idomeneo, Entführung, Figaro, Giovanni, Zauberflöte* and the Requiem if not highly unexpected leaps? Were they predictable in advance, like lunar eclipses? Are they perhaps calculable like the orbit of a comet?' (vol. 16, col. 810, and vol. 17, cols. 85, 103, 107, 122). Chrysander was right on all three points, and they have been taken that way or similarly by all serious writers on the subject ever since. What still awaits analysis, however, is the complex interplay between the various types of learning processes.

One of these processes, dominating the Salzburg years, is continuous and unbroken: Mozart's growing mastery of the composer's craft. Indeed, by the mid-1780s this process had led him to the apex of the humanly attainable. But inextricably linked with his progress toward mastery are a number of processes governed by conditions and laws which are different in kind from those of the figured bass.

It all began in play. Hardly had the boy turned four than he was *playing* instruments that he mastered like *child's play* and began to *play around* with the sounds he produced. This is more than mere punning. It may well be that, generally speaking, we master more things, and more kinds of things, by play than we realize. Mozart's lessons focused on the rules of the game, not on the meaning of the game itself. Years before he had learnt to imitate nature or 'affects' the boy knew what six-five chords and false relations are and how to resolve a dissonance. The circumstances under which his instruction took place also governed which genres he explored. Since his father was primarily a composer of instrumental music Wolfgang also started out as one. His first instrument was the clavier, the first models he encountered, through his sister's music lessons, were little pieces for the keyboard. Not until his trip to London did he write his earliest pieces for the voice, and by then he had already had two or three years' experience as a composer behind him. He was nine when he wrote his earliest sacred music – a motet, probably also a Kyrie – and he was ten when he wrote his first piece in that ambiguously defined category of divertimenti, cassations and serenades, which share the common feature of having to entertain listeners with variety and surprise. Mozart's earliest contribution to this genre, K32, is dated 1766 and entitled *Galimathias musicum*. Yet it is antedated by his first symphony, written when he was eight. Concertos and stage works entered his output at the age of twelve, and with his first string quartet of 1770, K80, written when he was fourteen, he emerged from divertimenti and serenades into the world of chamber music. We must note that between the ages of six and twelve Mozart had probed all of the genres that he would cultivate later in life, except for one: he wrote his first masonic song only at the age of sixteen.

The easiest path to retrace is the way the child learnt to master the rules which were valid at the time. When Nannerl was nine her father gave her a handwritten notebook containing lessons and exercises. It was from this notebook that little Wolfgang soon began to learn figured bass. Among other things it contains three exercises consisting of a bass line with figures indicating which chords to play. The way the player handles the separate parts so as to produce the requisite chords is, however, left to his own discretion within the confines of fixed rules:

This ability, too, Mozart acquired quickly. He was not yet seven years old when, as we can read in Melchior Grimm's *Correspondance littéraire* (Paris, 1 December 1763), the most highly trained Kapellmeister would have been unable to surpass him in the science of harmony and modulation. Leopold's teaching methods had obviously proved their worth, and Mozart clung to them when, in 1785, he gave lessons to his English pupil Thomas Attwood.

If figured bass was something tangible that could be written down and taught, it was not so simple with other, equally important aspects of the composer's craft. Even a subject so apparently cut and dried as musical form, a staple item in the training of nineteenth- and twentieth-century composers, did not exist in Mozart's day. As Peter Benary has put it in a penetrating study (1961, p. 148): 'In eighteenth-century music education the question of musical form was definitely secondary in importance.' Yet, as Benary also points out, this situation was beginning to change at the time Mozart was learning to compose. Concepts such as variation, variety, section and symmetry, as well as less tangible concepts such as *goût* or taste, found their way into composition manuals and music lexicons from mid-century. But none of them is to be found in Leopold Mozart's textbook, which admittedly dealt with violin playing, not with composition. And the work which Benary justly points to as the supreme eighteenth-century composition manual, the three-volume treatise by Heinrich Christoph Koch (1749–1816), did not begin to appear until the 1780s, at a time when Mozart's only remaining apprenticeship was with the Freemasons.

Besides instruction by rule, then, there was also another form of learning: instruction by imitation. Through imitation the boy learnt how to construct four-, eight- and sixteen-bar phrases, how to break up uniformity with contrast, how the sections of a piece of music should follow each other, and many similar things. In the aforementioned notebook, in which Wolfgang's earliest compositions were entered on blank pages, there is a minuet (now called No. 48) which he composed at the age of six-and-a-half but was unable to write down at the time. When his father wrote it out he added the following inscription: 'di Wolfgango Mozart d. 16ten July 1762'. Here are its opening bars:

Example 8

A year and a half later a set of six piano sonatas by Mozart appeared in print in The Hague. The first of these has a third movement made up of two minuets, of which the second, the trio section, is identical to the foregoing example. But it has undergone an improvement which, though slight, illustrates a principle of paramount importance. The first version syncopates the melody for the first four bars only, abandoning it in bar 5 and not returning to it later although the piece is twenty-two bars long. This is poor style, but the rule which proclaims this to be poor style is elusive.

The point at issue here is as old as music itself: the opening is left to the liberty of the player; the continuation is not. The question 'How do I start according to the rule?' posed by Wagner in *Die Meister-*

singer, is answered by Hans Sachs: 'You create it yourself, and then follow it.' His answer does not just apply to the age of the Meistergesang, nor just to Europe. Once a singer or instrumentalist chooses a particular technique – in our case the syncopation of the melody – it places him under obligation. A principle comes into play that unquestionably arises from and satisfies physiological needs calling for the unity or uniformity of the artistic result. Revealingly, European theories of art generally tend to account for departures from the rule of uniformity, using terms such as *varietas, modulatio,* development and so forth (see the relevant entries in the *Handwörterbuch der musikalischen Terminologie*). The rule of uniformity was obviously then, and is probably now, considered to be self-evident and 'natural'. But in fact the two – uniformity and departure – cannot be separated in the creation of art. Once the artist has set out on his chosen path he must both keep to it and depart from it, introducing new elements even to the point of the sharp contrast.

In other words the six-year-old Mozart, learning by imitation, had not yet grasped the rule of uniformity in this very early composition (we are talking about K6). In bar 5 the melody lands on the strong beats, in bar 6 there are six quavers, and in bar 9 twelve semiquavers. He has introduced too many new elements. But by the age of eight, in his new version, he had learnt to correct these shortcomings. Now the syncopation of the melody part continues in bar 5 and is picked up in bars 7, 15 and 17:

Example 9

In this way the basic rhythm now takes up more than a third of the total length, whereas in the first version it was a bit more than a fifth, isolated at the opening. Now the new elements can stand out properly. It may be that this correction was encouraged or carried out by his father, but that the eight-year-old composer had learnt the lesson need hardly be emphasized.

Still, we should always keep in mind the enormous amount of

material Mozart had to master during his childhood and teenage years. It ranged from amateur music-making in town and countryside to music of great learning and artifice, from church music to opera in all its various kinds, from comic songs to incidental music for tragedies, from music for convivial entertainment to music demanding thought and concentration, from vocal to instrumental music and even to spoken words with musical accompaniment. Moreover, all of this came in countless national variants and languages, not merely Italian, German, French and English but also the dialects of Bohemia, Vienna and the Alpine lands. Robert Schumann once made the clever observation (*c.* 1834, p. 207): 'Shut Beethoven for ten years in some godforsaken country village (a repellant thought!) and see whether he could produce a D-minor Symphony there.' Nor would Mozart have become what he did if he had not had the opportunity to absorb the music of half of Europe.

It is possible and, I feel, instructive to isolate one specific form of imitative learning. Let me illustrate this form first by taking an example from language.

In Vienna of the early twentieth century, a boy growing up in bourgeois circles (for girls things were different) was taught a greeting to be used when dealing with adults. This greeting was drilled into him with phrases like 'Say ...' If someone had asked him in first grade to write down the greeting on his slate he would probably have written *xtiant*. Years later it would strike the boy as a revelation to discover that this phrase, which he had parroted hundreds of times, broke down into words no less familiar – *küss' die Hand*, the familiar Viennese greeting meaning 'I kiss your hand'. Let us call this awakening of consciousness, in which new meaning is discovered in deceptively familiar things, *explorative learning*. Even that extraordinary child Mozart learnt his earliest musical entities not semantically but morphologically, as pleasant-sounding building blocks to be assembled in play. Only later, presumably aided or at least facilitated by the words of vocal pieces, did he discover that sounds can also express or 'imitate' something, as his father doubtless told him. The sources available to us are not so accurate that we can document this process during Mozart's childhood. But there is one example dating from Mozart's teenage years which can be readily explained as the result of explorative learning.

In addition to the revised version of *Thamos, König in Ägypten* K345, dating from 1779, two numbers from the earlier version of 1773 have also fortunately survived. In both versions the curtain rises to a large-scale choral number over 200 bars long in which the choruses of sun virgins and priests sing a paean to the rising sun. In verses less than brilliant we are told that the sun has dispelled 'the enemy of light, the night', and that it therefore 'brought new offerings ... from Egypt'. The musical style of the day demanded that any gaps in the choral melody resulting from the metrical pattern, and generally coinciding with breath rests for the singers, should be filled out with more or less formulaic instrumental interpolations. That is exactly what happens in this number. Two of these stopgaps – and in the first version that is fairly much what they are – are interesting because Mozart improved them dramatically six years later and the results of this improvement remained in his memory for another twelve years until the year of his death. These are the instrumental interpolations in bars 12 and 17 of the choral melody. The first enters after the words 'the enemy of light, the night' [*des Lichtes Feindin, die Nacht*], the second after the words 'brought new offerings' [*neues Opfer gebracht*]. Here is the first passage in the early version:

Example 10

The second appears on page 64 (Example 11). Something unexpected happened in the revision of 1779: the broken triads of the strings are also employed in the first of the two passages, and this in an orchestration which is unusual for Mozart, namely for two French

Taking stock of Salzburg

Example 11

Example 12

horns doubled at the octave by two trumpets. Since the fanfare rhythms are now given to trombones and timpani and the ascending oboe figures of the first version are now played by double woodwinds – and since the entire passage follows the fading night, sung *piano* by the chorus – what we now hear, supported by the entire wind section with timpani, is a radiant musical symbol of light (see Example 12 on page 64). The string figure of bar 17 of the chorus is retained at the same spot in the second version, where it is even doubled by the bassoons so that the attentive listener now hears it in a different way. In the first version this figure was a mere formula, just one broken triad among countless others. Now, however, having been so clearly articulated a mere five bars before, immediately following the word 'night', it has a significance that may have been latent in the earlier version but was unable to enter our consciousness, being inchoate and undifferentiated. Indeed, it presumably did not even enter the consciousness of the composer. At the age of twenty-three Mozart was able to discover new meaning in a deceptively familiar turn of phrase he had jotted down at seventeen.

That our interpretation of this process is not overdone is shown by an excerpt from the Requiem. When he wrote that incomparable passage at the words 'et lux perpetua' Mozart turned to the very same musical symbol he had used in *König Thamos*. It is probably the image of light spreading out simultaneously in all directions that inspired this figure, for he has retained not only the descending broken triad, emphasizing its initial note with a turn, but also the ascending motion in the other parts, this time transferring it to a rising sequence in the chorus:

Example 13

This figure deserves closer inspection. A related figure, perhaps felt by the composer to have the same meaning, is a constitutive element in *Figaro*. What we have referred to till now as a broken triad stands out from others in that it first begins normally:

Example 14

but then, while descending, twice skips a note only to recapture it from the opposite direction:

Example 15

These patterns:

Example 16

are familiar from yodelling. Mozart savoured them to the full in the slow movement of his Piano Concerto K537:

Example 17

where they appear five times within the space of four bars and countless times throughout the rest of the piece. (This is the concerto that Mozart played in Frankfurt in 1790, perhaps offering greetings from Austria to the River Main.) For singers, this type of broken triad has the advantage that they can remain longer within the triadic harmony; if they were to follow a normal arpeggiation of the triad they would soon reach the bottom of their range, and this seems to be the point of the figure when used in vocal music. After all, as Christian Kaden has remarked, this figure is not just melodic but also, perhaps even more so, a harmonic event.

In his overture to the ballet *Les Petits Riens*, written in Paris in 1778, Mozart has the rather conventional first theme followed by a charming second theme which, after unfolding for more than two dozen bars, is given an eight-bar codetta to round off the entire complex of some fifty bars. This codetta contains, three times in succession, the same figure we have been discussing, this time in a variant which, as we shall see, will be given special weight and significance years later from the lips of Susanna:

Example 18

But figures alone, whether melodic tags or harmonic entities, are not enough to make music. (This, incidentally, is what makes the publisher's claim for Gunthard Born's distinguished book – that it has 'deciphered' Mozart's musical language – somewhat inflated. To explore the meaning of figures without knowing the principles of construction by which they are assembled and combined with other elements is far from deciphering music. One might just as well decipher a language by exploring the meanings of its words without knowing its grammar.)

To account for the almost somnambulist assurance with which Mozart, even as a child, handled the principles of musical construction we must turn to yet another form of learning. This is an intuitive learning process distinguished by the fact that neither teacher nor pupil are able to pinpoint what is actually learnt. (Even composition teachers with a rational, functional approach, such as Hanns Eisler, often reserve a pained expression for phrases they find deficient or a vague gesture of the hand for things they find missing.) Let us consider Mozart's first symphony, called number 16 in Köchel's catalogue although it was preceded by some sixty other works preserved in writing. Mozart was a little over eight-and-a-half years old when he wrote it. It has survived in an autograph manuscript with corrections by Leopold, so that we can say, among other things, that Mozart's father found nothing to object to in the final movement. And he was right: we are dealing with a little masterpiece, and even the word 'little' applies only to its length. The movement is a mere 108 bars long and takes up little more than two minutes in performance. Its contrasts are handled with a self-confident aplomb that is almost eerie in a child of eight-and-a-half, being derived from the preceding material (an eight-bar theme) and put into balance with it.

Later, at the height of his powers, Mozart showed just how this should not be done but often was. In one of his most caustic jokes, *Ein musikalischer Spass*, K522 (June 1787), he confronts a bungling composer with the same problem that he had solved so brilliantly almost a quarter of a century earlier. Knowing that his bungler has to end his three-movement symphony with a fast movement, he likewise assigns him a Presto and invents a theme in F major which, though not brilliant, is at least usable, provided the composer knows what to do with it:

Example 19

Mozart is at once nasty and generous to his negative alter ego. Right at the beginning he makes him commit two howlers at once: 'parallel fifths' in bars 4 and 5 (strictly forbidden!) and 'hidden octaves' in bars 7 and 8, a minor peccadillo and easily corrected but nevertheless a sin. By the same token he grants him a quite respectable closing phrase for the first 'period' of the piece (the term was not coined until much later). After the somewhat unhappy turn to D minor, the so-called relative minor, in bar 8, he appends two bars that pleasantly upset the eight-bar pattern, returning admittedly somewhat noisily but efficiently to the main key (see Example 20 on page 69). But his imaginary composer does not know where to go from there. True, he modulates dutifully and very clumsily, but by the end of the first section he has

Example 20

neither left the main key nor, which is even worse, got away from the unceasing rhythm:

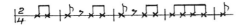

Example 21

We will not pursue his attempts to free himself from this strait-jacket, which even include a textbook fugal exposition, a horn solo and many another bold artifice. The point is that he is unable to escape monotony and merely rattles along in a meaningless rut.

With our eight-year-old composer it is quite different. The final movement of Mozart's Symphony No. 1 is likewise a rondo, and its sixteen-bar theme likewise has a periodic structure. Its first eight bars end in a so-called half-close on the dominant; the second eight bars, identical to the first apart from the final two bars, return to the tonic. The piece opens with a four-bar unison played by the entire orchestra, including strings, two oboes and two horns. This unison has three rhythmic figures:

Example 22

All three are put into action in the second four-bar unit. The quaver motion continues in the bass:

Example 23

The figure from bar 2 is taken up in bar 7 and transformed in bar 8:

Example 24

And the dotted crotchet is put into the melody part:

Example 25

Using these and a few more elements, Mozart deftly reaches the dominant, on which he constructs a sort of second theme from bars 5 and 6 of the first theme:

Example 26

In eight bars the descending melody line in the first violins spans a full sixth, while at the same time the three-note motif in the bass ascends more than an octave. This cannot go on for long, and anyone conversant with the music of the time will wait to see how Mozart will bring about the cadence. It, too, comes with a surprise: the complacent eight-bar pattern, broken down into two groups of four, is given a ninth and a tenth bar which, in the Neapolitan manner, supply the same final cadence that had concluded the first theme, namely, with six semiquavers in one bar:

Example 27

'I'his reminds us of a figure that Mozart drew in Nannerl's diary between 23 and 30 September 1780. The convex and concave parts of the figure are related like the two four-bar units of the theme, while the circular part to the right, though derived from the same basic pattern, differs from them in the same way as the theme's final two bars:

Now things really get going. Since the rondo theme occurs three times, taking up a total of forty-eight bars, there are fifty-seven bars left for the two interludes, or what in the nineteenth century were called 'episodes'. In other words, the interludes take up the major part of the piece. This is perfectly reasonable. Even as a boy Mozart knew how to handle the technique which constitutes, in essence, what was later called 'development' (in Mozart's day this term only applied to fugues). There is nothing unusual about mastering something intuitively that will only later acquire a name and, however flimsily, be codified in rules.

Whenever we want to know where Mozart, here or anywhere else, received a stimulus for a theme, we only need to consult Wyzewa and Saint-Foix. But they cannot tell us what enabled him to take the many component parts of that theme and to extract and elaborate their essence. In short, they cannot explain his principle of construction, or whatever we wish to call it. We have already seen in Chapter 2 that Mozart, at the age of three, four or five, could do things he had not yet been taught. Leopold and his friends could only assume that the boy had received these abilities from God. This enigmatic learning process was still at work when the boy was eight, as Leopold confirms in an impressive report from London on 28 May 1764. Writing home, he remarks that Wolfgang had played marvellous things on the clavier before the king. He then adds: 'In short, what he knew when we left Salzburg is a mere shadow compared with what he knows now. It exceeds all that one can imagine.' And they had left Salzburg barely a year before, on 9 June 1763. This phenomenon is a familiar one in psycholinguistics. Manfred Bierwisch (1989, p. 2) has put it succinctly as the problem

> that Chomsky summarized under the heading of 'Plato's problem'. It can be paraphrased by the question, 'How does a child form such a complex structure of knowledge on the basis of such limited experience?' Or, to put it more simply, 'How is it that we know more than we can possibly have learnt?'

One should avoid hasty analogies between language and music: these two systems of human communication differ fundamentally in too many of their structures and modes of operation. None the less, in the work of some linguists, including Noam Chomsky (1980, pp. 185ff.), or in astute linguistic dictionaries such as Lewandowski's under *Spracherwerb* ('language acquisition') and *Spracherwerbstheorien* ('theories of language acquisition'), we find entire passages which can be transferred to music without qualms. We must assume, for example, that embedded in the brain or nervous system of every human being are 'musical capacities' analogous to what in psycholinguistics are known as 'language capacities'. It follows, then, that any healthy child also has the ability to learn any kind of music provided it enters that particular musical environment at an early age, presumably before the age of two. Although to my knowledge it has never been tested under scientific conditions, we need not doubt that, say, a Chinese infant growing up in Germany would be able to express himself or herself just as easily in German music as a German child growing up in China would in Chinese music, or a Russian child in Arabic music, and so forth.

Mozart shared musical capacities of this sort with every other child on earth. His musical dispositions, probably unique in the full sense of the word, differed from those of his fellow humans by being available at an earlier age, by developing more quickly and apparently without limits, by extending to all areas of musical capacity (manual dexterity, memory, powers of invention, deductive powers and many others) whereas normal dispositions are more selective, develop more slowly and encounter limits.

What we are dealing with, then, are capabilities whose existence we can observe in children, whose results we can describe (approximately), and whose disposition must be postulated in the human genetic inheritance. Every normal human child has these capabilities to a greater or lesser degree, but not even the most highly evolved animals can approach them. Musical capacity is thus comparable to language capacity.

But at this point the similarity breaks down and the basic differences begin. Language capacity deals with logical operations, musical capacity with a complex adumbrated by terms such as symmetry and asymmetry, pleasantness and unpleasantness, preference and rejection. True, we sometimes speak of musical logic, but often put the word in quotes, and for good reason. Musical 'logic' is a matter of many things: parallelisms, repetition, the need for contrast, the expectation (perhaps frustrated) of particular continuations and connections during the act of music-making, a balance between similarity and dissimilarity, and many other things difficult to grasp. In non-poetic language, the colloquial language of everyday discourse, the objects denoted by these concepts are inessential and, at best, secondary. Only in poetry, a subcategory of language, is their presence as essential as in music.

Not even Mozart was immediately capable of dealing with these vague and ineffable qualities. To learn to deal with them he needed what he called, referring to his hard-won mastery of the string quartet, 'laborious toil' (*laboriosa fatica*). The fact that not even intuition can take wing without study, that many elements of this process can be isolated and examined, has hardly been noticed by musicology, and still less by the literature on Mozart. We would, of course, love to know what we are not, or not yet, capable of knowing. But we are still a long way from reaching this divide. To take an example, little has been written about how Mozart, during his years in Salzburg, began to treat music as a single vast and indivisible expanse while paying utmost attention to the minutiae of each genre. It appears that we only have the merest beginnings of a theory of music deserving of the name theory; that musicology, misled by a necessary division of labour, has for decades accustomed itself to compartmentalizing music into genres, subcategories, periods, styles and evolutionary stages. We have yet to tackle the task of examining how Mozart, against the advice of his father, gradually came to transplant techniques traditional in one genre into other genres; to take what he needed wherever he could find it, consciously infringing against time-honoured rules; to abandon rules learnt by rote in order to master new ones, and then still more new ones in turn. In all of this he followed a tendency evident in many of the major eighteenth-century composers and consciously expressed in calls to ignore national and stylistic boundaries. But the consummate mastery and consistency with which he was able to turn this tendency into miracles of art even transcended the abilities of a Joseph Haydn, whose operas remained by and large untouched by this process.

Those who reproached Mozart for writing church music that was operatic were perfectly right – in their recognition of the fact, not in their reproach. A melody like the one given below, taken from his *Litaniae Lauretanae* K109 and written when he was fifteen, probably for the court chapel of the Archbishop's summer residence (*NMA* I/2/1, p. ix), is the forerunner of numerous other secular-sounding turns of phrase in Mozart's sacred vocal compositions. It could just as easily be part of a singspiel:

Example 28

Even at the age of thirteen Mozart could accommodate a 'learned' or 'rationally' manipulated theme in the minuet of a cassation, even if its 'learnedness' is not so very recondite:

Example 29

And in *La finta giardiniera*, three ladies work out their problems of identity above a strict four-part texture which might easily have found its way into a string quartet, and in which the three female voices effortlessly merge. Passages like this had far-reaching repercussions on Mozart's style:

Example 30

We shall not lose track of the evolutionary currents illustrated by these examples as we look more closely at Mozart's music. In a certain sense, the hesitant, experimental and unpolished aspects of Mozart's music during the Salzburg period ('Here and there flicker the flames of genius' wrote Schubart of *La finta giardiniera*, composed when Mozart was eighteen) are more characteristic than are the perfect works of art. The same can even be said of that masterpiece which the twenty-five-year-old Mozart created at the end of his Salzburg period: *Idomeneo*. For however much Mozart valued and loved this opera, the great works of his decade in Vienna do not take it as their starting point. This is more than fortuitous, as we shall see. Chrysander's talk of leaps and bounds in Mozart's evolution as a composer proves to be all the more apt the deeper we probe into his life and music.

Chapter 10
The move to Vienna

This time Mozart's plan to take his life into his own hands was put into action. In order to understand his move to Vienna, with all its many consequences, we had best examine its worldwide preconditions from various angles.

It is relatively easy to assess those factors which we might call sociological, and which we can analyse with paper and pencil. Mozart's second tenure in Salzburg, which began in January 1779 following his Paris tour, was never intended to be permanent, not even by his father. Leopold thought of Salzburg as a base of operations which would allow his son to carry out commissions for other courts during graciously granted leaves of absence. Eventually he would take up a better position elsewhere, after which he would quit his Salzburg employment and summon his father and sister to join him. Indeed, Wolfgang had no objections in principle to this plan, but he literally took the second step before the first: he remained in Vienna without the assurance of a permanent position.

Admittedly the only account we have of the events leading to his final and irreconcilable breach with the Archbishop, and thus with Salzburg, is Wolfgang's own. But there is no reason to doubt that his version of the story, for all its emotional undertones, is largely accurate. Nor should we overlook his admission, on no fewer than three occasions (9 May, 12 May and 9 June 1781), that he had already resolved to remain in Vienna 'even without any particular cause'. When he left Munich he was already looking forward 'most eagerly to Vienna' where, he felt, 'good fortune is about to welcome me' (26 May). The Archbishop, in Mozart's own vivid words, functioned as a 'screen' (*Lichtschirm*) between him and the splendours awaiting him in Vienna, especially the possibility of direct contact with Emperor Joseph (24 March). It made him 'desperate' to think that on the very evening he and his Salzburg colleagues were made to give a 'shitty performance' for the Archbishop he had been invited to Countess Thun's, 'and who should be there but – the Emperor!' (11 April).

Small wonder, then, that a couple of weeks later Mozart invented a pretext not to return to Salzburg as instructed, thereby drawing upon himself a storm of abuse from his patron. His response was to declare his readiness to leave the Archbishop's service. This only produced new outbursts of wrath. Mozart now attempted, in vain, to submit petitions of dismissal to his employer. He had good reasons for insisting on a formal dismissal, which, it may be remarked, he was never granted. Perhaps he was aware of Johann Sebastian Bach's experiences in this regard. (In 1717 Bach had been held under arrest for four weeks for committing the same offence as Mozart's, when he tried to force his dismissal from the court in Weimar.) Two years later Mozart still worried that if he were to visit Salzburg the Archbishop 'might have me arrested' (21 May 1783). This clearly suggests that he knew full well about the outspoken Christian Friedrich Daniel Schubart (1739–91) who, at the time Mozart wrote his letter, had been in prison for years in Hohenasperg Castle. Whatever the case, Count Karl Joseph Arco, who as 'high steward of the kitchen' was also responsible for the Archbishop's musical repast, refused to accept Mozart's third petition, and, after a few words of amicable advice, terminated Mozart's Salzburg years once and for all with a kick up the backside that has gone down in history. With that, Mozart's contempt for 'court toadies' (23 January 1782) was joined by a healthy dose of hatred.

Mozart's object was to be free from the goodwill of such people in future. This wish was bold but not unrealistic. After all, Handel had been independent of aristocratic employment, though this was in England, the country with, at that time, the world's most highly developed economy. Gluck had also succeeded in obtaining a large degree of self-sufficiency, though by then he was already a famous man. Haydn was at least able to spend his final years in Vienna as a man of independent means, but only with the help of the money he had earned in London and an honorary annuity, and only after decades during which he had had, legally and in practice, the status of a court lackey. We can therefore thoroughly understand Leopold's concern. Mozart disclosed his plans to his father in the very first months of his stay in Vienna (12 January 1782): a permanent position at court, preferably with the Emperor himself (but only a position as composer, not one that carried burdensome duties by making him responsible for music at court); piano lessons; one opera commission each year; one public concert each year; and, finally, printed compositions sold by subscription. Not all of the five items in this programme were to materialize. The court appointment constantly eluded him. (At this stage Mozart was even willing to take up a suitable appointment elsewhere, though the imperial court in Vienna would have taken precedence.) All he was able to attain, however, was a position as 'musician-in-waiting' to the Emperor, with an annual salary of 800 gulden. As a comparison, the rent Mozart paid for his best lodgings, in Schulerstrasse (now Domgasse 5), amounted to 480 gulden annually. Yet his court appointment came too late even to cover this expense: it was not granted until December 1787, by which time the Mozarts had long been forced to leave their Schulerstrasse flat for financial reasons. As for opera commissions, Mozart received only four from the Viennese court over a period of eleven years. Nor did the publication of his music significantly increase his earnings. Piano pupils were more forthcoming, but this was an unreliable and, in later years, increasingly lean source of income which in any case little appealed to him. With regard to concerts Mozart's success in 1784 and 1785 was extraordinary. Twenty of them are documented in each year, and there may have been more. In March 1784 alone Mozart concertized at least eighteen times in houses of the Viennese nobility and bourgeoisie.

By and large, then, Mozart's calculations proved correct during his first five years in Vienna. When his father visited him there for the first and only time on 11 February 1785, sharing the life of the young family for about ten weeks, Mozart was a famous, much sought-after and highly paid virtuoso and composer, living with his family in the most comfortable and spacious quarters he was ever to occupy, the aforementioned Domgasse flat. Applying his dual criteria of 'honour and money', Mozart *père* could be more than satisfied. As far as honour was concerned, a mere five days after his arrival Leopold could report that his son had performed in public a 'glorious concerto' (most likely K456) so impressively that 'tears came to my eyes for sheer delight'. Even the Emperor was present, 'doffing his hat and crying "Bravo, Mozart!"' Leopold, as this same letter of 16 February informs us, also received confirmation of his son's abilities from the lips of the most competent judge of the age. Hardly had this opinion been uttered than the proud and happy father immediately passed it on to his daughter in Salzburg, and thus to posterity: 'Before God and as an honest man I tell you that your son is the greatest composer known to me either in person or by name. He has taste and, what is more, the most profound knowledge of composition.' The source of this opinion was none other than Joseph Haydn, the occasion being a performance of three string quartets that Mozart had dedicated to him. The performance was given in Mozart's own quarters, and he probably took the viola part while his father played first violin.

As for affluence, Leopold, always highly critical and cautious in his judgements, could reassure himself that his son, 'provided he has no debts to pay, can now put 2,000 gulden in the bank: the money is certainly there, and his housekeeping is extremely economical in point of food and drink' (19 March). True, he would no doubt have revised this opinion a few weeks later when he discovered that his son and daughter-in-law, for a visit to Salzburg which then did not take place, 'each had six pairs of shoes made to order which are now ready and waiting' (16 April). Later Leopold Mozart might have advanced much stronger arguments to prove that his assessment of the dangers of living without a permanent position had been correct. But he never witnessed the catastrophic decline in his son's circumstances. When Leopold died in Salzburg on 28 May 1787, Mozart's crisis had only just begun.

Apart from the financial aspect, the conditions under which Mozart wrote his music changed radically in a way that we cannot consider without touching on the substance of the works themselves. For the most part he now had to do without regular commissions that ensured a fixed income, a role formerly filled by, for instance, his compositions for the Salzburg court and church. What the Viennese court had to offer him in terms of regularly paid duties, ignoring for the moment the four opera commissions he received at irregular intervals, was limited to the composition of dance music. During his Vienna years Mozart did not receive a single commission for a piece of church music, apart from Count Walsegg's anonymous request for a Requiem which, as we all know, only reached him a few weeks before his death. Nor did Mozart have as many occasions to write light-hearted serenades, divertimenti and cassations; indeed, toward the end he had practically none at all. In their stead came other demands on his talents: piano concertos for his own use, operatic subjects of his own choosing, pieces written for occasions of his own making or offered to publishers. But, most important of all for a composer, these new demands brought new kinds of listeners into Mozart's musical arena.

This brings us to a point in Mozart's plans and expectations of which we can say with certainty that his calculations proved correct. What Mozart most wanted was the friendly, intelligent, appreciative and unstinting sympathy of people whom he could acknowledge, esteem and love in return. 'Mannheim loves me as much as I love Mannheim' is a typical remark, written on 12 November in Mannheim during his tour of 1778. In a letter from Paris, dated 1 May 1778, he found different words to express this same basic need: 'Give me the best clavier in Europe with an audience who understand nothing, or don't want to understand and who do not feel with me in what I am playing, and I shall cease to feel any joy.' He was about to find this sympathetic understanding more quickly than he had dared to hope. Scarcely had eight days passed after his arrival in Vienna than he was able to report: 'I have dined twice with the Countess Thun and go there almost every day. She is the most charming and most lovable lady I have ever met; and I am very high in her favour' (24 March 1781).

Wilhelmine, Countess of Thun, was at that time thirty-seven years old and by all accounts an extraordinary woman. An English traveller (quoted by Schenk 1975, p. 70) could write of her:

> No capital on earth can produce persons so distinguished by natural and acquired gifts, and by spirits so untrammelled and free, as the Countesses Thun and Pergen; their two houses are the meeting place of all who lay claim to good breeding, and the most valuable resource for the English during their stay in Vienna.

Another chronicler (quoted by Braunbehrens 1986, p. 167), again an Englishman and, to judge from the subtlety of his reports, a highly astute observer, wrote as follows:

> To a greater degree than I have ever known, the Countess [Thun] commands the art of maintaining and composing a gathering of people in such a way that they entertain themselves. For all her wit and consummate knowledge of the world she remains selfless at heart... One of her greatest delights is to remove prejudices from the acquaintances in her circle and to create and cultivate bonds of friendship... Never have I known anyone who possesses such a large number of friends and who knows how to bestow her own friendship so magnanimously on each of them. Within her walls she has created a microcosm of happiness of which she herself is the gravitating midpoint that holds all together.

Let us call one final witness whose competence in questions of human affairs we will have occasion to remark upon in the next chapter: Georg Forster. While temporarily residing in Vienna in the summer and autumn of 1784 Forster was welcomed into Countess Thun's circle. Writing to a lady friend on 3 September 1784, he described his impressions:

> When I compare the worthies of this place to those minor servants of lesser lords it is to the immeasurable advantage of the former. You cannot imagine how affable and amiable they are. Hardly does one find oneself among persons of rank than one is immediately encouraged to overlook their status and treat them on a familiar footing as kindred spirits. What transpires here when I am with Countess Thun (the finest woman in the world) and the Three Graces that are her daughters, I can only describe in the words: one *touches*.

Forster then goes on to summarize the Countess's virtues:

the most refined discourse; utmost delicacy united with complete candour; a wide knowledge of literature, all of it well digested and thought out; a pure and ardent sense of religion, far removed from any trace of superstition, within a gentle and innocent breast at one with Nature and Creation.

We are fortunate that Mozart's unusually warm opinion of the Countess can be confirmed by three reports written in such convincing language. They prove that his powers of judgement, which often let him down, particularly when he was trying to convince Leopold of the rightness of his decisions, were in this case completely trustworthy. It was Countess Thun who arranged his meeting with Count Orsini-Rosenberg, the 'General-Spektakel-Dircktor' (thus his imposing title), who in turn organized Mozart's commission to write *Die Entführung aus dem Serail*. The Countess was likewise responsible for the concert performance of *Idomeneo* that allowed Mozart to reveal his stature as a composer, at least to a small group of connoisseurs. It is even symbolic that the Countess followed the progress of Mozart's work on *Die Entführung* more closely than his father, who greeted the piece with indifference. As early as September 1781 Mozart had sent him parts of Act I together with his well-known trenchant précis of the work; other parts followed later. The expectations he placed on his father were high (31 July 1782):

> I thought . . . that you would hardly be able to open the parcel for excitement and eagerness to see your son's work, which, far from merely pleasing, is making such a sensation in Vienna that people refuse to hear anything else, so that the theatre is always packed. It was given yesterday for the fourth time and is to be repeated on Friday. Only – you couldn't find the time – – –.

Mozart's three final dashes conceal as much emotion as do the fermatas in his music. Leopold had sent 'such a cold, indifferent letter' in response that Countess Thun's warmth must have been doubly gratifying. At the beginning of August 1781 he had let her 'hear as much as was finished'; later, he had 'ridden up' (*vorgeritten*, Mozart's term for playing a piece at the piano while singing the vocal parts) the second act on 7 May 1782 and the third on 30 May. He could even rest assured that his newly-won friend would intercede actively on his behalf. And he could do with friends: at the first performance of *Die Entführung* 'the whole first act was accompanied by hissing' (20 July 1782). Even the première performance of *Figaro*, as we are told in the *Wiener Realzeitung* (Deutsch 1965, p. 278), was marred by 'obstreperous louts' who were paid to 'exert their lungs' and 'deafen singers and audience alike' with their hissing. Mozart had enemies in Vienna. They were quicker than he to realize that he belonged to the party of change, to the reformist camp of Emperor Joseph.

A good deal of what Mozart felt about the social fabric of his surroundings can be reconstructed (cf. Chapter 13). It was his firm conviction that, being a bourgeois musician, no prince was superior to him in light of his gifts and achievements. This belief sometimes found expression in touchingly naive forms of self-assertion. On 24 March 1781, for instance, in his very first days of independence in Vienna, he wrote to his father that he had received an invitation from Prince Galitzin. Etiquette required that the private valet hand him over to a lackey to show him into the inner chambers and escort him to the Prince. What in fact happened is recounted in Mozart's letter of 24 March: 'I took no notice, either of the valet or the lackey, but walked straight on through the rooms into the music room, for all the doors were open, – and went straight up to the Prince, paid him my respects and stood there talking to him.' To round off this picture we need only add the words 'just as if we were equals'. If we understand 'politics' in terms of the contemporary definition (quoted on p. 31) as contributing, or intending to contribute, to the common good, then this action was anything but politic. It was too plainly intended to draw attention to a proud young man named Mozart. But in the era of Emperor Joseph all of this was destined to change. To the extent that Mozart placed himself outside current conventions, he also joined forces with a circle for whom the flaunting of convention was part of a larger movement directed toward loftier goals. By battering down open doors in Prince Galitzin's palace Mozart left himself open for more far-reaching discoveries.

Among the earliest contacts Mozart reported to his father (26 May 1781) we find, alongside Count Rosenberg and Countess Thun, the names 'van Swieten and Herr von Sonnenfels'. Gottfried van Swieten (1722–1803) was no stranger to the Mozarts, who had made his acquaintance in Vienna as early as 1768. At that time Leopold had tried, without success, to astonish Viennese musical circles with the opera *La finta semplice*, K51, written when Mozart was twelve. All he achieved, however, was to have Wolfgang play the opera at the piano to a select audience, among whom was van Swieten. Van Swieten was sufficiently well-versed in music to appreciate the enormous strides Mozart had made in the intervening years. He was also present at the home of Countess Thun when Mozart played his *Idomeneo* at the piano. At that time van Swieten was not much more than the son of a famous man. His father Gerhard van Swieten, the personal physician of Empress Maria Theresia, was influential enough to secure from her one of the few concessions she was willing to make, namely to set up schools for training future generations of Austrian doctors. Now

Gottfried van Swieten had succeeded his father as prefect of the imperial library; he lived in his own house, received an annuity that was four times as large as Mozart's later income from the imperial coffers, and in 1781 had just become president of the Commission of Studies. In this latter position he was able to perform a critical role in Joseph's reform of the school system. He proved to be a steadfast friend of Mozart and supported him wherever he could, for example in the new concert series in Vienna's Augarten, which the Emperor had opened to the public in 1775. Van Swieten also deserves credit for introducing Mozart to some of the masterpieces of Johann Sebastian Bach and Handel, an event about which we will have more to say later.

Mozart also encountered once again two longstanding acquaintances. Tobias Philipp von Gebler (1726–86) had written the indifferent 'heroic drama' *Thamos, König in Ägypten* for which Mozart had composed choral numbers and entr'acte music as far back as 1773. He was now a member of the state council and a staunch collaborator of Emperor Joseph. Otto Freiherr von Gemmingen-Hornberg (1755–1836), whose acquaintance Mozart had made in Mannheim, had moved to Vienna in 1782. Both these men were Freemasons.

One of Mozart's many new acquaintances was Joseph Freiherr von Sonnenfels (1732–1817). His career is likewise typical of the circumstances then prevailing in Austria. Sonnenfels came from a Jewish family, his grandfather having been a rabbi. When he was still a child his father converted to Christianity, thereby, in keeping with the ethics of the time, gaining almost unimpeded admission to state offices and the upper reaches of society. Almost. Whatever the case, his father became a professor of oriental languages at Vienna University. Joseph was equally gifted linguistically, being at home in nine languages, and became a member and later the vice-president of the Court Commission for Legal Affairs. He was given a newly created chair in 'police studies and financial sciences' at Vienna University as well as a number of other positions. He is also credited, for better or worse, with having created Austria's bureaucratic jargon. Sonnenfels was a member of the masonic lodge *Zur Wahren Eintracht*. His collected minor writings were published from 1783 in ten volumes, of which the first four, possibly a gift from the author, were found in Mozart's library. In any event this influential and widely-known man, who was responsible for doing away with torture in Austria (partly during the reign of Maria Theresia), was one of Mozart's protectors – this time in the full sense of the word. Even Mozart's father paid him a respectful visit when he came to Vienna in 1785.

Even with all these things in common, including their association with the Freemasons, Mozart and Sonnenfels did not develop close relations. Their attitudes toward art alone could not easily be reduced to a common denominator; indeed, many of Mozart's views and decisions may, I surmise, have been made in deliberate opposition to Sonnenfels. For at the time that Mozart was working out the subject matter, material and techniques of his new operas Sonnenfels was elaborating rationalist views that must have come to Mozart's attention, being readily available in newspapers and pamphlets. These views could hardly have appealed to him, yet the two men were agreed that the theatre should become a moral institution.

One exciting aspect about Mozart's new surroundings was that representatives of a wide array of professions (manual ones excluded) could meet within a small area uninhibited by class distinctions. As Lessing complained, cobblers and carpenters were not to be found in these circles, and masons only in the figurative sense of the term. But Mozart doubtless met merchants and industrialists. At the time Mozart arrived in Vienna, Johann Thomas Edler von Trattner (1717–98) was the owner of a large enterprise in and outside of Vienna (see *Briefe* VI, p. 88). By 1759 he had founded a 'typographical palace' that contained everything needed for the most up-to-date methods of book production, 'from the type foundry to the retail shop'. Trattner owned paper factories, thirty-seven printing presses and eight bookshops and employed 200 people (Schenk 1975, pp. 463ff.). This man, too, was Mozart's protector. His young wife was one of Mozart's first piano pupils in Vienna, and the Trattners were godparents to no fewer than four of Wolfgang's and Konstanze's six children.

Another acquaintance was Johann Michael Puchberg (1741–1822), a manufacturer and wholesale dealer in silks, satins, linen and gloves. He was a Freemason, and by helping Mozart with generous loans at a time of need he saved him at least temporarily from falling into the hands of usurers.

Two other men deserve special mention in this context as Mozart's dealings with them betoken his lack of prejudice. Both were Jews. Raimund, Baron Wetzlar von Plankenstern (1752–1810), the son of a Jew who had converted and been raised to the nobility, was a banker and, for about half a year in 1782–3, Mozart's landlord. At first the Mozarts lived for three months in a house owned by Wetzlar, located in Wipplingerstrasse at the 'Hohe Brücke'. When they vacated this flat at Wetzlar's request they then moved to inferior lodgings on the Kohlmarkt, but again without rent. Wetzlar even paid the costs of their removal. He was the godfather of Mozart's first-born son, and subscribed to the Trattnerhof concerts along with his father and one of his sisters. Mozart called Wetzlar an 'honest' and a 'true and good friend' (21 May and 18 June 1783).

In Mozart's very first year in Vienna he had sublet from a Jew for eleven months, starting in July 1781. Braunbehrens is right to point out (1986, pp. 74ff.) that no Mozart biography bothers to mention this fact although it demonstrates the extent of his independence and lack of prejudice. Adam Isaac Arnsteiner, a financier and merchant dealer at the imperial court, was literally the only unconverted Jew allowed to rent a building at will. As a rule, Jews were made to live in specially assigned houses, wear a yellow patch and pay high tolerance duties. They were also forbidden to enter public inns and were not allowed even to look at Christian processions. Hilde Spiel (1962) has pursued the history of the Arnstein family (as they were later known) in order to shed light on Nathan's stepdaughter Fanny Arnstein, who maintained one of Vienna's leading salons with charm and esprit. This, however, took place after Mozart's death. Mozart surely must have met her; her husband Nathan Adam Arnstein likewise subscribed to his Trattnerhaus concerts. Nor is it implausible that Fanny Arnstein gave Mozart the copy of Moses Mendelssohn's *Phädon* that was found in his library (Braunbehrens 1986, pp. 77f.).

Another class of professionals whom Mozart met in the masonic lodges or greeted in the salons where he performed or at his own concerts was made up of scientists, scholars and university professors. In 1765 Joseph von Sonnenfels, writing in a bi-weekly periodical which he edited, had remarked (1783, I, p. 17):

> Vienna hardly suspects the existence within its bounds of a society of men dedicated to scholarship and the sciences, not in order to be proclaimed learned before the world, but to pursue learning for its own sake. In their meetings these men read their essays to each other in amity and friendship for the purpose of disclosing their imperfections. ... Such a society does truly exist.

Among Mozart's closest friends were the Jacquin brothers, Gottfried (1763–92) and Joseph Franz (1766–1839). They were sons of Nikolaus Joseph von Jacquin (1727–1817), a leading botanist in whose house and gardens Mozart was frequently an invited guest.

From the very outset Mozart tried to establish contact with those Vienna-based writers who held masonic and Josephine views. One of these was the poet Johann Baptist Alxinger (1755–97), the German translator, together with the composer, of Gluck's *Iphigénie en Tauride*. Mozart called him 'an excellent poet' and would gladly have had him translate *Idomeneo* (12 September 1781). Yet the collaboration never came about, nor did the two apparently ever meet. We do not even know which of Alxinger's poems Mozart read. But the poems Mozart set in the late 1780s show that the two shared many convictions. Perhaps they belonged to the same masonic lodge. Much the same applies to Aloys Blumauer (1755–98). Among Mozart's books was a collection of his poetry, published in 1784 in Vienna, and Mozart set one of his later poems, *Lied der Freiheit*, K506, which appeared in the *Wiener Musenalmanach* of 1786. Once again it turns out that Mozart's views overlapped on critical points with those of the poet he set. In the 1780s Blumauer edited a weekly periodical entitled *Wöchentliche Wahrheiten über die Predigten in Wien*, an exposé of sermons held in Vienna which was roundly attacked by the clergy. A specialist in this subject (Wangermann 1989, p. 7) has described the publication as follows:

> The *Wöchentliche Wahrheiten* tried to kindle public interest in the great dispute on religion. Congregations began to pay closer attention to the sermons they heard and even to form their own thoughts on the subjects dealt with. ... There is some indication that preachers who departed from strict traditionalism and attempted to bring Catholic dogma and its application into some sort of harmony with Enlightenment philosophy and the needs of the state had large followings in the populous new suburbs of Vienna.

Mozart's own serious efforts to harmonize Catholicism and Freemasonry become more intelligible with a closer knowledge of Blumauer's writings and readership.

Mozart also set poems by two other masonic poets. Joseph Franz Ratschky (1757–1810) wrote the words to a lied that Mozart probably composed on the occasion of his father's elevation to the second rung in the masonic hierarchy: *Lied zur Gesellenreise*, K468, dated 26 March 1785. Lorenz Leopold Haschka (1749–1827) wrote the words of Mozart's unfinished cantata *Dir, Seele des Weltalls*, K429.

We could go on with this list, but by now it should be clear that Mozart frequented a circle of men and women who offered him more than just recognition as a composer. During his Salzburg years he was linked to his audience by traditions and conventions which did not necessarily agree with his own convictions and thoughts, and which no one thought to question. Now, in Vienna, he experienced a new kind of relationship between the composer and his audience. Here his listeners expected, found and appreciated music that emerged from and took root in shared new values, conveying a new image of the world and articulating new moral qualities in opposition to the old world. This applied in particular to the Freemasons.

Like any class society, the society of absolutism tended to smother human relations beneath a thick blanket of privileges, dependencies and hierarchies. Its modes of thought and behaviour, class prejudices and obsequiousness, domination and subservience, envy and intrigue served merely as a veneer for blatant exploitation, producing an unfavourable climate for human relations.

But absolutism had been dealt a deadly blow. It was only able to maintain itself in its original barbaric forms on the periphery of Europe, and then only for a few decades. In England the aristocracy and bourgeoisie had begun to merge centuries ago, and France had assumed a vanguard position in this respect on the Continent. Even in the territories of Germany and Austria the feudal nobility had long ceased to be an economically and politically unified class. Centuries ago a process had been set in motion, one of whose results was that a small number of noblemen had been drawn to the courts of the centralized power, represented by kings, emperors or czars, and thus split off from the remaining aristocracy. The absolutist system gradually witnessed the rise of modes of production, transport and thought which in many ways conflicted with those of the ancient landed nobility, which thrived by mercilessly exploiting an unprotected peasantry. Artisans and merchants had settled in the towns; trade, even foreign trade, came into play; the town burghers gained in influence and power. All of this called for a free work force, whose release, however, was blocked by the ancient feudal nobility. It also called for increased production, safe roads and the abolition of feudal privileges.

It was here that royal power found a task and an opportunity. A precarious and unstable community of interest arose between absolute monarchs and town burghers. One important connecting link was the noblemen who had been attracted to court. This group provided ministers, civil servants and generals and helped to enhance the splendour of the court by its 'sense of style and capacity for ceremonial pomp, acquired over centuries in the exercise of power' (Krauss 1952, p. 8). In many respects the interests of the court nobility coincided with those of the burghers, the more so as they kept step with them even in the practice of modern modes of production. In France of the late eighteenth century, for example, a good half of all smelting works and coal pits were operated by the nobility. Similar developments, if not so dramatic, could be seen in other countries. Conversely, burghers who were *nouveau riche*, ennobled or otherwise close to centralized power did not find class distinctions to be irksome. Still, taken as a class, the aristocracy, even at court, had every reason to retain the absolutist state with its ancient system of hierarchy and privilege. Here they were fully in accord with their king or emperor. By the same token, the burghers had every reason to reform or, potentially, to overthrow this state. But this option was not yet on the agenda, not even in France, though it would arise there only a few years after Mozart's arrival in Vienna.

These tendencies, present throughout Europe, took on a special hue in Vienna, where they entered Mozart's awareness. If we take 'enlightened absolutism' to mean a regime that attempts to avoid revolution as a means of resolving conflicts by entering into compromises with the bourgeoisie, and at the same time curtailing the feudal privileges of the aristocracy, then even the reign of Maria Theresia (1740–80) falls into this category. Her eldest son Joseph (1741–90) had become Holy Roman Emperor and co-regent with his mother as early as 1765, following the death of his father. This year can thus be taken as the beginning of the Josephine era. Its culmination fell in the years from 1780 to 1790, when Joseph was sole ruler, and its decline and demise in the brief reign of Joseph's brother and successor Leopold (1790–2).

Tirelessly active, Joseph issued a flood of edicts and regulations and oversaw their execution. He was guided by a sober assessment of the usefulness of antiquated institutions and the measures to be adopted, and by extreme frugality, even in the budgeting of his court and his personal lifestyle. By abolishing serfdom, censorship and indentured labour, by granting freedom of religion with his *Toleranzpatent*, by introducing a judicial system, statutory law and facilities for tending the sick and poor, Joseph took on the appearance of a great new hope even in the eyes of Herder, Klopstock, Wieland, Lessing and Goethe. In Joseph's vision the Catholic religion assumed a major role: it was to function as a moral arbiter of the state – the ideas of the Italian theologian Ludovico Antonio Muratori (1672–1750) were at work here – but primarily under the stewardship of the Emperor and his civil bureaucracy rather than Rome and the clergy. Monasteries and monastic orders which did not perform useful services, for example by maintaining schools or tending the sick, were dissolved and their riches confiscated. Processions, displays of monstrances and similar celebrations were restricted or banned as superstitious.

We need not doubt that Joseph was a richly gifted man inspired by a genuine love of his fellow man. But he was unable to master many burning issues. The situation abroad was and continued to be threatening; it proved impossible to combine the preservation of the Habsburg empire with the ambitions of Prussia, France, Russia and Turkey. Wars of conquest or exchanges of territory by means of secret diplomacy between princes were not the way to achieve greater happiness in their populations. Rigid centralization and 'Germanification' were not the way to counter the aspirations of national independence. And there had already arisen more radical plans of action to confront internal social problems than existed within Joseph's intellectual purlieus. In his final years Joseph himself – and after his death his brother Leopold – had to retract many of the reforms he had taken such pains to introduce and institute. This was not primarily the fault of Joseph and his subordinates so much as the contradictions within his programme itself and the methods he chose to carry it out. It proved impossible to find a common denominator that would accommodate both the consolidation of absolutist society, whatever its state of reform, and the rise of a new society based on bourgeois methods of production.

It was, of course, not impossible for contemporaries to see through the complexities of this situation, but it was by no means easy. As far as Mozart is concerned, he came as close to fulfilling an old adage in Vienna as any artist has ever done, apart perhaps from Goethe, who at the end of his life put this adage into the following words in his conversations with Eckermann (1829, p. 285):

> It is not enough to have talent; it takes more than that to become wise. One must also be able to live in grand surroundings, to look into the cards of the leading players of the day, and to play oneself for loss or gain.

Mozart, it is true, never lived in 'grand surroundings'. But even as a child, with an inquisitive and soon acutely critical eye, he had had a chance to look into the cards of the leading players of his day. Now, in Vienna, he was playing the game himself, winning in the first half of the decade and losing disastrously in the second. He found himself taken up – perhaps not on so equal a footing as he might have wished – by a circle of men and women who had leading parts to play in the affairs of state, in the development of industry and trade in the Austrian territories, and in the making of public opinion.

The last-named of these opportunities, to give his music the greatest possible impact on the largest possible public, had been Mozart's expressed goal since the days of his youth. While rehearsing *Idomeneo* in Munich he brashly wrote, referring to a joke in his father's letter of 13 December, 'There is music in my opera for all kinds of people except the long-eared' (16 December 1780). Another celebrated passage from his letters, this time written in Vienna and referring to his piano concertos K413, K414 and K415, illustrates just how clearly he had thought out the problem of the interaction between composer and listener, how precisely he formulated his thoughts and how consciously he was able to carry out his intentions (28 December 1782):

> These concertos are a happy medium between what is too easy and too difficult; they are very brilliant, pleasing to the ear, and natural, without being vapid. There are passages here and there from which the connoisseurs alone can derive satisfaction; but

these passages are written in such a way that the less learned cannot fail to be pleased, though without knowing why.

And one of his last letters, written to Konstanze on 7–8 October 1791, records the reaction of the audience to *Die Zauberflöte*: 'But what always gives me most pleasure is the silent applause!'

This, then, provides a vantage point from which to investigate Mozart's new Viennese environment, namely, as an interlocking nexus of publicity and influence, all of it in a process of dynamic change. This nexus was more favourable than any he had hitherto encountered, but for this very reason it constantly opened up new vistas. When things are in such turmoil as they were at that time in Vienna, what limits can be placed on the growing audience? Why should a continual influx of 'non-connoisseurs' not be won over to the friendly gospel of music in addition to the small, but likewise growing, number of connoisseurs? It is no coincidence that in Mozart's final works the term *Menschheit* – humanity – also makes its appearance.

It was precisely in the 1780s that literature in Vienna experienced a previously undreamt-of boom. Censorship was relaxed, and there was a growing awareness that opinion-making should, and could, become a matter of public debate. The capital was inundated by a flood of magazines, newspapers, pamphlets, book reviews, theatre critiques and poetry collections. Even though a large part of this output 'falls under the heading of "waste paper"' (Blumauer 1782, p. 164), there was still a good deal of intelligent and accurate commentary, critical thought and ingenious humour to be found in the authors Mozart admired, and in some others as well. With their articles, reports and reviews they created a forum for the spread of Josephinism. We can now see why Mozart valued these men, apart from the fact that they shared many of his ideas. Alxinger was a gifted poet; Blumauer, like Mozart, had a humorous penchant for the foibles of society and his fellow man. We need only cast a glance at Mozart's own output in this area to appreciate his affinity to the popular forms of the Viennese *littérateurs* – and his reserve toward Sonnenfels.

Still, for all that, we must always remember that even in the ink-stained eighteenth century the printed word reached only a small fraction of the population. The same was not true of theatre, provided we understand theatre in all the multifarious forms characteristic of the century, particularly in Vienna. When Mozart returned home from one of his concerts or piano lessons – and he had a total of thirteen different lodgings during his years in Vienna – he would pass by one of those many stages that made up the complexion and life of the city, some of them nothing more than some planks of wood over a few barrels. They could be found, just a few steps away from Mozart's various quarters, on the Neuer Markt, the Hoher Markt, the Freyung, the Graben, even on the Glacis, that unbuilt strip of land, some of it park-like, some of it abandoned, that lay between the town wall and the suburbs. Others could be found in the suburbs of Landstrasse, Josephstadt, Lerchenfeld, Penzing near the newly erected imperial palace of Schönbrunn, and many other places besides. We know enough about Vienna's theatre life to say that it embraced both the brilliant and the tawdry, the timely and the ludicrous, genuine comedy and shallow entertainment. These qualitative categories were not measurable with the standards of 'high' and 'low' art.

Let us look at three short examples of products of this sort. First, *Die Braut von Ohngefähr*, a burlesque entitled, roughly, 'The Bride by Chance'. It begins as follows:

> To the strains of a ritornello of trumpets and kettledrums, enter Hanns-Wurst as an officer, singing an aria.

> *No. 1*
> Ihr Feuer-Mörser ins Gewehr!
> Ihr Säbel fort, rangirt euch her!
>   Ihr Pauken auf, und tummelt euch!
> Trompeten lärmt, und haust zugleich.
>   Bum bum! Tra ra!

> Ihr Martis Söhne kommt herbey,
>   Erhebt ein lautes Feld-Geschrey!
>   Und machet den Soldaten-Stand
>   Mit Ruhm der gantzen Welt bekannt,
>   Rufft aus!
> Bey bum, bum bum und tra ra ra,
>   Es lebe Mars! Victoria!

This doggerel might be translated thus:

> Ye mortars, come and join the fray!
> Ye sabres, close ranks and seize the day!
>   Ye drums, be off and beat tattoo!
> Ye trumpets blare, wreak havoc, too!
>   Boom boom! Tantara!

> Ye sons of Mars, to battle hie,
>   And raise a lusty battle cry!
>   Proclaim the soldatesca's lot
>   To all the world, with fame besot,
>   Cry ye!
> Bay boom, boom boom and tantara,
>   Long live Mars! Victoria!

The play runs its appointed course. Having broken into a house and paid court to the mistress, Hanns-Wurst is threatened by the master and, despite his murderous arsenal, has to plead 'full tim'rously' for his life. He saves himself by abandoning his designs on the mistress and settling for the maid Colombine, who is not at all disinclined. '"Are soldiers supposed to be bloodthirsty?" asks the Viennese Hanswurst in *Scipio*, Stranitzky's adaptation of an "heroic" opera libretto by Zeno, to which he himself supplies the answer: "More likely winethirsty!"' (Rommel 1952, p. 482).

Another play opens as follows:

Act I, scene 1.

An agreeable spot, two identical houses left and right. Off stage the sound of cracking whips and a post horn.
Enter Wurstl, pushing Leander in a wheelbarrow, blowing his horn and cracking his whip.

WURSTL (*emptying the wheelbarrow*): Here we are!

LEANDER (*picking himself up*): You clumsy oaf, what have you done now?

WURSTL: Giddyup! Whoa!

LEANDER: You confounded ass! Is this the way to treat your master? Small wonder if I broke an arm and leg! . . . But hold! – Luckily for you my desire to see my beloved Rosaura and hold her in my arms again, the sooner the better, is so great that I cannot waste time on a such wastrel as you, my liege lord Herr von Wurstl!

Our Hanswurst also wants to see his Trauterl. But not knowing which of the two identical houses belongs to their respective lady friends, the two men decide that Wurstl should eavesdrop at both as he will surely recognize his own ('She has a voice like a cowbell'). Before listening, however, he first does a bit of 'tasting'. Then he knocks at the doors after all and calls for his Trauterl, at which point the following ensues:

Scene 2.

GIANTESS: Here I be, what do you wish?

WURSTL (*recoiling*): Gadzooks, how she's grown! (*To the giantess*) Well, is it you or isn't it?

GIANTESS: Yes, my darling Wurstl, it is I, your dear, loving Trauterl. Come into my arms. (*She embraces him.*)

We can guess the rest. Out of the other house comes Rosaura, now a midget. After the two men have consoled each other at the thought that the one lady has become 'too much' and the other 'too little', Leander kneels to kiss the 'wee little hand' of his Rosaura. At this point, before a single piece of music has been heard (apart, presumably, from the entrance music), the fragment comes to an end.

Our third example is a song intended for a 'dim-witted gardener':

> Ein Weib ist das herrlichste Ding auf der Welt,
> Wer's leugnet, den schlag' ich, daß d'Goschen ihm schwellt.
> Oft zappelt's beim Manne, kein Geld ist im Haus,
> Sie jagt aus dem Schädel die Grillen ihm aus,
> Sie krabbelt dem Wildfang am Bart und am Kinn
> Und schmunzelnd sieht er auf das Weiberl dann hin.
> Wer's leugnet, den schlag' ich, daß d'Goschen ihm schwellt,
> Ein Weib ist das herrlichste Ding auf der Welt.

Or, approximately:

> A wife is the very most marvellous thing,
> And he who says nay, why, I'll make his ears ring!
> A man's often flighty, no money at home,
> She chases his whimsy and tells it, Begone!
> She coddles the blighter and scratches his chin
> Till he looks at his wife with a long sheepish grin.
> He who says nay, why, I'll make his ears ring!
> A wife is the very most marvellous thing.

All three of these plays deserve our attention. The first, with its motif of the swaggering warrior who is in fact anything but warlike, was elevated beyond recognition in Figaro's famous aria 'Non più andrai' (No. 9), where Figaro apotheosizes the reluctant soldier Cherubino into Miles Gloriosus. Hanns-Wurst's aria is taken from the oldest of the three plays quoted here. It was sung at the Kärntnertor Theatre presumably around 1740, and its author is either the celebrated folk actor Josef Felix Kurz-Bernardon (1717–83) or another actor-playwright from the same tradition (Pirker 1927, pp. vff.). The third play, with its hymn to the 'very most marvellous thing', merits our interest only in that Mozart wrote a set of variations on it for piano (K613). It comes from a farce by Emanuel Schikaneder called *Der dumme Gärtner aus dem Gebürge oder die zween Antons* ('The Dim-Witted Gardener from the Mountains, or The Two Antons'), the play with which he inaugurated his directorship of the Freihaus Theatre in 1789. This farce was so popular that it was given no fewer than six sequels.

Finally, the second of our three examples, the one with the augmented and diminutive lady friends, is especially interesting as it was written by Wolfgang Amadé Mozart. The occasion which caused this uncannily many-sided man to write this fragment in or around 1787 is unknown. It also has a companion piece, an even shorter fragment in Mozart's hand entitled *Der Salzburger Lump in Wien* ('The Salzburg Scallywag in Vienna'). There is no doubt who the scallywag is supposed to be: in the play he is called 'Herr Stachelschwein', or 'Mr Porcupine', another of Mozart's nicknames. What these two playlets (both are included in *Briefe* IV, pp. 167–73) signify is that Mozart took delight in Viennese popular comedy. Indeed, he says as much in one of his letters. Reporting on a sort of sequel to Martín y Soler's opera *La cosa rara* with words by Schikaneder and music by Mozart's first Tamino, the singer and composer Benedikt Schak (1758–1826), Mozart claims that he 'did not like it as much as "Die Antons"' (2 June 1790). This refers, of course, to the very same piece from which he took the theme for his set of variations.

Mozart was not alone in this opinion. One of the earliest eye-witnesses of Vienna's theatrical scene was the wife of an English diplomat, Lady Mary Wortley Montagu (1689–1762), who witnessed a comedy by Josef Anton Stranitzky (c. 1676–1726) while passing through Vienna in 1716. She wrote that she had never laughed so much in her life (Rommel 1952, p. 277). Her account, often quoted because of its curiosity value, has been questioned by those not willing to grant the lady a sufficient knowledge of German to judge the play, which was almost certainly, or at least in part, written in Styrian-Salzburg-Viennese dialect. Whatever the case, her report is highly interesting for several reasons. In 1710 Stranitzky became the first German-speaking actor to succeed, though with great effort and in hot competition with the Italian troupes favoured at court, in obtaining permanent premises for himself and his company: the newly erected Kärntnertor Theatre. This is indicative not only of the growing need for theatre in different strata of society, but also of changes which engulfed all aspects of theatre life in a maelstrom of events. Despite the constancy of many of their motifs and characters, the themes and plots of stage plays were in a process of change, as were their modes of production, the style of acting and the mechanisms for reaching their audiences. The fact that Lady Montague was encouraged by her friends to attend the newly built theatre, where this brilliant and irresistibly comic talent from the people was acclaimed by throngs of theatre-goers, none of whom was likely to have the Lady's rank, is remarkable. But it is also highly typical.

Similar observations apply to the Burgtheater, which of all the Viennese theatres has probably been studied the most thoroughly with regard to the make-up of its audience (Schindler 1976). Ever since it opened its doors in 1741 the Burgtheater had been attended by members of the high and ultra-high aristocracy, but the largest part of its audience came from various strata of the middle classes. Its boxes were set aside for the nobility and the grand bourgeoisie; the stalls, variously divided at different times in history, were reserved partly for the well-bred and partly for the less well-bred; the gallery, located in the first storey of the auditorium, changed in social value over the years. The upper balconies, it need hardly be mentioned, were never frequented by the cultivated public, not simply because one could not hear or see as well there, but also because tradition and etiquette played a part in the distribution of seats, which was principally regulated by ticket prices. (Theatre history urgently needs the kind of approach applied to the concert hall in 1983 by Hanns-Werner Heister, who has revealed the surprisingly ritualistic aspects of seemingly mundane and self-evident institutions, habits and forms of behaviour.) At this point we should note that in eighteenth-century Vienna it became standard practice for people of various levels of society to congregate under a single roof in order to partake of theatre performances. What is more, this practice had set in less than a century after the advent of those court ceremonies known as opera, where common people were admitted, if at all, only after the court had seen and heard its fill. By now, however, it was 'natural' for all Viennese theatres to have, like the Burgtheater, two, three or four balconies corresponding roughly to the strata of society.

The establishment of theatre companies in permanent premises was a phenomenon witnessed throughout the whole of Europe, and as always at watershed periods of history, for a long time the old institutions coexisted alongside the new. In addition to makeshift street theatres there were more comfortable buildings, temporary stages and wooden structures which also found room for a gallery and could offer flying machines and scene changes among their marvels (see Plates 1, 2, 4 and 5). There were also troupes that plied their trade in public inns. Mozart lived to see the two theatres in the town centre, the Kärntnertor Theatre and the Burgtheater, as well as the Josephstädter Theatre (built in 1779), followed by two additional theatres in the suburbs: the Leopoldstädter Theatre (1781) and the Freihaus Theatre (1787), also known as the Theater auf der Wieden or Wiedner Theatre (not to be confused with the Theater an der Wien, which first opened its doors in 1801 and is still in existence today). This unimaginably lively theatre scene was described exhaustively as long ago as 1925 by Emil Karl Blümml and Gustav Gugitz, to whom I am indebted for much of my discussion.

It cannot have escaped Mozart's notice that Vienna, being caught in the turmoil of these social changes, was also undergoing profound changes in its urban landscape. As demonstrated again and again by the redoubtable Lothar Kühne, our spatial environment is 'the fundamental element in the material conditions of our life' and represents 'social relations externalized in nature' (1985, p. 9). Most of Vienna's churches and aristocratic palaces were already standing when Mozart arrived. But a construction boom had begun that resulted in new types of buildings. Aside from providing the bourgeois with appropriate platforms for public display, commercial activities and business deals, it also affected Mozart's living conditions. For example, there was the Trattnerhof, a building scarcely four years old and owned by the publisher von Trattner (see Plate 3). It was a splendid, somewhat pompous bourgeois residential building of five storeys erected on the Graben in the place of six older houses and situated just a few steps from St Stephen's Cathedral, the centre of town. It had four staircases, two courtyards and two fountains and included a bookshop and a 'Lektur-Kabinett' or reading room. In the Trattnerhof one could read newspapers and pamphlets, drink coffee, take a meal, even hold concerts. Mozart took advantage of this last-named opportunity. On 6 December 1783 he wrote to his father of six projected 'subscription academies' of which the first three took place in a music room in the Trattnerhof, 'first floor no. 9', on three Wednesdays in 1784 (17, 24 and 31 March). On each of these memorable evenings Mozart played a new piano concerto: K449, K450 and K451. This was made all the more remarkable by the fact that in January of that same year Mozart himself had taken a flat in the Trattnerhof, 'second staircase, third floor'. Here he was not at the mercy of Herr Privy Chamberlain or Herr Lackey to escort him into the building's inner sanctum, as was the case with festivities in the mansions of the nobility. Here he was his own master and could receive his visitors as a man among equals. He greeted his guests in a music room under his own roof, as though he were a prince, but without all that elegant folderol which had become 'more intolerable to me every day' (16 December 1780). The subscription list for these Trattnerhof concerts has survived. It is indeed a mixture of high nobility and bourgeois scholars, of civil servants and men of trade – in short, the same mixture as was found in many of Vienna's salons and masonic lodges.

The Trattnerhof was not unique. Johann Pezzl, a shrewd observer and well-informed contemporary of Mozart's, has left a detailed account of the profits one could make by setting up large establishments of this sort. He called them 'earldoms in stone' because they could bring in as much or more income from rent alone as could an earldom from all its proceeds together. 'This is why', he explains, 'those who have purchased dissolved monasteries do not turn these buildings into glorious palaces'. (The great age of Viennese palace construction had taken place one or two generations earlier.) 'Instead', Pezzl continues, 'they are transformed into some fifty bourgeois residences, workshops and retail booths.' Even the building on the Graben where Mozart had lived in 1781 had, in addition to the living quarters, more than twenty rooms, ten chambers and three kitchens as well as three shopping arcades at ground level, three attics, two cellars, a carriage house, stables for six horses, and a hayloft (Braunbehrens 1986, p. 76). The bourgeois mercantile world came into existence noisily; Mozart purposely chose his room 'not looking onto the street for the sake of the quiet' (29 August 1781).

Besides these utilitarian buildings Mozart must also have been just as impressed as his contemporaries by the burgeoning public buildings, for example the General Hospital, started in 1784 at the behest of Emperor Joseph and still in use as a hospital today. Mozart's close friend Sigismund Barisani, as head physician, was given a residence in this building, which contained thirteen courtyards and occupied ten hectares of land. The most noble example of this type of construction project is perhaps the Military Physicians' Academy, which like the General Hospital still exists today (at Währingerstrasse 30). Italian architects took a leading part in the architectural history of the Josephine age. Combining beauty with practicality, these buildings are among the outstanding artistic achievements of the era.

One building which figured largely in Mozart's final year was probably anything but beautiful and noble: the aforementioned Freihaus Theatre. The 'Freyhaus', so-called because its owners, the princes of Starhemberg, were not obligated to pay taxes on it, was located about 500 metres beyond the Kärntnertor. It had existed for over a century, and had been expanded and renovated many times to become a miniature town within a town. In Mozart's day, an estimated 800 to 1,000 people (another estimate even gives 3,000) lived in the Freihaus, which was not dear and provided a healthier environment than the town could offer. In 1787 a theatre impresario lit upon the idea of building a theatre in the Freihaus. Duly inaugurated on 14 October 1787, it was taken over by another impresario half a year later. In July 1789 it received its third and final director, Mozart's longstanding acquaintance Emanuel Schikaneder, who remained in charge of it until the theatre was torn down in 1801. The Freihaus Theatre was a sturdy building with two balconies, wooden interior and masonry exterior and a stage approximately twelve metres deep. It was extended and improved many times; its second director had the footpath joining the theatre with the Kärntnertor illuminated with newly installed lanterns. Under Schikaneder the theatre had an attractive and broad-based repertoire, a top-flight orchestra and good singers. Among the latter were Mozart's sister-in-law Josepha Hofer and the highly cultured and talented Franz Xaver Gerl (1764–1827), an actor, singer and composer who later sang Sarastro in *Die Zauberflöte*. Mozart and Gerl soon became good friends. In the main the audience probably came from the petty bourgeoisie, although, to judge from the prices of some of the seats, visitors were also reckoned with from the upper classes. There was even a 'court box' which, in August 1791, was taken by Emperor Leopold, presumably after Schikaneder had entreated him during an audience to enhance the theatre's popularity with his presence. If music lovers went to concert halls in bourgeois tenement houses, theatre-goers went to theatres in their courtyards. Nestled in one of the many courtyards in a complex of tenement buildings, the Freihaus Theatre (see Plate 7) is a characteristic but not unique example of Vienna's changing urban lifestyle, cityscape and atmosphere.

A theatre is something sensual, corporeal and immediately accessible, a place where 'hearing and touch can stand side by side with the visible' (Weimann 1982, p. 63), where contact with other people ineluctably becomes part of theatrical experience. From a purely theoretical standpoint, then, it is inevitable that the theatre would also attract those who had not learnt the 'technique of reading and writing founded on the phonetic alphabet' (p. 63) or who had not made it their main form of communication with their fellows and their mode of confronting and comprehending the world. In Mozart's day the theatre was far and away the principal form of human communication in Vienna. Mozart's lifelong goal – 'to write operas' (4 February 1778) – reflects this fact.

The expectations and demands of the huge public that convened or was expected to convene in the theatres, none of which seated less than 1,000 persons, could only be met by following the advice of the theatre director in Goethe's *Faust*: He who offers a lot will offer something to many. The travelling theatrical troupes also knew how to present a lot. In keeping with their talents and possibilities, and no doubt at times exceeding both, they offered comedies and tragedies, farces, singspiels, pantomimes, ballets, burlesques and parodies, magic plays and *Maschinenstücke*, children's theatre and anything else that held promise of attracting an audience. It need hardly be mentioned that street theatre performances were not totally beholden to pieces written and composed for the occasion. But in the early decades of the eighteenth century such pieces existed, at least in Vienna: a large collection of printed comic songs and skits from the repertoire of the Kärntnertor Theatre, dating from about 1740 and entitled *Teutsche Arien*, was discovered by Robert Haas and Vladimir Helfert in the 1920s and edited by Max Pirker in 1927. These pieces are revealing evidence that professional writers, and perhaps composers as well, emerged from the ranks of folk actors who were capable of everything: they could declaim, sing and dance, write texts, skits and pieces of music, act from written texts or extemporize. The difference between what was transmitted orally and what was written down for a new play was generally not very great. For both types of literature proceeded from ancient and familiar material. The figures we meet in, say, the *Teutsche Arien*, together with their costumes and pranks, their sad destinies and their conflicts (inevitably leading to happy endings), were drawn from traditions that can be retraced through the whole of the Middle Ages to ancient Rome and Greece, eventually disappearing in the mists of pre-history. Yet even there they are not entirely inaccessible to research. Many, perhaps all human cultures produced similar forms of mimetic presentation (see Knepler 1988, esp. pp. 367ff.).

However long-lived many of its principles and motifs, the power of human invention gives rise to dazzling variety. If a society's productive capacity is sufficient to permit and encourage division of labour and vocational specialization it will also be capable of extraordinary creative achievements, provided that another precondition (necessary but often overlooked) is also met: namely, that the society is confronted with a need for major upheavals, testing both its intellectual mettle and, even more so, its practical capabilities. Just how, and under what preconditions, one of the most astonishing and inconceivable of human achievements came about – the writings of William Shakespeare in late sixteenth- and early seventeenth-century England – has been analysed in exemplary fashion by Robert Weimann (1967 and 1988). And among those preconditions was 'a complete rapprochement between the Renaissance's enhanced awareness of *poetic* form and the *acting* proficiency acquired from folk theatre' (Weimann 1967, p. 338). Like Elizabethan England, Vienna of the Josephine era 200 years later shows us just how deep are the wellsprings of genius, and how many sensory faculties genius seems to command in order to derive sustenance even from the naive, uncultured and crude. Mozart was acquainted with many if not all of the strands of tradition that remained alive in Viennese street theatre: its earliest roots from England (in the figure of Merry Andrew), its Italian version in the *commedia dell'arte* with its well-known stock characters, and more recent German traditions with Bernardon, Hanswurst, Thaddädl, Kasperle and Anton. Mozart's harlequinade of 1783 drew on the Italian tradition; *Die Liebesprobe* presents both 'Wurstl' and 'Kasperl' on the same stage. The *Salzburger Lump*, as already mentioned, introduces a 'Herr Stachelschwein' – Mr Porcupine – while *Die Liebesprobe* (unfortunately only in its cast of characters) also contains a 'Herr von Dummkopf' (Mr Deadhead) and 'Herr von Knödel' (Mr Dumpling) as, respectively, Rosaura's father and lover. These latter three figures obviously belong to the modern repertoire of travestied characters from the bourgeoisie. We have no right to consign these plays to the pejorative pigeonhole of 'occasional works': all of Mozart's works were written for particular occasions. This was customary at the time and says nothing about their artistic value or their status in his creative process. Like Goethe, Mozart might have compared himself to a gardener 'who possesses many beautiful flowers but does not take proper notice of or delight in them until someone asks him for a bouquet' (quoted from Dietze 1985, p. 390). His pleasure in poetry, Goethe explained, is rekindled when he is required to write an occasional poem. Popular comedy had a place in Mozart's arsenal of approaches and techniques. We can hear it in the music of Papageno, Leporello and Zerlina and in many passages from his instrumental music, including those significant and unexpected moments when the style of comic song bursts in amidst 'learned' thematic development. One special type of intellectual accomplishment has been described by the systems theorist Ludwig Bertalanffy: 'Human invention can be viewed as the new combination of existing elements' (1968, p. 26). Though Bertalanffy was not thinking in terms of the creation of art, much less of music, I have applied this idea, which has been expressed by other researchers and thinkers as well, to artistic creation in another publication (Knepler 1988), where I speak of *Leistungskonvergenz*. This concept – the convergence of human achievements – is not a simple one. It refers to mutual affinities and cross-fertilizations of elements from completely different areas of human activity. By themselves, these elements would never come together; nor can they be simply added or juxtaposed. The achievement lies in knowing that they can be made to coalesce and how this can be done.

The special point about this concept is that the act of composing is, strictly speaking, an instance of *Leistungskonvergenz*. 'Composing' is a very revealing word, one we might even call wise. Composers also combine or unite elements which do not necessarily fit or belong together, and human beings had been doing this for at least eight or nine centuries before Mozart started composing. His incredible creativity can be understood, among other things, as an example of *Leistungskonvergenz* at the very highest level. Mozart, in thought and deed, brought about the combination of many elements residing on different levels and previously unrelated to each other: the expectations of a new audience, the communicative possibilities of the theatre, the applicability of symphonic technique to opera, subjects drawn from contemporary events. In light of what has been said above we need not enumerate the new expectations of his listeners. The manner in which contemporary events entered his music, however, will be examined at the end of this chapter; and one of the threads governing the further course of this book will be to describe the union of opera dramaturgy and symphonic technique, initiated in opera buffa but carried by Mozart to unimagined heights.

No matter how unique Mozart's achievement, it lay entirely within a larger movement that had seized all of the countries of Europe: the union of popular and literary theatre. The great actor Friedrich Ludwig Schröder, for example, emerged 'entirely from the tradition of travelling theatrical troupes' and was principally concerned with 'expanding the powers of acting' (Rommel 1952, p. 274). (Schröder's formative impact on Vienna's Burgtheater occurred just at the time that Mozart was there to appreciate it.) One of the major tendencies of the age was to salvage the original, realistic acting techniques of popular comedy for the literary drama, transplanting them from travelling companies to permanent ensembles.

Astonishingly, this transplantation yielded a specifically musical by-product: *plot-related music*. In popular comedy this kind of music is taken for granted. Often the opening songs of comic characters introduce them as bustling with activity, putting their acting abilities in clear focus. In *Hanns-Wurst als MUSICUS* (Pirker 1927, I, pp. 141f.) Hanns-Wurst presents himself as follows in his opening song, singing and playing a number of instruments:

> Singen, blasen, leyren, pfciff'n,
> Geigen unds Bassetel greiff'n
> Kann ich la la, tu tu.
>
> (Sing and blow, strum and whistle,
> Thump a bass and scrape a fiddle -
> I can do it, la la, tu tu.)

Or he finds parallels in the animal kingdom for his tender feelings toward his lady friend. The result then looks something like this (*ibid.*, pp. 31f.):

> Ein jedes Vieh auf dieser Welt
>   Sucht das, was sich zu ihm gesellt;
>   Der Ochs ruft die geliebte Kuh,
>   Und singt: Muh Muh! muh muh!
> Der Löwe brüllt, der Budel murrt,
> Der Sperling pfeift, der Tauber gurrt,
>   Der Frosch folgt seiner Domina,
>   Und schreyt: Qua, qua! qua qua!
>
> (Every animal in this world,
>   Searches for his better half;
>   The ox calls his beloved cow
>   And sings: Moo Moo! moo moo!
> The lion roars, the poodle growls,

> The sparrow twitters, the pigeon coos,
>   The frog follows his paramour
>   And cries: Qua, qua! qua qua!)

In this way Hanns-Wurst brings into play more than a dozen animals. Kurz-Bernardon, perhaps the author or singer of these songs, also required music for scenes in dumb show. One of his comedies of the 1750s had music (now unfortunately lost) by the young Joseph Haydn. During a visit from the painter Dies, Haydn described how this came about (Dies 1810, p. 43). Kurz, looking for a performing musician, invited Haydn to his quarters and asked him to

> 'Sit down at the piano and play music appropriate to the pantomime I am about to perform. Imagine that Bernardon has fallen into the water and is trying to rescue himself by swimming.' He called his servant, flung himself lengthwise across a chair and had the servant drag the chair back and forth in the room. He then flayed about with his legs and arms like a swimmer while Haydn, in 6/8 time, imitated the movement of the waves and limbs. Suddenly Bernardon leapt up, embraced Haydn and nearly smothered him with kisses. 'Haydn, you're my man! You simply must write me an opera!' This is how *Der krumme Teufel* came about.

Another aspect of this picture is that, as a legacy of the travelling theatrical troupes, stage performers had not settled into specific types, at least not in Germany or Vienna. It was an everyday occurrence for tragedians to crop up in farces or actors to appear in opera. In this way, then, the various theatrical genres were able to learn from each other. In his *Geschichte der Schauspielkunst*, a history of acting published in 1848, Eduard Devrient frequently speaks of the beneficial influence exercised on 'the art of acting by its previously debased rival, opera, in the works of Mozart and Gluck'. He even goes so far as to pinpoint this influence (I, p. 534): it was 'that which acting most needed at this very moment, namely, the pulse and throb of artistic life: rhythm.'

Let us attempt to summarize what was gained and what was lost in the transition from a primarily oral tradition of theatre to one based on written texts. The virtues of the former are plain to see. Even if performances, including their dialogue and pranks, could hardly help but become fixed after countless repetitions, there was still ample room for real improvisation, for spontaneous new ideas and intuitive rephrasings, and especially for direct interaction with the audience – with its acquiescence, its laughter and applause, its displeasure and protest. There is much evidence that the reactions of the audience, including its shouts and spontaneous participation, were among the attractions of the popular stage. During his Vienna years Friedrich Wilhelm Schröder often attended performances of street theatre. The historian Rommel (1952, p. 429) records Schröder's impressions: 'Among the farces presented could be found genuine masterpieces. It is an irreparable loss that so many of them must disappear, nay, have disappeared already ... There is little hope of ever recapturing much that was invented so successfully.' Nor should we overlook the fact that many burning issues of the day found their way into street theatre precisely because of its capacity for improvisation and its storehouse of parody and travesty, mockery and innuendo. This was nothing new: Shakespeare's clown scenes sometimes present thoughts of deadly earnest amidst madcap nonsense. Similarly, Mozart delivers one of his most serious characters, Pamina in *Die Zauberflöte*, into the hands of the prankster Papageno as a partner in one of his most profound musical utterances, 'Bei Männern, welche Liebe fühlen'. But there is more to it than this. To present epoch-making issues by juxtaposing and interweaving petty and grand motives, sadness and merriment, tragedy and comedy, there must be a cogent and well thought-out plan and structure behind it. And this was beyond the power of even the best extempore theatre or the most successful improvisation.

The decisive question, then, is not *whether* improvised forms of musical theatre would be superseded by works permanently set down to the last detail in words, music and structure, but *how* this would come about. And in fact the transition took place amidst heated controversy. Sonnenfels, for example, had no notion that any loss might be involved. Mozart, as intimated above, disagreed. Sonnenfels wanted to see Hanswurst banned from the stage; Mozart on the other hand merely found (16 June 1781) that 'Hanswurst has not yet been banished from music, and in this respect the French are right' – a remarkable concession. Sonnenfels even went so far as to criticize Goldoni; Mozart had a libretto made from a specially commissioned translation of Goldoni's *Il servitore di due padroni*. Sonnenfels obtained a ban on improvisation at the Burgtheater; Mozart never entirely severed his ties to improvisation.

First of all, Mozart continued to improvise in the literal sense of the term as it applies to music. There are many accounts, even from Mozart himself, that he improvised at the keyboard for hours on end. Many of his public appearances also included free improvisation as part of their programmes. One special form of improvisation, on a given theme, he had mastered even as a boy. And there was more than one reason for the fact that he failed to write out the solo parts, much less the cadenzas, for some of his piano concertos. For one, it was unnecessary: he had the music in his head. But for another there were two advantages to not doing so: he could give free rein to his fantasy on the spur of the moment, and his concerto was protected from pirating.

Like improvised music-making, improvisation on stage derives from the earliest forms of mimetic communication, nourished on sources which sustained man's artistic behaviour before it was codified in rules, instructions and traditions. It is in this context that we should view Mozart's appearance as Harlequin (see pp. 8–9, 198–9), during which he improvised gestures, facial expressions and stage movement in panto-mime. Unfortunately no account of this performance has survived. In his letter of 30 July 1778 to Aloysia Weber, written in Italian, he advised her to follow a practice related to improvisation, being one of the oldest fundamentals of the art of acting: namely, to project herself into the psychological state of the character being represented.

Greater leeway was granted to comic characters, whose antics likewise arose in revolt against rules and regulations. When Papageno decides to 'ornament this tree here', then grants himself a lease of life by counting from one to three and interpolates a 'half-past-two' before the final three, Mozart would have been the last to object to this infringement of the sanctity of the written text. (Similar ideas, incidentally, can be found in the original libretto; see Dieckmann 1984, p. 109). When Richard Mayr (1877–1935), the admirable bass engaged for Vienna by Gustav Mahler, took the part of Leporello he allowed himself an even greater liberty. Where the original Catalogue Aria has 'mille e tre' he sang, in German, 'aber in Spanien schon tausendundzwei – nein – tausendunddrei, denn da seid Ihr auch dabei!' ('but in Spain there are already one thousand and two – no! one thousand and three, for there you are amongst them!') This, it is true, forced him to break down a few crotchets and quavers of the original into semiquavers, but in no way did it sin against the spirit of the original. When Mozart played Papageno's glockenspiel offstage during a performance of *Die Zauberflöte* he 'felt a sort of impulse' to play an arpeggio where none was written (8–9 October 1791). Schikaneder, taking the part of Papageno, saw Mozart in the wings, understood the joke and expected an arpeggio in the parallel passage, presumably in the second stanza. Mozart, however, left it out.

> This time [Schikaneder] stopped and refused to go on. I guessed what he was thinking and again played a chord. He then struck the glockenspiel and said 'Shut up'. Whereupon everyone laughed. I am inclined to think that this joke taught many of the audience for the first time that Papageno does not play the instrument himself.

Mozart, in other words, had nothing against actors dropping character in certain stage situations – an aspect of what Brecht called 'epic theatre'.

The same did not apply to the more serious roles, where the singer had to take back seat to the character he personified. The protagonists of the opera enact the plot in verbal or physical confrontations. Here, unlike the novel or the oratorio, there is no 'epic narrator' to relate the plot. At most, it is in accounts of events that have taken place off stage that an epic element comes into play, though here the emphasis does not fall on the music. Conversely, music is completely at home in moments of lyric dalliance, even in spoken drama. The many songs and musical numbers that Shakespeare prescribed in his plays are generally lyric moments couched among dramatic events. In opera seria, however, with whose stereotypes Mozart was permanently at loggerheads, the proportions had shifted completely in favour of the lyrical, namely, to arias, which were demanded by singers and audience alike. The stage action was dealt with dutifully and pro forma as a sort of embarrassing necessity – things had to get along somehow – mainly in the form of secco recitative. Even when produced by the hand of a master secco recitative cannot hold a listener's attention for long. Opera seria audiences made no secret of what they thought of recitatives: they ate and drank or let down the curtains of their boxes until the next aria finally came along. This mirrors the tendency in aristocratic opera (composers were always bridling at it) to nullify any semblance of conflict. The more closely real tragedy and disaster pressed against the theatre doors, the less one wanted to be reminded of it.

Mozart held this tendency in scorn. Instead, what he wanted for his music were plots and conflicts. In *Die Entführung* he demanded an 'entirely new plot' for a scene (26 September 1781). But, as already mentioned, it cost him a long period of hesitation, pondering and experimentation before he could assert the rights of drama in opera. For a while, around 1778, he thought he had found in melodrama a solution to this problem, but luckily he soon abandoned this idea. While working on *Idomeneo*, as we saw in Chapter 8, he seemed to feel that virtue lies in brevity. But even this insight circles the problem without striking its core. *Don Giovanni* is one of the most powerful dramas in existence, but there is no denying that several of its numbers are very long.

The core of any drama is collision, the confrontation of antagonistic characters, usually carried out in the medium of language. The category of collision was painstakingly analysed by Hegel (1955, especially pp. 224ff. and 1071ff.). Even today, as Gerhard Scheit has shown in a brilliant study of contemporary plays and dramatic theories (1988), it is still the central problem of drama, including opera. And, as Scheit reminds us (p. 11), 'there is always more at stake than aesthetics'.

At this point we should pause for a resumé and overview of Mozart's many and varied experiences during his Vienna years. As ready as he may have been to expand his horizons, to deepen his general knowledge and to apply the moral principles handed down to him by his religion, he could not have done so without the unexpected twists and cataclysmic events in which his hectic decade in Vienna abounded.

From his earliest childhood it had been part of Mozart's daily regimen to appraise critically whatever music he happened to hear from his contemporaries. But two musical events in Vienna left an especially deep impression on him, presumably because they co-incided with other experiences which were equally disturbing in their own right. The first was the publication in 1781 of Haydn's 'Russian' string quartets, op. 33; the second was his encounter with a large number of works by Handel and Johann Sebastian Bach at the home of Baron van Swieten, starting in April 1782. We should recall that as early as April 1781 Mozart had taken a room in the lodgings of Cäcilie Weber. True, he left the room by the end of August to take up new quarters on the Graben, a few steps away from the house 'Zum Auge Gottes' where the Weber family lived. But apparently he only did so because by then he already had serious intentions of marrying Konstanze Weber.

For the first time in his life Mozart felt he had found the conditions he needed to settle down permanently in a city. Of course he knew Vienna from earlier visits. But quite apart from the fact that Vienna had begun to change in appearance under Emperor Joseph, Mozart now looked at the teeming metropolis with new eyes: its colourful mixture of people from different professions, countries and walks of life, its cafés, inns and ale houses, its reading rooms and building projects, and of course its four theatres, soon to become five. He was also struck by the new listening habits of Vienna's audiences.

By the time a few years had passed Mozart was composing under conditions he had never experienced before at the same time and in one city. At least three types of audience were now at his disposal: the intimate but musically undemanding gatherings of the Freemasons; the larger audience, including connoisseurs, of the academies and concerts he gave at his own home and the homes of his friends; and finally the very large, anonymous theatre public, with its many subdivisions and its resultant dependence on readily intelligible effects. Yet these audiences did not exist in isolation, neither from each other nor from the aforementioned steady stream of information, communication and debate. Mozart was born into one of those rare moments of history when new ways of forming public awareness become not only possible but virtually imperative. Still, another discovery was required before Mozart could come to terms with this situation, a discovery he made only with difficulty.

As far as I know, Alfred Einstein has been the only writer to draw attention to and stress the fact that Mozart, having energetically liberated himself from the triumvirate of Archbishop, Salzburg and father, and having produced *Die Entführung*, spent several years of strange indecision in search of new operatic subjects. Indeed, nearly four years passed before he was able to complete his next opera score, *Figaro*. This is the period when, with feverish zeal, he 'looked through at least a hundred libretti and more' (7 May 1783) and took up the composition of at least four stage works only to abandon them. Of course we must always bear in mind that Mozart had to calculate his chances of being performed, to take careful note of who was in charge of the best singer-actors, and much else besides. There is a revealing letter of 21 May 1785 to a dramatist who had offered him a play in German with Rudolf of Habsburg as its protagonist. Apparently Mozart seriously considered setting the piece, which would have become his fifth attempt at a stage work, but wished 'to know beforehand whether its production has actually been arranged for a particular place'. He also points out that 'things are progressing very slowly' with the German opera, which may be 'targeted for ruin altogether'.

But apart from all this we are still left with the impression that Mozart himself did not know exactly what he wanted. We can see this first of all in the directions he gave to a potential new librettist, the Salzburg court chaplain Varesco (whose work on *Idomeneo*, however, had left Mozart less than satisfied). In a letter of 7 May 1783 Mozart itemizes the 'most essential things' in no uncertain terms. And what are they? First, the text should be 'on the whole quite comic'. Then he goes on to list the number and character of the singers to be engaged. Einstein is right to remark (1946, p. 432) that 'it looks as though Mozart was still thinking in categories, in typical roles, for which the typical protagonists were available in Vienna'. But the most convincing evidence of Mozart's indecision is supplied by the fragments themselves.

The one pursued furthest is a hopeless affair which Varesco finally sent to Mozart after repeated urgings: *L'oca del Cairo* ('The Goose of Cairo'). The hero is a young man who, with the aid of a mechanical invention, the Egyptian goose of the title, breaks into a tower where his beloved is being held prisoner by an evil old man. We stand the greatest chance of understanding why Mozart busied himself for months (from summer 1783 to the end of the year) with this absurdity if we assume that he wanted to capitalize on the same constellation that had given rise to the plot of *Die Entführung*: sclerotic tradition, as embodied in an old man, versus a young generation hungering for love and freedom.

Another libretto that captured Mozart's fancy as late as 1784 or 1785, showing just how widely he was willing to cast his net, treats us to two comic greybeards at once. It is a scene written to be inserted in an opera which had been performed in Parma toward the end of 1783 and whose composer Agostino Accorimboni, if we may believe the words of his contemporary Ernst Ludwig Gerber in his *Lexikon der Tonkünstler* (Leipzig, 1790–2), wrote music that 'betrayed a youthful and impassioned genius unfettered by rules' (I, 'Agosti', p. 15). The stage situation that evidently caught Mozart's attention once again involves a young man whose tender feelings for his beloved Livia enable him to achieve an ironic detachment from two fanatical and escapist savants, an archaeologist and a meteorologist. Mozart makes this conflict the linchpin of his sketch and even extracts from it some charming musical ideas. Even so, we can more readily understand why he abandoned this attempt after some 100 bars than why he took it up in the first place. The dramatic situation is too much beholden to traditional opera buffa to allow the composer to probe new conceptions.

The same cannot be said of another draft, K435, which probably also originated in 1783. We will doubtless never know whether Einstein was right in surmising that this tenor aria for a figure named Karl (together with the well-known 'Männer suchen stets zu naschen', one of Mozart's weakest pieces) was in fact intended for Goldoni's *Il servitore di due padroni*. Neither of the two pieces fits conveniently into the constellation of characters or the plot of this brilliant comedy. Whatever the case, Mozart was very serious in his plan to write a singspiel after Goldoni's play. In a letter to his father (5 February 1783) he reported:

> I am now writing a German opera *for myself*. I have chosen Goldoni's comedy *Il servitore di due padroni*, and the whole of the first act has now been translated. The translator is Baron Binder [probably an old acquaintance from the days of his Italian tours and roughly the same age as Mozart]. But we are keeping it a secret until it is quite finished. Well, what do you think of this scheme? Do you not think that I shall make a good thing of it?

Whatever the case, Mozart made a good thing of his aria 'Müßt ich auch durch tausend Drachen', whether or not it was intended for the Goldoni play. It is completely sketched out from the first to the last of its 143 bars, and several of its details, especially with regard to orchestration, are fully elaborated. Moreover, its final two bars (bars 142–3) are set aside for an artifice of which we will not find another instance in Mozart's entire œuvre: a kettledrum solo. The piece ends with a *forte* drum roll that resounds for a full three beats after the tutti cadence by the orchestra:

Example 31

But this is not Mozart's only extraordinary device. There can be little doubt that the aria draws on Pedrillo's aria 'Frisch zum Kampfe' (No. 13 in *Die Entführung*). Both are in D major and common time; one is marked *allegro con spirito*, the other *allegro con brio*; both have melodies built from triadic fanfare figures and descending scalar motifs; and both come from the world of trumpets and kettledrums – or, to be more exact, two trumpets in D and timpani on D and A. Note how similar are their underlying texts:

PEDRILLO:
Frisch zum Kampfe!

Frisch zum Streite!
Nur ein feiger Tropf verzagt.

Sollt' ich zittern?
Sollt' ich zagen?

Nicht mein Leben mutig wagen?
Nein, ach nein es sei gewagt!

KARL:
Müßt ich auch durch tausend
    Drachen,
die mit aufgesperrtem Rachen
Lischen Tag und Nacht
    bewachen,
eine blut'ge Bahn mir machen,
Drohte mir mit Schwert und
    Speer,
auch ein ganzes Ritterheer,
stritt ich ihnen Lischen ab –

(PEDRILLO: Off to battle! On to the fray! Only a coward would lose heart. Should I tremble? Should I quail? and not bravely risk my life? No, ah! no, I shall dare!)
(KARL: Should I have to pass through a thousand dragons guarding Lischen day and night with jaws agape, should I have to

pave my path in blood, should I even be threatened by an entire host of knights with sword and spear, I would wrest Lischen from them.)

Yet there is a significant difference. Pedrillo's text exhausts the repertoire of his emotions; Karl's does not. The last line in his text, quoted above, is followed by a timpani roll, once again played solo but this time piano. After this comes a line with important musical repercussions: 'oder sänk ins frühe Grab' – 'or sink into an early grave'. Mozart set this line as follows:

Example 32

The diminished seventh chord we are dealing with here was traditionally a symbol of despondence, pain, death. But it was unusual for this chord to appear in such a radical form in a buffo aria, with no fewer than five descending minor thirds following a solo kettledrum. Mozart's quest for new opera librettos was not limited simply to new subject matter; his setting treats the deadly alternative to victory with unusual seriousness. We might recall that before a decade had passed the composer of this aria and the man whose victory he counted as his own – Emperor Joseph – had both sunk into early graves. The optimism of the Josephine era was enshrouded in tragedy.

Mozart's next attempt at an opera, *Lo sposo deluso* of 1783 (K430), did not progress very far. All that survives are two arias, neither of them orchestrated, a terzetto marred by the fact that its opening and concluding situations are identical, the first number, and the overture leading into it.

On 23 August 1784 Mozart heard an opera which, as Einstein rightly assumes, must have struck him 'like a bolt of lightning' (1946, p. 442). Indeed, its impact on him can only be compared to his encounter with Johann Sebastian Bach two years previously (p. 440). This time, however, the effect did not come from the music. The opera Mozart heard was *Il re Teodoro in Venezia*, and it must have been Casti's libretto rather than Paisiello's music which took him by surprise. He fell ill that evening, and claimed that he had caught a cold by leaving the theatre without his cloak – and this in August! We will come closer to the true cause of his illness if we ask what it was about Paisiello's new opera that made him, in the words of Leopold Mozart (14 September 1784), 'perspire so profusely that all his clothes were drenched'. After all, this is not the only time that Mozart responded physically to inner agitation.

A second experience of the same sort was not long in the offing. In the very next year Mozart encountered the opera *La villanella rapita*. Here again it cannot have been the music, this time by Francesco Bianchi, so much as Bertati's libretto which struck him to the quick.

By this time Mozart, through the mediation of his then landlord Baron Wetzlar, had already made the acquaintance of Lorenzo Da Ponte early in 1783 and discussed operatic plans with him.

Mozart's musical output received an extra and decisive impetus from his encounter with the works of these three men: Giovanni Battista Casti (1721–1803), Giovanni Bertati (1735–1815) and Lorenzo Da Ponte (1749–1838). Instead of following the usual procedure and focusing our attention on their various adventures (these were heartless times and we cannot do justice to them by applying the standards of modern-day affluence), it would be useful to ask in what way their writings interacted with the Italian Enlightenment, and thereby indirectly with the French Enlightenment. For just as Diderot put contemporary problems and subjects on the theatrical stage, these three men opened up the operatic stage to a field which till then had remained outside Mozart's experience: the contemporary topic. It is, then, no accident that the two best opera texts Mozart ever received, indeed two of the most magnificent librettos ever written, *Le nozze di Figaro* and *Don Giovanni*, were the work of one of these men. Nor is it fortuitous that Mozart should turn precisely to him when, in a moment of destiny, he stumbled upon Beaumarchais's *Marriage of Figaro*. (For the time being I am deliberately excluding *Der Schauspieldirektor* of 1786, *Così fan tutte* of 1790 and *La clemenza di Tito* of 1791 as Mozart was not responsible for choosing the librettos. This, of course, is not to impugn the quality of these works.)

To be sure, *Die Entführung* has a sort of contemporary topic, too, but one filtered through its stereotype subject matter, through the oriental fairy-tale ambience that was so fashionable at the time. Casti, however, had boldly taken his subject from recent events and made no attempt to hide the fact. As was customary at the time, Mozart probably bought a bilingual copy of the libretto from the programme seller (a translation of its preface can be found in Appendix 2). As an experienced man of the theatre the topicality of the subject matter must have virtually leapt to his eye. But beyond that, in the first sentence of the introduction (called *Argomento* in Italian and simply *Stoff* in German) he could even read the decisive words 'political history'. The sentence runs as follows: 'Theodore, Baron of Neuhoff, is one of the strangest phenomena to have graced the political history of our century.' There now follows a brief account of this baron, a swindler who for eight months was really and truly king of Corsica but who was now living penniless in Venice. At the end of the preface the author points, clearly enough, to a 'charming sketch' which 'emanated from the pen of a celebrated writer in one of his most ingenious and widely read creations'. The reference is to Voltaire, who included the baron's tale in Chapter 26 of his *Candide*, published in 1758 when the events were then only about two decades old.

We have no way of knowing whether Mozart understood this allusion to a man whom, eight years before, he had grossly insulted. But even if he did not, the play can only have left him profoundly disturbed, for an epoch-making subject had found its way onto the opera stage. Three fallen crowns – one of them historical, one theatrical and one anticipated – are united in this work: the bizarre case of the eight-month king of Corsica, its comic reenactment on the opera stage, and the impending and, a few years later, actual fall of the mightiest European monarch of the age, the king of France. When we consider that only a few decades separated these events, that all upheavals have to be prepared beforehand in people's minds before they can become reality, that sarcasm and satire of the sort we find again and again in Mozart's letters are an operative part of this mental preparation, we can then form an idea of the explosive force of Casti's libretto.

Voltaire had made his hero lament: 'One used to address me as "Your Majesty"; now one scarcely calls me "Sir". I used to have coins struck; now I scarcely have a farthing. I used to have two ministers of state; now I scarcely have a servant.' Casti relates the tale from beginning to end without compromise or pity. In German the work is called, simply, *ein Singspiel*; the Italian uses a more accurate term, *dramma eroicomico*. Indeed, parodied heroism and unalloyed comedy merge so completely and perfectly that the hero can be introduced as follows at his first entrance. He is seated at a table in a Venetian inn, 'clad in a splendid dressing gown, sad and pensive. . . Enter Tadeo [the innkeeper] with a bill, followed by Lisette [his daughter, whom Teodoro is pursuing in hopes of salvaging his financial situation] with coffee, singing:

> Senza soldi, e senza Regno
> Brutta cosa è l'esser Re.

> (Without a farthing, and without a kingdom,
> it's a nasty business to be a king.)

Never before had Mozart been handed a text worded so pointedly and related so closely to the affairs of his time.

The opera ends consistently, if not in buffo style, with the penniless hero languishing in debtors' prison and comforted by his sister, who sings: 'Be merry, brother! Those who cannot pay always have the laws on their side.' None the less, and despite the prospect of liberation held out by his friends, Teodoro concludes with the words:

> In pace lasciatemi.
> Udir non vo più.
>
> (Leave me alone.
> I will hear no more.)

Admittedly the work has its weaknesses. Teodoro does not have an antagonist; the plot turns on the confusions and jealousies of the secondary figures; it is only loosely connected with Teodoro. In short, there is no opportunity for a conflict of opposing forces. But even so, for Mozart and Da Ponte it was an object lesson in a new outlook.

Bertati's plot is even more topical. A count gives money to Mandina, a peasant maid, in order to entice her into bed. Unsuspecting and naive, she accepts it as a token of his princely favour. Then, without any effort on her part, she winds up in the count's bed after all, having been drugged and kidnapped in the dead of night. With the clearest conscience in the world she can counter the reproaches of her fiancé by saying 'Ditte almeno in que mancai' – 'Tell me at least what I did wrong'.

These are the opening words of one of the two ensemble numbers that Mozart wrote for this opera (in place of two passages of secco recitative in Bianchi's score) when it was mounted at Vienna's Burgtheater in November 1785. The author of the words for these two numbers, though anonymous, was very likely Da Ponte, who at the time was competing for the favours of the Emperor, the court theatre director, Salieri and Mozart. Da Ponte was all the more likely and willing to turn to such explosive material since, despite the criticism he heaps on Casti's *Re Teodoro* in his memoirs, he must surely have realized the theatrical potential inherent in the great conflicts of his age.

In his two masterly ensembles for Bianchi's *Villanella rapita* (K479 and K480) Mozart, for the first time, seriously set about writing through-composed pieces where the librettist had only intended the customary secco recitative. This put him further along his path toward uniting music and dramatic action. In this case, no matter how harmless it may seem at first glance, he applied his craft to a vital issue. One of the major causes of the French Revolution was the revolt against the sexual rights of noblemen over the village girls subject to their rule. This issue, representing the subjugation of women in one of its most reprehensible forms, was the first epochal problem that

Mozart, without hiding behind allegory and metaphor, made a central conflict in his stage works. Within a span of scarcely two years he had handled the theme of a nobleman pursuing a village girl no fewer than three times: six months after *Villanella rapita* in *Figaro*, and one year later in *Don Giovanni*. And each time he handled it differently. The count who tries in vain to buy Mandina before resorting to kidnapping is not the same as Count Almaviva, who also tries to bribe Susanna for her favours, but harbours a real passion for the girl and has reason to believe that she is not indifferent to him. Nor does Susanna bear the faintest resemblance to the ingenuous Mandina: she is fully aware of what is going on and readily joins the game of disguise and intrigue. Giovanni, in turn, differs from Almaviva, embodying the aristocrats of all lands (and all operas) in a single character. Rather than being enflamed by a single woman he is enflamed by them all, driven by the lust for power and pleasure that is his raison d'être. Zerlina, for her part, is the only one of the three female figures that does not require a major effort of seduction to be won over: 'Vorrei e non vorrei' – 'I want to and yet I don't' – these are the first words she sings in that most famous of all duets, 'La ci darem la mano'. All six of these characters are sharply delineated and individualized.

But Mozart does not stop at the conflict between lecherous noblemen and attractive peasant lasses. The latter have their fathers (or uncles) and above all their fiancés. Mandina's and Zerlina's lovers are likewise peasants; Susanna's is a servant. Willy nilly, they are embroiled in their women's conflicts. Mandina's father and, especially, Figaro's (not to mention his mother) play highly ambiguous roles in the confrontations of the main characters, thereby helping to make them comprehensible. Most of all, however, it is the jealousy of Pippo, Figaro or Masetto that matters. The seducer is truly seductive, and finds himself abetted by the desires of his victims for the splendour, luxury and elegance lacking in poor Masetto. All the latter can say is 'ho capito' – he understands that he must remain silent. When the principal agents collide there is something objective, something beyond their powers to control, working tacitly in their collisions: the social situation in which they stand. On Mozart's stage, beginning with *Villanella rapita*, operatic characters become agents in a world drama, and stage constellations become ciphers for problems that are global in scope. And that simple thing which is so difficult to accomplish – revolution – enters on stage both in its simplicity (*Figaro*) and in its difficulty (*Don Giovanni* and *Die Zauberflöte*). Figaro strikes up a dance with the Count, and since both Susanna and the Countess play along, the servant and the peasant girl can impose their will – and their musical language – on their master. In the tragic counterpart not even Ottavio's pistol, by rights superior to Giovanni's sword, is of any use. It takes the intercession of supernatural powers before the 'extremely dissolute young cavalier' is borne off to Hell or, in *Die Zauberflöte*, goodness is allowed to triumph.

In all these individual creations and variants we can still descry the essential, the typical. This is not solely, or even primarily, the achievement of the plot: it is Mozart's music that reveals the essential and most characteristic feature of his time – the rise of a new age in history.

Mozart accomplished this miracle with an apparent lightness of touch which, in reality, masked exhaustive labours that only seem light-handed in retrospect. This was one of his secrets, and he was fully aware of it. We cannot discuss how he did this until we look more closely at the evolution of his instrumental music. For the moment, however, it should be clear just how many stimuli were required, and how many aspects of Mozart's unique gifts had to converge, in order to vouchsafe the success of his great work. He must have known what he was saying when, a mere eight or nine weeks after moving to Vienna, he wrote back to Salzburg (26 May 1781): 'it seems to me as if I *must* stay here.'

Chapter 11

Other remarkable lives

It was not only Mozart who thought this way. Some of his leading contemporaries equally felt that they *had* to live in Josephine Vienna.

One was Johann Pezzl (1756–1823), a writer of distinction whose prodigious oeuvre is made up of travelogues, portraits of cities, biographies of famous men, polemical pamphlets, and challenging and ingenious satires. Not only did he command the style of a sober reporter, compiling arguments from well-researched facts, he could also write with polished and scintillating sarcasm. His successful *Skizze von Wien* ('Sketch of Vienna'), published in six volumes between 1786 and 1790 with many subsequent reissues and sequels, falls into the first of these two categories. But even here Pezzl can suddenly shift to criticism when he sights prejudice, social injustice or the arrogation of privilege. In the best of his writings Pezzl recalls Heinrich Heine. He was a confirmed champion of the Enlightenment and a man of courage.

Pezzl is hardly mentioned in the literature on Mozart; not even Hildesheimer has anything to say about him. Yet one of his major works was found in Mozart's library: *Faustin oder das philosophische Jahrhundert* ('Faustin, or The Philosophical Century', 1783). It is a satirical novel with clearly autobiographical features. The hero of its title is a young man who, like the author, comes from Bavaria. From there he traverses half of Europe to see with his own eyes the century of philosophy and enlightenment and to make the personal acquaintance of Voltaire, whom his teacher Bonifaz has lauded as the *fons et origo* of tolerance and enlightenment. On his pilgrimage Faustin is mocked, chased, beaten, even threatened with murder when he or one of his companions is suspected of being a follower of the Enlightenment or a Freemason. Like Voltaire's *Candide*, one of Pezzl's models, the novel illustrates the cruel undoing of naive optimism. Yet the excerpts from Pezzl's writings given in the Appendix (see pp. 336–49) show just how little reverence the author of *Faustin* felt toward the creator of *Candide*. At the end of his wanderings Faustin arrives in Vienna, where he discovers 'Philosophy Enthroned' (thus the title of the penultimate chapter) in the form of Joseph II. He then resolves, as did Pezzl himself, to settle in Vienna, that 'capital of Germany so envied and denigrated by many a small-town burgher' (Pezzl 1783, p. 347).

It may well be that Mozart's Viennese plans, carried out with such firm resolve, were connected with Pezzl's. The latter, after all, had studied jurisprudence at Salzburg University from 1776 to 1780 (Rosenstrauch-Königsberg 1988, p. 331), and it is conceivable that the two young men became acquainted with each other during those years. Mozart's copy of *Faustin* may even have been a gift from its author in 1783, a seal, as it were, on a decision which Faustin, Pezzl and Mozart had all made in common. There can be no doubt that Mozart and Pezzl met regularly from 1784 in the masonic lodge *Zur Wohltätigkeit* to which they both belonged. And, as the present chapter will show, neither the *Wohltätigkeit* nor the affiliated lodge dominated by Ignaz von Born placed an emphasis on those clandestine rituals that have held so many later writers in thrall.

In Viennese Enlightenment circles Pezzl's writings were what we would now call an insider's tip. Georg Forster wrote that Prince Karl Lichnowsky – the same man who accompanied Mozart to Berlin in 1789 and who would later become one of Beethoven's patrons – read to him aloud from Pezzl's writings. Forster himself did the same during his visits to Vienna's salons (Steiner 1985, pp. 180f.)

Another man who came to Vienna for these same good reasons was Otto Freiherr von Gemmingen-Hornberg (1755–1836). Originally from Heidelberg, he became chamberlain to the Elector Palatine in Mannheim. There he befriended the Elector's brother, Wolfgang Heribert Freiherr von Dalberg, an important figure who directed the Mannheim theatre and wrote a *Mannheimer Dramaturgie* in 1779 (Schenk 1975, p. 346). Gemmingen thus stood right at the hub of the theatrical reform movement of his day. Mozart had known him since 1778. We may recall that on the forced return from Paris to his hated Salzburg Mozart made a stop in Mannheim. Here he used his proposed setting of a duodrama by Gemmingen (12 November 1778) as a pretext for extending his stay. (Regrettably, the play itself, a melodrama entitled *Semiramis*, is lost, as is Mozart's music.) Mozart was now, in 1782, to see Gemmingen too arrive in Vienna.

In the meantime Gemmingen had become famous. One of his plays, *Der deutsche Hausvater*, is said to have been more successful than Lessing's *Emilia Galotti*, with which it shares the same subject matter, the love of a nobleman for a young lady of the bourgeoisie. As literature we need not give the play a second thought; as an expression of the democratic tendencies of the Enlightenment, however, it is remarkable in spite of its weaknesses. The hero, a count, heads a family which seems at first sight to be intact but proves to be rent with problems and conflicts as the drama proceeds. The central conflict is that the father's youngest son, Karl, has fallen in love with the daughter of a painter, Lottchen, but feels compelled to give her up for the sake of his father, a career in diplomacy, and a liaison with a lady of the aristocracy. The father, however, having convinced himself that the painter is an honest man and that Lottchen genuinely loves his son, advises him to marry the girl. 'Believe me', he says to the two young people,

> flee the world; you no longer suit its conventions. Go to my estates. Karl, you shall take over their administration. You will have a few hundred underlings; make but two of those families happy and you will deserve a monument.

Lottchen, in a scene with Karl's lover, a Countess Amaldi, begs her in the following words to set him free: 'Ah, if you have loved, if you but knew – but people of your station do not love, do they?' And the following dialogue transpires between the two fathers, Karl's and Lottchen's: 'Nothing could move me to lay down this brush for an earldom!' The count's response is pure Mozart: 'That sentiment alone makes you more worthy than many a count.' The playwright neglects to mention that the painter does not have a 'few hundred underlings' at his disposal and thus has no regular income – a fact which Gemmingen, himself an underling, was as little likely to overlook as Mozart.

In Vienna Gemmingen apparently sought to earn his livelihood by editing periodicals. In 1782 and 1783 there appeared, pseudonymously but probably entirely from his pen, a weekly with the title *Der Weltmann*, or 'The Cosmopolite'. In a kind of preface addressed to the publisher (none other than Thomas von Trattner) he sets out the programme of his journal, which was intended for 'genteel' readers: 'One must write about them – of their overgilt fooleries, their overvarnished ignorance, their overweening pride. But one must also write for them.' And in the second issue, in an essay on the nature of the theatre and theatrical taste (p. 31), we find the following pronouncement:

> Banish from our stages all sartorial splendour and all the frippery of state: let the amiable characters always appear in the simplest and most natural attire, and drape the fools and villains in glittering junk. Turn the German stage into a school of simple manners, of contentedness, of peaceful and sociable behaviour.

Whether the 'cosmopolites' failed to appreciate these exhortations, and whether this explains why the journal perished in the avalanche of similar publications, is uncertain. In any event, *Der Weltmann* was succeeded in 1784 and 1785 by a *Magazin für Wissenschaft und Literatur*, and in 1786 by the *Wiener Ephemeriden*, a quarterly containing articles, reviews, announcements, statistical information on industrial development and, on page 57, the *cri de coeur*: 'How much remains to be done before the lovely flower of future affluence can blossom!' So much for the literary activities of the man who, in 1784, presided as Grand Master of the masonic lodge *Zur Wohltätigkeit*, the lodge Mozart chose to enter.

Being a 'Freiherr' or baron, Gemmingen was a member of the lower nobility, and thus had no part in the feudal exploitation of the peasantry. Most likely he and others of his station found it easy to support, in word and deed, Emperor Joseph's curtailment of aristocratic privileges. But Mozart's immediate circle also included members of longstanding feudal dynasties who had taken up the Josephine banner, for reasons which ought to be individually pursued. There was, for instance, the remarkable career of Count Franz Joseph Thun (1734–1801), the husband of Wilhelmine Thun. Ten years older than the countess, he already had a highly unusual life behind him by the 1780s. He discussed his career on 28 March 1783 in a masonic address (quoted in Irmen 1988, pp. 64ff., whose interpretation however I find wanting). By his own account, he had entered the masonic order over thirty years previously and had 'passed through thirty-three degrees'. Abandoning this 'pointless labour', he then spent twenty years outside the order. Alluding to the reasons for his estrangement from the Masons, he referred to 'wills-o'-the-wisp', namely, to the fact that many members were seeking the 'philosopher's stone' or 'pathways to the world of spirits', to 'prophesies and miracle-making, conjurings and superstition' (p. 66). In all of this he had taken an active part, only to 'discover much later, in the lodge *Zur Wahren Eintracht*, traces of what I was ever searching for but could never find' (pp. 64f.). Thun now gives an eloquent account of human misery, the alleviation of which by active charity, he maintains, should constitute the true philosopher's stone. I quote this passage in full (p. 66) since it was apparently similar motives that led Mozart, one-and-a-half years later, to join the *Wohltätigkeit* lodge:

> How many hospitals there are, full of the sick and wretched, left without care or attention, without ministrations or comfort, and begging for death ... How many sick are lying in their forgotten corners, languishing, known only by the death-knells announcing that they have finally found a place under the earth that was not granted them while they were on it! How many schools there are which, where not empty, are worse than empty, being in the hands of incompetents who draw a master's wages for

work unworthy of an apprentice! How many widows and orphans sigh beneath the yoke of injustice for a voice to plead their cause! And lastly, how many poor people lie naked and hungry, untutored and unattended, despised and cast aside from the great round of self-interest, voluptuousness and frivolity!

And when the count comes to speak of the class divisions that might easily separate him from other members of the lodge he waxes Josephinian and Mozartian: 'Well did I know your caution toward all those who are born to a state which – sad to relate! – so easily forgets man's first calling' (p. 65).

At least for some time Mozart's lodge had another interesting writer in its midst, Johann Kaspar Risbeck or Riesbeck (?1749/50–86). His work, though not of the same stature as Pezzl's, is nonetheless remarkable. The magnum opus of this man, whose life span was no longer than Mozart's, is his two-volume *Briefe eines reisenden Franzosen über Deutschland an seinen Bruder zu Paris* (1784). Much information not obtainable elsewhere, including facts on Viennese music life, have been taken from these 'letters of a French traveller to his brother in Paris'; Abert alone quotes Risbeck more than a dozen times. But Risbeck also wrote a four-volume history of the German people (*Geschichte der Deutschen*, 1788–90), and his study of monasticism, *Briefe über das Mönchswesen von einem catholischen Pfarrer an einen Freund*, written in 1771, went through three editions by 1780. Johann Pezzl published a biographical eulogy of Risbeck which I have included in the Appendix (pp. 351–3). A new biography is long overdue, for Risbeck too was one of those astute observers, tireless admonishers and incorruptible critics of the social injustices that Mozart and his masonic brothers had linked arms to combat. It is characteristic of the prettifying strain in recent Mozart scholarship that Erich Schenk (1975, p. 475) should reduce Risbeck to a 'writer of travelogues'.

Even in those stormy decades it would be difficult to find a life more remarkable than that of Georg Forster (1754–93). In the summer of 1784 he passed through Vienna on his travels, remaining there only about seven weeks. But his favourable impressions of the city, its surroundings and, above all, the people he met there led him to consider making Vienna his permanent abode. He quickly befriended a number of Freemasons who, as he reported to a friend, boisterously hiding his emotions, 'could have gobbled me up in friendship and would do anything to fetch me back' (*Werke* XIV, p. 16). Just why Forster was so impressed by Vienna's Masons becomes clearer when we examine his life and his unfortunate experiences of the early 1780s. I take my account from the definitive studies of Forster's complicated career by Gerhard Steiner (1968ff.).

Georg Forster was a man of extraordinary talents and touches of genius. Though not yet thirty years old when he arrived in Vienna at the end of July 1784 (he was only fourteen months older than Mozart), he was by then already a famous man. From July 1772 to July 1775 he and his father had taken part in Captain James Cook's second circumnavigation of the globe for the British admiralty. On this journey, at first under his father's supervision, he soon became an independently-minded researcher, thinker, illustrator and writer. It was his account of this journey and the drawings accompanying it – 'a compelling synthesis of scientific clarity and artistic sensibility' (Steiner 1977, p. 15) – that established his initial fame. After publishing this work at the age of twenty-three he was offered membership of several learned societies. He also approached the Masons seriously at an early date. As early as 1777 he had been accepted for membership in a Parisian lodge of a special kind: *Les Neuf Sœurs* ('The Nine Sisters'), founded by the astronomer Lalande at the instigation of Helvétius. Unusually, this lodge followed a conception drawn from Antiquity, taking its name from the Nine Muses. A short while later, under peculiar circumstances, the aged Voltaire was accepted into the same lodge. Here, according to the lodge's programme, natural scientists, poets, musicians, physicians and lawyers were meant to work together and 'hasten to the aid of mankind' (Steiner 1985, pp. 11ff.). This was, then, a fellowship of scholars and artists with lofty goals. In London, where the family lived, Forster's father had been forced to borrow enormous sums of money. The reasons were simple: those who did not wish to enter the services of a court as a librarian, tutor or Kapellmeister – who did not, as Christian Friedrich Daniel Schubart (1739–91) complained, want to become a 'cantor, school-master or town piper in Germany' (*Deutsche Chronik*, 29 September 1774) – or who did not possess the spiritual and physical powers of a Handel, were forced to live on the brink of ruin. No one with Enlightenment ideas in his head was immune to the fate that befell the intelligent, reflective and courageous poet and journalist Gotthold Friedrich Stäudlin (1758–96). Following Schubart's death, Stäudlin took over the editorship of the *Deutsche Chronik*, where he made no secret of his sympathies for the French Revolution, even in its second phase. Expelled by the duke from Swabia, where he had spent his entire career, he attempted to reestablish himself as the editor of a political journal, and drowned himself in the Rhine when all his efforts failed.

In 1778 – the year of Mozart's journey to Paris, which plunged his own father into nearly ruinous debts – Georg Forster undertook a tour of Germany to relieve his father's financial situation and to seek a position for him. Thanks to the high reputation enjoyed by this brilliant young man, he succeeded in both. He also met many of Germany's leading intellectuals, among them Goethe and Lessing, and was appointed Professor of Natural History at the University of Kassel. There he entered the masonic lodge and, fatefully, joined a circle of so-called Rosicrucians and 'Goldicrucians'. For almost four years Forster, with all the energy and dedication at his command, immersed himself in expensive, spiritually and physically taxing and strictly regimented attempts to create gold and to distil a life-elixir. It took years before he began to be plagued by doubts and reservations. As he wrote on 16 July 1783 to Christoph Friedrich Nicolai, an Enlightenment figure in Berlin, 'I have here a veil before my eyes that cannot easily be rent without instruction'. Scarcely a year later he was on his way to Vilnius (then part of Poland), where he had been offered a professorship. This same path brought him to Vienna.

As has often and correctly been claimed, it tells us little or nothing about the intentions or character of a late eighteenth-century figure to know that he was a Freemason. He may have joined a lodge from sheer opportunism, for in their heyday the Masons were highly influential. Or he may have joined what in the eighteenth century was known as a *Sauf- und Fressloge*, or 'booze and gobble lodge', these being fashionable at the time. He may have fallen in with charlatans, as Thun and Forster did for a while. Or he might have joined a circle of like-minded fellows to turn his concern for humanity into deeds.

At this point a brief outline of Freemasonry is called for in order to extract, from the mare's nest of parties and schisms that called themselves Masons or sympathized with them, the information that is germane to Mozart's own association with this order. I shall draw upon several studies of the activities of what Eva Balázs (1979, Preface) has called 'societies with universal goals'.

Freemasonry originated in England and was descended from the medieval craft guilds, some of whose members were masons in the literal sense of the word. In the seventeenth century, in ways which are still obscure, these groups gave rise to the 'free masons', who also maintained connections with the earliest learned body in Europe, the Royal Society. The great upsurge of Freemasonry on the Continent, affecting almost all the nations of Europe, was a product of the eighteenth century. 'Within the larger phenomenon of the Enlightenment', observes H. Wagner (1979, p. 69), 'the proliferation of the Masons also had its niche.' Wagner goes on to itemize their original goals (p. 70):

> an interest in the exact sciences ... a striving for tolerance toward various Christian denominations and, shortly thereafter, toward other monotheistic religions as well; the propagation of the

Christian doctrine of the equality of all men before God; the abolition of class privileges (by treating all masons equally in the lodges); and an active intercession on behalf of the categorical rights of citizens.

The most important contemporary essay on Freemasonry in German was probably Lessing's *Ernst und Falk: Gespräche für Freimaurer* ('Conversations for Freemasons'), written in 1778–9. In words that have lost none of their force today, Lessing's pamphlet takes up the meaning and potential of bourgeois society, showing concern for the development of the individual and the malignity of privilege and prejudice.

Before long, tendencies had arisen within Freemasonry that worked against its avowed goals: 'an almost endless proliferation of hierarchical degrees and systems, an increasing adaptation (whether overt or not) of hermeticism and alchemy, mysticism and spiritualism, theosophy and Christian cabalism'. Among these currents were the aforementioned Rosicrucians, who exercised a pernicious influence in southern Germany and the Habsburg monarchy (Hammermayer 1979, pp. 11f.).

In contrast, some of the outstanding and most radical representatives of Enlightenment ideas could be found in the 'Illuminati', an association founded in the Bavarian town of Ingolstadt by Adam Weishaupt (1748–1830), a professor of canonical law at the university there. They, too, attempted to establish themselves as a learned society (Hammermayer 1979, p. 32) and penetrated masonic circles. But they tended to work in secret, and by the mid-1780s, after a mere ten-year existence, the organization was suppressed, first in Bavaria and then elsewhere. Nonetheless, its influence may have continued here and there. There is some likelihood that Mozart, while still in Salzburg, pursued the goals of the Illuminati in a group of like-minded young men of his age, and did so with a sympathy also shared by his father (see Leopold's letter of 14 October 1785). We will take up this thread again later.

It is no accident that in the eighteenth century the terms humanity, humanitarian and human rights assumed a significance which, though in danger today of degenerating into catchphrases, still harbours a previously undreamt-of potential for dynamic change.

Far and away the most learned and influential Freemason working in the same Vienna circles as Mozart and Georg Forster was Ignaz von Born (1742–91; see Plate 9). His life was remarkable enough. But since there is no scholarly biography to outline the world-view of this extraordinary man with greater accuracy than I can attempt here, I shall base my discussion primarily on two reliable early sources: a biographical study by Pezzl (1792), and the *Biographisches Lexikon des Kaiserthums Österreich* (1856–91) by Constant von Wurzbach, a redoubtable scholar who in the course of forty years produced a biographical dictionary in sixty-four volumes with more than 24,000 painstakingly researched entries on the outstanding men and women of imperial Austria.

Born, originally from Transylvania, received a Jesuit education. However, after a mere sixteen months he fled their tutelage and moved to Prague, where he read law and eventually took up the study of the natural sciences. He profitably combined these studies with extended journeys through Germany, the Netherlands, France, Hungary, Transylvania and Carniola, and was especially interested in mineralogy, mining and coinage. At about the age of twenty-eight he suffered a serious accident, the consequences of which made him a semi-invalid for the rest of his life. Apparently he was poisoned by fumes in a mine shaft while trying to acquire first-hand knowledge of a technique for extracting ore. Later he was poisoned in another way when he took an overdose of opium to alleviate the unbearable pain.

In 1776 Born was summoned to Vienna by Maria Theresia for the purpose of 'ordering the Royal Imperial Cabinet of Natural Curiosities'. Before long, however, he was able to turn to one of his main preoccupations, a method of extracting gold and silver ore which not only produced greater yields than previous methods but was also less dangerous to those involved and more sparing of wood. Emperor Joseph introduced Born's method throughout his Austrian domains, and Born took a share of the considerable amounts of money saved by his method, though he had to bear a third of the costs of its development. It seems that Born fell into financial difficulties during the reign of Emperor Leopold (Irmen 1988, p. 155, n. 5). At his death he is said to have left behind stupendous debts.

But at first all went well. Born had an opportunity and an imperial brief to convert his scientific knowledge into practice. This fact, and the fact that he worked in conjunction with the reform of a mighty empire, were also decisive for his activities in the Masons. Born's aim was nothing less than to transform his masonic order into a society of learned men. Although Austria was not actually to receive such a society until 1847 with the founding of the Academy of Sciences, Joseph II had toyed with plans of this sort as early as the 1760s, even before he had ascended the throne as sole ruler. These schemes are documented in the letters of Lessing, who at one point was meant to be summoned to Vienna. On 11 December 1771, for instance, he wrote 'that the Emperor intends to establish an academy of sciences in Vienna, and I know of others whom he has likewise summoned'.

Even Maria Theresia was convinced of the need to support technology, medicine and the natural sciences lest the Austrian empire fall apart. But there seems to have been powerful resistance toward any attempts to free philosophy from its role as the handmaid of theology. To the present day it has proved difficult in Austria to bring about this necessary interplay of the exact sciences and theoretical cognition.

Born's aims and accomplishments are well documented: he saw to it that they were. The *Journal für Freimaurer*, edited by Sonnenfels and Blumauer, appeared from 1784 to 1786 in twelve stately volumes, each of them recording a quarter of a year of masonic activities and related news from throughout the world. Moreover, from 1783 to 1788 there appeared a publication whose title page, characteristically enough, presents Born as a member of no fewer than seven learned societies between St Petersburg and Toulouse: *Physikalische Arbeiten der einträchtigen Freunde in Wien*. The British Library in London preserves four octavo volumes of this journal with hundreds of pages of essays on geography, botany, zoology and mineralogy by the 'harmonious friends in Vienna' – essays which do not overlook the lives and living conditions of working people. This series of publications superseded two earlier ones which Born had edited during his stay in Prague (Rosenstrauch-Königsberg 1979, p. 105): *Prager gelehrte Nachrichten* ('Prague Scholarly News', 1771–2) and *Abhandlungen einer Privatgesellschaft in Böhmen* ('Proceedings of a Private Society in Bohemia', 1775–84).

Born's activities as an editor evidently arose in extremely close connection with the work in his masonic lodge. Thus, the title-page vignette of the first volume of his *Einträchtige Freunde* shows a female figure in antique garb, holding in her left hand a pair of compasses with which she measures a globe, and in her right a carpenter's square of the sort commonly used by the Masons in their coats of arms. An emblem of compass and square also adorns the *Journal für Freimaurer*. Even Born's seemingly modest proposal, made and carried out in 1782, of changing the name of 'instruction lodge' to 'training lodge' had conceptual underpinnings. Members were meant to hear lectures on subjects ranging from morality to mathematics and 'natural philosophy in the broadest understanding of the term', as well as papers by non-Masons to be submitted in writing, appraised by specialists and discussed in the lodges. This latter plan encountered resistance and could only be partially implemented. But Born was able to take decisive steps in the direction he wanted (Rosenstrauch-Königsberg 1979, pp. 103–5).

Born, Sonnenfels and Alxinger were clandestine members of the Illuminati (H. Wagner 1979, p. 78). Credible evidence survives to indicate that Born intended to enlist Emperor Joseph in the Freemasons. His plan did not succeed, but neither was it far-fetched, given that Joseph's father, Franz Stephan of Lorraine, had been a Mason since 1731 and Frederick II of Prussia since 1738.

As the Freemasons began to be persecuted and the Illuminati were banned in Bavaria, Born and his comrades-in-arms showed their mettle. On many occasions from 1784 onwards they published news of these and similar persecutions. When Adam Weishaupt was accused of trying to acquire Bayle's *Dictionnaire* (one of the great achievements of the early French Enlightenment) for the university library in Ingolstadt, Born published in his *Journal* two open letters to the most prominent oppressors, proudly proclaiming his allegiance to Freemasonry in the one and announcing in the other that he not only made diligent use of Bayle's famous book but even possessed his own copy (Rosenstrauch-Königsberg 1979, p. 110).

As Johann Pezzl neatly put it (1792, pp. 234f.), the lodge over which Born presided was

> more a kind of learned society, and in it were assembled most of Vienna's scholars, writers and friends of literature. Other lodges were permitted to labour on the system of the Knights Templar, to seek the philosophers' stone or to do whatever they wished. In the *Wahren Eintracht* one occupied oneself with literature, and on certain days during the winter months there were so-called 'training lodges' [*Übungslogen*] consisting of public lectures. Three or four members each read an essay of his own choice, in prose or verse, on topics from history, ethics, philosophy, and usually something on the history of the ancient or modern mysteries and secret societies. All of these essays then appeared in print in a journal for Freemasons.

There we have it. The very first issue of the *Journal* carried, on pages 17 to 132, a long treatise by Born on the 'Mysteries of the Egyptians', which, notwithstanding the expectations aroused by its title, is intent on presenting a sort of history of science, technology and the arts in ancient Egypt. Mozart probably knew this essay. (The hotly debated question as to whether Born was the original model or paradigm for Sarastro is put the wrong way around: it is not Born himself but rather the spirit of his life's work that came alive in *Die Zauberflöte*.) The second number of volume 1 of the *Journal* has an article entitled 'On Magic' which, far from probing the mysteries of occult doctrine, attempts to do the very opposite and explode them. Here is a characteristic statement of summary: 'Genuine concepts are doubtless the first step toward enlightenment, and no one who thinks seriously about the matter will enter the path of magic.' An essay on the masonic ceremony is no less critical of that ceremony than another on the masonic oath is critical of the oath (both are in issue no. 2 of 1784). The twelve volumes have been reprinted with a useful commentary that alerts us to an address by Ratschky (in volume 1) containing a profound thought which had already been put forth years earlier by Lessing in his *Ernst und Falk*. There, in somewhat obscure words (1875, p. 8), we can read: 'The true deeds of the Freemasons are done for the purpose of making dispensable virtually everything that generally goes by the name of good deeds.' Ratschky's address (Giese 1988, p. 41) put it differently: charity means more than caring for the poor; instead, it hinges on what the Greeks called *aretē*, a mixture of virtue, perfection and righteousness. The ideal masonic lodges, as envisioned by Lessing and partially instituted by Born, sought nothing less than the perfection of human society, in which men were to become active for the good of all in accordance with their abilities.

Born's stature and thought become more manifest if we consider a publication of quite another kind, one which caused an extraordinary uproar on its simultaneous appearance in 1783 in Latin, German and English, with a French edition to follow in 1784. The Latin version, *Specimen Monachologiae*, is attributed to 'Physiophilus'. The English version, on the first page of a thirty-page preface, calls it the work of 'Baron B*** of Vienna', a 'naturalist' well known in England. The German title, *Neueste Naturgeschichte des Mönchthums, beschrieben im Geiste der Linnäischen Sammlungen*, might be translated as 'A Most Recent Natural History of Monasticism, Written in the Spirit of Linnaeus's Collections'. For this work Born invented a pseudonym that at once conceals and discloses his identity and is in itself a small compendium on the art of displacement of authority. Playing on the fact that he has the same Christian name as Ignatius of Loyola, the sixteenth-century founder of the Jesuits, Born acidly adds the surname Kuttenpeitscher (roughly, 'Whipcowl'), but keeps the name Loyola as a fig leaf and even retains the initial P for Pater ('Father'). This, then, is the name Born chose to use: 'P. Ignaz Loyola Kuttenpeitscher of the former Society of Jesus'. In so doing he assumed the role of a 'father' who refuses to hide behind his monk's cowl. The title page shows a wolf with sheep's mask delivering a sermon to a flock of sheep.

As the feudal nexus of production, government and society disintegrated it left behind an ethical vacuum. The authorities that once pronounced judgement on what was right and just, or good and evil, had begun to topple. To be sure, a large majority of even the shrewdest advocates of the Enlightenment, the most upright Masons and most radical revolutionaries were unwilling to disavow the existence of a Guiding Hand as the ultimate arbiter of morality – a Supreme Being, Master Architect or whatever other name they chose to apply. 'Call Him Jehovah, or God; call Him Fu or Brahma' wrote the Mason Ziegenhagen, in lines set by Mozart in 1791 (K619). Still less had the religious world-view weakened among the common people.

Nevertheless, the traditional mediators between God and mortals – the emperors and kings, the spiritual and temporal princes, the priesthood and the monks – had largely forfeited their credibility. Joseph II revealed sound political instincts when he sought to base his good standing on the rationality of his attempted reforms rather than on his inherited imperial sceptre. It is symptomatic of the loss of prestige suffered by the clergy that Leopold and Wolfgang rarely had anything positive to say about them, unless it had to do with the personal integrity of those in their own circle of friends. Again and again their correspondence uses the derogatory term *Pfaffe* for 'priest' (11 October 1771, 3 December 1778, end of May 1781, 17 November 1781, 21 March 1783). Their distinction mirrors a rift within the clergy itself, especially in Austria.

At that time so-called 'reform Catholicism', originally an Italian development, played an important role in the Austrian territories, and especially so in their Slavic regions. Austrian historians such as Eduard Winter (1896–1978), Fritz Valjavec (1909–60) and Ernst Wangermann (Professor of History at Salzburg University) stress that large segments of the Catholic clergy took part in instituting Joseph's programme of reforms – some dutifully, some reluctantly, but many with gusto. Josephinists could even be found among the Jesuits. Braunbehrens, for instance, informs us (1986, p. 466, n. 6) that according to the admittedly incomplete records there were at least forty-five clergymen in the masonic lodges: priests, monks, canons and so forth. Even the odd bishop or two were said to be clandestine Freemasons. In other words, Joseph's campaign against superstition and the cult of saints, against pilgrimages and corruption among clergymen and monastics, was not directed toward the Christian faith as such. On the contrary, a formidable programme of education among clergymen was designed to integrate them into his reform schemes as teachers of children or as ministers to adults. Part of this project involved a constant stream of revelations on the extent of depravity among the clergy, and especially among monks. On 1 February 1782, for example, four monks held captive for years in the underground vaults of the Capuchin monastery were discovered and set free, as was a friar who had spent fifty-three years of his life there (Steiner 1985, p. 176).

Not even Ignaz von Born, presumably an atheist, ventured against religion. In his own words (1783b, p. 4v.) he was convinced that 'two-thirds of all Roman Catholics are enemies of monasticism'. What Born described in his exposé was the abuse of high-minded ideals as a pretext for crimes. Drawing on Linnaeus's taxonomy of the plant and animal kingdoms, he enumerates these crimes with vicious sobriety, neatly categorizing them by monastic order. Born does not mince words. One order 'is more akin to predatory animals than to human beings' (p. 5v.); another is made up of *Unmenschen*, or fiends (p. 6); and they are all 'blood enemies of the human species and of sound judgement' (p. 9), being 'plagued with an unquenchable thirst and a constant craving for flesh' (p. 39). And these are among his milder characterizations.

Our picture of Born's personality would be incomplete if we failed to mention the personal charm he evidently radiated. Wurzbach (1857, p. 73) described Born as 'a never-ending source of cheer, wit and high spirits', making 'one's dealings with him as pleasant as they were highly instructive'. And Johann Pezzl, who, of course, knew Born at first hand, had this to say of him in his biography (1792, pp. 252f.):

> Born was all things to all men; he had a quite natural and unique gift for capturing one's affection. People who were indifferent to or even predisposed against him would sometimes become his most ardent admirers within the space of a few hours' conversation ... When Born was in a mood to spout sarcasms it was a delight to hear, for the spirit of Lucian and Swift seemed to reside doubly within him. But woe to the fools or folly upon which his satire descended!

Georg Forster, recently fled from the labyrinthine mazes of para-science, was spellbound by Born. The two men soon developed a close friendship, probably encouraged by their common interest in the natural sciences. They were together almost on a daily basis; Born's name appears more than eighty times in Forster's diary. The impressions Vienna left on Forster were all the more profound in that he encountered Josephinism well beyond the confines of the intellectual elite. The cultivated circles he frequented spanned a wide variety of classes and professions, and their approach to nature and dealings with the arts, their discussions and even their games, were those of a culture that held out much promise – indeed, more than it could possibly fulfil.

In principle, the Freemasons also appreciated music. In some lodge meetings the brethren sang songs and performed works for chorus and small orchestra specially written for the occasion. Indeed, many songs and their musical settings were printed in the *Journal*. But it is remarkable that the *Journal* does not once mention the name of Mozart. And when Joseph Haydn was admitted to the lodge a Brother Holzmeister delivered a speech on harmony (volume 2, number 2) which had nothing more profound to say than that it was music's 'delightful purpose' to touch and cause pleasure (p. 177). It then went on to conclude, in words which, we may assume, probably left Brother Haydn less than moved: 'To sing the praises of that celestial being, Harmony, to you, our newly admitted Brother Apprentice ... would be a futile endeavour.'

How it came about that Forster and Mozart never met is impossible to fathom. Forster's painstakingly detailed diary contains the names of the men and women he met in Vienna. And if we compare his diary with the subscription list which Mozart circulated a few months previously for his three Trattnerhof concerts we discover that Forster met at least twenty-six of the 176 highly placed persons living in the imperial capital and mentioned in Mozart's list. Indeed, the number may have been as large as thirty-four, since in many cases the incomplete entries and imprecise orthography leave room for ambiguity. This was roughly one-fifth of Mozart's Trattnerhof audience. We have already seen how both men frequented the home of Countess Wilhelmine Thun, whom they held in equally high esteem. They had other common acquaintances as well, Gemmingen in particular. And on at least one occasion they could both be found under the same roof. This was on 23 August 1784, when they both attended the first performance of Paisiello's *Re Teodoro*, the performance at which Mozart, as mentioned on pages 111-12, fell ill. Forster noted the date in his diary: 'Then, to the new opera by Abbé Casti with music by Paisiello ... Magnificent music and many scurrilous, witty and satirical ideas in the text.' But if the two had actually met Forster would certainly have made note of it.

Perhaps someone told Forster that Mozart was in the audience, for the only time the name of Mozart crops up in Forster's writings is in connection with Paisiello. This happened as follows: Between late March and the beginning of May 1790 Forster heard a performance of a singspiel by Dittersdorf in Dunkirk, at that time under military occupation. As annoying as he found the loud conversation of the officers before the curtain rose, it was even more annoying that they bellowed along with the wretched actors during the arias. Forster went on to conclude (*Werke* IX, pp. 337f.):

> The cruder the man, the more coarse the jolt required to satisfy his senses. The art of Mozart and Paisiello is lost on these Midas's ears, which are only attuned to the street songs of a Ditters[dorf].

Chapter 12

'Mozart of the *Wohltätigkeit*'

Why did Mozart let three years and nine months pass before deciding to enter a masonic lodge? We cannot say. Nor can we say why he ultimately decided against joining the prestigious lodge *Zur Wahren Eintracht* where Born was Grand Master. Perhaps the smaller lodge *Zur Wohltätigkeit*, headed by Gemmingen, was more congenial to Mozart for a number of reasons. Only two of its members were noblemen – Gemmingen himself and Lichnowsky, both of them Mozart's age. Pezzl, too, was of the same generation as Mozart. Perhaps a circle of some two dozen men, most of them his own age, seemed more suitable to him than Born's far more substantial lodge, which must have had a good 200 members at the time Mozart joined the Masons, including many older and more distinguished than he. Or it may have been that Mozart's choice was not as free as is generally assumed. He was, to be sure, a well-known composer ever since the performance of *Die Entführung*, and we should not think that Ignaz von Born had no feeling for music. His Latin entry in Mozart's album is friendly and warm-hearted, and his praise of Mozart's music no more trite than Brother Holzmeister's praise of Haydn's. Born, too, proceeds from the concept of harmony, and finds it remarkable that Mozart's music – which he calls *grata*, meaning welcome and gratifying as well as graceful – unites the widest imaginable variety of tones: 'high and low, merry and earnest, long and short ... and all without contradiction'. This entry, however, dates from April 1787. It may be that Born did not recognize a potential ally in the composer of *Die Entführung*. This might also explain why he did not introduce Forster to Mozart.

We stand no more chance of reconstructing Mozart's actual motives than the outward stages of his masonic career. The least we can do, then, is to recount the few known facts. O. E. Deutsch's short essay on this subject (1932), Paul Nettl's article on Freemasonry (1955) and, more recently, the labours of Katherine Thomson (1977), Braunbehrens (1986) and Philippe Autexier (1984, 1986, 1987) have unearthed much archival material and suggested a number of interpretations.

Irmen's book on Mozart (1988) deserves special mention for publishing many previously unknown documents, some of which I shall cite, but not for its unjustifiably slipshod interpretations.

Mozart was admitted to the lodge *Zur Wohltätigkeit*, or 'Charity', as an Entered Apprentice on 14 December 1784. By 7 January 1785 he was already a Fellow-Craft, and probably by spring of that same year (the exact date is unknown) he had been made a Master Mason. At the time Mozart entered this lodge it was directed by Gemmingen in the same spirit as Born's. True, no minutes of its meetings of the sort published in the *Freimaurer-Journal* for the *Eintracht* have survived. But in the twenty-third issue of his periodical *Der Weltmann* (1783, pp. 190–2) Gemmingen welcomes the publication of Sonnenfels's writings (of which Mozart owned four volumes) and expresses his 'gratitude and reverence' for this fellow soldier, who 'has almost always stood alone.' In the same year, as a visiting lecturer in Born's lodge, Gemmingen delivered a speech offering support to Born in his efforts to confront 'mystical errors'.

Mozart attended the meetings of the Freemasons regularly and enthusiastically. Even Deutsch, writing in 1932 (pp. 23–6), was able to document eleven visits, and there were many more than that. As it was customary for members of one lodge to attend the meetings of other lodges and to register their names in a visitor's book, we possess a priceless combination of Mozart's name and that of his lodge, all in his own hand:

However, he did not remain 'Mozart of the *Wohltätigkeit*' very long. As early as December 1785 Emperor Joseph commanded the eight Viennese lodges to be reduced to three. Thus, in January 1786, Mozart's lodge joined two others to form the lodge *Zur Neugekrönten Hoffnung* ('Newly Crowned Hope') while Born's, likewise combined with several others, was renamed *Zur Wahrheit* ('Truth'). The lodges did more than exchange visitors: the better equipped rooms of Born's lodge were often hired out for the meetings and ceremonies of the smaller lodge of which Mozart was a member.

Joseph's decree did not work out as he had evidently intended. To a certain extent the Emperor sympathized with the Masons and wished to integrate the cultured and well-intentioned men who worked there into his reformist schemes. But he felt compelled to put them under his supervision, together with what he insultingly called their 'conjurings'. Mozart, like Born, attempted to put the best and most benevolent interpretation on Joseph's proclamations, claiming that the Emperor wished to place the Masons under his protection. The consequences of this benevolence, however, were disastrous. As Joseph's decree coincided with the suppression of the Illuminati it marked the first step in the state's harassment of Freemasonry, leading within a few years (after Joseph's death) to its complete prohibition. Nor were the internal tensions within the Masons alleviated by Joseph's intercession. On the contrary: whatever his intentions may have been, he only succeeded in strengthening the hand of those within the order who opposed the model of the learned societies and the Illuminati, and thus Born's concept as well. The year 1786 witnessed a general crisis in the movement, during which even Born turned his back on it. It is at this point that the Freemasons lost their function as a force for social change.

Mozart remained true to the Freemasons even during these years of crisis. A mere three weeks before his death he conducted, in his own lodge, the last composition he was ever to complete.

Sadly, one document that might have shed invaluable light on Mozart's thoughts regarding Freemasonry has disappeared. A few years after Mozart's death Konstanze wrote a business letter to Breitkopf & Härtel (17 November 1799) with a postscript that reads as follows: 'I have enclosed a few preliminary notes describing Mozart's life. You are aware that he was a Mason.' Then, after adding various items of information, she remarks: 'He also wanted to establish a society with the name "The Grotto" [*Die Grotte*]. I have only been able to discover a fragment of his essay on this matter.' Later, she listed a number of writings and objects lent to the Leipzig publishing house 'for use in a biography' (21 July 1800). Heading the list is

an essay, largely in my husband's hand, concerning an order or society he intended to found, called *Grotta* [this time Konstanze uses the Italian spelling]. I am unable to provide any further information. Stadler, the court clarinettist here [Anton Stadler (1753–1812)], who wrote the remainder, could do so, but hesitates to admit that he knows about it as the orders or secret societies are very much hated.

The essay has disappeared. But the fact that Mozart wrote it at all implies that he was dissatisfied with the existing masonic order, for otherwise why should he want to found a new one? Furthermore, Konstanze's information is trustworthy, being of no use to her at a time when secret societies were prohibited and 'hated'. As Mozart was in close contact with Stadler from 1784 it is reasonable to date the essay from this period.

Grottos, of course, were widely popular in the eighteenth century, but it is likely that two particular grottos, which had impressed Mozart in his youth, were partly responsible for the name he chose for his proposed society. 'The little house is nothing much, but the countryside! – the forest, in which my host has built a grotto which looks just as if Nature herself had fashioned it! The whole is magnificent and very delightful.' This is how Mozart (13 July 1781) described a grotto in the palace grounds of Count Johann Philipp Cobenzl, situated in the slopes of Kahlenberg in the Vienna Woods, where he was a frequent visitor. By good fortune we have a description of the same grounds from the hand of Georg Forster (*Werke* XII, p. 128), who was likewise the count's guest in 1784:

> Wherever one turns there are fresh, exceedingly beautiful, charming and variegated prospects... Deep, overgrown vales open to view, their nethermost chasm filled with a babbling brook ... A grotto that makes us shudder in humility as we enter, entire veins of ore, the walls bedecked with precious stones and crystals, a stream slowly passing through, a bench of solid rock and arched arcades of dark masonry ... Suddenly, at the end of the dark archways, a tiny portal opens and we again find ourselves betwixt shady trees and shrubbery, where a slender footpath leads across a narrow meadow and into the woods.

Another grotto, this time located in Aigen near Salzburg (see Plate 14), played a still greater role in Mozart's youth. Its design, we must imagine, was probably similar to that of Cobenzl's grotto. Information on it is supplied in a slender volume published in 1911 by Richard Koch, a Freemason and the director of the health resort at Bad Reichenhall. Koch, however, bases his account mainly on secondary sources such as local Salzburg histories or studies of the Illuminati; moreover, he presents his findings in such an amateur manner that modern researchers ought to return to his sources. On the other hand, so closely does his account match the documented facts of Mozart's life that the outline presented here is probably tenable.

In the 1780s (Koch 1911, pp. 28ff.) Salzburg had two masonic lodges, of which at least one had been founded by the Illuminati. Of the nineteen names listed by Koch as members of these lodges (p. 33) some eleven played a part in Mozart's life. Among them are the canon of Salzburg Cathedral and Mozart's early patron, Count Waldburg zu Wolfsegg und Waldsee (1729–1820), along with two members of the Gilowsky family and Augustin Schelle (1742–1805), a professor of philosophy, jurisprudence, history and oriental languages. The latter, together with another close friend of the Mozarts, Lorenz Hübner (1753–1807), edited the *Salzburger Staatszeitung* from 1783 and later published a literary journal, the *Oberdeutsche Allgemeine Literatur-zeitung*. Even Leopold Mozart, though absent from Koch's list, had strong sympathies with the Illuminati; this explains his close ties to Count Wolfsegg, from whom he borrowed money. Paul Nettl's claim (*MGG* IV, col. 894) that Leopold expressed 'highly negative opinions' of the Illuminati in a letter of 14 October 1785 is inaccurate. What Leopold actually does in this letter is to underplay reports from Munich on the persecution of the Illuminati, calling them – incorrectly, as it turned out – exaggerated. He imagines that the authorities had merely proceeded against the 'hardheaded' and 'eccentric' members, against 'this fanaticism', but not against 'genuine Freemasons'. This quintessentially Leopoldian turn of phrase was doubtless aimed subliminally at the 'fanaticism' of his own son, who is not mentioned once in this letter to Nannerl. The letter also confirms that one of the men on Koch's list, Count Friedrich Franz Joseph Spaur, was indeed an Illuminato.

Still more precise and germane to our discussion, though the source reference is unfortunately incomplete, is Koch's quotation from Lorenz Hübner, who played a part in Mozart's life in other respects as well. First of all, we know from Mozart himself that Hübner was in Salzburg toward the end of September 1780 even though he did not reside there at the time. Writing in Nannerl's diary (23–30 September 1780), Mozart notes the date – 'the 24th in the cathedral' – and then adopts the voice of his sister to continue: 'I, the victorix [referring to their games of target practice], ... Monsieur Hübner and Ceccarelli also present'. Further, it is significant that Hübner studied at the University of Ingolstadt, where Adam Weishaupt had founded his order, and later taught at the grammar school there. Finally, we owe a debt of gratitude to Hübner himself for supplying information on a matter which we will take up here. On 19 February 1785 Mozart, clad as an Indian philosopher, attended a masquerade. Here he distributed a printed leaflet containing eight riddles of his own devising and at least fourteen 'Snatches from Zoroaster's Fragments to be Taken to Heart'. (The most caustic of the latter can be found in the next chapter on p. 151.) We would have known nothing about them if Mozart had not sent a copy – now lost – to his father. Leopold forwarded it to Hübner, who in turn printed parts of it in the *Oberdeutsche Staatszeitung* of 23 March 1786 (reprinted in *Briefe* III, p. 506). It was Hübner who reported that 'Privy Councillor Ernst von Gilowsky was fond, even by starlight, of holding amicable revels in the wild and beautiful wilderness surrounding the grotto, together with his friends Amann, Mozart and Barisani' (Koch 1911, p. 34). At this point we should mention that Gilowsky owned property in Aigen, where the Barisanis also had a villa, that the aforementioned grotto was situated on this property, and that Mozart maintained unusually close relations with members of these three families even during his Vienna years. It was his longstanding acquaintance Ernst Gilowsky (1739–89), for instance, whom Mozart retained in 1787 to settle the affairs of his inheritance following Leopold's death, and Franz Xaver Wenzel Gilowsky (1757–1816) was best man at Mozart's marriage to Konstanze on 4 August 1782. Even the unfortunate Basil Amann (1747–85), who apparently died insane, had Mozart's sympathy. I cannot agree with Eibl's conclusion (*Briefe* V, p. 231) that Leopold, in his letter of 27 February 1770, was being ironic when he claimed that 'Herr Basilius's misfortune ... has cost Wolfgang many a tear'. Mozart, for his part, was sincere when he wrote on 7 June 1783 that he was 'very sad for Basilius Amann'.

Mozart felt closest to the Barisani family. He maintained contact with no fewer than eight of the nine children of the Barisanis, an Italian couple who had moved to Salzburg. In the early 1770s he paid court to one of their daughters, and Sigmund Barisani (1761–87), who later became head physician at Vienna General Hospital, was always ready to come to Mozart's aid with medical advice. (He also tended Leopold during the last weeks of his final illness.) There were few people whom Mozart loved as dearly as 'Sigerl'. When his friend died on 3 September 1787 Mozart confided his thoughts to his own chapbook in words which otherwise never fell from his pen. Writing on 3 September, he called Barisani 'this noble man, this best and dearest of friends and the saviour of my life', adding that 'all those who knew him well will *never* recover ... unless we are reunited in a better world'.

In sum, we gain the impression that Mozart maintained intimate contact with a small group of young men of whom, in the late 1770s, none was older than twenty-four or twenty-five and many were younger. Further, these young men often met and enthusiastically discussed the new Enlightenment doctrine from Ingolstadt, where at least one of them already had connections – namely, the doctrine of the Illuminati. It would convey a false picture to claim that they were also members of the Illuminati, who in any event granted no diplomas and maintained no membership lists. But they centred their activities in that very grotto in which one of their fathers had built a portal more reminiscent of a masonic temple than a 'witches' cave', as the grotto was called by the local population (Koch 1911, p. 31). It was probably this grotto – or *grotta*, as the elder Barisanis would have put it – and the events that took place around it that Mozart had in mind when, as Konstanze tells us, he set out to 'establish' an 'order or society' and to call it *Die Grotte* or *Grotta*.

Even if we did not know from Mozart's own works and his surviving written remarks (see the next chapter) that he belonged to the Enlightenment wing of the Freemasons, we could infer it from the titles in his library, which, as mentioned in Chapter 4, contained no fewer than seven Enlightenment authors. We could also infer it from his desire to enter into contact with Blumauer, Alxinger, Ratschky and Haschka upon his arrival in Vienna. And the only time that the word 'mysteries' occurs in the texts he set to music – 'sich den Mysterien der Isis ganz zu weihn', from No. 21 of *Die Zauberflöte* (bars 233f.) – it alludes to Born's essay *Über die Mysterien der Ägyptier*, a treatise on Egyptian science rather than a compendium of mysticism.

Hence, Hans-Josef Irmen is surely on the wrong track when he tries to enlist Mozart in the mystical doctrines of the 'Asiatic Brethren', a prime example of how conscientious documentation can be given an unconscientious slant. Irmen's evidence is slender, resting on nothing more than two of Mozart's signatures, each followed by two triangular figures in his own hand. By 'merging' these two triangles in our imagination we obtain 'the official emblem of the Asiatic Brethren' – or so Irmen surmises (1988, p. 213), overlooking the fact that triangular figures of all shapes and sizes were a basic component of *all* masonic symbolism. If this style of argument suffices to establish Mozart's membership in the Asiatic Brethren, it also makes him an adept of *gematria*, a cabbalistic technique involving the assignment of numeric values to letters of the alphabet. In the present case this means assigning 1 to 'a' and so forth, with 9 being assigned to both 'i' and 'j', 20 to 'u' and 'v', and 24 to 'z'. It then transpires, according to Irmen, that Mozart distributed the note heads in the score of *Die Zauberflöte* in such a way that their total number within certain sections invariably has deeper significance. Counting the note heads in the first violin part of the Introduction to No. 1, for example, we arrive at a total of 129, a veiled reference to the word *Zauberflöte*.

Although Irmen is aware, and even states, that 'the entire numerological game' is open to 'many interpretations' (p. 292), he recklessly plunges into this game himself and has Mozart coding dozens of secret messages via the note heads in his manuscript, including the birth year of Christian Rosenkreuz, the founder of the Rosicrucians, and the year in which his *Chymische Hochzeit* originated in the fifteenth century. We need only add up the note heads in certain sections of the score and then 'interchange the last two digits of the two figures'. Admittedly these messages can only be extracted from the autograph manuscript since, as Irmen correctly points out, Mozart's copyists wrote out his abbreviations – e.g. his use of a single note with two strokes through the stem to indicate four semiquavers – and thereby produced a completely different total number of note heads in their copies. What Irmen either did not know or did not bother to consider is that Mozart's conductors, singers and other fellow musicians were never given his autographs but only these manuscript copies. Thus, Mozart must have undertaken this immensely time-consuming counting game for the sole purpose of sending an ambiguous message to his copyists. Surely this is a nonsensical assumption.

Instead of adding up note heads it is more fruitful to read them. When we do, we find ourselves confronted with the fact that those of Mozart's works which are more or less closely linked to Freemasonry are no more uniform from a standpoint of compositional technique than are, say, his mature operas. Efforts to find specifically masonic elements or components in these scores have not led very far. Einstein (1946, p. 365) claims that 'Mozart presumably had to create his own musical symbolism: the rhythm of the three knocks, ... the slurring of two notes, symbolizing the ties of friendship, ... the progressions of parallel thirds'. 'Furthermore', he goes on to say (*ibid.*), 'tonality takes on symbolic meaning: E flat major is gently heroic and humane.'

This is certainly correct as far as it goes. It is entirely plausible that Mozart took musical commonplaces such as two-note slurs (in K468):

Example 33

or parallel thirds, which were as good as unavoidable in eighteenth-century music, and signified them in his own way to form a musical symbol of fraternity. No doubt his music was never more 'masonic' and compelling than when seemingly at its most simple:

Example 34

But there is no shortage of compositions in which the above-mentioned features are related to the Masons only precariously, if at all, just as there are pieces that lack these features though plainly inspired by the spirit of Freemasonry. Sarastro's aria, No. 15, for instance, is not in the 'humane' key of E flat major, which would more neatly fit into the tonal and conceptual scheme of *Die Zauberflöte*, but in E major. (I venture to guess that it would otherwise have been too low for his friend Gerl, for whom he wrote it.) Nor does it contain more than a few of those two-note slurs indicative of friendship. Admittedly there are some parallel thirds to be found, but no more here than elsewhere. In their stead, however, precisely at the crucial words 'hand of friendship' (*Freundeshand*), Mozart devised a series of ascending and descending scalar motives with sustained notes in the middle parts:

Example 35

Reinhold Hammerstein (1956, pp. 19f.), referring to this passage, speaks of the 'graphic "sensualized" image of two people walking' – to which we might add 'toward each other' – and indeed of the rendering of human action in Mozart's stage music as a whole. But the point is that such things are not limited to the masonic music.

A more promising approach is attempted by Paul Nettl in his article on masonic music for *MGG* (IV, col. 896). Mozart's masonic works, he claims, are 'united by a distinctively Mozartian humanistic style'. Yet Nettl, and still more A. V. Heuss, whom he quotes, can only offer a vague characterization of this style. Today we can and must go beyond this, as I will attempt to do in this chapter and the analytical ones to follow.

It would be pointless to deny that whenever Mozart took up his masonic vein he drew on certain specific keys and rhythms, instruments and melodic shapes. Yet this in itself is not sufficient to characterize his masonic music. We must not lose sight of our claim (discussed in Chapter 9) that no matter for whom Mozart worked he had his vast musical universe at his disposal. And it was a constructed universe.

It is all the more striking that Mozart never – with one exception – rose above artistic mediocrity in the works he is known to have written for lodge meetings. Certainly, the cantata *Laut verkünde unsre Freude*, K623, is a charming piece of music and would be touching even if we did not know that its composer was to die three weeks after first conducting it. Its recourse to *Die Zauberflöte*, premièred six weeks earlier, deserves special mention as an illustration of the way Mozart semanticized his musical material.

One of the greatest moments in *Die Zauberflöte* is the thirty-bar passage in the finale in which the voices of Pamina and Tamino join with those of the two Armed Men to form a vocal quartet in F major. Here, as so often, Mozart's music is at its most gripping when confronted with a situation in which dangers, confusion or chaos must be overcome to achieve desired and attainable goals. (A similar instance is the scene in which Anna, Elvira and Ottavio appear masked at Don Giovanni's banquet, at first expressing their anxiety to an accompaniment of agitated D minor figures in the strings, then imploring heaven for protection in a solemn B flat major *adagio* interrupted by the Minuet. Another piece of similar design, likewise in D minor, is the *Rex tremendae majestatis* from the Requiem. In Chapter 20 I will show that Mozart stood in no need of the theatre in order to depict situations of this sort.)

In the quartet from the *Zauberflöte* finale, the moment immediately preceding the ordeals by fire and water is transfigured into music in a manner that is perhaps best described in the language of semiotics: the difficulty of the undertaking is mirrored in the effort required to produce the 'signifiers'. True, a high A is not particularly troublesome for sopranos and tenors; any Mozart singer should be able to reach it without undue effort. In this case, however, it appears several times in succession within a few bars: first three times for Tamino, then three times for Pamina, and finally, in a sort of canon, four times for the first Armed Man, making a total of ten occurrences in fourteen bars, all within an unbroken string of *andante* quavers. Example 36 shows the point of greatest intensity. The perilous difficulties essayed by the Freemasons – not so much in their rituals, which they need not have taken very seriously – have been turned in a highly original manner into music. (The effort involved in producing musical signs that

Example 36

indicate difficulty or danger can be experienced viscerally in works for full orchestra, where the audience can see just how hard musicians have to 'work' in order to convey acoustically an underlying sense of menace.)

The duet for tenor and bass in Mozart's last masonic cantata alludes directly to this quartet from *Die Zauberflöte*. It has the same flowing quavers in a triple-metre *andante*, the same high A for the tenor (answered with a lower C by the bass) and likewise deals with labour and toil:

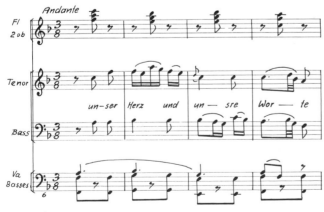

Example 37

For all their similarities, however, this duet, like the cantata as a whole, and indeed like all of Mozart's masonic music, has virtually nothing of the urgency and grandeur of *Die Zauberflöte*. Mozart wrote his masonic pieces for listeners with no musical background. Being educated men, the Masons knew full well that music was part of the grand scheme of things, as their eulogies to Mozart and Haydn attest (see pp. 129–30 and 131), but they understood little about it. Under such circumstances Mozart, by his own admission (see p. 80), never gave his best. K483 and K484, *Zerfliesset heut', geliebte Brüder* and *Ihr unsre neuen Leiter*, are three-part accompanied choral songs on weak poems written to open and conclude a lodge meeting. They contain perhaps the most banal music that ever flowed from Mozart's pen. And the cantata *Sehen, wie dem starren Forscherauge*, K471, for tenor, three-part male chorus and orchestra, has as little claim to immortality as does *Die ihr des unermesslichen Weltalls Schöpfer ehrt*, K619, a setting for tenor and piano of a poem by Ziegenhagen, composed in the year of Mozart's death. To appreciate fully the gap in quality we need only recall the sacred music he wrote at the same time. The much-praised and much-sung *Ave verum corpus*, K618, for instance, is a veritable miracle in sixty-four bars that leaves us at a loss to say which is more incredible, the ease and inevitability with which the piece flows along, or the mastery with which light and dark, dissonance, imitation and modulation are made to occur at important compositional junctures. Not to mention K626, the Requiem.

Nevertheless, as intimated above, there is one masonic composition which can stand alongside these and other masterpieces of Mozart's maturity: the Masonic Funeral Music, K477. Its solitary position among the masonic pieces leads us inevitably to ask whether it really was intended 'to commemorate the deaths of Brothers Mecklenburg and Esterhazy', as Mozart claimed in his catalogue of works. For Mozart gave his best only with great inner commitment, which was hardly required of him in the case of these two deaths. Moreover, the dating of the Funeral Music poses problems. Mozart clearly entered this piece in his catalogue as the first item under the heading of July 1785; Mecklenburg and Esterhazy, however, did not die until the following November.

To explain this state of affairs Philippe Autexier has offered an elaborate hypothesis (1984, 1986) which, among other things, postulates the existence of a lost original version of the Funeral Music for three-part male chorus. It would be unfair to judge this or Autexier's other hypotheses regarding Mozart's masonic music before his projected book on the entire complex has appeared. I will therefore content myself with extracting the most plausible features from a line of argument which, at present, I am not able to follow in all points.

According to Autexier, Mozart performed his Funeral Music on more than one occasion. And in fact it really does exist in two versions, the second having two basset horns and a *gran fagotto* (perhaps a contrabassoon) in addition to the six winds and the strings of the first. The première performance, we must assume, was occasioned by an event that took place on 12 August 1785, the day on which Carl von König, a Freemason born in Venice, was accorded the rank of Master Mason in the Viennese lodge *Zur Eintracht*. It was not this man's elevation that occasioned the work, however, but the fate of the Venetian lodge to which he had previously belonged. This lodge had been forcibly dissolved, its furnishings burnt in public, and König banished from the city. An address held on that day (in Italian) confirms that these events were the actual reasons for the ceremony. The speech, reprinted verbatim by Autexier (1984, pp. 43f.), praises the steadfastness and strength of spirit shown by Brother König in the face of such adversity. The Enlightenment followers in Vienna's lodges, and especially the Illuminati, interpreted these events – correctly, as it soon turned out – as the beginning of the end of Freemasonry in the Austrian territories.

For his contribution to this ceremony Mozart chose the technique of chorale variation, a method new to him which he had no doubt acquired from his recent study of Johann Sebastian Bach. He was to apply the same technique six years later in the scene of the Armed Men in *Die Zauberflöte*. It is virtually a casebook example for Brother Pezzl's polemical essay (1787) against those Protestants who accused Roman Catholics of intolerance. Against these accusations Pezzl counterposes the genuine tolerance of Enlightenment Catholics: Montesquieu, Voltaire, Diderot, Beccaria, d'Alembert. He might well have added, as another example of Catholic tolerance, Mozart's unselfconscious integration of Protestant forms within his own compositional style.

Essentially, the technique of chorale variation consists in presenting a section of a hymn tune against a contrapuntal texture that interprets and comments on that hymn by means of freely invented motifs in the other parts. The section Mozart chose to set is taken from the 'Gregorian *lamentatio* sung during Holy Week' (*NMA* IV/11/10, p. ix). Yet the motifs he associates with it are not homogeneous, as was usually the case in chorale variations, but fall into at least three different types. The piece is full of contrasts in other ways as well. I would be hard pressed to name another piece by Mozart, or by any of his contemporaries, that pays such close attention to the dynamic levels at which its separate strands are to be played. Normally Mozart writes one 'p' for *piano*, or one 'f' for *forte*, which then applies to an entire section of the piece and to entire groups of instruments. In the

Funeral Music, however, he has painstakingly placed *piano*, *forte*, *crescendo* and *decrescendo* hairpins in literally every stave of his score. As a result, even the very first eight bars have more than four dozen such marks, the piece as a whole well over 200. By comparison, the chorale variations of the two Armed Men, occupying forty-four bars of *adagio*, make do with a total of eleven dynamic marks, all of them saying the same thing: *piano*. The Funeral Music, on the other hand, frequently alternates between *piano* and *forte* in adjoining bars. Its sole *'cresc.'* ends in a *subito piano*, and the winds repeatedly interfere with the *piano* of the strings by adding sustained chords, swelling and receding. The longest dynamically uniform passage consists of a mere eleven bars of *forte*, leading into the final third of the piece with a modulation from C minor to E flat major. In the opening bars we hear the swelling and receding lament of the winds, beginning with two oboes:

Example 38

The entire first third of the piece has the character of an introduction. Only then, in the second third, does the chorale enter, now plaintively emphasized, now pathetically submerged by the strings. Winds and strings stand in mutual opposition. The ending takes a fully unexpected turn: the final cadence, in a halting *pianissimo* (the first in the piece), dissolves in a C major chord played by the full orchestra for an entire bar, swelling and receding. It is a perfect counterfoil to the opening measure. The lament turns into an accusation, sorrow becomes a cry of protest, repeatedly and helplessly falling back until the final bar raises a faint hope. The approaching demise of a mighty movement with which the composer felt a spiritual kinship has inspired a superb and unique piece of music.

Mozart performed the piece once again for the funeral service of the two deceased masons. Later he entered it in his catalogue, deliberately neglecting to mention the first performance. It may have seemed to him not entirely safe to admit its true occasion.

A comparison with the scene of the Armed Men shows just how different two basically similar pieces can be. Both are sets of chorale variations; both are in C minor; both have the chorale melody in the winds and contrasting motifs in the strings; both have a central modulation to E flat major (coinciding in *Die Zauberflöte*, as Hammerstein points out on page 17, with the word *erleuchtet*, 'illuminated'); and both end in C major. But these points in common are offset by striking differences. The hymn sung by the Armed Men, in octaves doubled by seven wind instruments, is contrasted contrapuntally with a single motif in the strings and by submotifs derived from it. From its first bar to its last the entire piece, as mentioned above, never rises above *piano*. The striding motifs in the strings, in constant quavers, manifest the difficulties encountered on the 'road full of hardship', the subject of the hymn. But calmly and soothingly the listener is assured that whoever faces up to these difficulties will 'surge heavenward'. The chorale tune, then, is conceptually in accord with the counterpoint.

By now it should be clear that Einstein's criteria are insufficient to characterize a piece of masonic music. He, too, is exceedingly cautious: 'If one wished', he writes (1946, p. 366), 'one could find all the symbols of Freemasonry in the 69 measures' of the Masonic Funeral Music. But this hardly holds true for the scene of the Armed Men; and in both pieces, as Einstein fully acknowledges, the principles and details of construction are more important than the presence or absence of parallel thirds. Agreed, we have no more right to ignore these 'stray' symbols than the tone-painting that occasionally occurs even in Mozart's music. But we must hear them in context.

Katharine Thomson (1977, pp. 159ff.) has marshalled convincing evidence that Mozart secretly inserted characteristic masonic rhythms into several numbers of *Die Zauberflöte*. As Autexier informs us, the Viennese lodges made use of three types of 'knocking' figures:

- ‿ ‿   for the first degree, the Entered Apprentice
‿ - ‿   for the second degree, the Fellow-Craft
‿ ‿ -   for the third degree, the Master Mason.

Mozart, he continues, has the overture begin with the rhythm symbolizing the first degree:

Example 39

(The minor objection that we hear five knocks rather than three is dispelled by Autexier in 1987, p. 98.) In the middle of the overture we are then given the second rhythm, indicating the Fellow-Craft, and this three times in succession:

Example 40

Up to now, however, no one has noticed that Mozart concludes the overture with the rhythm of the Master Mason:

Example 41

A second semantic level of meaning comes into play as well. As so often, Mozart symbolizes the degree of Master Mason by the three flats in the key of E flat major, and accordingly assigns the second degree the key signature of B flat. By this line of reasoning the overture should actually begin in F major. It does not, of course, for reasons just as obvious as the fact that the overture is made up of more than rhythmic symbols.

The symbolism of Freemasonry occupies the same position relative to Mozart's complete output as do the Masons themselves 'within the larger phenomenon of the Enlightenment' (see p. 122). Throughout his life Mozart never abandoned those ethical imperatives which, in religious drapery, had become second nature to him since his childhood. But he was not so convinced that the church and its representatives were best equipped to administer them. The outlook of the Masons seemed to him more concrete and more in touch with the spirit of his times. They enabled him to maintain a stance of critical detachment toward the church without sacrificing his faith. The commandments of Freemasonry, compared to those of religion, were like new administrative regulations added to an existing body of law. In this sense, the title that Katharine Thomson gave to her study of Mozart's masonic music – *The Masonic Thread in Mozart* – is perfectly apt. When we listen to Mozart's masonic symbolism we are dealing with a thread or weave in the fabric of his music. Or, to choose a different metaphor, we are dealing with building blocks whose place in the edifice we can only understand by examining the structural principles according to which they were assembled by Mozart, the Mason.

Chapter 13

Convictions and thoughts: a closer look

Mozart's commitment to Freemasonry and the Enlightenment as understood by Lessing and Born's circle cannot be denied. The following quotations, arranged in chronological order, show just how consistent was Mozart's political thought. Most of these statements are taken from letters to his father. After their correspondence had begun to diminish around 1782, for reasons both intrinsic and extrinsic, Mozart never found another correspondent even remotely as intimate.

Mozart's quotations are placed alongside others from his contemporaries. This is not meant to suggest that he knew the statements and poems quoted; some of them, although written by his contemporaries, he could not possibly have known.

When a social order is borne to its grave, a number of views, modes of thought, metaphors and images, some of them identical in their wording, arise independently in different minds.

If Mozart's statements are few in number, their counterparts had to be selected from a practically unlimited set of possibilities.

Social status and human dignity

Let there be no fawning for I cannot bear that.
> Letter to his father,
> 10 December 1777

I often hear much wild lament of the arrogance of the great. Their arrogance will not abate until our fawning relent.
> Gottfried August Bürger, *Mittel gegen den* Hochmut der Grossen (Remedies for the arrogance of the great), 1787

At Salzburg I never know how I stand. I am to be everything – and yet – sometimes – nothing! Nor do I ask so much nor so little, just something – I just want to be

What is the Third Estate? Everything. What did it used to be? Nothing. What does it want? To become something.
> Emanuel Joseph Sieyès,

something.
> Letter to his father,
> 15 October 1778

This slavery in Salzburg!
> Letter to his father,
> 12 November 1778

For on my honour it is not
Salzburg itself but the Prince and
his conceited nobility who become
every day more intolerable to me.
> Letter to his father,
> 16 December 1780

At last my blood began to boil, I
could no longer contain myself and
said, 'So Your Grace is not
satisfied with me?' 'What, you dare
to threaten me – you scoundrel?
There is the door! Look out, for I
will have nothing more to do with
such a miserable wretch.' At last I
said: 'Nor I with you!' 'Well, be
off!' When leaving the room I said,
'This is final. You shall have it in
writing tomorrow.'
> Letter to his father,
> 9 May 1781

Tell me now, most beloved father,
did I not say a word too late rather
than too soon? Just listen for a
moment. My honour is more
precious to me than anything else
and I know that it is so to you also.
> Letter to his father,
> 9 May 1781

What Is the Third Estate,
> 1789

Servitude, servitude, and again
servitude!
> Rousseau,
> *Confessions*, Book III,
> 1781

It is sad always to be a slave.
> Joseph Haydn,
> letter to Marianne von Genzinger,
> 27 June 1790

Even servile souls can hate a
tyrant; only he who hates tyranny
is noble and great.
> Goethe, *Xenie*

The services of the mighty are
dangerous and not worth the
effort, the compulsion, the
humiliation they entail.
> Lessing,
> *Minna von Barnhelm*,
> Act V, scene 9,
> 1760–3

Every man is obligated to claim
his right and to see that it is
not tread underfoot; for otherwise,
if he casts away his right he
thrusts his humanity aside.
> Immanuel Kant,
> lecture on moral philosophy,
> given twenty-eight times
> between 1756 and 1789

It is the heart that ennobles a man;
and though I am no count, yet I
have probably more honour in me
than many a count.

Letter to his father,
20 June 1781

Virtue alone, not birth, bestows
dignity.

Johann Heinrich Voss,
Gesang der Deutschen,
1793

Social status and human relations

His, I daresay, is again one of
those money matches and nothing
else. I should not like to marry in
this way; I want to make my wife
happy, but not to become rich by
her means ... Herr von
Schiedenhofen was obliged to
choose a rich wife; his title
demanded it. People of noble
birth must never marry from
inclination or love, but only from
interest and all kinds of secondary
considerations. Again, it would not
at all suit a grandee to love his
wife after she had done her duty
and brought into the world a
bouncing son and heir. But we
poor humble people can not only
choose a wife whom we love
and who loves us, but we may,
can and do take such a one,
because we are neither noble, nor
highly born, nor aristocratic, nor
rich, but, on the contrary, lowly
born, humble and poor; so we do
not need a wealthy wife, for our
riches, being our brains, die with us.

Letter to his father,
7 February 1778

You know well that the best and
truest of all friends are the poor.
The wealthy do not know what
friendship means, especially those
who are born to riches.

Letter to Abbé Bullinger,
7 August 1778

Wealth is a greater burden to
talent than poverty. Under
thrones and mounds of gold
there perhaps lies buried many
an intellectual giant.

Jean Paul,
Selbsterlebensbeschreibung,
1818

It is very remarkable that
everywhere on earth the mildest
and most humane of nations
are those who have almost no
property or those who have not
introduced it to the generality.

The most evil of men, as
everywhere, are those most
interested in things material,
the most miserly, the most
deceitful.

Morelly,
Kodex der Natur,
1755

All wealthy men count their
gold before their inner value.

Rousseau,
Emile ou de l'éducation, Book V,
1762

Social status and intelligence

For a cavalier can't do the work of a Kapellmeister, but a Kapellmeister can well be a cavalier.
> Letter to his father,
> 9 July 1778

... aristocracy of talent...
> Rousseau,
> *Confessions*, Book VII,
> 1781

If we were at the mercy of the knowledge of those in power we would perhaps still have no grain to nourish us and no scissors to cut our fingernails.
> Claude-Adrien Helvétius,
> *De l'esprit*,
> 1785

If you are a poor dunderhead, become a clergyman. If you are a rich dunderhead, become a leaseholder. If you are an aristocratic dunderhead, but poor, become whatever you can for money. But if you are a rich aristocratic dunderhead, become whatever you want – only not a man of reason, that much I forbid you.
> Mozart on a leaflet which he
> wrote himself and handed out at
> a masked ball, dressed as an
> Indian philosopher,
> 15 February 1785

ARISTOCRATIC COUNCILLOR:
My father was a baron of the empire! And yours, may I ask...?

BOURGEOIS COUNCILLOR:
So low, my lord Baron, that were you his son I believe you would be tending the swine.
> Johann Heinrich Voss,
> *Stand und Würde*,
> 1792

Nationhood

'Even in pre-revolutionary Germany patriotic sentiments were virtually equivalent to political opposition': Werner Krauss (1965, p. xxvii).

But then, perhaps, the German national theatre which is sprouting so vigorously would actually begin to flower; and of course that would be an everlasting blot on Germany, if we Germans were seriously to begin to think as Germans, to act as

On the kind-hearted notion of bequeathing the Germans a national theatre although we Germans are not yet a nation!
> Lessing,
> *Hamburgische Dramaturgie*,
> 1768, nos. 101–4

Germans, to speak German and,
Heaven forfend, to sing in German!!
Letter to Anton Klein,
21 May 1785

The military

What appears to me to be truly
ridiculous is the horrible military
– I should like to know of what use
it is.

Letter to his father,
18 December 1778

For whom, thou goodly German
folk, art thou equipped with arms?
For whom dost leave thy wife and
child and hearth for foreign parts?
For princes and for noble rabble
and the blather of the clerks.

Gottfried August Bürger, 1793

New music

If we composers were always to
stick so faithfully to our rules
(which were quite good at a time
when no one knew better), we
should be concocting music as
unpalatable as their libretti.

Letter to his father,
13 October 1781

Those [earlier] good writers
would perhaps have been farther
along than we today if others
had preceded them and paved the
way. We owe it to the very light
they kindled for us that their
writings are no longer useful for
our purposes.

Marmontel,
Poétique française,
1766

Chapter 14
A traditionalist?

The term comes from Alfred Einstein. 'Mozart', he writes (1946, p. 151), 'is a traditionalist; it is not his intention to make something which is, at all costs, novel. He does not wish to make it different but better.'

We know what Einstein means. Mozart had a grasp of tradition second to none. His unique opportunity of visiting the leading musical capitals of Europe while still a child or adolescent, his phenomenal memory for music and his no less astounding capacity for grasping the essence of a piece and using it for his own purposes – all of these, taken together, lend credence to Einstein's dictum 'not different but better'.

Mozart concedes the legitimacy of the old style in church music (12 April 1783) without actually submitting to it himself in *Ave verum corpus* or the Requiem. Otherwise he distinguishes between 'the ancients' and 'the moderns' (29 March 1783), leaving little doubt as to where his own sympathies lie. In clear opposition to his father, Mozart, newly come of age, came to the conclusion that there can hardly be too many new things in music. Even at the age of twenty-two he could wish his father 'as many years of life as are needed until nothing new can be produced in music' (8 November 1777); while working on *Die Entführung* he distanced himself unequivocally from the early rules of music, 'which were quite good at a time when no one knew any better' (13 October 1781); and when he decided to lay his opera *L'oca del Cairo*, K422, to one side, perhaps to take it up again at a later date, he was certain that 'of all the operas which might be performed before mine is finished, not a single idea will resemble one of mine' (10 February 1784). He even goes so far as to 'guarantee' this, doubtless thinking of his large-scale ensembles in symphonic style.

These are not the words of a traditionalist. They might, however, have come from a man who has discovered the wisdom – applicable no less to music than to social and political upheavals – that if revolutions are to be genuine and profound rather than mere flare-ups of protest they must be directed, not against the old, but against the obsolete. There are deep reasons for this. In all stages of its evolution the human species has produced genuine expressions of humanity alongside rank barbarism. And it is a maxim of revolutionaries not to jettison the former while surmounting the latter. The uninitiated are not likely to associate the name of Lenin with a pronouncement such as 'We must not dispense with the old'. But not only did he utter it in 1922 (volume 33, p. 426), he made it a guiding principle in his attempt to erect a new order. We have already confronted this problem in the realm of music. It lurks behind Chrysander's rejection of the attempts by Otto Jahn to belittle Mozart's predecessors (see pp. 57ff.). One of Mozart's many secrets was his ability to take over and critically adapt anything brought forth by his forebears and contemporaries, with the emphasis lying on the word 'critically'. Neither as a child nor as an adolescent had he been able to do this. In Chapter 8 I argued the likelihood that it was Melchior Grimm, himself a man at the centre of critical thought in eighteenth-century Europe, who directed Mozart's critical faculties to musical problems.

However it may have come about, Mozart's confrontation with his musical surroundings took on a new quality during his great Paris journey of 1777–8 and his gradual maturation. As he wrote to his father from Mannheim with justifiable pride (7 February 1778): 'As you know I can more or less adopt or imitate any style of composition.' Mozart scholars have not overlooked this talent. Practically the main thrust behind the monumental Mozart biography of the French writers Wyzewa and Saint-Foix (1911–46) is to retrace the ideas that Mozart received from each of his models and exemplars. What their five mighty tomes fail to show, however, is that it is more important to see what Mozart did with an idea than where he got it. Their value and their limitations reside in their grasp of stylistic history, which, however, always falls short when applied to out-standing figures. In this case our writers subdivide Mozart's evolution into no fewer than thirty-four stages. In contrast, Reinhold Hammer-stein (1956, pp. 1–24) has pointed out where Mozart's encounter with his forebears eventually led: 'What may have been "adoption and imitation" during Mozart's period of growth and maturity – emulation, stylistic copy, the study of models – has, by the time of his late works, become a free and sovereign mastery of all styles and genres.'

This also implies that Mozart knew perfectly well what he did *not* want. True, his projected critical manual on composition never materialized. In the same year as his completion of *Die Entführung* Mozart intimated to his father that he 'would like to write a book, a short critical study of music, illustrated by examples' (28 December 1782). What did materialize, however, was a broadly executed example that might have found its way into this book, and indeed may have been intended for it: *Ein musikalischer Spass*, K522, dating from June 1787 during Mozart's most mature period. (We have already examined one movement from this work in some detail on pp. 68ff.) Here Mozart pillories the same sort of thing as Thomas Mann in the famous speech of Mynheer Peeperkorn in *The Magic Mountain* (1978, p. 667). With meaningful brow and decisive, penetrating and expressive gestures and demeanour, he addresses a small gathering as follows: 'Ladies and gentlemen. – It is well, all very well. But I ask you to keep in mind and not for an instant to lose sight of the fact that – Nevertheless …' And so it continues all the way to Mynheer's resounding conclusion: 'Done, ladies and gentlemen! Completely done! I know us to be in agreement in all these matters. And therefore: to the point!' At which the narrator drily remarks: 'He had said nothing'. Mozart's tacit commentary on this abortive symphony by his untalented contemporary is much the same.

After attending Paër's *Leonora* Beethoven is said to have told the composer, 'Your opera pleases me, I shall compose it.' This, of course, is a witty but spurious *bon mot*. But there is no doubt that ideas of this sort motivated Mozart in many of his countless borrowings of ideas, themes and principles of construction from other composers. He wanted to demonstrate what can be done with them, given the necessary talent. Nor can we doubt that when he did so he sometimes gave free rein to his mockery and pride. His only true model, he felt, was Haydn (Joseph Haydn, of course; Michael Haydn does not fall into the same category, although Mozart also learnt much from him), followed by Handel and all the members of the Bach family. (His arrangements of Handel's oratorios do not belong here; Mozart merely adapted these works to meet the taste of his day and performance conditions at the house of Baron van Swieten.) And for all his esteem of Gluck, even during his Paris journey he knew himself to be that composer's peer.

Now, how did Mozart go about 'saying' something in his music, and moreover saying something new? How did he traverse that path which, as Einstein (1946, p. 226) rightly remarks, referring to the symphonies but applicable to the other genres as well, advanced 'from the decorative to the expressive, from the external to the internal, from mere ceremonial to spiritual avowal'?

We must take the term 'spiritual avowal' seriously. Mozart himself alluded to it when he claimed (see pp. 13ff.) to be able to express convictions in his music. And unless we try to trace convictions and spiritual avowal in the fabric of his music, we will not notice the novelty that Mozart so avidly posited for his art. In the following chapters we shall use selected examples to show how Mozart went about 'doing new things in music' without dispensing with the old. We shall have to delve into details, especially as Mozart was fond of presenting even his boldest musical constructs as though they could be done in no other way. At least this is how it seems to us; his contemporaries were often startled, confused, dismissive.

Pointing out the irregularities and asymmetries of Mozart's themes, Arnold Schoenberg quotes the theme of the minuet from the B flat major String Quartet, K458, and shows that its structure is far more complicated than it seems. Its eight bars, it turns out, are assembled in units of 3 + 1 + 1 + 3. Schoenberg then concludes (1975, p. 410): 'The whole theme comprises eight measures; thus the irregularity is, so to speak, subcutaneous (i.e. it does not show up on the surface).' The same can be said of his music in general. In his 'journey through the keys' (15 October 1777) Mozart does not overlook a single tonality and undertakes completely unexpected modulations. At times we need hardly notice that we are in B major, E flat minor or B flat minor. But he never takes B major, F sharp major, C sharp major, D flat major, G flat major or C flat major as his tonic key, i.e. as the key in which a piece begins and ends. And when a piece, the only one in his prodigious output, does happen in fact to end in B major there are deep reasons for its doing so (see pp. 202–6). His handling of dissonance is no different. It is hard to believe, but the harshest dissonance Mozart ever wrote occurs in one of the gentlest numbers of *Così fan tutte* (see pp. 255–6). Others, even harsher than those in the so-called 'Dissonance' Quartet, K465, can be found in a slow movement from one of his piano concertos (see pp. 254–5). They might escape our attention entirely, so subtly are they woven into the musical texture.

Moreover, as Nicolaus Harnoncourt rightly complains (1984, p. 121), Mozart's musical idiom is all too often 'flattened, ironed smooth, sweetened and made bland' in performance. Harnoncourt himself has attempted in his writings and performances to reinstate Mozart's works 'in their original form, by now virtually unknown'.

We shall proceed to examine a very wide array of musical examples: short and long, melodic and harmonic, timbral and pointillist, some consisting of no more than a single note, others going beyond the movements of an instrumental work or the numbers of an opera. Again and again we will have to be guided by the realization that it is not the 'notes' that make the music, but the context.

Chapter 15
The question of imitation

When the Terzettino in *Così fan tutte* (No. 10) conjures up gentle waves and zephyrs we hear soft murmurings in the strings:

Example 42

In *Figaro* (Duet, No. 2), flutes and oboes imitate the sound of the Countess's bell:

Example 43

A few bars later horns and bassoons give us the Count knocking at Figaro's door:

Example 44

And when Susanna, in her garden aria (No. 28), sings of babbling brooks and caressing breezes, dulcet tones are heard in the winds:

Example 45

Similar instances can be found in Belmonte's second aria in *Die Entführung* (No. 4). Indeed, Mozart himself describes them in his celebrated letter to his father of 26 September 1781. Having sent 'a little foretaste' of his opera to Leopold in Salzburg, he explains in detail how he set the words to music. 'Even [Belmonte's] throbbing infatuated heart is depicted', Mozart writes, 'by two violins in octaves':

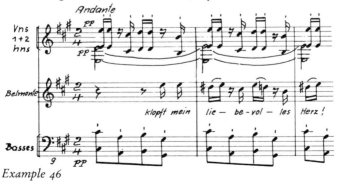

Example 46

'You hear the whispering and the sighing', he continues. Rightly so, for he even distinguishes between whispering (*Lispeln*):

Example 47

and sighing (*Seufzen*):

Example 48

Belmonte's 'trembling and faltering' and his 'swelling breast' are likewise transmuted into music. Switching from 'you hear' to 'you see', Mozart writes: 'You see how his swelling breast heaves'. As so often with Mozart, this apparent carelessness in wording conceals an insight. For indeed the audible elements (whisperings and sighs) and the visible signs of agitation (the heaving of his breast, his trembling and faltering) are given equivalent expressions in the music, the latter 'by means of a crescendo'. This crescendo, which allows us to 'see' Belmonte's swelling breast, shares with it the quality of expansion. Rousseau, in the entry on *imitation* in his *Dictionnaire de musique*, coined a phrase to capture this sort of translation of visual perceptions into musical ones: 'Music seems to transport the eye into the ear.'

Mozart does not have much more to say about this aria, although he might have added many further points to his discussion. The word 'feurig', for instance, meaning 'fiery' or 'ardent', is set a fourth higher than the word 'ängstlich' or 'anxious'; and the basses cling – anxiously, as it were – to a single note in bar 2 only to plunge ardently into the lower register two bars later. Another device deserves our attention. The first measure begins *piano*, followed by a crescendo. But whereas the crescendo mentioned by Mozart – the one expressing Belmonte's swelling breast – extends over a full three bars (35 to 37) and ends in a *forte*, this one breaks off after the first bar and ends as it started, *piano*. Consider small children or animals who attempt something beyond their capacities: they start off with gusto, stop, and then pretend that nothing had happened. In the language of behavioural psychology these are known as 'intentional movements' (Tembrock 1980, p. 167), in which an action is initiated but not carried to its conclusion. There is hardly a better way of rendering anxiety in music than by presenting an intentional movement in the form of a dynamic build-up leading to nothing – a procedure frequently encountered, on a much larger scale, in Schubert.

What prompted Mozart to draw his father's attention to his great success in Vienna? While still a child he had been taught that 'in all pieces of music one should approximate the natural wherever possible'. These words are to be found in a violin method whose author was Leopold Mozart (1756, p. 109), and we may be certain that Leopold, as the teacher of his son, did not fail to mention what he had set down so intelligently and convincingly in his book. As an adolescent Mozart had heard similar ideas in similar words from his friends in Paris, Mannheim and Vienna. Now it was time for him to prove to his father that he had learnt his lesson and knew how to apply that doctrine of imitation that formed the cornerstone of Enlightenment aesthetics. Even his choice of words – 'express' (*exprimieren*), 'display' (*anzeigen*), and so on – follows the contemporary vocabulary.

Worldly and down-to-earth, the doctrine of imitation played a decisive part in supplanting the theocentric music aesthetics inherited from medieval scholasticism. Beginning embryonically in the Renaissance, it posited three principal objects of imitation: our natural surroundings, 'affects' or emotions, and the declamation of human speech. The latter form will be considered in the chapters to follow.

Imitation of nature is the least problematic part of this doctrine, largely coinciding with what we now call word-painting or onomatopoeia. There is no question that it plays its part in musical cultures everywhere, today extending even as far as *musique concrète*, electronic music and pop music. Nor is there any dearth of examples from Mozart and his contemporaries that might be added to the ones mentioned above.

Things become more difficult when we turn to the imitation of 'affects'. Mozart himself claimed that it is possible to translate audible and visible signs of agitation into music, and showed how this can be done. What he could not have known, but what behavioural psychology has taught us, is that the observation of outward signs of internal states and their impact on the observer form the starting point of mimetic communication.

Yet not all internal states need produce outward signs, quite apart from the fact that the signs can also be suppressed. The doctrine of imitation has nothing to say about the extent to which this coincides with the imitation of nature. The two types of imitation may often overlap. Unlike the sighs and whisperings of Belmonte's aria, the murmuring, caressing woodwind chords in Susanna's aria conform to the gentle trochaic rhythm underlying the number rather than introducing new movement into the music. This lets us know that Susanna is at one with nature, with herself and Figaro, with the world. They say just as much about her as they do about nature. This is a point which we would do well not to overlook.

In the Duet, No. 2 from *Die Entführung*, Osmin tries to prevent Belmonte from entering the house of Bassa Selim. At the climax of the number Osmin sings the following phrase:

Example 49

At the word 'Fort!' – 'away!' – Mozart writes a *sforzato* for all instruments, reinforced by grace notes in the violins and woodwinds. We might be content to conclude that we are listening to Osmin's 'affect' were it not for the fact that these grace notes are of a quite unusual sort. Mozart has the instruments play no fewer than four different sets of grace notes simultaneously, one of them additionally doubled at the octave:

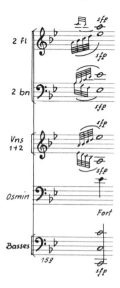

Example 50

The listener is unable to single out any one of them. This passage was evidently inspired by the image of a cracking whip made up of several thongs, each of them capable of producing a noise different from the others (Osmin is traditionally armed with a prop of this sort). Since noises really are the result of a number of simultaneous events generating irregular sound waves, Mozart, with his superb ear, has correctly analysed this phenomenon and imitated it in his music. Osmin's 'affect' is combined with a physical event caused by this affect, and so we are dealing with a fusion of two forms of imitation at once, with Osmin's rage as well as his whip. Osmin in his anger cracks his cat-o'-nine-tails with special vehemence; his anger is transformed into movement, the movement into violent noise. Just as movement and state of mind are mutually conditioned in the stage figure, onomatopoeic and emotional elements merge in his musical representation.

Enlightenment thinkers were not as fixated on imitation as were many of their teachers, who often set out from the presupposition that a musician cannot convey an emotion convincingly to his listeners without projecting himself into that very same emotion. In similar words this was said countless times, once in no uncertain terms by Mozart's father (1756, p. 260) and again by Mozart himself when he set about being a teacher. On 30 July 1778, at the height of his courtship of Aloysia Weber (she was in the process of learning 'Ah, lo previdi', K272, his Andromeda scena of 1777), he wrote her a serious and didactic letter in Italian on the art of stage acting. There we read: 'I advise you to think carefully of the meaning and force of the words, to put yourself in all seriousness into Andromeda's predicament, and to imagine that you really are that very person.'

'Wrong!' is what Diderot would have said of the last two clauses. In his *Paradox sur le comédien* he argues at length against the naive doctrine of empathy or projection, according to which what an actor requires most of all is *sensibilité* – empathy with the character being presented – after which the success of his performance is assured. Diderot rejects this with the argument that nothing occurs on stage exactly as it does in nature, and that a 'special system of principles' (1968 II, p. 483) and an 'ideal model conceived by the author' (p. 492) must intercede between the character presented and his representation on stage. Poet and actor must be keen observers and require perspicacity and sound powers of judgement (p. 484); their power of empathy, on the other hand, is not at issue. 'Exaggerated empathy makes mediocre actors; mediocre empathy makes the swarms of bad actors; and the complete absence of empathy is the prerequisite for outstanding actors' (1968 II, p. 489). These ideas were taken up by Brecht, who thought very highly of Diderot, and worked into his theory of alienation. As we can see, they far transcend the theory of imitation and empathy. (Diderot apparently belittled *sensibilité* for the sake of his main argument. We can well imagine an actor following Diderot's principles and yet adding a dash of *sensibilité*, just as a comedian can be amused at his own jokes.)

Mozart may have been aware of this theory. It was already five years old when he stayed at the home of Baron Grimm, who was familiar with Diderot's ideas and may have touched on them in conversation. But whether or not he came into direct contact with it, Mozart wrote his music in the manner prescribed by Diderot. We can distinguish between several levels or stages in this process. First, there is the artist as observer. We often meet Mozart the observer in his letters, with their precise, acute, often sharp-tongued verbal portraits. To a certain extent, they form preliminary studies to his musical portraits. A composer is even less able than an actor to transmit his stock of observations directly to his audience. A 'system of principles', to use Diderot's phrase, must be set in operation in order to transform into sound what he has seen, heard, felt and appraised. We will have many occasions to see that Mozart performed transformations of this sort quite consciously. Another stage in the process of musical representation lies in storing up observations together with the musical transformations assigned to them. Just how precisely this functions in Mozart's mind can be seen by the fact that many of the transformations invented in his early years remained with him for his entire life as his personal musical vocabulary or, one might also say, as his personal repertoire of musical signs. Lastly, the composer must discover a mediating level or vehicle, an 'ideal model conceived by the author'. Mozart often found this vehicle in stage situations. In Chapter 10 we saw how Mozart came to discover a new mediating level in contemporary events.

Goethe, who is well known to have placed great stock on Diderot, also dealt gingerly with the doctrine of imitation, emphasizing its dangers for the arts no less than its indispensability. In a delightful essay entitled 'Der Sammler und die Seinen' ('The Collector and His Family', *BA* XIX, pp. 207–74) he strictly distances himself from the usurpatory properties of imitation, which will not rest 'until it has gone so far as to set the copy in place of the original' (p. 230). Taking Bello, the proverbial household dog, as his example, Goethe argues that 'we would not advance very far' by producing a perfect imitation for then we would have 'at best two Bellos for one' (p. 243). Art has completely different dimensions.

It is plain to see that music, even viewed superficially, is never entirely taken up with imitation. Mozart, for example, omits to mention several items in his invaluable letter on *Die Entführung*. He evidently considered it superfluous to draw his father's attention to the fact that in No. 4 the horns sustain a note in octaves for several bars, that the woodwind offset the voice with gentle turns of counterpoint, that the strings provide additional accompanying parts, that the basses rise as the voice descends, and so forth. To men of the trade this was all self-evident. But if we wish to know how Mozart 'semanticized' his music we will have to ask what these and other elements accomplish if they do not serve the purposes of imitation – whether imitation is the only or even the preferred means of relating music to reality. And the best place to direct this question is to a piece by Mozart in which imitation is important but, as we shall discover (not to our surprise), only one means among others to this end.

Chapter 16
Zerlina and the three modes of music

When Zerlina sings her second aria 'Vedrai, carino' (No. 18 in *Don Giovanni*) Masetto is in a pitiable state. First she played a nasty trick on him: if Donna Elvira had not intervened with her warnings Don Giovanni's masculinity, pride and superiority would have driven the girl into his arms on the very day of her marriage to Masetto. Now she finds her Masetto roundly thrashed and full of pain. After making certain that none of the bodily parts that matter to her have been damaged she sets about applying salves and medicines not to be obtained from the apothecary. Mozart was well versed in such things:

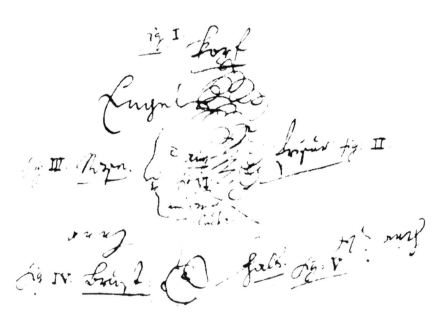

Maria Anna Thekla Mozart, the 'Bäsle' of Mozart's correspondence, drawn by Mozart in a letter to her of 10 May 1779.

But Zerlina's medicines would not be so irresistible, neither to Masetto nor to the listeners of the scene they are acting out, if she were to speak instead of sing, and if she did not have thirty or forty musicians to accompany her. After merely singing natural remedies of reconciliation for some fifty bars of *andante* she begins to become physical. As a stage direction indicates, 'she lets him feel her heart'. Knowing full well that Masetto cannot feel the throbbing heart of his lover without raising his own pulse, Mozart gives us more to hear in the music than just the heartbeats. But he makes them audible too, indeed in three different ways. First, we hear eight bars of throbbing semiquavers in the cellos and double basses:

Example 51

Three bars later we hear:

Example 52

no fewer than six times, and a few bars later:

Example 53

166

again six times – or more precisely five-and-a-half, for here something remarkable takes place. With the final semiquaver of the above quotation the voice detaches itself from the ticking woodwinds – which obligingly stop ticking at precisely this moment so that Zerlina's voice can stand out unaccompanied – and goes its own melodic way to the words 'toccami qua, qua', 'touch me here, here':

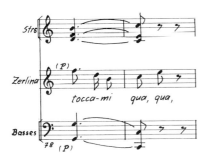

Example 54

It is easy to hear what that way is: the voice follows the lilt of the words, just as it failed to do in the preceding two bars while subordinating itself to the mimetic rendering of the heartbeat. But what Zerlina can do, the instruments can do as well, for example in this figure, doubled in three octaves by the woodwind:

Example 55

Obviously the woodwind are anticipating the 'sentilo battere' of the voice, but not in the same way as the basses. The latter direct the listener to 'battere' – the heartbeat – by in turn beginning to throb, transforming themselves in a manner of speaking into a pulse or, if you will, a heart. The woodwind, on the other hand, anticipate the inflections of the words in a cantabile phrase that Zerlina herself does not deliver until eight bars later. It sometimes happens that instruments adapt themselves so closely to the mode of texted vocal parts that they can even 'pronounce' words not found in the text itself. One example of this is found in bar 52. Zerlina concludes the second period of her aria with a question: Would you like to know, she asks, where I keep this natural and harmless medicine that I want to give you, cloaking her question in the words 'dove mi sta'? Hanns-Werner Heister points out that the question is answered in the orchestra: 'là!', 'here!':

Example 56

Both these ways of anticipating words – the mimetic technique in the basses and the word-related one in the woodwind – take place simultaneously for eight bars, beginning at bar 53. Music can do this sort of thing.

But there is still more. Two further musical events are unfolding at the same time. Within these few bars the violins and violas, gently and unobtrusively, resolve four times from dominant to tonic:

Example 57

These are filler parts, bridging the gap between the bass and melody lines and sustaining the harmony of the eight-bar period together with the basses. This, at any rate, is how a composition teacher would put it, and his description would be right as far as it goes, albeit decidedly incomplete. Softly and placidly, restrained rather than throbbing, the chords are heard several times over a pedal point. Schematically, they might be represented as follows:

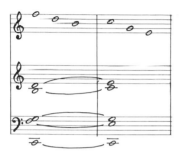

Example 58

They, too, contribute to the overall effect. So do the sustained notes in the horns. Sustained notes are the exclamation marks of music. To realize their importance one need only omit them in performance; not only trained musicians, but halfway experienced listeners will feel something important is lacking. In principle, these elements fall into the same category as those expressing Osmin's rage, except that in this case they are tender and soothing.

At this point I may be allowed some observations which are no less surprising for being sober and statistical. With regard to its harmonic scheme Zerlina's second aria has no parallel in the whole of Mozart's output, nor do I know of anything comparable by another composer. The piece is rightly called an aria for it comprises five sections with clearly contrasted melodic material, and yet it has the restricted harmonic range typical of a lied. Among Mozart's lieder with clavier accompaniment, however, there is only one that approaches the length of Zerlina's aria – 'Abendempfindung an Laura', K523 – and it modulates through more than half a dozen keys. All the others which make do with one modulation to the dominant are considerably shorter. Zerlina's song is, in this respect, most readily compared with Papageno's entrance number in *Die Zauberflöte* (No. 2), which is likewise called an aria. This, however, has a mere fifty bars of which ten, a fifth of the piece, are in the dominant. The figures for Zerlina's piece are quite different, almost beggaring belief. Of its 104 bars only eight are in the dominant, and the remaining ninety-six touch the subdominant region in only seven-and-a-half. This unique piece, then, is in the key of C major for ninety-two percent of its total length. In a ninety-six-bar orgy of C major we hear the progression dominant-tonic no fewer than forty-one times:

Example 59

In some of his less ambitious closing numbers or final movements Mozart also limits himself occasionally to dominant-tonic progressions over long expanses with scant melodic material and stereotype rhythms. Here, however, we have no call to speak of scant material, stereotypes or lack of ambition. It is the *semblance* of simplicity and naturalness that Mozart gives us here, though with a refinement and artistic mastery which not even he commanded until the mid-1780s. Later this point will be documented with some detailed evidence; for the moment, however, we will examine the effect that lies couched in these filler parts.

Behavioural psychologists (see Wallin 1992, pp. 320f.) distinguish between two kinds of utterances: 'attractors' and 'detractors'. The former are friendly and beckoning (e.g. mating calls), the latter hostile and defensive (cries of warning or terror). Not only animals are startled by acoustical events that reach a loud volume after a rapid increase in amplitude. Conversely, sounds which are soft, sustained, and rich in overtones are also attractive to humans. If the sounds expressing Osmin's rage and whip were 'detractors' (see pp. 161–2), we now hear 'attractor' sonorities from Zerlina's orchestra. Yet we hear other sonorities as well, shifting unexpectedly from soft detractors to the gentlest of attractors, but restrained and well-ordered, as always in eighteenth-century music.

Musical parlance has a term to express the change from something painful to something soothing: 'resolution'. A dissonance is said to 'resolve' into a consonance, and this process can be made a musical metaphor for any release from tension or pain. Processes of this sort were described in elevated if non-technical language by Hegel. One passage of his *Ästhetik* (1955, p. 850) mentions several composers, the last two of them being his contemporaries Mozart and Haydn:

> The serenity of the spirit remains intact in the works of these masters; pain, of course, finds expression as well, but it is always resolved. The poised symmetry never reaches an extreme;

everything coheres within the bounds of restraint, so that jubilation never degenerates into wild ranting and even lamentation exudes the most blissful calm.

Nothing in eighteenth-century music could capture the inevitable release from pain, the 'blissful calm' of lamentation, more perfectly than the ever-recurring and familiar tonic resolution of the dominant, with its relatively mild dissonance (at times distinctly stressed by Mozart in this piece). Toward the end of the number the 'biogenic' methods – the term will be explained below – begin to accumulate, including an increase in volume and a rise in tessitura. For the first and only time the voice reaches a high G with a concomitant increase in intensity. This increase is, as Mozart would have put it, 'expressed by means of a crescendo', likewise the first and only one in the piece. With this high G Zerlina leads us triumphantly – and, of course, again by way of the resolution of the dominant – into the ritornello, this time *forte*, again for the first and only time in the piece. 'Toccami qua, qua, toccami qua!' Just touch me here, she says, and all will be well:

Example 60

In No. 18 of *Don Giovanni*, then, we have isolated a number of musical elements which cannot be reduced to a common denominator. Many unmistakably imitate nature in the sense that they are onomatopoeic; others mobilize the 'affects'; still others follow laws comparable to those that govern human speech. It is quite obvious that we are dealing with phenomena which are responsible for more than just the magical effect of Zerlina's song of seduction. They apply to all European music, and perhaps to music as a whole. As an aid to describing and analysing these phenomena I have suggested in another book (1980) using the terms 'logogenic', 'biogenic' and 'mimeogenic' to describe the methods or 'modes' of human music-making and the 'elements' in the music thus produced.

Logogenic elements are analogous to language. These are the elements found most frequently in eighteenth-century music. Of these, the most frequent in turn are those passages resembling the melody – or what linguistic theorists would call 'intonation' – of human utterances, chiefly poetically formed utterances with an underlying metre and rhythm. As can be seen in the various kinds of recitative, the lilt of prosaic or vernacular language has also left its mark on special forms of music. However, it would seem that since the Middle Ages the metrical qualities of poetic language have been the driving force behind European music, the ordering principle to which the other properties of music are subordinate. Here it should immediately be remarked that these metrical qualities of poetic language cannot be completely accounted for in logogenic terms; the order imposed upon them derives from the rhythms of bodily motion. In the USA there recently appeared a book on Mozart (Allanbrook 1983) which proceeds on the assumption that Mozart's music, and indeed classical music as a whole, derived primarily from rhythmic patterns, particularly those of the dance, and must be understood from that angle. The book's many stimulating remarks and ideas notwith-standing, it is wrong to think that music derives from, and can be explained on the basis of, one single element. It is presumably due to the prominence of music's linguistic and metrical qualities that the other types of musical behaviour and elements are generally played down.

Biogenic methods can be traced back in evolutionary history to the origins of humanity and beyond to the behaviour of higher animals. They involve an entire world of processes of the most varied kinds. Acoustically perceivable processes inside a living being – faster or louder heartbeat, heavier breathing, groans, cries – are symptomatic of mental states. In the course of evolutionary history they may be stylized to form deliberate signals for purposes of communication with other sentient beings, and hence to become components of musical languages. Hegel viewed the 'cadenced interjection' as 'probably the starting point of music' (1955, p. 818). It was, he claimed, 'the natural outburst of emotion, a cry of horror for example, or a sob of pain, the shouts and trills of high-spirited pleasure and merriment, and so forth' (p. 849) – all of them biogenic elements – that constituted the origins of music, though admittedly not in their natural form but 'cadenced', i.e. ordered into a system. With our greater knowledge of musical cultures we will treat biogenic elements not as *the* starting point of music but merely as *one* of its starting points.

One particular distinction between two types of biogenic methods is of critical importance to music. According to a hypothesis advanced by Günter Tembrock (1983, p. 185), it probably derives from the different ways in which man's vegetative system and his motor abilities operate. The former probably accounts for the endlessly varied nuances that man can bring forth in his singing, in addition to high and low, loud and soft, and the transitions between them. By activating the larynx the most subtle nuances of man's inner being can be made audible, even in speech and all the more in singing. Nor is there any doubt that instruments too can sing, producing even greater extremes of register and more refined nuances than the best singers. In this regard rhythmic regularity plays no part.

With man's motor abilities things are fundamentally different. Whether walking, running or beating (on one's own body or on the ground), whether stamping, dancing or, much later in human evolution, performing physical labour, the organized regularity of movement is paramount. And from these activities organized rhythm found its way into mimetic communication and joined forces with the modulating sounds of the human voice.

This helps us to understand a musical phenomenon that occupied Mozart. In a lengthy passage from a letter of 23–5 October 1777 to his father he expostulates on the necessity of reconciling unity of tempo with expressivity in performance. The former, he maintains, is the 'chief requisite in music', but unless one can play 'expressivo' one will not 'get good results' from the clavier. This, however, is easier said than done. For expressive playing demands a freedom of delivery which is not always compatible with strictness of tempo. 'Everyone is amazed', Mozart continues,

> that I can always keep strict time. What these people cannot grasp is that in *tempo rubato* in an Adagio, the left hand should go on playing in strict time. With them the left hand gives way.

In short, two modes of performance take place simultaneously, the one in strict time, the other kept free for the sake of expressivity.

This, of course, also applies to Zerlina. When she sings 'sentilo battere' she has to keep strict time for the sake of the motoric and mimetic impulse. But when she sings 'toccami qua', for instance, we must grant her certain liberties in her delivery. What I propose to call 'multiple processes' are a basic feature of European music.

Mimeogenic methods derive from the necessity in humans (and animals) to imitate much of what they are able to perceive acoustically. This is part of the strategy of assimilation by means of adaptation.

Small children imitate the voice of their mother and the sounds of animals, those of today even the internal combustion engine. In mimetic performances human beings have imitated wind, rain and water, animals and their fellow humans for as long as humankind has been in existence. Adorno was certainly correct to say that without imitation man would never have become human.

Verbal languages, too, have biogenic and mimeogenic elements at their disposal in the form of interjections and onomatopoeic words. But they play a relatively minor part, and many could be done away with entirely without causing language to cease being language. In music, on the other hand, they are part of its basic equipment, and it is crucial that they be produced recognizably, incisively, and with many shades and hues of volume and timbre.

In order to make this possible the human species has evolved a veritable arsenal of man-made musical instruments. They bear witness to the fact that biogenic and mimeogenic methods of music-making are no less indispensable than logogenic methods. For musical instruments are capable, to put it crudely, of being louder and softer, higher and lower, more penetrating and more richly nuanced than the human voice. No writing about music will be worth its salt unless it takes into account the fact that across the globe there is not a single system of music that does without man-made instruments, nor any linguistic system that requires them.

The most profound reason why musicians have drawn on man-made instruments, however, is probably that their use can make multiple processes the rule rather than the exception. 'Vedrai, carino' illustrates just how many musical events can proceed simultaneously. Take sustained notes. It seems plausible to look for their origins in calls between spatially separated people, enjoining alertness and establishing a bond over the distance. In any event they are an acoustical guarantor of the presence of fellow human beings. In many cultures there are singers who would not be able to sing their melodies at all unless accompanied by sustained notes from other singers or instrumentalists. Moreover, certain instruments such as bagpipes or hurdy-gurdies are built in such a way that they always produce sustained notes, either unison or in octaves, when a melody is played on them. Drones, pedal points or, as in Zerlina's aria, sustained notes in the middle, high and low registers were among the ubiquitous features of composed music in the eighteenth century. Our piece opens with a C held for four bars in three low-register octaves to support the delivery of the main melody, like an archetype of biogenic performance techniques. This is one reason why the piece is so irresistible. If one wanted to hold someone fast with music, this would be the way to do it.

1 The Schottenplatz. Engraving by J. A. Delsenbach after a drawing by Joseph Emanuel Fischer von Erlach (1693–1742) dating from the first half of the eighteenth century. It was on this square, known in Mozart's time and thereafter as the 'Freyung', that a certain Georg Hofmann performed 'ha'penny comedies' (*Kreuzerkomödien*) in which every member of the audience paid one kreuzer for each act.

2 Market spectacle around the year 1785, after an etching by Franz Anton Maulpertsch (1724–96). The stage was presumably set up somewhere just outside the town walls (note the gate in the background). The actors, one of whom is being consulted as a dentist, are presumably announcing the start of a performance.

Opposite 3 View of the Graben toward the Kohlmarkt in Vienna. Combination of coloured copper engraving and etching, drawn from life and engraved by Carl Schütz, Vienna, 1781. During his Vienna years Mozart lived in the Graben on two separate occasions: first in building no. 17 (upper left corner at the intersection with the Kohlmarkt), and again in the Trattnerhof, Graben no. 29 (the first building on the right). Living in the centre of town had advantages for Mozart's concertizing and for giving piano lessons. In his years of crisis Mozart was twice forced to move to the suburbs, where rents were lower but the trips by carriage or foot were longer. For about half a year he lived on the Landstrasse (1787), and for the same length of time on the Alsergrund (1788). All his other lodgings were but a few steps away from the Graben. The same applied to the aristocratic or bourgeois homes he frequented, as well as the Burgtheater and the Kärntnertor Theatre, the former being conveniently reached via the Kohlmarkt, the latter via the Dorotheergasse, whose intersection with the Graben can be seen in the lower left-hand corner of the engraving.

4 The 'Golden Ship', a
bourgeois building (no. 198)
near the Nussdorf Line.
Detail from *Vogelschau der
Stadt Wien* ('Bird's-eye
View of the City of
Vienna'), surveyed from
1769 to 1777 and engraved
in copper in 1785 by Joseph
Daniel von Huber.

5 Bauernfeind Hall (no. 70)
in the Lerchenfelder Strasse.
Detail from *Vogelschau der
Stadt Wien*.

6 View towards the suburbs of Wieden and Wien. Combination of coloured copper engraving and etching by Johann Ziegler, Vienna, 1780. From the left to the middle of the engraving we can see the River Wien, in the middle the Freihaus. The latter, as can be seen from a town plan made seventeen years later (Plate 7), was expanded during Mozart's lifetime. Though only located some eight hundred metres from the town walls and the Kärntnertor Theatre, the Freihaus was set in a different world, a world Mozart entered when he visited its theatre (built in 1787) and mounted his *Zauberflöte* there in 1791.

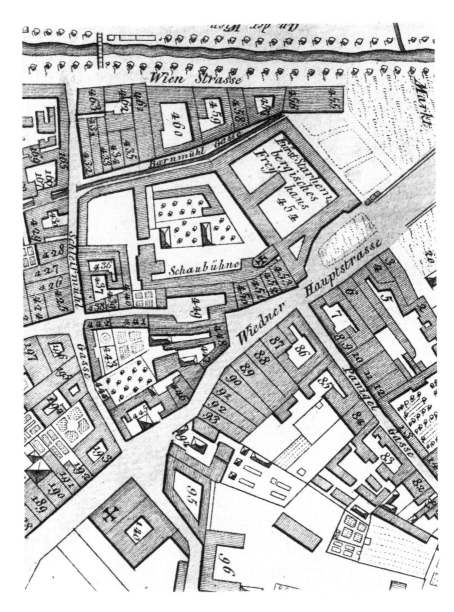

7 The Theatre in the Freihaus. Detail from a town map by Maximilian von Grimm, 1797. The word *Schaubühne* (stage) marks the location of the Freihaus Theatre. It was situated in a landscaped courtyard between Schleifmühlgasse and Obstmarkt, known today as 'Naschmarkt', in the Vienna district of Wieden. As with Plates 4 and 5, this offers further proof that theatre directors, rather than relying on audiences to come to them, even went so far as to establish their companies in bourgeois residences.

Viel Orth hab ich durchreist Su Wien will ich verbleiben
Ich bitt mein Herr last mich in eüre *Bande* schreibe

8 Hanswurst (J. A. Stranitzky) seeking admission to the grand theatre. Engraving
from *Lustige Reiss-Beschreibung* (1716). Comic figures did not have to grovel to
appear in grand opera: indeed, without the critical attitudes they introduced and
the stage situations and acting techniques they made possible, the genre would
have perished of its own inertia. Mozart's style is inconceivable without the
historical process captured in Stranitzky's ironic genuflection. Not only Pedrillo,
Leporello and Papageno but even Figaro come from the world of comic figures.

9 Ignaz von Born. Portrait in oils by Johann Baptist Lampi the Elder
(1751–1830), *c.* 1790 (see pp. 123–9).

10 *Liberty or Death*. Gouache by Pierre Etienne Lesueur, *c.* 1790 (see p. 257).

11 Lorenzo Da Ponte. Engraving by Michele Pekenino after Nathaniel Rogers, *c.* 1800.

12 Giovanni Battista Casti. Contemporary engraving by Antonio Lanzani, c. 1770.

13a Page from the autograph score of the Sinfonia (Overture) to *Le nozze di Figaro*, showing that Mozart originally intended the overture to have a slow middle section in D minor (see p. 266).

13b From the autograph score of *Figaro*: Figaro's recitative introducing his Cavatina, No. 3 (see p. 185).

14 Grotto in the bottomlands of the Gilowsky estate in Aigen near Salzburg.
Photograph from the second half of the nineteenth century (see pp. 133ff).

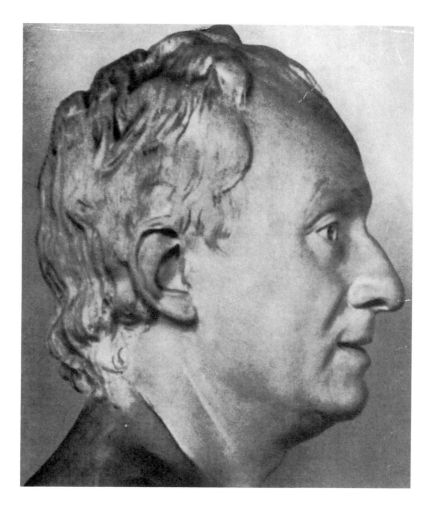

15 Denis Diderot. Detail from the portrait bust by Jean-Antoine Houdon, 1771. Though he probably never met the man, Mozart came into contact with Diderot's ideas in 1778 through the mediation of Melchior Grimm. among the notables whom Leopold Mozart, writing in early 1778, urged him to visit was 'Mr Diderot'.

16 Anonymous engraving from the mid-eighteenth century. Comic figures, including Pantalon, Pierrot, Scapin and Harlequin, observe the world of fools from behind a screen so as to 'learn from them successfully to play their parts'. Mozart, who was fond of identifying with Hanswurst and Harlequin, would have seconded the couplet's concluding line that 'many find their likeness in the dramatic arts'.

17 *Die Zauberflöte*. The first scene of Act II, described by Mozart as the 'solemn scene', as staged by Walter Felsenstein in 1954 for the Komische Oper, Berlin. Photograph: Jürgen Simon (see p. 319).

But the complications are not over yet. We must bear in mind that only in exceptional cases do the three types of elements occur in a pure form, clearly distinguishable from each other. Normally, over the vast expanses of time in which musical systems have emerged, the separate techniques have been combined, superimposed and hybridized. The same, of course, applies to Zerlina's singing. To be sure, she behaves as if she emphasizes now the one, now the other, while seemingly neglecting the remaining elements. But if we look more closely we notice that things are more complicated than that. What holds the entire piece together is, first of all, metre, a biogenic element. Logogenic formations also occur throughout. The mimeogenic elements, though only evident toward the middle of the piece (see Examples 51 to 53), are already foreshadowed in bar 2:

Example 61

Both the grace notes and the rhythm of this bar are later repeated to the word *battere*, signifying a heartbeat:

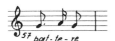

Example 62

They thereby anticipate the mimeogenic mode, as do the figures in the woodwind and violins:

Example 63

The mimetic impulse is at work before it becomes manifest. We are confronted with the disturbing fact that in Zerlina's aria, as in music everywhere, the melody, an accompaniment figure, a harmonic progression, even a single note may derive from two or even all three modes. Even when one mode commands our attention we must always ask whether the two other modes are not functioning as well, and if so, how.

Consider an example. We have referred to heartbeat rhythms as mimeogenic elements. This makes good sense: the words, the musical events and the stage scene (Zerlina directing Masetto's hand to her bosom) all unite to form a prime example of mimetic representation, turning an inner process into an experience we can both see and hear. But the externalization of inner processes is also a defining feature of biogenic methods. We are dealing with a superimposition of two modes.

Eventually musicology will be forced to direct its attention to the physiological and psychological aspects of music's worldwide origin and evolution. This challenge is all the more imperative as the impact of musical creations is no less complex than are those creations themselves. We perceive music with different components of our brain and nervous system. The studies published by D. E. Berlyne and his collaborators (1965, 1973, 1974) offer proof that many musical figurations take precedence over others, for reasons no less obscure to the researchers than to musicians and listeners. Even those biogenic elements that make Zerlina's melodies seem so graceful (Mozart has given No. 18 the tempo mark *grazioso*), so sweet and ingratiating, impinge on areas of our nervous system which are not primarily involved in discursive thought. We find ourselves in the realm of the biotic. But by the time we enter the mimeogenic we are not so far removed from human consciousness, since the perception of mimeogenic elements presupposes the existence of accumulated experiences. If we did not know subconsciously that hearts beat so many times per minute, or if the basses and woodwind in Zerlina's aria were to tick twice or half as fast as they do, we would not be able to associate them with heartbeats. A bit of cognitive thought is involved. And as for logogenic formations, it is well known that even toddlers will warble speech-melodies before they can utter words, and that we produce verbal logogenic creations constantly from early childhood, this being at least in part a conscious process.

Today we have better chances than ever of understanding those complex creations that musicians and music lovers have to deal with. We are living in the age of a 'cognitive revolution'. For the last three decades or so we have been within reach of a 'unified theory of knowledge' (*Science*, 24 July 1988) in which cognitive and aesthetic forms of knowledge stand side by side. Methods of musical analysis which extract a single element or complex of elements and ignore the others are obsolete.

To return, yet again, to 'Vedrai, carino'. Its wealth of mimeogenic effects and its full exploitation of biogenic possibilities (already evident in the superabundance of dominant-tonic figures) are offset by a key scheme that is simplicity itself. But this simplicity is semantic: Zerlina is one of those 'low-born' figures who, as Mozart sarcastically noted (7 February 1778), are neither bad nor ingenuous. Zerlina's sensuality is pitted against Don Giovanni's, and her second aria virtually crackles with eroticism. As this sensuality, to paraphrase Mörike, takes the form of 'marvellous new desires and temptations every hour of the day' – indeed almost every second – we can see how the indescribable wealth of variation and nuance that Mozart lavished on this aria has a semantic purpose. We need only consider, and hear, Zerlina's voice in proportion to the instruments accompanying her. It begins straightforwardly enough with the first violins doubling the voice in unison, as one might expect, and the other strings subordinate. But by the time we reach the second eight-bar phrase (bars 19ff.) the violins retire discreetly to the lower octave so that Zerlina can stand out a shade more clearly. And when, six bars later, the violins return to Zerlina's register, the bassoon adds a nasal voice an octave below, perhaps to mock the apothecary (*lo speziale*) who is at a loss to produce the natural tinctures and potions of love. Four bars later a new constellation arises: Zerlina's 'no!', underscoring her superiority to the apothecary. This 'no!' is unaccompanied (we hear her delicate voice by itself for the first time), and flutes and bassoons take the word from her lips by entering unexpectedly on the upbeat, albeit this had been anticipated in bar 7 of the ritornello:

Example 64

The 'certain balm' of bars 34–5 is accompanied by two bassoons in the lower register, 'that I carry about with me' by a flute in the higher register two bars later. The constellations begin to change in more rapid succession. A new one occurs with the words 'sentilo battere' (bar 56), where Zerlina must surmount a full tutti chord in the orchestra. This chord, however, carefully omits the very note on which Zerlina enters, and the same device takes an entirely new twist when, in bar 76, all six woodwinds accompany the voice, courteously parting in the middle to give her a chance to stand her ground against this strange mixture of timbres (see Example 53). The fluttery bars 17 and 18:

Example 65

play a special part insofar as they are among the very few that are repeated. Three times they recur unchanged, but at the fourth recurrence (bars 93–4) they usher in the second of the piece's only two interrupted cadences. Each of these recurrences presents the G–C resolution in a different rhythm:

Example 66

In the very next bar this looks as follows:

Example 67

With 'sentilo battere' the dominant begins to expand – something we had not encountered up to now – first over one bar (bars 51, 56, 58 etc.), then over three bars (bars 63ff., 69ff.) before being resolved. The piece begins to oscillate, even to vibrate, and yet it still exudes calm and repose. The effect is indescribably profound: small wonder that Masetto is powerless to resist. Adorno (1952–3, p. 37) claimed of the postlude that it 'seems to reconcile the divided house of humanity itself'. And indeed, when the postlude begins to declaim Zerlina's refined yet innocent melody *forte* and with full orchestra (both for the first time) only to dismiss us with a *pianissimo* (again the first in the piece), by the time we reach the forty-first resolution to C major it seems it is not only Masetto's pain that has vanished.

Chapter 17

The 'genuine natural forms' of music

The expression, applied to poetry, comes from Goethe. Writing in his *Notes and Commentaries on the 'West-östliche Divan'* (1816–18, *BA* III, pp. 232f.), he advanced the theory that 'there are only three genuine natural forms of poetry: straightforward narrative, impassioned depiction and personal action: epic, lyric and dramatic'. This view, as Goethe well knew, was anything but novel, and inevitably directed the discussion several aeons behind European developments. Taking this into account, although his essay is barely two pages long, he added Homer's epics to his argument. Yet given our present-day knowledge of human evolution and anthropo-sociogenesis, and our new theories of the origins of man's aesthetic faculties (summarized by the present author in Knepler 1988), we are not only able but obliged to take up mimetic communication, which is as old as humanity itself. Mimetic performances and all that they involve – rhythmically regulated movement, impersonation, disguise, utterances of all kinds – are designed to elevate man above his daily surroundings to exactly the same extent that they are rooted in those surroundings. Epic poetry, lyric poetry, drama and music all obey a single formula: they all stand above the everyday in order to make pronouncements upon it.

Provided we leave this vast historical dimension open-ended and keep present in our eyes, ears and minds not only the points in common between language and music but also their differences, it is revealing to apply Goethe's argument to Mozart's music. (It goes without saying that we will not be focusing on the genesis or foundations of music.)

Goethe has his essay culminate in the sage counsel to search for 'classical exemplars' (*Musterstücke*) in which 'each element separately predominates', and other instances that 'tend to one direction or the other until all three ultimately seem to unite'. If we follow his advice we will certainly have no difficulties with the second of his natural forms. Lyrical elements abound in Mozart's instrumental slow movements and opera arias. In this respect the difference between Mozart and earlier, contemporary and later composers is at most qualitative. And he remained true to the lyrical to his dying day.

It is a striking fact that lyric vocal pieces make do with few words, often no more than four lines of verse. Once the opening word of Konstanze's second aria, 'Traurigkeit' ('sadness'), had been uttered, little more was needed to stir the composer's imagination. To be sure, 'an able poet, that true phoenix' (13 October 1781) may be on hand to provide further poetic felicities such as the lovely image (discussed on pp. 220–1) of the zephyr wafting back the lover's plaints. This may give the composer additional stimuli, perhaps provoking him to apply techniques of imitation. As a rule, though, lyricism in music relies primarily on biotic elements, many of which only achieve their effect on a large scale, whether by repetition or by developmental elaboration. Expressive phrases may recur again and again; accompaniment figures, whether quiet or 'impassioned', fill out time and space; sustained notes resound through the texture either softly, urging alertness, or threateningly. The uninhibited outburst of joy or lamentation is the very source of musical lyricism.

In the works of his youth and early manhood, particularly in his opera seria arias, Mozart often clung to the tripartite form with contrasting central section that was traditional for lyrical pieces. But as he matured, he distanced himself from this convention, too. As lyricism favours a constant and unimpeded flow, a lack of contrast in the words may be welcome. While working on *Idomeneo*, the first opera that the young composer approached conceptually and critically, he came to the conclusion that 'strained or unusual words are never fitting in a pleasant aria' (5 December 1780). The implication, mentioned in the same letter, is that preference should be given to single-section arias. Simple lied forms might even be the most appropriate. In the event, however, this development was counteracted by another, namely Mozart's urge to incorporate his arias into the action. At this point we leave the domain of the purely lyrical, and other demands begin to rear their heads.

Narrative form, too, is relevant to opera. Opera cannot do entirely without messages or accounts of events that take place off stage or before the rise of the curtain. As we know, singspiel handles epic demands differently from other forms of music theatre by including spoken dialogue, and even monologues. For a while Mozart took a lively interest in the so-called melodrama – he called it 'duodrama' (12 November 1778) or 'monodrama' – in which the orchestra responds to spoken passages with interpolations 'in the manner of obbligato recitative' (*ibid.*). But after *Zaide*, K344, of 1779 he wrote nothing more in this genre, probably because the alternation between spoken text and short instrumental passages offered neither words nor music an opportunity for genuine development, the less so as the spoken passages were delivered by opera singers, who are usually ill-equipped to handle them.

The preferred narrative form of eighteenth-century opera was recitative in both its variants: *recitativo secco* (from the Italian word for 'dry', i.e. accompanied solely by a keyboard instrument with cello and/or bass), and *recitativo accompagnato* or *obbligato* (accompanied by the orchestra). Wherever genuine narrative or reportage occurs it must necessarily differ from the lyrical in its handling of the relation between music and text. Not only must the words stand out, there are generally a good many of them, and music must concentrate largely on its logogenic options and underplay its other possibilities. We can see this most clearly in the way ancient epic poems are recited, as is still done in many parts of the world. When they are sung, or when the manner of delivery approaches song, the music consists of a stereotype formula repeated dozens, even hundreds of times, often interrupted by a second formula to mark points of articulation. This second formula can even be given to instruments, thereby creating a sort of strophic form.

Secco recitative inherited some of the musical spareness of ancient epic poetry. Even in Mozart's hands it satisfies its musical requirements merely by approximating the speech-melody of the words as spoken and negotiating the necessary modulations, thereby functioning as a connecting link between the opera's numbers. Deadline pressures forced Mozart to entrust the recitatives of *La clemenza di Tito* to that 'court jester' (?June 1791), 'Snai' (24 or 25 June 1791) and 'idiotic oaf' (2 July 1791), Süssmayr. But no pressure could have been great enough for him to subcontract even the briefest aria so long as he was still able to hold pen in hand.

Because recitative resembles colloquial speech, the eighteenth century perceived and referred to it as musical prose. This is not surprising: even when opera librettos were written in verse, as were Da Ponte's, the composer could dispense entirely with regular four- and eight-bar periods, or with what Heinrich Besseler referred to as 'correspondence melody' (1954), once he had resolved to set a particular passage in secco recitative. The spareness mentioned above likewise added to the prose-like character of recitative: the listener might almost forget that he was dealing with an art form at all.

Carl Dahlhaus and Hermann Danuser have demonstrated just how complex and contradictory are the interrelations between what is considered poetic in music and what is considered prose. Rhythm, harmony, and the accentuation of the beats in a bar, as Dahlhaus rightly maintains (1978, pp. 139f.), cannot be viewed in isolation. Even when Mozart writes a seemingly regular eight-bar period its subdivisions may prove on closer scrutiny to be irregular, and thus closer to colloquial speech. Danuser (1978) claims that we must view two contrary processes in combination: a 'prosification' of regular periodic structure, and a 'poeticization' of elements originally akin to prose. If we consider all music to be a product of man's mimetic communication the distinction between prose and poetry in music becomes purely quantitative. Even the driest of recitative, which is 'by nature' closest to colloquial speech, has enough elements which are completely alien to everyday life: fixed pitches for the voice, underlying metrical divisions, modulatory schemes, the support of musical instruments.

Just how appropriate recitative was thought to be as a vehicle for narration becomes apparent when we consider the Terzetto, No. 7 from *Le nozze di Figaro*. As a whole, let us recall, this is a dramatic number. The Count discovers Cherubino cowering in Susanna's armchair while Susanna and Basilio look on. But first he relates how he had already caught the page earlier that same day. As Susanna and Basilio, though for different motives, want to know when, where and how this happened, it pleases the Count to distract attention from his own escapades by recounting Cherubino's, and he launches into a narrative. This calls forth a recitative in the midst of an otherwise dramatic piece of music:

Example 68

But as Goethe points out – and emphasizes – straightforward narration may incline toward the other two natural forms. He chooses the following example:

Yet listen to the modern impromptu speaker in public market places as he treats a subject from history. For the sake of clarity he will first narrate; then, to kindle interest, he will speak as an historical agent; finally he will wax ecstatic in order to transfix his audience. So curiously interwoven are these elements, and so infinitely varied the poetic modes, that it is difficult to establish an order in which they can be placed next to or behind one another.

Mozart's handling of recitative confirms this observation. Since he tends to incline even reports and narration toward the dramatic we seldom find, in his music, straightforward narrative comparable to the messenger's announcements in Greek drama. We are far more likely to encounter dialogues that quickly flow into self-contained dramatic numbers. The passage of recitative in which Susanna explains to Figaro why she does not want to move into the room vacated by the Count merges almost imperceptibly, *attacca*, into the Duettino, No. 2, in which they continue a dialogue that might otherwise have remained in recitative. Here, as everywhere else in his mature works, Mozart gives precedence to self-contained numbers. He even finds opportunities to make the ordinarily barren secco recitative musically and conceptually more fertile. We need only think of the unforgettable role of the bass in the recitative preceding Figaro's Cavatina (No. 3).

(A delightful play on the diminutive in the first scene between Susanna and Figaro should not be overlooked. In the recitative between their two duets Susanna refers to her fiancé, with a combination of tenderness and pity for his dull-wittedness, as 'caro il mio Figaretto', an expression rendered in English, weakly, by 'my dear little Figarolet' or something similar. In No. 2, this time certainly not from tenderness, she uses a similar diminutive, 'il caro Contino', in reference to the Count, whom Figaro up to then has only spoken of as 'Conte' or 'padrone'. Not until the Cavatina, when he resolves to strike up a dance with Almaviva, does Figaro finally bring himself to use the diminutive title 'signor Contino'.)

In the recitative immediately preceding the Cavatina Figaro might be said to be conducting a conversation with himself. The instrumental bass serves as his interlocutor, partly by almost exactly duplicating the vocal part (bar 44), partly by giving Figaro's words a non-verbal continuation (bars 46–7), and on one occasion by an unexpected outburst of emotion (bar 51). When the name 'Susanna' appears, Mozart sticks faithfully to the libretto by putting two or three dots after the word in his score, as he often does in his letters when he is unable or unwilling to say more (see Plate 13b), and giving a legato phrase to the cello:

Example 69

What we have here is an intermediate form between dry and accompanied recitative.

The latter, to use Goethe's terminology, distinctly tends toward 'impassioned depiction' and the dramatic. It is no coincidence that Mozart, in his handwritten catalogue of works, often indicates when an aria is preceded by an accompanied recitative, many of which are among his most profound inspirations. One example is the superb self-contained number of sixty-nine bars in which Donna Anna recognizes Giovanni as the man who stole into her room and murdered her father. The orchestral interpolations make do with two elements – a rhythmically agitated motif marked *allegro assai*:

Example 70

and another in placid quavers as Ottavio attempts to console the frenzied woman or as she takes control of herself:

Example 71

There are no fewer than seven changes of tempo, some of them sudden, some gradual, and no fewer than nine modulations to new keys, many of them almost violent. Moreover, Anna begins her tale of

Giovanni's forced entry into her room in the very rare key (for Mozart) of E flat minor:

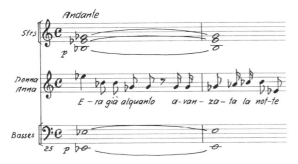

Example 72

What most merits our attention, though, is the way Mozart marshals the potential of symphonic writing in order to expand the dramatic function of music. Nor has this close congruity between stage action and symphonic technique been ignored in the Mozart literature. Abert drew attention to it as early as 1919 (I, pp. 416, 646, 922 and passim). In 1954 Hans Engel studied the manner in which formative properties of the symphony found their way into Mozart's opera finales. Charles Rosen (1971, p. 289) alerts us to the enthusiasm felt by Mozart as a young man when he 'discovered that music on the stage can do more than meet the requirements of singers or express sentiment, but can become one with plot and intrigue as well', and that 'the classical style moves with the least strain in its depiction of comic intrigue and comic gesture'. I have already mentioned the commendable attempt by an American authoress (see p. 172) to discover 'rhythmic gestures' in Mozart's music, namely the elementary forms of dance and march. Similarly, Stefan Kunze (1984, pp. 244f.) sees a 'common denominator between dance and theatre'. All of these considerations, I would suggest, should be enlarged in scope as deep and as far back in history as our knowledge will allow. In mimetic ceremonies, all those strands which later evolved over millennia into the separate arts (more or less independently of each other) originally worked together as an undifferentiated whole.

But to return to the more recent and tangible past, Mozart too stood in a familiar tradition. Opéra comique, opera buffa and singspiel had begun long before to import symphonic techniques into the opera orchestra. Repeated motifs were used as an instrumental background for the vocal parts; orchestral crescendi prepared the way for dramatic climaxes; there were even hints of developmental variation in the portrayal of conflicts; and more besides. Mozart, however, went far beyond this.

Mozart's music is always analogous to language of a particular kind – poetry. 'Verses are indeed the most indispensable element for music' (13 October 1781). Hence, his music is metrically structured, providing a grid in which not only the sung words but every element in the piece finds its place. But they do so in contradictory ways. Allanbrook was certainly correct to claim that Mozart's very choice of metre and tempo, associated as they were with familiar dance, march and other musical forms (in Mozart's case we must not overlook church music), points the listener in a particular direction, sets a mood, kindles expectations. These latter may either be satisfied, or they may be deceived, frustrated or led astray in the most various ways. In Chapter 22 we shall see how this can happen, taking the march from *Figaro* as our example.

Mozart has no difficulty incorporating externals of the plot in his opera scores by simply adopting the technique of imitation. We hear the approaching steps of characters making their entrance, the make-believe pain in Figaro's ankle following his alleged leap from the window, the approach of the serpent which threatens Tamino, and countless other examples of this sort. But they would hardly suffice if his music did not have more to offer. For Mozart's opera scores also have at their disposal the inexhaustible repertoire of biotic methods. Some of these we have already discussed in the chapter on Zerlina, and we will continue to encounter them every step of the way. It is they that largely provide the crucial aspects of art; they give human beings an inkling of how to live.

Goethe's essay – to return to it one final time – puts an equal if not greater stress on the union of the three forms of poetry than on their separation. 'In the briefest of poems', he writes, 'one often finds them side by side, and it is this very union within the narrowest of confines that brings forth the most splendid creations.' After pointing to ballads and Greek drama Goethe then continues: 'In French tragedy the exposition is epic, the central section is dramatic, and the fifth act, with its passionate and ecstatic denouement, might be called lyric.' Shakespeare's *Merchant of Venice*, it might parenthetically be mentioned, follows exactly this same pattern. This pattern, however, is foreign to Mozart. Even so, it is the 'union of the three natural forms within the narrowest of confines' that constitutes the magic formula underlying his mature operas.

The way this is accomplished can be observed in the incomparable Sextet, No. 19 from *Le nozze di Figaro*. It has no lack of surprising turns of event, although Marcellina's discovery that Figaro is her and Bartolo's son takes place in secco recitative prior to the number itself.

The object of the sextet is to portray the contradictory impact of this new family arrangement on those involved. It opens with a short lyric effusion by the three major participants (bars 1 to 12). This is a piece *à la gavotte* (Allanbrook 1983, pp. 135 and 352) which places the parents in an old-fashioned and straight-laced but by no means unsympathetic light. Mozart's happy choice of this basic mood, so amiable yet slightly detached, explains why we have such difficulty knowing for certain whether the tears that spring to our eyes result from emotion, the comedy of the situation, or joy at the unexpected resolution:

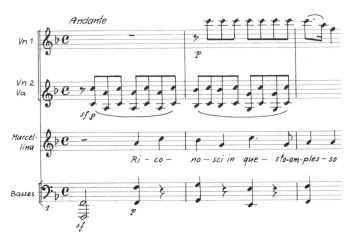

Example 73

This basic mood is left unchanged by the garrulous quavers of the disappointed Count and his bribed magistrate (bars 13–16), which are integrated with the other voices to form a gently disturbing background (bars 17–23):

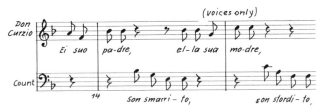

Example 74

They are interrupted by Susanna in bars 24 to 32 as she produces a thousand doubloons (or ducats or pieces-of-eight or whatever else *doppie* might be) so as to release Figaro from his promise to marry Marcellina. Here we are indeed dealing with forms within the 'narrowest of confines'. First there is Susanna's announcement, unmistakably a narrative. Then comes the comically affecting family bliss, mingled with the mumbled protestations of the Count and Don Curzio. Indeed, Susanna's announcement, introduced in the dominant like the second theme of a symphonic movement, is set in a style approaching recitative, with soft, sustained chords in the strings. Every word is meant to be clearly audible:

Example 75

But what just a few moments ago would have been a crucial item of news now passes unnoticed. The comedy of this scene resides in the fact that the billings and cooings of three of the characters, and the grumblings of the other two, continue as if nothing had happened (bars 33–9). At this point the music becomes dramatic, in a technical sense of the term as well (bars 40–7). Susanna and Figaro collide; she showers him with reproaches and will hear none of his explanations (see Example 76 on following page). But this does not last long (mm. 43–6), and even the slap that Figaro is made to suffer six bars later takes place against an undulating lyricism and the consolatory sound of two oboes, sustained for eight bars. The orchestra, representing the other characters and the audience, all of whom know that the confusions are about to be unravelled, hardly takes notice of Susanna and her outburst. This is a remarkable passage. An inconspicuous little motif, which, in numerous variants, nonetheless typifies the music of *Figaro* as a whole, is associated with Susanna in a very particular manner, as we shall see later. Now a variant of this motif is taken up twenty times by the orchestra (bars 48–65). But Susanna apparently

Example 76

does not hear it; in any event it does not calm her, and she remains beside herself with rage. Instead, as is only fitting, she finds herself in league with the very character who is otherwise her antagonist – the Count, whose words and music she now mimics:

Example 77

It is only logical that Marcellina should be the one to save the situation. She walks up to Susanna, embraces her and explains how things stand. It is no accident, and by no means extraneous to the musical design, that Marcellina's conciliatory music (bars 72–4) should adopt the character of a transition to the recapitulation, moving from a dominant C major to the tonic key of F major, and that her explanations should function as the recapitulation. Her opening theme resounds in the wind in three octaves:

Example 78

while she, in counterpoint with her own theme, explains to Susanna that her erstwhile rival is now her mother-in-law. There follows that well-known passage, one of the greatest scenes in the world's dramatic literature, in which Susanna, unable to believe her ears, has Marcellina's words separately verified by every character on stage. The same game is then repeated for Bartolo's paternity. It is the merriest and most congenial form imaginable of what is known in the theory of drama as stichomythia.

Now is the moment for lyricism to make an appearance (bars 101–40). It does so *sotto voce* in the voices, and *piano* or *pianissimo* in the instruments, with the Count and Don Curzio only able to remonstrate in the form of curt interjections (see Example 79 on following page). The four main characters now conclude the number as it began, in concord and harmony.

Not all conflicts are resolved so easily, and not every Mozart ensemble has such opportunities for comic development. But each of his ensembles, the heart and soul of his musical dramas, has its own manner of 'combining and juxtaposing' the epic, lyric and dramatic in rapid succession.

These are not products of chance. The eighteenth century was the century of motion. Nothing is more frequent in the writings of the Enlightenment than accounts and discussions of upheavals and revolution, in both the political and the general sense of the term. In the article 'Encyclopédie' for his magnum opus of the same title (1755,

Example 79

p. 157), Diderot, in a manner typical of its author, linked together the different areas of life and human activity: 'What changes occur daily in the language of the fine arts, in machinery, and in techniques of labour!' Even one of Mozart's letters contains the French word *motion* in an important connection (see pp. 293, 304).

In sum, we are dealing with a confluence of many sorts of knowledge, intuitive insights, familiarity with traditions, and insistence on innovation. First, Mozart correctly realized – or perhaps we should say sensed or guessed – that in the age of enlightenment and change the theatre was the right place to reach those masses of people who would ordinarily never open a book, newspaper or pamphlet. But, of course, it had to be an opera: opera was his 'great longing and passion' (14 February 1778); the mere thought that he might be commissioned to write an opera made his 'whole body seem to be on fire' and made him 'tremble from head to foot' (31 July 1778). In Paris he came to the firm realization that operas had to be structured differently from the ones he had written in his youth. And in Vienna, in a process that presumably cost him no small amount of effort, he learnt that the way to reach audiences was by choosing contemporary subjects. It was his own discovery, probably nurtured by the experiences listed above, that the multiple processes of music are ideal for creating a broad array of events on different levels – some of them conflicting, some taking place in a matter of seconds and changing as they do – and for bringing them to life on stage, together with their emotive values and the compliance of the audience.

It turns out, then, that the union of Goethe's three natural forms within the narrowest of confines, as carried out in music, cannot be understood in isolation. Rather, their union is linked to an achievement that was nothing less than epochal. The great problems of the age had reached a point at which the need to solve them, and the possibility of doing so, had entered general awareness. It was in this intellectual atmosphere that a great creative mind found, in the crucible of this awareness, the means of fashioning musical works of art of a new kind.

Chapter 18
Musical portraits

How did Mozart experience the links between the currents of his age and individual persons, himself as well as his family and friends? And how did he turn these experiences into music? These questions, though far from peripheral, have not yet been given the attention they deserve.

There is only one piece of music, the Andante from his Piano Sonata K309, of which Mozart himself claimed (6 December 1777) that it 'closely fits the character' of a particular person, meaning a person from real life rather than a fictional one. When he played it, the letter continues, the piece was an 'extraordinary success'. A junior colleague confirmed his impression: 'It is really a fact. She is exactly like the Andante.'

This 'she' was Rosina Theresia Petronella Cannabich, the daughter of Mozart's Mannheim friend and thirteen years old at the time, although Mozart thought she was fifteen (he was not quite twenty-three himself). In a letter of 6 December 1777 he described her as

> a very pretty and charming girl. She is very intelligent and steady for her age. She is serious, does not say much, but when she does speak she is pleasant and amiable.

For some time it was uncertain whether the piano sonata in question was K309 or K311. Since 1985 opinion has settled in favour of the former (*NMA* IX/25/1, pp. xiiff.). Before then Alan Tyson (1987, p. 29), the doyen of Mozart autograph studies, wrote that 'to attempt to assess which movement corresponds more closely to Mlle Cannabich's character is certainly an unusual dating technique!' Tyson is, unfortunately, quite right: the art of identifying particular characters in pieces of music, even when the composer tells us his intentions, is not highly developed.

The Andante has an unusual design, being half in tripartite lied form and half a set of variations. The theme consists of sixteen bars in two eight-bar phrases; the first has a half-close on the dominant while the second varies the first by reinforcing the tonic. The same thing happens the second time round, except that the melody is richly decorated. Then comes a middle section which sets out solidly in the dominant C major. It, too, has a middle section, which is yet another variation of the same eight-bar phrase of the opening. When C major returns the left hand is likewise given a rich figuration that must have caused little Rosina many hours of practice since, as Mozart discovered (14 November 1777), 'her left hand, unfortunately, is completely ruined'. Following this thirty-two-bar middle section we return as expected to the first theme – or, more precisely, to its second half, also with figurations. And since the coda gives yet another variation of the opening half-period, we hear it, varied and decorated, a total of seven times.

Equally striking are the dynamics. Though clearly indicated, they are not always immediately intelligible. As Nannerl commented: 'The Andante requires indeed great concentration and neatness [*Nettigkeit*] in playing' (8 December 1777). Here we should bear in mind that in Austrian dialect *Nettigkeit* means, roughly, orderliness and exactitude. The very first four bars have no fewer than eight dynamic markings:

Example 80

Unusually, only the three notes linking the first half of the theme to the second (both marked *piano*) are to be played *forte*:

Example 81

Equally unusual is the *pianissimo* link at the end of the theme:

Example 82

The sonata is 'strange', remarked Leopold Mozart (11 December 1777), adding a question mark that leaves us in the dark as to whether he meant to question the work or his opinion of it. 'It has something in it of the *mannered* Mannheim taste', he chided, only to end on a conciliatory note: 'but so very little that your own good style is not spoilt thereby'. He had, of course, noticed that despite its *Manieren* (ornaments) the Andante is carefully structured.

This sonata, together with its Andante, stands at the crossroads of several historical trends which have been explored in particular by Heinrich Besseler. One of these is the emergence of the 'instrumental character theme' (1951, p. 347), whose 'variety of contrast' (1958, p. 448) is made to cohere by a 'uniform progression' (1951, p. 337). Another is the appearance of the concept of 'musical character' (1954, p. 97, and 1958, p. 447). This concept is not only theoretical; it also has a practical, compositional aspect that eventually gave rise to a vast number of character pieces.

It is useful to add a psychological slant to these various theoretical and compositional aspects. Mozart expressed himself very precisely on this point: he clearly stated that he wrote the sonata to fit the character of a particular person of his acquaintance. Later, while discussing his music for Osmin (26 September 1781), he revealed that he applied a specific compositional device – what we would today call a mediant shift – to express a particular state of mind, namely, a fit of anger. Both instances undercut the common claim that Mozart composed his music without reference to reality. In fact, Mozart the shrewd observer and Mozart the musical inventor are one and the same person. This leads us to several conclusions with important consequences for a theory of music.

Rosina Theresia Petronella was not the only person in Mozart's surroundings whose character he attempted to portray musically according to the taste of his time. The method he applied here is, in principle, no different from those he used to create his operatic characters, apart from the fact that the latter are given words as well. Even without a model along the lines of Rosina Theresia, the result may be a character piece. Music is not firmly attached to a particular object. It can also draw on stored experiences.

As far as the Andante from K309 is concerned, Mozart captured what he considered the 'pleasant and amiable' side of this pretty girl in his theme, as he often did without directly referring to a specific person. The fact that he repeated the mood-setting half-period seven times, merely altering its figuration, is perfectly in keeping with the steadiness and consistency he saw in the girl's character. Mozart was fully capable of rendering contradictory and split personalities in music by means of unexpected turns of phrase and outbursts. We need only think of Osmin or, in an entirely different vein, of Leporello. But not even Rosina is without her surprises. The capricious dynamics are proof enough that Mozart viewed her as something more than a meek little lamb. True, the surprises remain within bounds, but they are still there. Even the energetic middle section:

Example 83

shows Rosina from an angle other than the her 'pleasant and amiable' side.

Another unique and unduplicatable piece has unfortunately only survived in a very fragmentary state. Only once in his life did Mozart compose a stage appearance for himself – and what a role he took! In the pantomime which he conceived, composed and performed (with others) for the Carnival festivities of 1783 he cast himself as none other than Harlequin. We have already looked at this piece on pages 8–9; all that survives of it are two violin parts, the first a sketch, the second a finished version, sections of which have disappeared. Mozart's music for the 1783 Carnival season was not one of his mightiest creations. This is evident even though many details were lost with the disappearance of the other parts for the presumably small instrumental setting. Nonetheless, it is interesting to note the amount of agility and caprice in Mozart's conception of himself as Harlequin:

Example 84

By bar 9 it is already time for an Adagio:

Example 85

which, however, returns to the Allegro a mere six bars later. There is certainly no shortage of contrasts, least of all in the character of Harlequin.

Even if Mozart never again appeared in one of his own works, there can be little doubt that traits of his own personality can be found in many of his stage characters, if not before then during his Vienna period. Great dramatists, it would seem, can proceed in no other way. Mozart did not need to state – at least he never did so in writing – that he identified with Figaro. Yet both have the same station in life, the same troubles, and the same way of dealing with them. As a couple, Susanna and Figaro are conceived musically in a manner completely different from any other of his leading characters. (We will have more to say of this in Chapter 22.) But we must also consider the possibility that parts of Mozart's personality entered figures with whom he had less in common than with Figaretto. Sarastro comes to mind, or Papageno, or the Count, perhaps even Leporello. Nor is it absurd to assume that we might find one or another trait of Mozart's personality scattered among his female characters.

These problems appear at their knottiest in those figures which are presented negatively in the plot, stage situation or musical setting. Consider how well Mozart knew the words which Da Ponte gave to Don Giovanni, and how seriously he took them:

Senza alcun ordine
la danza sia,

Let the dancing be
without any order,

chi'l menuetto,	have some dance the minuet,
chi la follia	others the folía
chi l'alemanna farai ballar.	and others the allemande.

True, Mozart did not compose this scene 'without any order'. But he followed Giovanni's instructions to Leporello to the letter by having the assembled guests perform three dances at once. This suggests, even if it does not prove, that Mozart may also have detected in Giovanni's other requests and commands some secret desires of his own – certainly not in his lack of scruples or his contempt for women (and men), but perhaps in his unbridled sensuality.

Mozart commentators have often wondered how to interpret the paean to freedom 'Viva la libertà!' which Giovanni strikes up in the finale of Act I, followed by all the on-stage characters and the orchestra, with trumpets and kettledrums in a radiant C major for thirty-two bars (371–403). Interpreting the scene, we must recognize that the significance accorded to these words by the various fictitious characters, the effect of their words on the other characters, and the reaction of the various groups in the Prague audience of 1787 or the Vienna audience of 1788 do not coincide.

I have reasons to assume (the most important of these is set aside for Chapter 20) that the figure Mozart identified with most strongly in *Die Entführung* was Pedrillo rather than Belmonte. Whenever Mozart applied a special compositional device in one piece only, we can be certain that the number has been singled out for special meaning. Pedrillo's Romance, No. 18, is a piece of this sort. Never before and never again did Mozart write a piece which within a mere seventeen bars (the full length of the Romance) reaches no fewer than seven keys – B minor, D major, A major, C major, G major, F sharp minor and F sharp major – six of them with full cadences and one (C major) by means of one of those same mediant shifts used to portray Osmin's rage. Further, the piece is also unique for being, basically, without a main key. Its ritornello begins in B minor while the voice – and remember that we are dealing with a vocal number – never once touches this key, beginning instead in D major and ending in F sharp major. Nor does the number even end in B minor, the only key that might possibly qualify as the tonic. In fact, it does not actually end at all. Instead, it simply stops after Pedrillo has sung his four stanzas and spoken his interludes and postlude to the ritornellos, but without cadencing in D major. Did Mozart, who otherwise planted his music so firmly and securely in the mother earth of tonal harmony, wish to depict Pedrillo's uprootedness and distance from home – and perhaps his own as well?

Similarly, third parties may also have found their way into the composer's imaginative world, as in the following case. In May and June of 1781 Mozart had been expelled from the Archbishop's service with a brutality that left permanent scars on his psyche. The words that flew about triggered his musical imagination. Three times in a row he quotes the words of the Archbishop in letters to his father, as if writing a protocol. 'There is the door ... I will have nothing more to do with such a miserable wretch'. Thus reads his first letter on the subject (9 May 1781), the same letter in which he exclaimed: 'I hate the Archbishop to the point of madness.' A mere three days later he quotes the Archbishop's outburst twice again within the space of a few lines: 'Clear out!' A month later he speaks bitterly of the second expulsion, this time by Count Arco, who 'hurled me out of the room and gave me a kick up the arse'. The letter is dated 13 June. In July Mozart started work on *Die Entführung*.

Given the profusion of letters in which Mozart bares his soul to his father, we are in the fortunate position of being able to watch his artistic imagination at work. Among other things, we note that a process of artistic transformation or distillation took place, or whatever else we might want to call the following sequence of events. Many qualities of these two very real figures – the Archbishop who humiliated and cursed his young Kapellmeister, and the Lord Steward who threw him out of the house of the Teutonic Knights (today Singerstrasse No. 7 in Vienna) – were transplanted to the fictional figure of the malicious overseer in the seraglio. This becomes plain to see when we place the invective Mozart invented for his employers alongside that for the fictitious Osmin:

The Archbishop or Count Arco as described in Mozart's letters of April to June 1781:	Osmin as portrayed in his letters of September to October of that year:
Erzlümmel (arch-rascal), 101	grober Flegel (coarse booby), 163
Menschenfeind (misanthrope), 105	Erzfeind von allem fremden (arch-enemy of everything different), 162
zornig (furious), 111	zornig, 162
dumm, Sottise, Dummheit (stupid, stupidity), 110, 114, 125	dumm, 167
grob (coarse), 126	grob, 163, 167
impertinent, 110, 114	impertinent, 163

One thing is certain: the hatred kindled in the young composer by his recent experiences has been projected onto the figure of Osmin. This was a step away from Mozart's conventional negative figures – the one in the nine-year-old composer's *Perfido* aria, for instance (see pp. 10–11), or the hard-hearted sultan of *Zaide* – toward those tinged with political reality in his later operas. Osmin, then, bears traits of real and living persons, but without lessening his general validity as a stage figure. On the contrary, the volatile unpredictability that makes Osmin so dangerous, his unexpected eruptions of malice, doubtless closely observed by Mozart in living persons and transformed into notes, make Osmin's music suitable material for pieces on a higher level of abstraction. We will encounter Osmin again in Mozart's instrumental music.

To conclude our discussion we shall draw on a piece of instrumental music which was probably, though final proof is lacking, intended as a musical portrait: the Adagio in B minor for piano, K540, a piece which Mozart scholars have frequently referred to as mysterious and enigmatic.

To begin with, the piece is not exactly 'in B minor': it ends – at first hesitantly, then almost exuberantly – in B *major*. This alone places it in the category of Mozart's unique creations. As often as he otherwise touches on this key, even settling there in the middle sections of pieces in other keys, there is no other work by Mozart that ends in B major. We are dealing with a completely worked out sonata form. Its first theme is modelled after a *Kyrie eleison*:

Example 86

while the second, accordingly, would seem to intimate a *Christe eleison*:

Example 87

This suggests that the Adagio may have been patterned after a church sonata. Mozart contributed several pieces to this genre during his years in Salzburg, all of them in sonata form, but none of them in the minor or adagio.

The Adagio is earnest, almost tragic in character. It has a melodic style remarkably similar to two wordless canons (K229 and K230) that Mozart had composed years earlier, perhaps in 1782. These pieces, given here with words by the German poet Hölty, begin as follows:

Examples 88a and 88b

Albert Dunning, the editor of the volume of canons for the New Mozart Edition (*NMA* III/10, p. xvi), maintains that these contrafacta texts were popular

> because they closely matched the musical character of these canons. We need only mention the text given to the chromatic descending fourth at the opening of K229. This interval embodied a figure from early baroque compositional theory (*passus duriusculus*) that had long established itself in the musical imagination as a vehicle for musical threnody.

In the *musica poetica* of the baroque period, the *passus duriusculus* (Latin for 'somewhat difficult step') was felt to express lamentation. Accordingly, Mozart's publishers selected for it the words 'Sie ist dahin' ('She is gone') from Hölty's *Elegie auf eine Nachtigall*. Threnody is the ancient Greek word for a dirge or funeral ode. In our Adagio the chromatic descending fourth occurs several times:

Examples 89a and 89b

No less remarkable is the melodic connection between the opening of the piece and the beginning of K230, which was given the words 'Selig alle sie, die im Herrn entschliefen!' ('Blessed those who passed away in the Lord') from Hölty's *Elegie beim Grabe meines Vaters*, an elegy at the grave of the poet's father. Interestingly, when Franz Mozart composed a festival chorus for the unveiling of a monument to his father, he used this piece as a slow middle section.

As already observed the Adagio is serious and tragic, apart from its final six bars. There are frequent *sforzati*, as in the theme itself, and frequent contrasts of forte and piano. Harsh dissonances occur:

Example 90

and the development section modulates in a mere thirteen bars through six keys, at times with unexpected boldness. If Mozart intended that this remarkable piece 'closely fit the character' of a particular person, that person was certainly no Rosina Cannabich.

When dealing with sonata movements in the minor mode it is always useful to note whether the composer 'sticks to his guns'. If the second theme appears in the relative major, the recapitulation presents him with two options. Either he can choose the strict procedure where the second theme follows custom by appearing in the tonic (and hence in the minor), in which key the piece then comes to a close. Or he can relent, as Mozart and Haydn often do, and have the second theme, and thereby the piece, end in major. The Adagio, however, is especially remarkable in that Mozart takes *both* options, first ending the piece strictly in the minor mode and then appending its unique six-bar coda.

The coda begins with the descending fourth given in Example 89b. In this way it arrives at the dominant, where it remains, undecided, for half a bar. The process is then repeated, this time with the interval expanded to form a chromatic descending minor sixth. There follows yet another repetition, in which the descending sixth is pianistically embroidered and the final minim (marked with a cross in Example 89b) is subdivided into four quavers. The final resolution to B major is thus postponed and yet, at the same time, made to seem inevitable:

Example 91

Now let us turn to the extra-musical evidence. On 2 June 1787 Mozart responded to the news of his father's death by sending a letter to his sister. In matters which touched him deeply he was not one to write at length. This gives special weight to his remark 'as our loss is equally great': only Nannerl and he could know what the deceased man had once meant to them. A short while later he promised his sister some 'new things from me for the clavier' (1 August 1787). However, a year was to pass before he posted these pieces (2 August 1788), remarking: 'This, I hope, will make everything all right again'. Almost certainly they included the Adagio, which was entered in his handwritten catalogue on 19 March 1788. I assume, therefore, that K540 was written in mourning at Leopold's death.

It fits our picture of Mozart's thought and action that he should silently dedicate a piece of music to the memory of his father and allow it to be performed by his sister, the only other person to suffer the same loss as he. Its unmistakable proximity to church music is likewise part of Leopold's legacy: this was an area in which their views most frequently coincided. The only works by Leopold that Mozart requested for performance purposes were pieces of church music. If we further assume that the Adagio, like the Mannheim sonata K309 and many other works, was written to capture the character of its dedicatee, we have little difficulty in retracing its concept. A 'close likeness' is only one of the factors we may expect to find. Music never merely clings to an object, no matter how closely it may approximate or even resemble that object. As Goethe would have put it (see p. 164), music has neither the intention nor the capacity to produce a 'second Bello'. The subjective force of the composer's mind permeates, shapes, and largely determines the object of representation. Seen in this light, Mozart's enigmatic piece in B minor/major turns out to be a character study of a stern, serious-minded man lacking gentler traits no less than unexpected outbursts of emotion, a man with harsh, puzzling qualities that combine to form an absorbing and rounded portrait. The composer senses and creates a character of coherence, consistency and unity, but he does so with the eyes of filial love, undimmed by the estrangement that came between them. And then the six-bar coda with its major mode – hesitantly achieved, luxuriously caressed, continually reconfirmed. This major mode goes beyond the portrait of Leopold and merges with that of Wolfgang. It is part of the concept of this marvellous piece of music that it never tells us who relents, who forgives, and who reconciles himself with whom.

Chapter 19

How opera was dramatized by the symphony

At Mozart's request, we may recall, an ensemble number was added to *Die Entführung* – the Quartet, No. 16, which he then turned into the first large-scale model of his new operatic world. Made up of eight sections differing greatly in tempo and key, it also exemplifies the interplay, discussed in Chapter 17, of narrative, lyric and dramatic forms within a small compass. First, while Konstanze and Belmonte protest how dearly they have longed for this day of their reunion, Pedrillo and Blonde exchange instructions for the hour of liberation until finally all four voices unite in a lyric effusion of anticipated joy. In the next section the men falteringly doubt the faithfulness of their ladies – and are brusquely rebuffed in turn. Then begins a short scene which merits closer attention.

It occupies a mere twenty-and-a-half bars, all in *allegro assai*, and takes no more than forty seconds to perform. The first thing that strikes us is how quickly the music modulates, landing with full cadences in D minor, C minor, B flat major and G minor within the space of a few bars. The modulatory passages last no longer than one-and-a-half bars each, and each complex of keys no more than three-and-a-half to five bars. No key remains in the ear for longer than ten seconds. In the entire opera only the overture and Pedrillo's Romance, No. 18, change harmonies as rapidly as this. The final section of the Quartet, for instance, remains in the tonic key of D major for its entire duration of over 100 bars, lasting nearly two minutes, almost twelve times as long as any key in our scene. The harmonic mobility is matched by the movement that has entered the events on stage. Till now, Belmonte has stood next to Konstanze, and Pedrillo next to Blonde. Now, however, the women put their heads together while the men reassure one another that they are cured of their jealousy. Each of the four entries is accompanied by a stage direction: Blonde speaks to Konstanze, Konstanze to Blonde, Pedrillo holds his cheek (he has just been enlightened with a slap) and Belmonte speaks to Pedrillo. All four must change position on the stage, and this walking about accords with the internal movement in the music until a moment of catharsis (in Aristotle's sense of the term) is reached in which jealousy and displeasure are forgotten.

Movement, meaning the ordering of time, is a property of all music, even of the slowest. (We may assume that what is felt to be fast or slow in music depends on the number of events – melodic, harmonic, rhythmic and timbral – that take place between two human heartbeats.) Rapid movement can be made a musical sign for unrest, bustle, mobility. It may even signify labour, as becomes clear in an example from *Die Zauberflöte*.

Having arrived in Sarastro's realm, Tamino asks:

> Wo bin ich nun? – Was wird mit mir?
> Ist dies der Sitz der Götter hier? -
> Doch zeigen die Pforten – es zeigen die Säulen,
> Dass Klugheit, und Arbeit, und Künste hier weilen.

> (Where am I now? what is my fate?
> Is this the dwelling place of the gods?
> Yet the gateway and columns tell me
> that Wisdom, and Labour, and Art reside here.)

Up to now we have been listening to accompanied recitative. In the next two lines, however,

> Wo Tätigkeit thronet und Müssiggang weicht,
> Erhält seine Herrschaft das Laster nicht leicht.

> (Where Diligence reigns and Idleness relents,
> Vice will not easily maintain its sway.)

the recitative gives way to an *allegro* passage typical of busy symphonic writing, with a leading melody, active bass, off-beat quavers in the strings and sustained notes in the bassoons:

Example 92

Human labour, performed on myriad occasions over the millennia, has left mimetic traces in music, and when music is meant to represent activity the orchestra has to 'work'. The same point can be demonstrated from the opposite direction. Haydn's lied 'Lob der Faulheit' ('In Praise of Idleness'), after a poem by Lessing, ironically reproduces the curious paradox that the object of its praises is at the same time an obstacle to their expression ('Yet I cannot sing thee, for thou dost prevent my doing so'). Several times the active figuration slows down or comes to a stop, and the piece ends, fittingly, at a point of minimum motion:

Example 93

Not so in our scene from *Die Entführung*. A single motif:

Example 94

alternates bar by bar between the first and second violins throughout the entire scene, twenty times. In the two modulatory passages the demisemiquaver figure appears twice in each bar, compounding the unrest:

Example 95

Then come the voices. In even crotchets they articulate a regularly structured four-bar theme outlining a progression of tonic-dominant-tonic:

Example 96

The theme retains its melodic contour and harmony in all four of its occurrences, but the sequence of pitches is altered, partly to satisfy the declamation, partly to depict the characters. In any event Pedrillo, and he alone, is given dotted crotchets with quavers, apparently to accommodate the iambic rhythms which are generally assigned to him elsewhere (e.g. in the Romance and some sections of his Aria, No. 13):

Example 97

Taken together, these devices strike a curious balance between regularity and irregularity. The theme of the vocal parts, as we have seen, retains its four-bar periodic structure. Yet the associated tonal regions are of different durations, being respectively four-and-a-half, four-and-a-half, five, and three-and-a-half bars long. The sustained notes – some entering in mid-modulation, others after the modulation has reached its goal – have still different durations: four-and-a-half, five-and-a-half, six, and three-and-a-half bars. And then, of course, there is the motif in the strings, constantly transposed to different registers. In sum, three elements – the theme, the string figure, and the sustained notes – overlap in rapid succession and ever-new variants, along with the rapid changes of harmony. The result is a kaleidoscope of new combinations which will not remain still for a second. The scene is vibrant with the same sort of energy we find in the development sections of symphonies. Indeed, this scene has the same position within the quartet as do symphonic development sections. They, too, appear at that juncture where conflicts are enacted before a resolution is brought about, whether in the recapitulation or, as here in the Quartet, in the quieter final sections.

The point is not that Mozart transferred to the opera the fixed techniques and forms of symphonic writing: they did not exist at the time. Nor did he infuse new symphonic life into fully-fledged operatic forms: these did not exist either, apart from the lied, aria and so-called '*couplet* finale'. What Mozart discovered in the process of composing was that there was, at that time, no procedure more suitable for depicting dramatic events than the then nascent instrumental style with its symphonic techniques. After *Die Entführung*, Mozart's symphonic writing (in the broadest understanding of the term) and his stage works evolved in parallel to previously unknown heights. And as Mozart scholarship – insofar as it deals knowledgeably with his music at all – generally treats genres separately or categorizes his works by genre rather than shedding light on their interaction, it stands little chance of doing justice to this problem.

Not that the problem has been ignored. In his two books on the classical style (1971, 1980) Charles Rosen, in particular, has richly documented not only the origins but also the evolutionary history of symphonic technique, including a discussion of opera. Just what sort of problems we face becomes clear when we consider one of Mozart's supreme achievements.

This is Scene No. 16.3, in B flat major, of the Act II Finale in *Figaro*. It begins at the point where the Count briefly leaves the stage in order to search Susanna's room for Cherubino, whom he suspects of hiding there. Abert (II, p. 328) considers this scene to be 'a completely free rondo'; Stefan Kunze (1984, p. 318) at least speaks of the 'action-based layout [*Aktionscharakter*] of the musical structure'; Arnold Schoenberg also gave some thought to this scene, stating that it contains 'an astonishingly great number of segments' with variations of 'five little phrases in constantly changing order' (Schoenberg 1975, p. 412). Two years later, though without referring to Schoenberg, Hans Engel (1954, p. 126) described the number as 'rather like a sonata-allegro form with development section and recapitulation'. This is exactly right. We are dealing with a unique instance in Mozart's work of a vocal-instrumental symphonic movement which, if the piece were not already so familiar, might be performed as a purely instrumental piece without noticeably differing from others of the kind.

Like so many of Mozart's themes, the principal theme of this scene is in conflict with itself. The fluttering violin quavers in the first four bars express the agitation of the Countess, while her halting delivery of its principal notes express the very breathlessness of which she speaks. Here the mimeogenic method and the logogenic are at cross-purposes (see Example 98 on page 212). The second four bars soothe the distraught Countess as Susanna points to the window through which Cherubino has escaped. Voice, violins and bassoon all share in a broadly arched melody (see Example 99 on page 212). Three mimeogenic *forte* hammer-blows now accompany the reappearance of the Count, who has searched the adjoining room in vain for his rival. This is a transitional section leading to the second theme, in which the

Example 98

Example 99

Count, logically enough, avails himself of the agitated motif of the Countess (see Example 100 on page 213). But he soon recovers his composure and, every inch a count, expounds the second theme: let no one ever again attempt such cruel pranks as he has just been made to suffer. But he gets no farther than that. If Susanna countered the agitation of the Countess, expressed in the first half of theme 1, with a

Example 100

soothing continuation, it is now both women who interrupt the Count halfway through the second theme. He has no claim to sympathy, they exclaim, singing in chattering quavers:

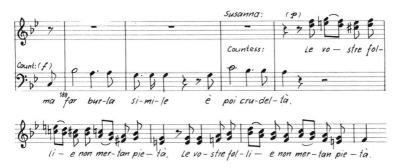

Example 101

Dramaturgically, we have reached a sort of stalemate: both parties have stated their positions, musically as well as verbally. Formally, we have arrived at the end of the so-called exposition: the two themes of the symphonic movement have been presented, the dominant key of F major attained. The so-called codetta that often occurs at this point, reinforcing the dominant and preparing the way for the development section, is heard here as well. To conclude the thirty-two-bar opening section of the piece, four bars in a gentle F major state Susanna's motif of reassurance while the Countess wards off the Count's protestations of love. Now comes the development, as we would call this section today (the term was used only for fugues in Mozart's time), in which the exposed themes and motifs are led through a wide range of keys, even passing from major to minor and vice versa. They are now varied, inverted, truncated, given new instrumental garb, combined with fresh motifs – in short, 'developed'. The extraordinary thing about it is that both types of processes – the one in the orchestra and the one on stage – dovetail as though it were the most natural thing in the world. Let us take a closer look at how they do this.

The Countess begins by playing her trump card: she is always being suspected of something. What could be more appropriate musically than to have her (only partly feigned) displeasure expressed by the second theme, the same one which the Count, just a few seconds earlier, had called upon in a vain attempt to prohibit such pranks. The Count takes up the second half of the theme, set in the minor mode to underscore his humiliation as he now seeks Susanna's assistance to calm his irate wife. The theme is also combined with a motif which, though rhythmically displaced, is otherwise – and probably by coincidence – identical to the beginning of the overture:

Example 102

That the characters constantly interrupt each other is in keeping with the argumentative nature of this scene, just as the rapid flow of contrasting thematic fragments belongs to the developmental nature of this section in a symphony. Once again, it is Susanna who rebuffs the Count with a variant of the second half of theme 2 (see the latter half of Example 101):

Example 103

Inverting the Count's theme (Example 101, first half), the Countess now goes on to the offensive:

Example 104

And so it continues until virtually the exact mid-point of this seventy-two-bar development, when we reach the first moment of relaxation, in A flat major. Using a variant of her reassurance motif, Susanna comes to the Count's assistance: he has been punished enough. The Countess is now half assuaged, and for the first time all three voices are united. Then, however, the Count asks why, if everything was so harmless, was he told the story of the captive page, why was the Countess so distraught, why was he surreptitiously handed a letter? When he learns that all this was merely meant to put him to the test and that – so the women explain in their chattery quavers – Figaro passed the letter to Basilio, the Count tries once again to fly into a rage. Helplessly and comically, he falls into the same chattery vein in which he had just been reprimanded. The same thing promptly happens again following this new outburst, in which he is allowed to indulge for only two bars.

With this, peace is restored and we reach the recapitulation. It starts off in the subdominant key of E flat major, a procedure which, though found in Haydn and later in Schubert, is quite rare for Mozart. The recapitulation is identical to the exposition in its sequence of themes and its duration, but there is one important difference. For the first time, all three characters present their eight-bar themes without interruption: the Count promises to forgive everyone; the Countess doubts whether anyone will ever believe a woman's anger (using the first theme in a minor-mode variant whose indescribably sweet pathos is one of the supreme moments of the score); and Susanna concurs with the Countess, using the melody of the quaver theme one final time. This takes us to the tonic, in which key the coda now sets out, bringing this incomparable piece of music to a conclusion by developing Susanna's reassurance motif alone for thirty bars.

Musical aestheticians ought to be troubled at the thought that a symphonic movement and a busy sequence of stage events should converge so effortlessly. It is certainly nothing to be taken for granted. Our difficulties begin, strictly speaking, with the way we describe this convergence in the first place. If we want to claim that music is the crucial element in opera, that it sustains the stage action, then we shall have to confront the fact that Scenes 18 to 20 of Act II of Beaumarchais's original play sustain the same action very well without music. If, conversely, we want to claim that the symphonic movement accompanies the stage action, we will have to explain how it can be perfectly satisfying, delightful and exciting as instrumental music. Finally, if we want to tackle the problem by claiming that music adds something to the stage action – whether by reinforcing, intensifying or commenting upon the drama – we will not be able to stop at this generalization. The fact that instrumental music can be used to dramatize this special form of vocal music – opera – raises the complementary question of how vocal music can be used in turn to semanticize instrumental music. This question takes us to the next chapter.

Chapter 20

How instrumental music was semanticized by vocal music

The mountains of prejudices mentioned in the Preface are nowhere more in evidence than in the problems to be taken up in this chapter. The concept of 'absolute music', as Carl Dahlhaus has established (1978, p. 9), originated in German romanticism and applies to instrumental music. Today, with greater or lesser consistency, it is considered to mean 'music with no bearing on reality', and is often bandied about without qualifications as though this was how the term was understood in Mozart's day. For Mozart, however, there was no hard and fast boundary between vocal and instrumental music. This is plain to see everywhere in his output, but particularly so in the way he handled the relation between overture and opera. And the words he set to music clearly refer, of course, to a reality of some sort outside the world of art.

At the time of Mozart's childhood it was customary for an opera to be preceded by an interchangeable three-section piece of instrumental music. By the time he was a young man composers had set about creating musical, and hence conceptual, links between this introductory piece of music and the events in the opera. This development does not apply only to the history of opera: we should not forget that the operatic overture was one of the roots of the symphony. Even as late as 1786, at a time when Mozart had long considered it a matter of course to relate his overtures in one way or another to the stage events they 'opened', he called one of these overtures a *sinfonia* – namely, that of *Le nozze di Figaro*.

Mozart found ever-new ways of relating the overture to the opera. Even *Il re pastore*, K208, written for a festive theatrical performance at the Salzburg court when he was only nineteen, reveals one such possibility. The overture, a *molto allegro* in C major, merges directly with the first vocal number 'Intendo amico rio', a song-like aria in 6/8 metre, marked *andantino* and likewise in C major. This aria in turn derives from an instrumental piece, namely, from an idea in the slow movement of the Symphony in C, K96, which Mozart had written at the age of fifteen. As the *Neue Mozart-Ausgabe* puts it (II/5/9, p. xvii), 'the beginning of "Intendo amico rio" sounds for all the world like the major-mode version from the symphony'. And when, in the same year as the opera, Mozart needed to write a symphony he simply used the overture to *Il re pastore* as a first movement and an instrumental version of the aria as the slow movement, to which he then added a Presto (K102/213c).

In several scenes of *Idomeneo* there is a motif which recurs as a musical symbol, related, of course, to the words and plot (see Floros 1979, pp. 34ff.). This motif only comes to full fruition in the final section of the overture – the last number to be composed – where, in the style of a symphony, it is intensified in descending sequences and takes on an unexpectedly tragic significance.

The fragmentary opera *Lo sposo deluso*, written in 1783 between *Die Entführung* and *Figaro*, applies a fresh device unique in Mozart's output. Beginning in the style of a symphonic *allegro* with trumpets and kettledrums, the overture then settles into a charming *andante* dominated by the woodwind. Now it is time once again for an *allegro* section, perhaps a repeat of the opening *allegro*, as in *Die Entführung*. That is what happens here, too, but with a surprising difference. The curtain rises and the *allegro* of the overture expands to become a quartet, the orchestral part of which elaborates the material of the *allegro* and puts it through different keys as though it were part of a symphony.

In *Don Giovanni* Mozart takes yet another approach. The broadly planned confrontation between the hero and his adversary in the Act II Finale – itself drawn from the spirit of the text (note the confrontation between *Sì* and *No*) – is tightly compressed in order to form the slow introduction to the overture. The main section of the overture, on the other hand, does not take up the musical themes of the opera.

Finally, the motto *Così fan tutte* which gave Mozart's like-named opera its title is presented *vocaliter* in the final act and *instrumentaliter* in the overture.

Mozart's ritornellos (the name given to instrumental preludes, postludes and interludes in vocal pieces) likewise overstep the boundary between instrumental and vocal music. Harry Goldschmidt never tired of reminding commentators of this problem. Ritornellos form a key issue in our discussion since, though untexted, they cannot be completely understood without reference to the words.

In Mozart's music pieces from completely different genres are often thematically interlinked. The Mozart literature abounds in more or less convincing examples. As early as 1939 Walther Siegmund-Schultze identified several hundred 'motivic-thematic relations' in Mozart's vocal and instrumental music.

One example which, to my knowledge, has yet to attract attention is a theme that so caught Mozart's fancy that seven different versions of it can be demonstrated. The first occurs in *Zaide*, namely in the Quartet, No. 15, which Mozart wrote in Salzburg in the year 1779 or 1780. Though the last existing number of the piece, the Quartet does not form the opera's conclusion, which in fact was never composed since Mozart abandoned the work. This number suffers from the fact that, dramatically, it remains rooted to the spot. A cruel sultan is determined to execute two lovers for attempting to flee; a well-meaning friend who tried to help them in their flight begs the sultan for clemency; Zaide does the same, but only for her beloved Gomatz, who in turn wishes to take her place. This unhappy predicament remains the same from the first bar to the last. Mozart, then, can think of nothing better to do with the ritornello than to repeat it verbatim without altering the course of the music. It first appears as a purely instrumental introduction to the Quartet. Then it recurs in the middle of this long number of 250 bars, this time with added vocal parts, in which form it is heard twice again. The following example shows this second form, which is identical to the first apart from the added voices:

Example 105

The lovers sing of their weariness with life while the sultan observes that their entreaties are in vain.

Mozart ultimately abandoned his plan to finish and mount the work, and the music lay fallow. It therefore comes as no surprise that the composer – evidently suspecting, correctly, that there was more to be had from his theme than he had extracted from it in *Zaide* – should take it up again.

In purely instrumental form our theme occurs in the first movement of Mozart's C major Symphony of 1780 (K338), where it unexpectedly appears in the second thematic group with the following melodic variant:

Example 106

Roughly one year later Mozart, now in Vienna, wrote Konstanze's second aria for his *Entführung*. After expatiating on the marvellous 'Traurigkeit' theme in G minor, the piece modulates, as might be expected, in order to reach a second thematic complex in B flat major. This is what we then hear:

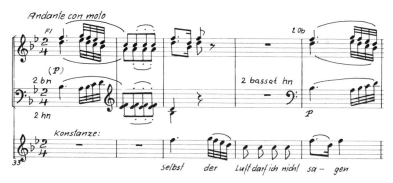

Example 107

As we can see, it is identical note-for-note, including the key and orchestration, to the ritornello from No. 15 of *Zaide*. Compared to the Allegro number its note values are reduced by half, so that even in Andante the pulse of the theme remains exactly the same. But there is one crucial difference. Following the instrumental statement the voice, largely unaccompanied, takes up the melody to words which Mozart, with justification, claimed were 'not bad' (13 October 1781):

> Selbst der Luft darf ich nicht sagen
> meiner Seele bittern Schmerz;
> denn unwillig ihn zu tragen,
> haucht sie alle meine Klagen
> wieder in mein armes Herz.
>
> (I cannot even tell the breeze
> of the bitter pain in my soul;
> unwilling to bear the pain,
> it wafts all my laments
> back to my poor heart.)

But the vocalization of the instrumental theme has its price in poor declamation. The highest pitch falls on the unaccented definite article *der* with an added burden of four demisemiquavers. In compensation, the *Zaide* theme has not only been rescued from the oblivion of its unused score, it has also been instilled with new poetic meaning. The contrary motion of bassoon and oboe in the original may have been inspired by an image of clemency simultaneously sought and denied. In *Die Entführung*, this musical configuration has been given the added conceit of a breeze wafting laments back to the very heart from which they came. Mozart promptly seized upon this contrary motion for the decisive words in the vocal part:

Example 108

In sum, we are dealing with an example, typical for Mozart, of semanticization.

Version 4 also comes from *Die Entführung*, namely, from the draft of an Act III Finale which Mozart later rejected and left incomplete. This finale would have opened with an aria for Belmonte containing, once again in B flat major, the following phrase, repeated after four bars:

Example 109

This brings us to version 5. In the autumn of 1781 Mozart finished Act I of *Die Entführung* plus three pieces from Acts II and III, including the 'Traurigkeit' aria and the aforementioned draft. In a letter of 26 September 1781 he called the text of the latter 'a charming quintet or rather finale'. Then came an interruption, necessitated by Mozart's wish to transfer this charming finale from Act III to the end of Act II. This made it essential to change the text of both acts substantially, and 'that requires a bit of patience' (26 September 1781). But by 6 October he could write: 'Well, I am beginning to lose patience [and] am composing other things in the meantime.' Among these other things was the Sonata for Two Pianos, K448, dated November 1781. Mozart wrote it for himself and one of his female pupils, and 'even later was fond of playing it in public' (Schmid 1955, p. 10). Small wonder! The second movement, an Andante in G major, bears a fascinating relation to *Die Entführung*. It opens with a cantabile theme whose bearing on the opera, if intended by the composer at all, is not obvious. Beginning in bar 13, however, something unexpected happens: Mozart establishes a musical connection between Konstanze and Belmonte. He does this by first having both pianos play the Konstanze theme from the *Traurigkeit* aria for eight bars. This is followed, playfully divided between the two instruments, by figurations taken from Belmonte's aria, No. 4, where they were associated with the 'whisperings' and 'sighs' of his lady friend (see Example 110 on the next page). By combining musical elements from Konstanze's and Belmonte's arias Mozart, in his own mind and in those of contemporary connoisseurs, also drew a relation between the poems of the two respective passages. Konstanze's words, already quoted above (see p. 221), were now joined by the following words from Belmonte:

> Ist das ihr Lispeln?
> Es wird mir so bange.
> War das ihr Seufzen?
> Es glüht mir die Wange.
> Täuscht mich die Liebe,
> war es ein Traum?

Example 110

(Is that her whispering?
I tremble with dread.
Was that her sighing?
The blood rushes to my cheek.
Has love deceived me,
was it a dream?)

Three years later, in the Adagio of his String Quartet in B flat major, K458, Mozart presented a breathtaking harmonic version of this same theme against a variant of Belmonte's second aria, 'O wie ängstlich, o wie feurig' (No. 4) of *Die Entführung*. Another three years later, in *Don Giovanni*, the theme is used again, this time to denote hopeless and unrequited love. When Donna Elvira (Terzetto, No. 16) sings her plaint from the window, knowing that her efforts are doomed to failure, Mozart turns to the *Zaide* theme, its seventh version.

This interpretation, though based on musical findings which cannot be doubted, will encounter resistance among many musicians and musicologists – that, too, cannot be doubted. And this resistance is deeply entrenched in the recent evolution of thoughts on art and the world. In the final chapter of this book I will take a closer look at this issue. For the moment, however, I will allow myself a brief digression.

Sonate, que me veux-tu? This question, originally posed by Fontenelle (1657–1757), a leading proponent of the early French Enlightenment, quickly became famous. In English we might translate it as 'Sonata, what do you want of me?' or 'What are you trying to tell me?' It is easy to see what the question is driving at: it harbours misgivings toward instrumental music. These misgivings might be summarized as follows: If music paints 'nature' or 'affects' in intelligible colours, or if it is accompanied by words or stage events which call for music in real life – in a dance, for example, or the delivery of a song – then we have no trouble going along with it. But if music appears without these justifications and accoutrements – naked, as it were – what is a reasonable person to make of it?

We would do eighteenth-century music theory an injustice if we were to reduce it to its shortsightedness or deafness toward instrumental music. Obviously, we cannot judge art theorists entirely by how accurately they were able to predict the future course of art at the great junctures of history, even if artists were already treading new paths at the time. First came the songbirds, then the ornithologists. We must not close our eyes to the limitations of the Enlightenment figures and demand from them a water-tight theory of music, something we still lack today. If we bear these limitations in mind we will find their writings full of intuitive insights into the nature of music, astonishing anticipations and scientifically productive starting points. None the less – and we must bear this in mind as well – at the very moment that Haydn and Mozart were creating their miracles of quartets, sonatas and symphonies in interaction with pan-European currents of history, serious reservations and misgivings were frequently being voiced against instrumental music.

Even Jean-Jacques Rousseau (1712–78) ends his article 'Sonate' of 1765 for volume XV of the *Encyclopédie* (lightly revised two years later for his own *Dictionnaire de musique*) with Fontenelle's question, quoted verbatim. In the preceding sentence he even speaks of 'sonata rubbish' – *fatras de sonates* – and ironically advises composers to proceed in the manner of those clumsy painters who are forced to write beneath their creations 'this is a tree, that a human being'.

The shortcomings of music aesthetics begin at the zenith of the Enlightenment. Immanuel Kant (1724–1804) posited for music, as for art as a whole, a lofty rung in his moral picture of the universe and a significant role in human relations:

Instrumental music semanticized by vocal music

> The beaux arts ... constitute a mode of representation which has
> a purpose in and of itself and which, though of no practical
> import, helps to promote the cultivation of our emotions into
> convivial discourse.   (1790, § 44)

But Kant's lack of understanding for the way music functions is no
less profound than his general conception. He maintained that
'music speaks entirely with sentiments and without concepts', and
that as a result its beauty 'belongs to the same species ... as the
parrot, the hummingbird, birds of paradise and a good many
crustacea of the sea', or 'wallpaper' (1790, § 53 and § 16). We can
well imagine Mozart's expletives in response to these comparisons,
if he had ever read them.

With only slight exaggeration, we might say that the situation is
much the same today. Specialists in aesthetics and the philosophy of
art know little or nothing about the specific qualities of music.
Conversely, composers and performers claim to understand nothing
of what philosophers or theorists of art and music have to say, nor do
they have to understand it: if need be, they can produce their own
private theories. This is not to deny, however, that there are notable
exceptions in both camps.

By the nineteenth century there were some who could not accept
the chasm between aesthetic theory and musical practice. In particular,
Hermann Kretzschmar (1848–1924) was responsible for furthering the
theoretical foundations of practical music-making. In arguments
which are still worth considering today, he specifically insisted on the
need to establish a well-grounded and well-informed science of the
interpretation of instrumental music. To this art of interpretation he
gave the name 'hermeneutics', for which he then coined the German
neologism *Dolmetschkunst*, a highly revealing term that casts instrumental music in the role of a foreign language. Kretzschmar lamented,
with justification, that this art of interpretation had 'fallen into the
hands of dilettantes, especially philosophers inadequately trained in
music' (1902, pp. 168ff.).

But right from the very start the founders of hermeneutics
committed two fateful errors, neither of which arose from the nature
of the subject itself. Neither Kretzschmar nor his friend and protégé
Arnold Schering (1877–1941) began their discussion with the instrumental music of Haydn and Mozart. Kretzschmar dealt with Haydn
but not Mozart. Schering, after publishing major studies of Bach in the
1920s and 1930s and calling, completely within reason, for a field
devoted to musical symbolism, wrote a single article on Haydn's so-
called programmatic symphonies and ignored Mozart entirely. He
then took a roundabout path via Liszt to arrive at Beethoven, whose

instrumental works he then interpreted in the 1930s as though they were programmatic creations of the New German School.

Now, there may very well exist conceptual and musical relations between instrumental music and works for the theatre, and we need not deny Schering's instinct for tackling problems which have been widely avoided. But by attempting to prove that all of Beethoven's sonatas, string quartets and symphonies were instrumental reenactments of scenes from Goethe, Schiller, Shakespeare, Wieland, Jean Paul, Cervantes, Euripides and Homer, he led hermeneutics in the very direction that Kretzschmar had warned against:

> Anyone who believes, however, that the aim of musical hermeneutics is to detect stories, novels and playlets in instrumental compositions has understood neither the purpose nor the nature of this discipline. (1905, pp. 289f.)

Undaunted, Schering claimed to be able to prove that Beethoven followed the sequence of scenes in his presumptive literary models word by word. 'The ascending and descending arpeggios (bars 12ff.) symbolize the outspread arms of the Queen as she rushes hither and thither', is a characteristic pronouncement from Schering's embarrassing exegeses of Beethoven. The Queen in this case is Mary Stuart, the piece the Piano Sonata op. 110, which was 'written on two scenes from Schiller's tragedy' (1936, pp. 521 and 525). As if this were not enough, Schering adopted the unfortunate method of attaching words from his chosen dramas to Beethoven's themes, generally producing not only unconvincing associations but clumsy declamation as well. Small wonder that Schering's interpretations of Beethoven have failed to take hold, especially as he dedicated an essay of 1934 to 'the New Germany' and railed against 'racially alien music'. As a rule, this aspect of his work has been sheepishly overlooked by his admirers and editors, probably for reasons of political expedience no less than scholarly rectitude.

Mozart's Sonata K448 is not, of course, an instrumental reenactment of a scene from *Die Entführung* of the sort that Schering was fond of discovering in Beethoven. Instead, the slow movement conveys a poetic idea which, though latent in the opera, was not worked out conceptually, scenically or musically. Belmonte claims to hear Konstanze's voice although she scarcely dares to speak at all. This imaginative and ingenious conceit is all the more credible in that one of the ideas of the aria is a ban on verbal utterances. In the Andante of K448, Konstanze speaks with no words at all, and Belmonte hears and understands her. Indeed, the two numbers are almost casebook examples of those passages 'from which connoisseurs alone can derive satisfaction, but which are written in such a way that even the less learned cannot fail to be pleased, though without knowing why' (28 December 1782). The less learned who fail to notice the allusions in K448 because they do not know or recognize the themes and motifs from *Die Entführung* will be satisfied with the delightful play of melody. Perhaps they will even hear fluttering hummingbirds, and though they are unlikely to have visions of crustacea they may well imagine butterflies. Connoisseurs will derive greater satisfaction. The coincidence that the opera's heroine is called Konstanze may have caused Mozart to take especially seriously the sighs, whispers and laments mentioned in the aria's text. He was, after all, in a similar predicament when he wrote the piece. It is a paradox that the more a work of art is filled with the particular, the more forcefully its ideational contents cry out for generalization. This paradox is at work here. Instrumental music, being released from the necessity of having to cling to words or plots, can yield to music's innate propensity to go its own way without necessarily abandoning the possibility of incorporating hints, allusions and metaphors. Instrumental pieces are ideal for drawing generalized conclusions from particular instances. No longer are we confronted with Konstanze and Belmonte: lovers can understand each other even without words. This is what K448 wordlessly conveys.

In Mozart's musical world, semantics are not bound to particular subjects – in our case the lovers Zaide and Gomatz – but neither are they completely disembodied. Once characteristic musical structures have been presented and semanticized by words or plots, structure and semantics become allied in Mozart's imagination. Stimulated by quite conventional or even banal material, the musical creation becomes capable of expressing the most subtle thoughts and emotions. Mozart's music falls under the general conditions that governed art in the eighteenth century, conditions which were formulated as follows by Goethe (1826, XVII, pp. 595f.):

> What applies to all my writings, and hence to my minor poems as well, is that after being stimulated by some greater or lesser occasion they all arose in direct contemplation of some object. Thus, even if they do not resemble each other, they share the common property that in certain extrinsic and often mundane circumstances something general, intrinsic and more exalted presented itself to the poet's eye.

Again and again Goethe complained that most readers of literature cling to the material – the subject matter – and fail even to perceive the general, intrinsic and more exalted.

The conditions governing the reception of music are no less complex, and perhaps even more so. In fifty highly instructive pages

Christian Kaden (1984, pp. 201ff.) has pursued the functions of musical communication, pointing out just how different are the needs, interests and motives of those who create or listen to music. We may enjoy music, love it (or its performers) or be 'music buffs' without having the slightest inkling of its full potential.

Working our way into Mozart's output, we soon encounter a difficulty which, though certainly not unique to Mozart, is perhaps especially applicable to his music because it often seems so 'simple'. Mozart's musical ideas grew in his mind, retaining many of their characteristics and shedding others. In so doing they were able to expand, metamorphose and renew themselves in such a way that the germ of the original idea need no longer be recognizable. In consequence, it has become more difficult for us to probe the connections that existed for the composer. This does not apply to Mozart's sets of variations, which follow the traditional rule that the theme being varied must always remain recognizable. Nor does it apply to the related principle of thematic development. But music happens to have creative processes which cannot be entirely subsumed within terms such as variation, thematic development, symphonic processes, or whatever.

The insights, few in number but great in significance, which Mozart himself gives us into the workings of his musical imagination offer us a starting point. Writing to his father from the latter's native town of Augsburg, Mozart, not yet twenty-two, describes a lesson in improvisation that he gave to the canons of the Augustine monastery of Heiligkreuz (23–5 October 1777). First he asked for a theme, and having received it he proceeded as follows:

> I put it through its paces and in the middle (the fugue was in G minor) I started off in the major key and played something quite jocular, though in the same tempo; and after that the theme over again, but this time arseways. Finally it occurred to me, could I not use the jocular character [*das scherzhafte Wesen*] for the subject of the fugue? I did not waste much time in asking, but did so at once, and it went as neatly as if Daser had fitted it.

Daser was the Mozarts' family tailor in Salzburg. 'Arseways' (*arschling*), a term still in the repertoire of the Viennese comedian Hans Moser, though now apparently out of fashion, means, of course, 'from behind'. Translated into musical terms, this can only mean the familiar medieval technique known as cancrizans, whereby a series of notes is played back to front, though not necessarily with pedantic exactitude. Music examples 130 to 135 illustrate how this technique looks in Mozart's hands.

Mozart had probably been taught the practice of creating contrasts, including the alternation of 'learned' sections with others of a 'jocular' character. But he had mastered it without considering the role that seriousness and humour play in the lives of human beings. Not until he had begun to think for himself did he stumble upon that process which I have called 'semanticization'. But since the technique of musical contrast is itself a product of the mental states and needs of mankind, the question as to which came first – contrast derived from the subject matter of poetry and deliberately related to the material world, or contrast derived from the imitation of musical models – recalls the age-old and unanswerable question of the chicken and the egg.

Still, at least we know some of the musical procedures that went on in Mozart's mind, though we have no right to assume that he did not devise others as well. Let us now look at several examples that shed light on the most inventive, or perhaps we should say the most sophisticated, of his musical devices.

To begin with, we should not overlook direct quotation, a technique which, though not exactly frequent, occurs repeatedly in Mozart's works. Perhaps the strangest quotation is found in the Jupiter Symphony, K551. The first movement opens with a celebrated theme of ebullient dignity leading to a no less celebrated lyrical theme. It then enters a grandiose and impassioned *forte* passage for full orchestra, beginning in the minor mode, whose eighteen bars make it nearly as long as the first theme and exactly as long as the second. At this point something unexpected happens which cries out in vain for a 'purely musical' explanation. Introduced by a gracefully descending figure in the violins, we are now given a third theme, a highly unusual occurrence at this stage in Mozart's career. And this theme is quoted from an aria which Mozart had composed two or three months previously for the baritone Albertarelli, the singer of the Vienna *Don Giovanni*, for insertion in an opera buffa by Anfossi. The voice part, of course, is omitted, but otherwise the passage is quoted note for note, merely being transposed from F major to G major, adapted to the instruments at hand, and reduced from twenty bars to ten since the original is written in 2/4 metre rather than the symphony's 4/4. Here, to jog our memory, is the theme's opening:

Example 111

How did a 'kiss of the hand' (mentioned in the aria's text) come to enter the Jupiter Symphony? Hardly because Mozart wanted to include a pretty tune in one of his large-scale works, perhaps to add to its popularity. Here is the text of the passage he quotes:

Voi siete un po' tondo	(You're a bit of a boor,
mio caro Pompeo,	my dear Pompeo;
l'usanze del mondo	go and study
andate a studiar.	the ways of the world.)

This quotation (the Italian word *tondo* means 'round' or, figuratively, 'unpolished') should be heard in the same way as Beethoven's 'O Freunde, nicht diese Töne!' In a lilting dance tune Mozart ironically allows the operatic character, an affected courtier, to teach the composer a lesson – the same lesson that he had directed to 'dear Pompeo'. There is no need to fly into a passion, he declares; if you study the ways of the world you will find more amiable ways of saying what you have to say. The other movements of the symphony, particularly the finale, show how Mozart meant this lesson to be understood.

In July 1782 Mozart was commissioned to write a symphony in honour of his Salzburg friend Sigmund Haffner. When the commission reached him Mozart was not in the best of moods. *Die Entführung*, performed for the first time on 16 July and for the second time three days later, was a rousing success, but the 'cabal' at the second performance was even worse than at the first ('the entire first act was hissed'), and the terzetto that concludes Act I was 'bungled'. 'I was beside myself with rage.' Furthermore, Mozart intended to arrange the opera for wind instruments before anyone else could 'secure the profits' by doing so – which, in the event, is exactly what seems to have happened. Reluctantly, he then set about writing the symphony. All of this can be learnt from his letter of 20 July 1782. And since he had not overcome his anger at Osmin – who, we may recall, was something more than the overseer of the Pasha's harem – an agreeable piece of music is the last thing we should expect.

Osmin dominates the opening movement. We hear a passage taken from his second aria 'O, wie will ich triumphieren' (No. 19), expressing the malicious and sly side of his character:

Example 112

Its principal features, the upward leaps of an octave within a descending melody line, are recast as follows:

Example 113

The upward leap of one octave has been expanded to two; the *piano* has become a *forte*; grace notes, upbeats and trills have been added; and a contrast depicting Osmin's antagonists has been worked into the continuation of the theme (bars 6ff.).

A second malicious turn of phrase from Osmin's music entered the opening movement of the Haffner Symphony. When, in No. 2, Belmonte attempts to contact Pedrillo by way of Osmin he is rudely rebuffed (see Example 114 on page 232). The features of this phrase, too, appear in the symphony in exaggerated form. If the motif rose a fourth in the opera, it spans more than an octave in the symphony.

Example 114

Once again, semiquaver upbeats have been added, and not just a *forte* but no fewer than eight *sforzato* thumps:

Example 115

We need only hear a recording by Otto Klemperer – and doubtless other conductors as well – to realize that the first movement of the Haffner Symphony, far from being amiable and capricious, is malicious, threatening and dangerous, and that the characters imperilled by Osmin (most of all Blonde, one presumes) also appear in the score. But Osmin's phrases have undergone an enormous metamorphosis.

After *Le nozze di Figaro* had been completed and given its première on 1 May 1786 Mozart wrote, among other things, a string quartet. This work, the 'Hoffmeister' Quartet in D major, K499, which was finished on 19 August of the same year, contains a number of motifs from *Figaro*. In the Act IV Finale Figaro, believing himself to have grounds for jealousy, sings the following phrase, doubled by the strings in three octaves:

Example 116

This little motif is taken up a good dozen times by Figaro, by the orchestra, and by Susanna, who pokes fun at his jealousy. It even appears in D major and is finally shorn of its two final notes, so that it takes on virtually the very form in which it entered the string quartet:

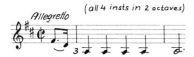

Example 117

Here it is raised three times to higher pitch levels, ultimately arriving at a short four-bar period that merits closer scrutiny. In the Sextet, No. 19, Susanna and Figaro, and Marcellina and Bartolo, agree to celebrate a double wedding on that very day. There then follows a recitative which concludes, unusually, in a terse and ironic little triumphal march beginning and ending *pianissimo* and aimed at the Count (see Example 118 on page 234). Note for note – or more precisely with forty-one of its fifty-one notes (the discrepancies leave the substance intact) – this little phrase has been transplanted from the opera to the string quartet, where the four instruments assume, as it were, the roles of the four operatic figures.

The theme of the string quartet containing these two quotations begins with a melodic turn which, though reminiscent of Susanna's motivic material, does not occur in the opera in this form. The entire complex – I have examined it more closely elsewhere (Knepler 1976) – is too striking to be described simply as a montage made up of one newly invented figure and two quotations. We will come closer to the truth by assuming that what was 'buzzing in Mozart's brain' (13 October 1781) not only included musical ideas but also the conflicts

Example 118

and dramatic situations that gave rise to those ideas. A deep relationship between two people, an upsurge of jealousy, the ultimate triumph
over adversity – all this has been turned into twelve bars of this
quartet theme, a theme made up of three mutually antagonistic
components and yet all of a piece.

In her second aria, No. 20, the Countess is given words that neatly
outline her role in the drama: 'The memory of this bliss [has] not left
my bosom'. She sings them to the following melody:

Example 119

The same melody, slightly altered, recurs in the slow movement of the quartet:

Example 120

and is taken up in the coda, where it undergoes a significant development:

Example 121

Something highly characteristic has taken place. Just as the Countess's motif is taken beyond its limits in the quartet, so the operatic subject matter transcends its own bounds. It is no longer merely the Countess who is voicing her sorrow.

Another motif from *Figaro* reappears in an instrumental work, namely, in the D major 'Prague' Symphony, K504, completed on 19 December in the same year as *Figaro*. Its final movement makes use of the four-note motif that underlies the Duettino, No. 15:

Example 122

In the opera Susanna and Cherubino scurry hither and thither in the locked room, apparently about to fall victim to the Count's wrath, until Cherubino finally resolves to save himself by leaping from a window. As a musical genre this scene is a sonata-allegro movement which, as befits the general panic, is left incomplete: instead of a recapitulation the development section leads directly into the coda. The symphonic movement, on the other hand, lasts three times as long and is scored for full orchestra rather than the string section as in the opera. The orchestra plays at full throttle, extracting anything and everything it can from this little motif and the events on stage. And, of course, the movement indeed turns out to be a fully-fledged sonata allegro. But the transformation already begins with the motif itself. When presented in the opera, as the germ-cell of the entire scene, it takes up no more than four bars – eight if the scene were written in the 2/4 metre of the symphony finale. In the symphony the motif is given a syncopated continuation and repeated, with variations, on the supertonic, thereby forming a fully rounded sixteen-bar period.

At this point we can isolate one motive on the part of composers – a psychological motive – that can lead them to transplant ideas from stage works to instrumental music. Without abandoning the subject matter that inspired the music of a given operatic scene, they can give that music grander dimensions and a higher level of abstraction, just as they can allow their powers of invention far more of that expansiveness that music requires.

Two examples from the Duettino can clarify this point. Four bars, occupying no more than eight seconds in performance, are devoted to Cherubino's make-believe pathos before he performs his daring leap for the sake of his adored Countess. Accordingly, the stage action is slowed down with a quick detour to the minor mode. The symphony, on the other hand, has completely different means with which to retard the action: a good dozen keys are touched upon in the development section. Take another example. In the opera, the orchestral figures that accompany Cherubino's leap do not even fill the two concluding bars. The analogous passage in the finale of the symphony takes up sixteen bars. By relaxing the connection to the events on stage and the need for brevity, Mozart gives his musical signs the means necessary to denote concepts which are at once blurred and broadly conceived. In other words, the finale of the Prague Symphony is not about jumping out of windows – as might have been suggested by the Prague setting – but about boldness of action per se.

An even more far-reaching transformation of the initial musical material took place when Mozart composed his G minor Symphony K550. The germ of the first-movement theme is to be found in that scene in *Don Giovanni* in which Donna Anna discovers the body of her murdered father (No. 2). The psychological and emotional links are plain to see. At some time in late March or early April 1787 Mozart learnt of his father's illness; on 4 April he wrote him a letter in which, to comfort the dying man, he describes death as 'that best and truest friend of mankind'. At about the same time he took up work on *Don Giovanni*. Scene No. 2 and the aforementioned letter, then, were both written within the same short period. Both passages, the operatic scene and the theme of the symphony, have a low, supporting G against which are set dissonant semitone 'sighs', which then rise by an interval of a minor sixth. In other words, three elements from Mozart's original idea (indicated by numbered brackets in Example 123) found their way into the theme of the symphony. The opening G, assigned to an accompaniment figure in the violas, is unique in that no other Mozart symphony has a similar introduction to the entry of the theme. Then there is the semitone motif; in the opera it enters at various pitch levels, among them E flat–D, which in the symphony is retained and made a formative element. Finally, there is the upward leap of a minor sixth, likewise retained in the symphony (see Example 123 on page 238). Those who are uncomfortable with the notion that a theatrical event – a daughter chancing unexpectedly upon her father's corpse – can be the stimulus for a symphonic movement should compare the opera's woodwind motifs (not shown here), modulating to extraordinarily remote keys as Donna Anna loses consciousness, and the similar woodwind motifs and modulations found in the development section of the symphony.

The six string quartets dedicated to Joseph Haydn occupied Mozart for (by his standards) an unusually long period of time – more than two years, from at least December 1782 to January 1785. When Mozart had them published by Artaria in September 1785 he prefaced

Example 123

the quartets with a dedication to 'mio caro amico Haydn', informing the reader that they were 'the fruit of long and laborious toil'.

Mozart's statement is confirmed by the many surviving sketches or drafts, jottings and fragments associated with these quartets. (We should, I believe, follow Alan Tyson's suggestion (1987, pp. 82–105) and not consider all of Mozart's incomplete pieces of music to be fragments. The term fragment should be reserved for passages which were written out but later rejected, such as those in that 'charming finale' discussed on page 222. Sketches or drafts came about when Mozart, exceptionally, worked out certain aspects of a composition on paper, such as a complex passage of counterpoint, before entering it in his score. Jottings arose when Mozart wrote down and elaborated ideas for possible use at a later date. Sometimes he returned to these ideas, often he did not.) From no other period in Mozart's career do we have so much material of all three kinds than for the years of the Haydn Quartets.

One reason for this, among others, was Mozart's discovery that operatic conflicts and symphonic techniques can mutually cross-fertilize each other. *Die Entführung* haunts many pages of the Haydn Quartets, as is apparent in the way that both unite a buffo quality with deep earnestness. And the vehicle for this buffo quality is Pedrillo.

Pedrillo's harmonically unique Romance pursues a rare and curious progression of keys from A major to C major to G major in bars 8 to 13. The same progression, but even more concise, is heard in the minuet of the D minor Quartet, compressed into bars 4, 5 and 6. This movement, too, modulates rapidly, reaching nine different keys in twenty-seven bars, an average of only three bars per key. Granted, there are no obvious melodic references to the Romance, but is Pedrillo not audible in the harmony?

Mozart himself, in his celebrated remarks on Osmin's anger in his *Entführung* letter, describes how harmony may be used to represent states of mind. Now, Pedrillo is not angry, least of all while singing his Romance, the signal for the planned abduction. But he can lack heart, being in this respect no different from his composer. 'I am a little anxious as it is', Mozart can write without provocation (25 June 1791); and Pedrillo, before launching into the Romance, exclaims: 'Courageousness is a capital foolish business. If you don't have it, no amount of trying will give it to you. How my heart is pounding!' Just as his composer can express, at an unexpected moment, 'a kind of longing which is never satisfied' (7 July 1791), so Pedrillo, using the boldest of harmonies, turns the Romance into an image of the insecurity felt by uprooted persons at moments of danger. It may be that Mozart discovered the harmony of Johann Sebastian Bach at the time he wrote this piece. 'I go every Sunday at twelve o'clock to Baron van Swieten, where nothing is played but Handel and Bach', he reported to his father on 10 April 1782. *Die Entführung* occupied him until the end of May, and of its twenty-one numbers the Romance is fourth from last. But not even in Bach could he have found such a dense concentration of harmonic shifts (from A major to C major in bars 9 and 10), reinterpretations (G major as the so-called Neapolitan sixth of F sharp minor in bar 14) and tonic-related keys (F sharp minor and major in bars 15 and 17), all in a piece belonging to a light genre. To reach a better understanding of the connections between Pedrillo and the Haydn Quartets we will have to combine musical analysis with psychology, namely, with the theory of personality no less than the psychology of artistic creation. We must again cast an eye at Pedrillo's harmony in order to do justice to another passage which migrated from *Die Entführung* into the quartets. Pedrillo's aria 'Frisch zum Kampfe' (No. 13) is also an unusual piece of music. To begin with, we should not overlook that the trumpets and timpani which, in *Zaide* (as elsewhere), were reserved for persons of the Sultan's rank, are now used to give courage to a bourgeois protagonist. The aria is based on a six-bar phrase which, slightly varied, we again encounter in the string quartet. Here, too, the question is one of plucking up courage. The aria, for all its D major brilliance with trumpets, horns and drums and rushing scales in the strings, does not quite succeed in this: it is followed by the lines, quoted above, on Pedrillo's lack of 'courageousness'. The six bars are structured as follows:

Example 124

This little theme occurs five times, always in the tonic, always with the same scoring, four times with voice and once with instruments alone, making up almost a third of the entire piece. It almost takes on the appearance of a refrain. Standard four- or eight-bar periods are avoided; what stand out melodically are the two four-note groups in bars 13 and 16, and harmonically the first cadence on the supertonic, E minor. At this point, on the word *verzagt* (to quail), there is a 'slip' which Mozart, like every good student of composition, had been taught to avoid: namely, not to double the third in a first-inversion triad. That, however, is exactly what he does here (in bar 14), although he mostly obeys the rule.

The first movement of the G major Haydn Quartet, K387, has a second theme whose bouncy lyricism, as one might expect, contrasts sharply with the theme that opens the movement. Here the voice of Pedrillo rings out loud and clear (see Example 125 on the following page). Immediately in the first bar we notice the four F sharps, now playfully extended to six. In both cases the first turn of the harmony leads to E minor. In the quartet we even hear, in bar 4, that same 'slip' which struck our ear in Pedrillo's aria. And both phrases are six bars long.

A similar relationship between an earnest first theme and a buffo second theme occurs in the String Quartet in E flat major, K428. Here, too, we find the Pedrillo theme, now expanded to eight bars, transposed to B flat major and incorporating some additional melodic material. The same characteristic four notes are heard, harmonized as a cadence in G minor. After a conventional mid-point cadence in the dominant, F, there is an unexpected detour into C minor before the return to the tonic, B flat (see Example 126 on the following page). The semiquaver figure in bar 42 of this example harbours another

Example 125

Example 126 (continued on next page)

Example 126 (continued)

hidden allusion to Pedrillo. This figure derives from the so-called gypsy scale, which however was not yet in use in Mozart's day. The reason why it sounds at once so strange and familiar becomes clear when we compare it with a turn of phrase from the Romance:

Example 127

There is further evidence for the *Entführung* atmosphere of the Haydn Quartets. For the penultimate work in the series, the A-major Quartet K464, there exist two final movements, one of them complete in every respect, the other unfinished although Mozart had written out 170 bars (perhaps two-thirds of its projected length) in his most ingratiating style. It is the longest of all Mozart fragments; indeed, it would even bear performance as it stands. The reason why Mozart rejected the finale becomes clear when we discover that it has been drawn from *Zaide* (see Example 128 on following page). This theme obviously derives from the Terzetto, No. 8, in which Zaide, her beloved Gomatz and the faithful Allazim announce that their 'sorrowful fate' is about to be dimmed by the rising sun (see Example 129 on following page). In the middle section of the Terzetto, to the accompaniment of *sforzati*, tremolos and chromatic semiquaver figures, we hear 'bloody comets' ascending amidst rumbling thunder – only to disappear after eight bars. This stage thunder, too, entered the unfinished finale of the quartet. Mozart's imagination, as Goethe would have put it, has been 'kindled by a lesser occasion', one whose

Example 128

Example 129

emotional and ideational world the composer of *Die Entführung* had long outgrown.

However, the newly composed quartet finale arose, once again, from a metamorphosis of a musical idea contained in the opera. Note, first of all, that in three of the Haydn Quartets, *allegro* movements are suddenly interrupted by passages dominated by semibreves and minims. These three passages are, moreover, melodically related (see Example 130 on page 244). Since it is by no means customary for string quartets to have such strikingly similar passages, the question naturally arises as to their source. And here we discover a passage in *Die Entführung* where an Allegro movement is similarly interrupted in order to state, in words and music, one of the opera's mottos (see Example 131 on page 244): *Es lebe die Liebe!* – Long live love! In the Quartet, No. 16, this idea has been given the simplest musical setting imaginable, being nothing more than a segment of a scale which, even if played in inversion or retrograde, still yields nothing more than a segment of a scale. But things begin to look different the moment we consider the chromatic version alongside the diatonic. The following example, taken from the above-mentioned Duettino in *Figaro*,

Example 130

Example 131

illustrates just how quickly and easily Mozart can slip from one version to the other:

Example 132

In his Haydn Quartets, Mozart took a motto rich in significance and 'put it through its paces'. He subjects the core of his theme to various processes of transformation, presenting it in its original form and in inversion, in its diatonic and chromatic versions simultaneously, and

244

giving them different harmonizations and dissonant modulations, all expressive of the perils of love. Not slavishly following the order of scenes in the opera, but neither abandoning the essence of its plot, he allowed its themes and motifs to kindle a myriad musical formulations and contrasts in his instrumental music. Without pretending to be exhaustive, I should like to cite a few more of his recastings of the *Es lebe die Liebe!* motto. The theme of the final movement from the A major Quartet:

Example 133

is derived from the germinal motif in its chromatic variant, but this time 'arseways'. At least three passages in semibreves and minims, comparable to the ones cited in Example 130, prove to be related:

Example 134

Those who are still unwilling to accept the relation to *Die Entführung* are invited to compare the scalar motifs accompanying the motto in the opera with those from its occurrence in the A major Quartet (quoted in Example 130). They turn out to be virtually identical:

Example 135

It will not do simply to think of these as variants, variations or even developmental manipulations of a theme. As in many of the pieces we have looked at and listened to up to this point, we are forced to conclude that Mozart must have occupied himself with techniques fundamentally different from those captured in traditional musical terminology. As he wrote to his father while still in Paris: 'You know that I am, so to speak, soaked in music, that I am immersed in it all day long and that I love to speculate, study and meditate' (31 July 1778). At least from the time of *Die Entführung* his repertoire of musical procedures must be said to include metamorphosis, a concept which, as we well know, played an important role in Goethe's theories, and which Harry Goldschmidt (1985, pp. 228ff.) has applied successfully to Beethoven's technique of composition. This enables us to investigate obvious similarities in character between pieces of music which have no noticeable thematic or motivic overlaps, but which share structural properties such as those indicated in the examples given above. The principle of the thing will not disappear for want of attention.

This chapter, using some two dozen examples from Mozart's instrumental music, has demonstrated the need to expand our analytic methods with regard not only to musical structure but also to ideas and emotions. For, to quote Harry Goldschmidt once again (p. 250), 'musical and cognitive processes merge'.

What we have attempted here reveals but the tip of the proverbial iceberg, and raises more questions than it answers. This is fully in keeping with the present precarious state of music aesthetics, which – with a humility unfortunately all too justified – have capitulated before Mozart's instrumental music instead of illuminating it with innovative questions and methods.

Chapter 21

Conclusions from endings

Every Mozart opera has a *lieto fine*, a happy ending, and the overwhelming majority of his instrumental works end with a quick, cheerful finale. In this respect they are no different from literally thousands of other operas, sonatas and symphonies of the eighteenth century. An older contemporary of Mozart, Johann Adolph Scheibe (1708–76), wrote in his *Compositions-Regeln* that a quick final movement may be followed by another, but it 'must likewise be very high-spirited and agreeable' (*c.* 1730, p. 84). And so it was, an untold number of times, in accordance with a tradition which is doubtless long-standing and rooted in dance and ritual. No matter how serious, sad or tragic the occasion that brings people together to make music, they do not as a rule part company without having struck a merry note. A funeral ceremony may be performed in deep mourning with all the customary prayers and observances only to switch, often with brutal suddenness, to an unrestrained piece of music or a wake or both, in obedience to the dictum that life must go on – as indeed it always has, at least up to now. Certain human needs tend to find their way into all forms of society.

But should we really be satisfied with these unquestioned données, which are still found in most histories of music today? Two thoughts deserve consideration. The earliest large-scale form of written music in European history – the Mass – follows a different pattern. Its final section, the *Agnus Dei*, concludes with a plea for peace. Instead of offering an unbridled finale that casts all cares to the winds, it demands composure and contemplation. That is the first point. The second is that scarcely had one or two decades passed after Mozart's death before composers began to cast doubt on the *lieto fine* in operas and symphonies, and there arose what is characteristically called the 'finale problem'. Even Beethoven's triumphant finales betray a superhuman exertion that was completely alien to Mozart, and Bruckner and Mahler required still mightier efforts in order to give their listeners a triumphant vision of humanity before releasing them from the concert hall. Many of Alban Berg's works – the second movement of the

Chamber Concerto, the *Präludium* of the Three Orchestral Pieces, the third movement of the Lyric Suite and, rather more freely, the entire opera *Lulu* – proceed in retrograde from their mid-point. Hans F. Redlich interpreted this phenomenon as early as 1957 (pp. 157 and 367): the retrograde technique 'becomes a musical symbol of an artistic yearning which would actually prefer to disenact the musical events altogether.' As a musical sign, this ingenious technique offers a bitter answer to the question of man's future perspectives. Obviously, events of the times and man's images of them are decisive. The finale problem is not simply musical in nature.

In the early history of the symphony and chamber music, a period extending into Mozart's youth, these two genres were criticized and abused by their opponents and detractors, and not entirely without reason. 'The general uproar of a modern symphony or overture neither engages attention, nor interrupts conversation', opined one of these naysayers (Hawkins 1776, p. 919) without the slightest inkling of the possibilities latent in this uproar. Even decades later one could still read the following:

> Listening to the predictable and noisy recurrence of the half-closes in Mozart's symphonies, it seems to me, at least, as though I were hearing a musical setting of the clatter of crockery at an aristocratic repast.

The words are Wagner's (1860, p. 126). Applied to Mozart's post-1780 symphonies, and to many of the earlier ones as well, the remark is senseless. But it points to the subservient function of that species of instrumental music which indeed left audible traces in many of Mozart's early symphonies, not to mention the early divertimenti and cassations. As we know from hundreds of glorious examples, Mozart never lost his love for the lightness, grace and accessibility that can distinguish this type of music. He even seems to have realized where this sort of music had its origins. His observation that 'Hanswurst has not yet been banished from music' (16 June 1781) goes hand in hand with his preference for farces not to the taste of the literate and cultured, and for all kinds of buffoonery. The more mature he became, the more he raised this kind of music to a higher level.

Mozart tackled this problem from two different angles. Either he combined themes or motifs from the popular sphere with others from elevated music, or else he subjected them to musical devices of a sophistication and subtlety that other composers were unable to demonstrate even in their most sublime creations. We have already seen one extraordinary example of this in 'Vedrai, carino'.

At this point attention should be drawn to a peculiarity of Mozart's endings. In longer pieces he loved to add a little closing idea or codetta to the end of a section: short, graceful, surprising – and superfluous according to all existing rules. This device derives from the divertimento, where playful surprises were part of the game. Three examples will suffice, although they could be multiplied ad infinitum.

For a divertimento composed in Salzburg, probably around 1780, Mozart wrote, as was the custom, an introductory march (K445) which comes to an end after a little more than fifty bars. In its last few measures the final cadence is heard a good four times, first *piano*, then *forte*, then *forte* again. But no, the piece is laid out so that, at the very last moment, the cadence recurs yet again to delight the listener, this time in a completely unexpected *pianissimo*:

Example 136

In the first of the string quartets dedicated to Haydn, K387, completed on the last day of that eventful year 1782, the exposition reaches its conclusion. The composer then appends another playful cadence, the merest bagatelle of a musical idea, unrelated thematically to the rest of the piece but all the more diligently exploited in the development:

Example 137

There also exists a vocal counterpart of this kind of cadential flourish, namely, the four-part passage (cited in Example 118) that brings the recitative following the Sextet in *Figaro* to its satisfying conclusion.

A second peculiarity of Mozart's happy endings is that, in his mature works, he generally does not let them have the final word until after he has plumbed the depths of seriousness and tragedy. This is particularly true of his slow movements, but sometimes even of those movements still called minuets although they had long been nothing of the sort. Contemporaries, whether approving or not, were aware of this quality. 'Mozart leads us into the depths of the spiritual realm', wrote E. T. A. Hoffmann (1810, p. 38). 'Dread seizes us ... Love and melancholy resound in sweet spectral voices; night ends in iridescent purple.' In short, this highly imaginative man was exalting precisely that jumble of opposites that left other listeners so frightened.

There is something touching in the thought that even the great Lessing puzzled over the question of when a composer may be allowed to 'leap, for example, from placidity to tumult, from tenderness to cruelty'. A poet can make such leaps intelligible, he argues,

> but how can this be accomplished by a musician? ... First we dissolve in sorrow, then suddenly we are supposed to seethe with anger. How? Why? Against whom? ... Music cannot determine any of this. It leaves us in uncertainty and confusion.

Lessing then concludes that 'a symphony that expresses different and contradictory passions in its various movements' must be condemned as 'a musical monstrosity' (*Hamburger Dramaturgie*, no. 27, pp. 128–30). Mozart was eleven years old when these pages were written. We should not judge lesser lights too harshly who were also bothered by similar questions. Thus, we will have to indulge Leopold Mozart for wanting to set aside 'the natural and popular, which is readily understood by everyone', for special genres such as singspiel or 'German opera'. 'The grand and sublime style is suited to grand subjects. Everything in its place', he wrote on 3 November 1777, as though the lesser figures who peopled the stage in popular genres had no right to deep emotions.

Still, at a time when seemingly immutable things, institutions and persons of a different magnitude were being forced to give way, we can hardly expect the substance of music to remain untouched. In a process of worldwide dimensions, thinking people were discovering that the mighty are unable even to invent a pair of fingernail scissors, that a Kapellmeister can be a cavalier, and that dignity is also a right of ordinary people. This same process disclosed to Mozart that one does not have to be an aristocrat to feel sadness, despair or mortal fear. He ennobled musical figures from the buffo stage by conferring upon them the compositional laurels traditionally set aside for elevated genres. Leopold Mozart never understood this, thereby adding a new, and perhaps the deepest, conflict to an already insoluble father-and-son complex and irritating Mozart with his continual harping on the popular. In all likelihood, or so it seems to me, one of Mozart's most extreme scatological remarks refers precisely to this conflict: 'It's one thing if Papa shits the filth, another if I eat it' (22 November 1777).

To understand Mozart's endings we have to know what they are supposed to end. Not until we have a grasp of Mozart's expressive world in its entirety, including its gloomier side, will his cheerful endings fall into perspective. What we are confronting is nothing less than the question of artistic truth. No matter which genre he cultivated, Mozart also confronted the tragedy of the human condition. Even his singspiels find room for sorrow, supreme sacrifice and icy reserve. This is one reason why traditional generic terms no longer suit Mozart's mature operas. If *Die Entführung aus dem Serail* is a singspiel, then it has numbers never heard in a singspiel before. *Don Giovanni* refuses to bend to any of the subtitles bestowed upon it: it has something of an *opera buffa*, agreed, and something of *opera seria*, *dramma giocoso* and *opera semiseria* as well. But most of all, these are works of a new kind.

Scarcely a gloomier piece flowed from Mozart's pen than the Rondo in A minor for clavier, K511. It was written in March 1787 at a time when Mozart was brooding on *Don Giovanni*, and shares with it one of the techniques that gives this opera its unique flavour (how it does this will be explained later). This technique is the interplay between various segments of the chromatic and the diatonic scale. The principal theme itself contains both:

Example 138

Note the ascending chromatic line in bars 2 and 3, reinforced with a crescendo and spanning a fifth, and the diatonic line in bar 4, descending and encompassing a full octave. The chromatic figures mostly remain within the compass of a fourth or fifth; sometimes they go beyond this, and one, in the middle, major-mode section of the piece, spans an octave plus a sixth. Occasionally they are tightly compressed: there are eleven of them, for example, in the six bars from 49 to 54. Sometimes diatonic and chromatic figures collide in a narrow space, as in the theme itself. In general, as close listening reveals, the chromatic figures predominate: there are more than sixty of them as compared to half as many diatonic figures, many of which become chromatic on repetition. The technique which, in the Haydn Quartets, was made a vehicle of cheerful contemplation has been modified in such a way that here, and in *Don Giovanni*, it signifies tragedy. Even the core of the theme (bar 1 of Example 138) can be construed as a sigh. This is exactly how it is treated in the final five bars, where it fades away twice into inaudibility, bereft of its continuation:

Example 139

Mozart takes a similar tack in the first movement of one of his mightiest creations, the String Quintet in G minor, K516. It was composed only two months after the work we have just looked at, and hence certainly during the writing of *Don Giovanni*. Again, it shares with *Don Giovanni* the combination of diatonic and chromatic shapes, and its first movement ends in much the same way as the A minor Rondo. This time a fragment from the second theme (see Example 140 on following page) is set beneath descending chromatic scales and rising diatonic figures, its failing voice seeming to denote a vain and helpless cry (see Example 141 on following page).

   The G minor Symphony, K550, as we know, clings relentlessly to the minor mode. Other pieces by Mozart do the same thing. Among them is one which is still little-known, doubtless because the instrument for which it was intended cannot do it justice: the *Orgelwalze*, *Flötenuhr*, or whatever else one might want to call the

Conclusions from endings

Example 140

Example 141

musical apparatus displayed in Müller's Art Gallery in Vienna, apparently in several models. We can only nod in agreement with the editor of this piece, Wolfgang Plath (see *NMA* IX/27/2, pp. 80–94 and ixff., with further information on the *Flötenuhr*, 'Müller' and his 'art gallery'), when he remarks that Mozart's dislike of the 'Adagio for the clock-maker', expressed in his letter to Konstanze of 3 October 1790, cannot possibly have referred to the F minor Adagio, K608. Mozart could hardly have written a piece of this unity, consistency and dark grandeur against his will, nor would he have belittled the piece while writing it. In this case nothing that we might call an original version has survived. We can only hope that, some day, a composer will make a worthy arrangement of K608 for full orchestra, meaning an orchestra of the size that impressed Mozart (11 April 1781), with forty violins, ten violas, eight cellos, ten basses, six bassoons and double woodwind!

We should not attach undue importance to connections between events in a composer's life – even the death of a loved one – and the genesis of a composition. The romantic image of Mozart being upset by some recent sadness and throwing himself into the composition of a sad piece of music will have to be revised, if only because the way a composer writes his music necessitates his detachment from the initial impetus. This is not to deny the existence of that impetus, but completely different mental processes are also at work besides the initial emotion.

Many of Mozart's gloomiest works were apparently part of larger cycles. The tragic G minor Symphony, K550, was preceded by the festive E flat major Symphony K543 and followed by the serene Jupiter Symphony in C major, K551. All three works, it goes without saying, are organized on the basis of related structural principles. Similarly, the G minor String Quintet belongs to a cycle of four string quintets (perhaps more were planned) which, rather than nullifying its tragedy, place it in perspective. We are reminded that in the most tragic of Mozart's late operas, *Don Giovanni*, life emerges victorious over what in *Die Zauberflöte* is called *Tod und Verzweiflung* – 'death and despair' (the sequence, first death and then despair, is anything but absurd to a Catholic who believes in damnation). Later we will take a closer look at how this is accomplished. What serious or tragic movements achieve in macrocosm within cheerful pieces, or tragic works within cheerful cycles, is accomplished in microcosm by dissonances and their resolution. It may be surprising to learn that the harshest dissonances Mozart ever wrote are found in his most graceful and poised pieces of music. In one of his most popular and frequently performed pieces, the slow movement in F major from the C major Piano Concerto K467, Mozart divides the violas – a practice otherwise seldom encountered in his mature music – thereby producing five string groups instead of the usual four. These are then available for five-note chords of an unheard-of level of dissonance. There is no doubt that the reason why the phrase:

Example 142

radiates such heavenly calm and grace is that it is preceded by dissonances which, though played *piano* by muted strings and immediately resolved, are among the harshest Mozart ever conceived. Example 143 shows these dissonances in schematic outline, beginning with the moderate dissonance of bar 12, advancing to the stronger one of bar 14, to the extreme harshness of bar 15 and the milder harmony of bar 16, which then lead to the resolution in bar 17:

Example 143

It is hard to believe, but nevertheless true, that Mozart invented a dissonant *seven*-note chord precisely for a piece that otherwise revels in euphony in order to lull the winds and the waves. But he maintained an ironic detachment: the audience and one of the three singers know that the journey which the elements are asked to protect will in reality never take place. Twice in succession, at the word *desir* (desire), these seven notes resound for a full bar, and two of them chafe against the others seven times within that bar, generating a uniquely translucent sonority of mingled pain and pleasure. I know of no harsher dissonance in Mozart's entire output. It is found in the Terzettino from *Così fan tutte* (No. 10) and assumes the following form, once again in schematic outline:

Example 144

The notion that dissonances may, indeed must, resolve – that the world is not entirely condemned to Hell, and that in consequence the vast majority of musical works are allowed to end in a symbolic major – this notion is not unique to Mozart. 'Like unto lovers' quarrels are the dissonances of this world: they are reconciled amidst the fray, and all that was once parted is reunited.' The lines are taken from Hölderlin's *Hyperion*. Similar ideas were expressed by Johann Jakob Wilhelm Heinse (1746–1803) in his *Ardinghello und die glückseligen Inseln*, a work of 1787 that roused attention with its erotic liberties:

> Pythagoras was right: the world is a work of music! Wherever the power of consonances and dissonances is at its most crowded and entangled, there is life at its fullest; and all unhappy persons must take solace in the thought that no dissonance in nature can remain as it is.

A little-known pastor from Württemberg named Johann Ludwig Fricker went even farther to link the technical treatment of dissonance to that which it signifies and evokes in the listener's mind. In the *Musikalische Real-Zeitung für das Jahr 1789* – perhaps Hölderlin read the essay – this pietist and natural philosopher wrote the following remarkable words: 'In actuality, beauty consists only in the resolution of dissonance into consonance, [conveying] a vision [of] the way in which all the dissonances of the world will ultimately resolve into a single eternal harmony.' (All the above quotes are taken from Heise 1988, pp. 56f.)

Not even the greatest composer can decide what his fellow men feel about their world. The problem of dissonance, like the finale problem, is answered at a level above the individual. The effects of this supra-individuality have been described in a thoughtful essay by Ivan Nagel (1985). The two principal species of eighteenth-century opera, he maintains, reach their happy endings according to different principles. Nagel proposes *mercy* and *autonomy* as antithetical concepts within a historical process in which 'the sovereignty of the single person gives way to the freedom of the individual' (1985, p. 12). In opera seria, so his argument goes, the plot moves from 'the pronouncement of a judgement of divine-monarchical rage ... to its eventual mitigation'. Clemency – mercy proclaimed from on high – is the normal ending of an opera seria. Not so in opera buffa. Mozart's *Figaro* and *Così fan tutte* are governed by

> the daily interactions of equals in rehearsal for a potential humanism within the world of mankind – the only world they have. They know nothing outside this world: no deity, no sovereign, no secret society will mildly and obligingly 'come to their assistance through the agency of quite unexpected external beings' [the quotation is taken from Goethe]. The ancient apparatus of comedy is instilled with its often forgotten meaning: genuine self-assistance for everyone, the totality of which – the ensemble – presses onward towards a happy ending. (p. 40)

This is a convincing and impressively worded analysis which, I feel, Nagel spoils by failing to apply it with sufficient thoroughness.

Sarastro and his priestly followers claim the right to punish and protect, even to decide over life and death, for the benefit of mankind. Nagel cannot and will not accept this claim. This is all too understandable, given the abuse to which such claims have been put since then and are still being put today. But Mozart wrote *Die Zauberflöte* at a moment in history when negative experiences of this sort were not available. Nor were there any recipes for making 'superstition vanish' and 'the wise man conquer', for banishing evil to Hell, much less for turning the happy ending of an opera into a symbol for the fortunate demise of the ancien régime.

Susanna and Figaro reached their goals by virtue of their wit, cunning and bare hands; only the Count was armed with a sword. Yet by 1787, in *Don Giovanni*, not only does Ottavio have 'a pistol in hand' (bar 509 of the Act I Finale), even Masetto (II, 4) is given a flintlock and pistol, modern weapons pitted against the poignard of the aristocratic lord. The figure in Plate 10, though unrelated to *Don Giovanni*, might have represented Masetto or any of the peasants with whom he joined forces in order to 'butcher' Giovanni – *trucidarlo* (II, 4). After all, the two earliest librettos of the opera (1787 and 1789) show the peasants armed with swords and firearms. In *Die*

Zauberflöte injustice is swept aside by lightning, thunder and tempests, albeit under the administration of the good characters. In the late eighteenth century the question of violence looked very different from the way it looks today. We would hardly think Mozart capable of the following thought: 'Had it been absolutely necessary for me to die, I should have taken at least a couple of them with me into the next world.' Yet he wrote these very words in a letter of 30 December 1780 to his father, describing a singer murdered in his own home by 'three or four assassins'.

To Nagel, *Don Giovanni* is governed 'neither by forgiveness nor by mercy' (1985, p. 46). This is undoubtedly correct. But Nagel overlooks that something else is also at work, something felt at the time to be justice. Otherwise he could never have concluded that *Don Giovanni* 'is one of the very few operas of its time which ends badly' (p. 48) – badly because 'happiness perishes' at Giovanni's demise (p. 46). This, however, is not the meaning that Mozart and Da Ponte gave to their opera. *Il dissoluto punito o il Don Giovanni* reads Mozart's entry in his manuscript catalogue of works: 'The Libertine Punished; or, Don Giovanni'. They considered their work to be an opera buffa or a *dramma giocoso* and titled it accordingly. The end of the opera – we will take a somewhat closer look at it later – would be unintelligible if its creators had construed Giovanni's downfall as a disaster rather than a redemption. Nor would the finale of *Die Zauberflöte* have become as we know it today if Mozart had viewed its priestly fellowship – to whose real-life counterpart, after all, he belonged to the end of his days – as an 'elitist male fraternity' (p. 33) and Sarastro as an autocrat.

A generation that has accumulated bad experiences with political parties and the exercise of power may look askance at Freemasonry, which was indeed a forerunner of modern parties, or at the notion of a party being the 'instrument of power to do good' (p. 46), or certainly at the use of force to ward off evil. For all the contradictions, narrow-mindedness and buffoonery in which the libretto of *Die Zauberflöte* abounds, Mozart clearly took it very seriously without taking every word of it literally. It is revealing in this respect to compare how Mozart treated the downfall of the negative characters in *Don Giovanni* and *Die Zauberflöte*. Both operas make use of trombones, the instruments of earnestness, tragedy and danger. But in both works the trombones have disappeared by the time the opera ends. In their stead, Mozart applied a device which merits our very closest attention.

In the penultimate scene of *Don Giovanni* we see the Don descend into Hell while cowardly Leporello hides beneath a table. In the final scene, divided musically into three sections, the two remaining male figures and the three women enter along with representatives of justice (*ministri di giustizia*) in order finally to impose earthly laws on Giovanni. Only when she sees him in chains, sings Donna Anna, will her pain subside. Instead, she learns from Leporello that justice has already been meted out. This leaves them in no doubt as to the identity of the shadow they had just encountered. As Anna sings this passage her voice descends chromatically for more than an octave, recalling the ominous scales of the overture and the Commendatore scene:

Example 145

Heaven, then, has appointed Hell to carry out its verdict. Leporello, quickly accustoming himself to his recent loss of an employer, claims to know the exact spot at which the Devil swallowed (*trangugiò*) his 'former' master. This concludes the first section of the finale, the Allegro assai. With the words 'Now, my dearest, since heaven has avenged us all' – *vendicati siam del cielo* – Ottavio opens the middle section, a Larghetto of which more than half belongs to him and Anna. In a lyric duet full of decorative instrumental detail – exactly what Leopold Mozart would have called 'grand things' (*grosse Sachen*) – they reach an understanding: Ottavio consents to Anna's wish for a year in which to console her heart before putting an end to his anguish. The others then announce how they intend to shape their lives. Elvira will return to her solitude (the convent is a translator's invention); Zerlina and Masetto will go home to a meal with their friends; Leporello will search in the nearest tavern for a better master. At this point the grand style of the duet, though many of its elements are retained, is gradually transformed into a buffo style in the mouths of the low-born figures. Mozart accomplishes this with great artistry.

Then something again quite unexpected happens. Returning to the pathetic style and high-flown phrases, the low-born figures, and only they, express the hope that the scoundrel Giovanni will remain in the realm of Proserpina and Pluto. (Perhaps Anna's and Ottavio's unwillingness to sing these lines is explained by their superior education, which tells them that Giovanni has gone to the Christian underworld, not to the Hades of Antiquity still believed in by common folk.) Similarly, the transition to the *presto* section that concludes the final scene, and hence the opera, belongs to Zerlina, Masetto and Leporello alone. Dropping character and turning to the audience, whom they address as 'you good people' (*o buona gente*), they ask everyone to join in the ancient lay, which, however, is again initiated by the two high-born women. The music of this 'ancient lay' brings the fusion of high and low styles to a culmination. It is a *fugato* in the ecclesiastical manner, evidently based on a Hallelujah model. But almost at once, in the fourth bar of the strict fugue subject, a light-footed buffo flourish dances in to accompany it:

Example 146

Perhaps we would not attach any importance to this figure if it did not recur twice, including one appearance in the bass, and if a similar figure did not occur somewhat later:

Example 147

Moreover, the entire complex ends with the original figure. Only ten bars before the curtain falls it recurs again, this time wittily presented in a spare, two-part texture in the violins, with the descending chromatic line which we have heard so often in the course of this opera. Tragedy has not been banned from the world, but life has triumphed.

In principle, *Die Zauberflöte* ends in exactly the same way, though with quite different material. In the final scene (II, 30) trombones resound as the forces of the Queen of the Night are 'confounded and destroyed'. They also accompany the victors' hymn of praise and thanksgiving. Then, however, we hear a melody (bar 847 of the Finale) which is more likely to have come from the lips of Papageno than from Sarastro and his fellows, and in which the trombones have nothing to say. This melody expresses not so much the jubilation of victory as serene superiority:

Example 148

In this way the opera approaches its conclusion, gracefully and *piano*. Not until the final eight bars do we hear a reinforcing *forte* from the full orchestra – without trombones.

As in opera, so in Mozart's instrumental works. Ludwig Finscher (1988, p. 27) has made the interesting observation that in three of Mozart's most majestic creations the conclusion is brought about by a combination of contrapuntal texture and buffo theme. The first of these, as we have just seen, is the finale of *Don Giovanni*. The second is the finale of the G major String Quartet, K387:

Example 149

The third is the finale of the Jupiter Symphony:

Example 150

This is but one of the methods whereby Mozart oversteps the time-honoured boundaries separating the popular and clownish from the 'grand things'. It may be that he learnt his music more quickly than his politics, that he created techniques of musical expression for emotional contents whose full potential he only realized in the course of mastering the composer's craft. The age of the common man had dawned, and with it the first stage toward the autonomy of the individual. Susanna and Figaro emerge victorious against the Count; Papageno enters the realm of the elect, albeit at a lower level; even Leporello has a spot reserved for himself, and may perhaps find a better master. Nocturnal gloom resolves in the major; suffering, death and despair are banished; and with a harlequin bow from the composer the curtain descends on a world of hope.

To transform this world into music Mozart invented new

techniques, constructive principles and instrumental colours. But he was right not to forget the dark hues. A few decades later the dream of a world of free and active human beings had become a utopia. Today there is even some danger that the curtain will ring down on a human tragedy of a darkness beyond the imagining even of Mozart.

Chapter 22

Building blocks and principles of construction

Among many other things, the correspondence between Goethe and Schiller turns on the problem of the relation between poetic impulse and deliberate construction. Writing from Jena on 27 March 1801, Schiller formulated this problem in a way that probably applies to the creation of all works of art, and most certainly to works of music. Recounting a debate with Schelling, he notes in passing that 'for the sake of their ideas, the honourable idealists take all too scant notice of experience'. He then explains that a poet 'starts with the unconscious', after which comes 'the clearest awareness of his operations'. He, the poet, may consider himself lucky to rediscover 'the initial, obscure, all-embracing idea [*dunkle Totalidee*] of his work' in the finished product. Then Schiller adds:

> Without an obscure but powerful all-embracing idea to precede one's technical exertions it is not possible to produce a work of poetry. And poetry, it seems to me, consists precisely in expressing and communicating this unconscious impetus, in translating it into an object.

Our chances of describing that 'obscure but powerful all-embracing idea' or retracing its origins are probably slim. But we may well be able to pursue its 'translation into an object'. After all, this object lies ready to hand – in our case in the form of an autograph score. Yet there is no branch of musicology that deals with questions of this sort, even though musical analysis, if carried out with sympathy and expertise, is always stumbling upon them. The so-called problem of the final movement (see pp. 247–8) also belongs to this complex of questions.

It should be mentioned that Rousseau saw and described this problem after his own fashion. His *Dictionnaire de musique* contains an article on *dessein*, by which he understood draft, plan, or even intention. Here he was not concerned with any particular beautiful aria or harmony but rather with a basic principle (*sujet principal*) that relates all the parts of a whole and forms that whole into a unity.

Similar words can be found in his article on melodic unity (*unité de mélodie*) and, unexpectedly, under original intention (*prima intenzione*), where he speaks of a process in the composer's imagination resulting in a piece of music 'di prima intenzione'. (Oddly, Rousseau assumed that this process did not exist in French music, hence his use of the Italian term.) The result, he claimed, is a piece of music that 'occurs to the composer in its entirety and with all of its parts, just as Pallas Athene sprang fully armed from the head of Jupiter'.

Though obviously indispensable, not even the most subtle analyses of individual passages, pieces or movements will suffice to answer the questions we are addressing here. This much is self-evident. Many useful and stimulating essays (including Frits Noske's of 1977) would, I feel, make greater headway if they were to pay more attention to what Schiller called individual 'operations' and how they relate to an 'all-embracing idea'. In our case, these operations consist in thematic and motivic variation, developmental techniques, in modulations and key schemes, in the distribution of sonorities, and many more things of the sort.

We can hardly imagine composers working in any other way. When Mozart read *La Folle Journée ou Le Mariage de Figaro* for the first time he must have formed – to use Schiller's unsurpassable phrase – an 'obscure but powerful' general concept of the work. Presumably this was accompanied, half consciously, half unconsciously, by a few technical ideas that could barely be captured in words, i.e. vague notions such as 'it should be in D major', or 'lots of ensembles and not much recitative', or 'almost everything in the major and cheerful'. Related ideas of a quite different sort must have occurred to him when Da Ponte (we assume) approached him with the proposal to set the Don Juan legend.

The nonexistent branch of musicology devoted to these questions will, it would seem, reach its destination most quickly if it concentrates on large and complex works and applies the method of comparison. This is what we shall try to do now. As always, restraint is recommended in the coining of new technical terms. We shall use the term 'building blocks', as earlier in this book, when speaking of motifs and themes, i.e. relatively clearly defined entities. By 'principle of construction' we mean the method (or methods) whereby motifs, themes, pieces, movements of a work, or acts of an opera are combined to form a whole. Our object is to compare *Le nozze di Figaro* and *Don Giovanni*, since the fundamental differences between these two works virtually demand this sort of treatment. They were composed within the span of a mere two years, between October 1785 and October 1787. Both operas are beholden to opera buffa and 'go from D', as Mozart would have said ('ex D gehen'), and both are written in Italian and set in Spain. Yet one could scarcely find four bars transplantable from the one to the other – and this in a century when entire arias were commonly borrowed from other stage works, even by other composers. This is perhaps the most incredible of the many incredible things about Mozart.

Of the several principles of construction which could probably be discovered in both these works, I will concentrate on four:

> the use of timbre
> the opposition of major and minor
> the choice of compositional models
> the singling-out of specific building blocks.

To start with, we should not underestimate the dimension of timbre. It might seem that the timbre of the eighteenth-century orchestra, and the assignment of vocal types to roles, was so completely codified by tradition that Mozart had little freedom to create original orchestral or vocal colours. Six pairs of winds, two timpani, five groups of string instruments – this is the normal disposition of his orchestra. Similarly, the choice of who was to sing tenor, soprano or bass was largely predetermined. By and large, Mozart managed perfectly well with twelve-stave manuscript paper, which even gave him enough room for the vocal parts. Only very rarely did he have to write wind parts on separate sheets. As for additional instruments, *Don Giovanni* and *Die Zauberflöte* call for three trombones; a mandoline accompanies Giovanni's serenade, No. 16; and Papageno has a glockenspiel (Tamino's flute belongs to the standard orchestra). Only one aria – Zerlina's first, No. 12 – requires an 'obbligato' instrument, in this case a solo cello. The three lightly scored on-stage orchestras in the first finale of *Don Giovanni*, and the somewhat more richly scored wind band in the second finale, supply colours which are lacking, for example, in *Figaro*, where the March in the Act III Finale might in principle have been entrusted to an on-stage orchestra. In *Così*, at a critical point in the drama, stage music is heard with a chorus behind the scene.

But this is only part of the story. *Figaro* is dominated by the sound of strings with woodwind and horns. Trumpets are heard, of course, in the Count's aria, No. 18. But except for that – and except for the final numbers of Acts II and IV, where they reinforce the orchestral tutti – they only appear in the ironically martial numbers: Bartolo's revenge aria (No. 4), the heroics imposed upon Cherubino by Figaro in No. 10, and the march parody in the Act III Finale.

In *Don Giovanni* the trumpets are handled quite differently. From the very first bar of the Overture they play a crucial part in the opera's tragic and gloomy undertone until, together with three trombones, they accompany Giovanni's descent into Hell in the Act II Finale. Hence, the relatively uniform orchestral sonority of *Figaro* contrasts with the richer palette of *Giovanni*, with its on-stage orchestras, trombones, mandolin, solo cello, and more liberal use of trumpets.

The second principle of construction – the opposition of major and minor – is also applied more liberally in the later work. Indeed, statistically the minor mode is of little importance in *Figaro*. Apart from short minor-key episodes, such as that of the Countess in No. 16.3 (mentioned above on p. 215), there are only two major-minor oppositions in the whole of the *Figaro* score. (A third was deleted by Mozart: the Overture, as the autograph clearly reveals, was originally intended to have a middle section in the minor. All that remains of it after the deletion and elimination of several pages of score is a single bar, reproduced in Plate 13a, of which we can only say that it would have become a siciliano in D minor. Mozart may well have wanted to preserve the major character not only of the Overture but of the entire opera.) Of the two minor-mode pieces, Barbarina's Cavatina, No. 24, devotes fewer than forty bars to her sorrow over the lost pin. There is nothing tragic or ominous about it; at the first Vienna production this piece, which raises the curtain on the fourth act, was sung by a twelve-year-old girl.

On the other hand, the second piece is among the most powerful juxtapositions of major and minor to be heard even in Mozart's works, and it is introduced with utmost sophistication. It is found in the finale that concludes the third act with some 230 bars of music, and is made up of four distinct pieces: march, chorus, dance, and shortened reprise of the chorus. This sequence may be regarded as a tripartite A-B-A form with the following overall pattern: introduction (march), part A (chorus), part B (dance), part A (reprise of chorus). But in view of the significance of the stage action in this finale, a purely musical explanation of this sequence is not enough.

With seemingly untroubled festive joy, the March introduces a spectacle which has been arranged in advance by Figaro. But here, as anyone with ears can soon hear, appearances deceive. This is a C major march of a special character whose very metre is ingeniously unstable. It consists of two groups of four alternating phrases, the first modulating to the dominant G major, the second to the tonic C major. But the groups are unevenly emphasized. Those leading to the dominant, in which of course the March cannot conclude, are disproportionately expanded into 8 + 14 + 14 + 8 bars. Those leading toward the tonic have to make do with 3 + 3 + 3 + 4 bars, as if they were short of time. Hence, forty-four bars lead to the dominant, but a mere fourteen to the resolving tonic. This is a hidden message to the Count: the ceremony he so abhors is not meant to come to an end.

The composer is permitted to express scorn where his characters must, for their various reasons, remain silent. But this scorn is given an even more explicit voice of its own. At first played softly by single instruments, then with ever greater insistence, and finally *forte*, the woodwind add a nagging, wailing three-note ornament on the strong beats in ever-new combinations of timbres, spread over three or four octaves:

Example 151

The figure is heard a total of twenty-four times – to the great detriment of the festive spirits. But the actors play their parts perfectly, and at some point the march reaches a conclusion after all. Now, in the most innocent of all allegrettos, the peasant lads and lasses sing the praises of their 'so very wise master' (*sì saggio signor*) for abandoning an offensive and degrading aristocratic privilege. And they do this no fewer than eight times. The Count is forced to listen, and Figaro's plan moves another step closer to fruition. The Count must be made to repeat his promise not to obstruct the wedding, and he must do so publicly before the entire village.

At this point there now begins that minor-mode section which provides the contrast upon which the whole scene is planned: the Fandango. Mozart has borrowed not only the theme of the piece from

Gluck's ballet *Don Juan* – which in turn took it from an Andalusian dance – but also its entire design. This design, both in its original form and in Gluck's recasting (the two versions are reprinted in Abert, II, music supplements pp. 16 and 17f.), has something unpredictable about it, probably because its theme, though strongly defined at the beginning, does not come to a conclusion but is simply spun out with motivic fragments and, unexpectedly, a few fresh motifs as well. Mozart's breathtaking mastery resides in his ability to bring the theme to a clear conclusion after eight bars (themselves irregularly constructed) and even to repeat it three more times, yet all the while intensifying its mood of unpredictability and menace.

To do this Mozart applies three devices. First, the theme is given a different continuation at each of its appearances. Second, the woodwind take part, sometimes doubling the violin melody at a higher or lower octave, sometimes adding sustained notes or disturbing contrapuntal sigh motifs to the texture. Third, the writing is interspersed with unexpected new motifs, one of them taken from Gluck's Fandango – maliciously, one almost wants to say, as though Mozart wished to show how to handle this sort of thing. For there is no denying that Mozart's Fandango has about it an eerie gloom against which Gluck's piece, wonderful as it is, pales in comparison. The plot does not stand still as the masters and servants dance their fandango. While the Count grandiloquently performs the ceremony of the bridal cap Susanna hands him a billet-doux inviting him to a tryst in the garden – a tryst which, however, will turn out quite differently from what he imagines. Opening the letter, he pricks his finger. This is observed by Figaro. He, however, is unaware that Susanna and the Countess have meanwhile continued the intrigue in a manner which, though not exactly thwarting his own designs, will cause him grief in the future. These seemingly harmless events on stage have a social dimension of historical proportions, though we must keep in mind the different levels of social awareness both in the stage figures and in their creators. In the event, the day was not far away when not only aristocratic privileges but the entire aristocracy would be abolished, at least in France to begin with. With a bit of arithmetic we discover that the first performance of *Figaro* was separated from that fateful day by a mere four years and two months. The Fandango is well and truly a dance on a volcano.

But the volcano fails to erupt. At the end of the Fandango the Count, every inch the benevolent sovereign, announces that the wedding will be celebrated with due pomp on that very same evening. He says this on the assumption that he will be able to spend a 'certain half-hour' with Susanna beforehand, having received her sham invitation for this very purpose. The concluding repeat of the villagers' chorus again seems to evoke the harmless atmosphere of singspiel.

The opera spans an arch from the D major of the overture to the D major of the final scene, thereby creating a unified key scheme. (Mozart, of course, since he wrote the overture last, completed this arch in reverse order, incorporating allusions to the finale into the overture.) In the midst comes that colossal scene in A minor, the Fandango, which in turn is embedded in the ironic C major of the Act III Finale.

Don Giovanni has a completely different design. Seen as a whole, it proceeds from D minor to D major, with far-reaching consequences. *Don Giovanni* is the only one of Mozart's mature operas that spans an arch from a minor-key opening to a major-key conclusion. In this respect it has only one predecessor in his œuvre: *Betulia liberata*, a work by the fifteen-year-old composer which likewise begins in D minor and ends in D major. *Don Giovanni*, in a manner of speaking, has redeemed the promise of Mozart's maladroit earlier effort.

Don Giovanni, as is well known, opens with the music of the figure who will bring the philandering hero of its title to justice. The *adagio* section of the Overture – likewise the last number to be composed – is a thirty-bar précis of the Commendatore scene, a section some six times longer in the Act II Finale that concludes the opera. What is important, and often overlooked, is that this scene too, leading to Giovanni's descent into Hell, ends in D *major*. In other words, the turn to the major mode is not reserved for the *scena ultima* that follows upon the Commendatore scene. The libertine's downfall is designed, not as a catastrophe, but as a liberation.

If the D minor of the opera's opening is intimately linked with the D minor of its conclusion, the same cannot be said of the two D major complexes, that of the overture and that of the final scene. There are good reasons for this: the major-mode section of the Overture depicts Giovanni's *joie de vivre* while that of the Act II Finale, examined somewhat more closely in the preceding chapter, is devoted to the future lives of the characters left behind.

In *Don Giovanni* Mozart made the juxtaposition of major and minor, or the transition from one to the other, a sustaining principle of construction. The very first number in the opera – the nocturnal scene in which Giovanni surprises Donna Anna, the Commendatore dies in a duel, and Leporello in his hiding-place protests that he cannot think what to say or do – follows a course that is unusual for Mozart, namely, from major to minor. Leporello's reluctant sentry duty begins in a brisk and uneasy F major, while the scene that concludes the number – a terzetto for three basses (likewise unique in Mozart's operas) uniting the voices of the dying Commendatore, the triumphant Giovanni and his servant – ends in F minor. The *dramma giocoso* begins tragically, the minor-to-major of the overture being immediately opposed by a gloomy major-to-minor. But we have not

been released from D minor yet. The duet between Donna Anna and
Don Ottavio, No. 2, returns again and again to the relentless D minor
in which it begins and ends whenever Ottavio attempts, in B flat
major, to soothe his distraught fiancée. Another instance is Donna
Anna's next important scene, No. 10, an accompanied recitative and
aria in D major which climaxes in a cry for vengeance:

Example 152

It, too, has a D minor episode, introduced by dissonances, in which
Anna recalls the wound in her father's breast:

Example 153

Another D minor scene, this time of nearly fifty bars, is found in the Act I Finale – the magnificent Terzetto between Anna, Elvira and Ottavio before, masked and armed, they enter Giovanni's banquet hall:

Example 154

If we count the other major-minor oppositions in the opera – one leading to B minor in Elvira's aria No. 8, another in B minor in Giovanni's aria No. 11, one in C minor and G minor in the Sextet, No. 19 – we arrive at a total of nine, of which six are in D minor. This is a significant and audible difference from the *Figaro* score, which has only two even if we include Barbarina's Cavatina. These two operas, then, are evidently based on quite different 'all-embracing ideas'.

The third principle of construction which distinguishes these two works, the choice of compositional models, must be seen in connection with the fact that *Figaro* is closer to opera buffa and *Don Giovanni* to opera seria. One consequence is that large-scale arias in the seria style do not figure significantly in *Figaro*. Only the Count is given such an aria – No. 18 – and it is used to isolate him from the other characters. In *Don Giovanni*, however, if we include the aria later added for Elvira (No. 21b), there are five.

This generic distinction is even more decisive in the ensembles. Mozart's great achievement of fusing stage action and symphonic technique can, of course, only come to full fruition where dramatic action truly does take place on stage. Take, for example, *Così fan tutte*, which is not laid out to provoke a collision of antagonists or antagonistic groups. As the plot is almost completely internalized, there is little room for symphonic technique. It is symptomatic that

Despina's change of identity is the key prop of the exterior plot not just in one finale but in both, neither of which by any means constitutes the high point of the work.

Figaro thrives on deliberately contrived confrontations, enacted on stage, between antagonistic groups of characters. In scenes such as the one between the Countess, Susanna and the Count (see pp. 211ff.) or the Sextet (see pp. 188ff.), the action is bursting with drama, and epic, lyric and dramatic sections alternate within a matter of seconds. These scenes are typical of *Figaro*, which contains a good dozen of the sort.

Nor does *Don Giovanni* lack its antagonistic groups of characters. But since it is in the nature of opera seria that its figures are inclined to proclaim and lament their conflicts in song rather than to resolve them in action, the score is laid out in a completely different way. All we know of Giovanni's amorous conquests is hearsay; despite Ottavio's many demands for and pledges of revenge, he fails to pull the trigger when Giovanni is finally cornered; Giovanni is either allowed to escape or he turns out to be the wrong man (No. 19, the Sextet); Masetto knows that he must grovel before his betters, and when he joins forces with others of his own kind he allows himself to be outwitted; and Elvira is passivity incarnate. As a result, compared with *Figaro*, symphonic development is of lesser importance in *Don Giovanni*. Instead, we are given musical set pieces more closely resembling the sequence of movements in a symphony than a symphonic movement itself.

There are two kinds of operatic ensemble. In the first, the composer's imagination is kindled by the personalities of his characters and their rapid changes of mood, which are in turn conditioned by the contingencies of the plot. We can call this type the *individual* or *action ensemble*. The other type might be called a *contemplative* or *situation ensemble*. Here the individual personalities of the characters seem to be temporarily suspended while they are held spellbound by an emotion: pain, fear or, more frequently, confusion. In this case the composer has to invent a thematic framework in which the individual characters can take their places.

Rossini was a master of the situation ensemble. A splendid example of this genre occurs in the Act I Finale of *Il barbiere di Siviglia*, culminating in a final scene with the words:

> Mi par d'esser colla testa in un orrida fucina.
>
> (I feel as if my head were in a horrible forge.)

The scene begins with a thematic framework from which, almost wilfully, any semblance of individual characterization has been expunged:

Example 155

Obviously the theme expresses not so much the characters' horror as the harmlessness of its causes.

The score of *Don Giovanni* is full of situation ensembles, but they are of a completely different kind. They reflect a moment in history at which – shortly before the volcano erupted – the classes held each other in check, not yet willing to press their advantage. The courage with which Susanna, Figaro and the Countess take fate in their own hands and publicly expose their adversaries is not to be found in the characters of *Don Giovanni*, perhaps precisely because the moment had drawn nigh at which this courage would be put to the test. Nor do the conspirators invoke the Commendatore: he is sent by Heaven. In sum, we are given impressive juxtapositions of characters in groups fraught with almost unbearable tension – a tension which, however, is never discharged. It is almost symbolic of the way conflicts are handled in this score that, in the Act I Finale, three dances from different levels of society – aristocracy, bourgeoisie and peasantry – can be heard simultaneously.

The manner in which Mozart combines action ensembles and situation ensembles in *Figaro* sheds revealing light on the opera's underlying concept, its all-embracing idea. We have already looked at one typical action ensemble in some detail (see pp. 211–16). In a finale, to quote the witty Da Ponte (1823–7, I, p. 202),

> all the singers, even if there be 300 of them, must appear on stage – singly, in pairs, in sixes, in their tens, in their sixties – in order to sing arias, terzettos, sixtiettos and grand choruses; and if the plot of the drama will not allow it, why then, it is the poet's task to find a way, no matter whether he thereby offends all common sense and breaks all the Aristotelian rules and precepts in the world.

Da Ponte did not have to go to such extremes in *Figaro*, but it nevertheless happens that seven persons find themselves in a state which some of them describe as:

Son confusa, son stordita   I am confused, benumbed,
Disperata, sbalordita.   desperate, perplexed.

and others as:

Che bel colpo, che bel caso!   What a stroke! what a turn!
è crescendo a tutti il naso.   Their noses have all grown
                                       a bit longer.

This calls for a situation ensemble. The one that concludes the finale looks as follows:

Example 156

In the finale of the last act Mozart takes the exact opposite approach. The garden act opens in a state of imbroglio – of tumult and confusion, of undiscovered disguise and dissimulation – calling for a thematic framework which limits the scope for individual characterization. For this purpose Mozart invented the following:

Example 157

But with the untangling of the imbroglio the personalities again step forward, and individual ensembles are used for the reconciliation of Susanna and Figaro and for the Count's unmasking and exoneration.

The larger pattern, then, is as follows: the Act II Finale moves from the collisions of the individual ensembles to a situation ensemble of general confusion, while the Act IV Finale, conversely, proceeds from the confusion of the situation ensemble to its resolution in individual ensembles.

Once all the conflicts have been resolved, however, general agreement reigns among the characters, now nine in number. Beginning *andante* and *sotto voce*, they express this agreement once again in a situation ensemble. But what an ensemble, and what a situation! The Count is humiliated and all are satisfied, but the manner in which they are satisfied has been determined by the Countess and – as we shall soon see – by Susanna. Enlightenment is not just mankind's escape from his self-imposed immaturity (in Immanuel Kant's incomparable phrase), it is also women's escape from domination by men. In this ensemble Mozart, once again, found novel ways of expressing a 'conviction'.

What a situation, and what an ensemble! Calculated from the Countess's words of forgiveness, it occupies no more than twenty-one bars, six of which, beginning at bar 430, are exquisitely beautiful. Let us try to trace the enigmatic origins of that beauty.

The underlying text consists merely of two short lines from Da Ponte's libretto:

> Ah tutti contenti
> Saremo così.
>
> (Ah, in this way
> we shall all be satisfied.)

They are sung by the nine characters, now united in an ensemble, using the same melody with which the Countess, six bars previously, had forgiven the Count, saying:

> Più docil'io sono,
> E dico di si.
>
> (I am more open to good sense
> and say, Yes.)

Her feeling of superior sense is warranted, and not only compared to the Count: men in general are seldom masters in the art of understanding and forgiveness.

Before the ensemble takes the Countess's melody from her lips, we hear a sublime figure in the violins. This figure has been described in poetic terms by Ivan Nagel (1985, p. 39):

> Mercy itself seems to fall earthward in the unison of the violins, whose descending quavers weave gently into the paean of the

ensemble, not as bookish tone-painting, but like a rediscovered blessing from a language antecedent to Babel.

But miraculous though this violin figure may be, it is also one of the building blocks of the *Figaro* score, and it owes the quality of its earthward-descending mercy to the fact that in the course of four acts we have heard this particular kind of broken triad (already pointed out in Chapter 9, pp. 66–7, and in Examples 13 to 18), now similar, now identical, nearly 100 times in more than a dozen numbers. It is first announced by Susanna, to whom it belongs in a highly specific way. In her very first duet with Figaro she draws attention to herself, and away from his pedantic measurements, by singing:

Example 158

He then takes up this little motif, and their two voices unite in the shortest love duet in all opera:

Example 159

In Act IV this duet will be rounded off to form an equally short love duet based on the same broken triad:

Example 160

277

In the Duettino, No. 5, Susanna leaves it to the violins to proclaim her triumph over Marcellina:

Example 161

But she herself divulges her semi-infatuation for Cherubino:

Example 162

In the utter consternation brought about by the Count as he stumbles upon Cherubino putting on a dress and cap, Susanna alone keeps a clear head by singing a melody to her motif:

Example 163

One of the tart responses heaped on the Count in Scene 16.3 of the Act II Finale (already discussed above) takes the form of Susanna's tune:

Example 164

It is only logical that the Count, in the Duettino, No. 17, should warble an inversion of Susanna's motif to express his delight that she is finally about to yield her favours (see Example 165), and no less logical that she should defend her ruse with the very same inversion (see Example 166). In the Sextet, No. 19, the

Mi sen− to − dal con − ten − to

Example 165

Scu − sa − te − mi — se − men − to

Example 166

orchestra, as already mentioned, plays this inversion to her a dozen times without being able to quell her anger:

Example 167

In her Aria, No. 20, the Countess slips into a variant of Susanna's motif, just as she slips into her clothes in the plot:

la me − mo − ria di − quel be − ne

Example 168

Susanna then expands this in the Garden Aria, No. 28:

Deh vie − ni non tar − dar, oh gio — ia bel − la

Example 169

and

in − co − ro − nar ———— di ro — se,

Example 170

279

Figaro sarcastically exaggerates Susanna's – and his – motif as he feigns his love for the Countess:

Example 171

after which the two grant themselves eight full measures of sweet rapprochement in the 'Pace pace' scene (see Example 160).

And then the ineffable violin figure in the final scene! By now we have already heard it many times, usually sung, sometimes played by the orchestra, generally somewhat faster and more compact, but sometimes in the same andante and with the same expansiveness. But never before have we heard it played *unisono* by all the violins, beginning *piano* and leading downwards with a *crescendo*:

Example 172

280

Thus, the figure is able to sound at once familiar and yet novel, summarizing all that has happened to it beforehand and yet sounding as though it had dropped from heaven. It is a miracle of constructive artifice, using a tiny building block which another composer might have considered scarcely worthy of notice.

There is much wisdom in giving this little motif first to Susanna rather than to Figaro. She sings it to the words 'sembra fatto inver per me' – 'it seems made precisely for me' (see Example 158) – referring to the hat she is trying on. But the words seem exactly to fit the motif that Mozart has invented for her, and truly for her alone. The motif of self-assertion belongs first and foremost to Susanna: Figaro adopts it from her; it is Susanna who first opens Figaro's eyes to the schemes of the Count; it is she and the Countess who rescue Figaro when the Count drives him into a corner with his inquisitorial questions; and it is also the two women who take control of the master plan to outwit the Count and carry it out in their own way, thereby also teaching Figaretto a lesson. We are, after all, dealing no less with the marriage of Susanna than with that of Figaro. Mozart's music brings this to life by giving musical precedence to her. It is only logical that Susanna's motif should also usher in those exquisite bars of conciliatory resolution. Now let us observe how Susanna's motif of self-assertion is made to dovetail with the Countess's melody of reconciliation.

The first thing we notice are the dynamic marks: the ensemble that takes up the Countess's melody sings it *sotto voce* – softly, with subdued voice – while the accompanying wind play *pianissimo*. The violins entrusted with Susanna's motif, on the other hand, play it three times *piano* – and *crescendo*, although it is directed downwards. Evidently the practically-minded Mozart did not wish its lower notes to vanish in the overall sonority; at each occurrence the motif is meant to be audible to the very last of its seven notes. This is an unusual, even unique method of handling levels of dynamics. Both of these musical phrases – Susanna's and the Countess's – are meant to stand side by side on an equal and independent footing, as do the two women themselves.

First, as we note in bar 430, Susanna introduces the ensemble with a sort of improvised prelude; the two women overlap for no more than two quavers. The reason for this is that the voices enter with the Countess's gentle melody before the violins have reached the end of the motif. The second version, in E minor (bar 432), retains its introductory character since, of course, it leads into the second phrase of the melody. But because the violins elide with the singers, and vice versa, this time there are five quavers of overlap. In the third version (bar 434) the overlap is extended to seven quavers as a long, sustained note in the voices virtually invites the motif to join in. Finally, in bar

435, Susanna's motif and the Countess's melody, resounding together for nine quavers, coincide.

Thus, Susanna's motif sets out in the first number of the opera and enlivens the work throughout until, blending with the melody of the Countess, it resolves the conflicts to the satisfaction of all and concludes the plot. Always euphonious, occasionally rebellious, never averse to cunning, deception or reversal, it unfolds in irresistible litheness and grace, garlanding the melody of the Countess.

The same litheness and grace, here the result of a contrapuntal masterpiece, were also heard in No. 21 when the two women, their voices joined in seductive euphony, devised their sham billet-doux inviting the Count to a tryst. But by the end of the work female cunning has triumphed and is no longer required. It was Figaro who had taken up arms against his master; it was also he who won the first stage of the battle, forcing the Count to repeat in public his renunciation of the *jus primae noctis*. But only the cunning of the female characters was able to force the Count to renounce this right in deed as well as word. Without cries of victory, without vengeance, without gestures of superiority or other insignia of male domination, the two women offer us a prevision of how human conflicts, once they have become unbearable, might be resolved.

This is an impressive example of how the fourth of our principles of construction – the preference for particular building blocks – functions. As this amiable and light-hearted musical element is heard over and over again, usually as a brief motif but sometimes expanded into a theme, it has a decisive impact on the character of the entire work.

Don Giovanni, on the other hand, is dominated throughout by a dark and ominous element: scales or scalar segments, diatonic and chromatic, major or minor or mixtures of both. These are not the quick rushing scales traditionally used (even in *Figaro*) in cadential passages, but rather scalar figures ascending or descending in slow or moderate tempo. They can be heard as early as bar 23 of the overture:

Example 173

These figures give the opera its basic material. Segments and transformations of them permeate the entire drama as a constant forewarning of impending catastrophe.

This sort of musical commentary is heard as early as the death of the Commendatore:

Example 174

And the duet which follows, between Anna and Ottavio, has the figure in both its ascending and descending forms:

Example 175

Even Leporello's seemingly comic itemization of Giovanni's conquests (No. 3) warns of the doom with which he is playing:

Example 176

In Elvira's Aria, No. 8, the scalar figures occur in multiple variants, emotionally intensified:

Example 177

It is Anna who introduces the chromatic descending version in the Quartet, No. 9:

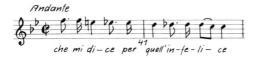

che mi di — ce per quell'in-fe- li — ce

Example 178

And it is the oboe and bassoon that present a diatonic version in Anna's Aria, No. 10:

Example 179

The D minor Terzetto, that of the three maskers in the Act I Finale, highlights the descending lines of the vocal parts by reiterating various figures of this sort:

Example 180

Their second Terzetto, entreating Heaven to aid them in their perilous enterprise, ends just before the ballroom scene with the same scalar motif as was given to Anna, this time played *adagio* by four woodwinds:

tra-di- to a— ze — lo del — mio

Example 181

Also in the Act I Finale is the realization, expressed by all three, and once again in the form of a descending scalar motif, that the miscreant Giovanni is no longer in a position to deceive them:

Example 182

Nor can we even discount the possibility that the ascending scale which forms a countermelody to the theme in Zerlina's Aria, No. 18 (analysed in Chapter 16), falls into the same category:

Example 183

Whatever the case, scalar motifs are all the more plain and unambiguous in the Sextet, No. 19. To mention but two passages, Elvira's plea for clemency for her purportedly faithless husband, and Leporello's appeals for mercy after disclosing his true identity, are filled with many of them (see Example 184). Leporello's whining, continued in his Aria, No. 20, though at a quicker tempo, also fits into this category (see Example 185). Even Ottavio's Aria, No. 21, composed of quite different thematic material, ends in a brief orchestral postlude with the familiar chromatic descent (see Example 186). Nor is it surprising that the fear-ridden

Example 184

Example 185

Example 186

Leporello should provoke two types of descending scales from the orchestra when he is made to invite the statue of the Commendatore to dinner:

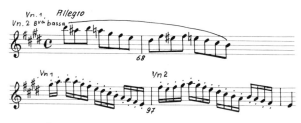

Example 187

And we have already mentioned (see Example 145) that Anna's voice descends more than an octave when she speaks of her eerie encounter with the Commendatore in the final scene.

We now know that there exist two different types of mental activity – the one spontaneous, holistic, quasi-automatic, the other logical, analytical, expressible in discourse. It also seems likely that the two hemispheres of the human brain work together in both these forms of mental activity. Knowing these things, we stand a better chance of understanding Schiller's thought quoted at the outset of the chapter. Mozart, then, with complete awareness of the musical 'operations' he performed, was able to take the 'obscure but powerful all-embracing idea' that sprang to his mind as he absorbed these two mighty operatic themes with all his senses, and to 'translate this idea into an object' – and by way of that object to his listeners, or at least to those of them with ears. Nevertheless, the way he accomplished this is and will ever remain a miracle.

Chapter 23

'A hostile fate – though only in Vienna'

Mozart's supreme creations did not pay off financially. On the day the Bastille was stormed in Paris, eight years after his move to Vienna, Mozart sent a harrowing letter to his fellow Freemason Michael Puchberg, asking urgently for money. He described his situation in the strongest possible language: he would be lost, together with his sick wife and child, if Puchberg did not help him. This same long letter (14 July 1789) contains the following passage: 'Unfortunately Fate is so hostile to me, *though only in Vienna,* that even when I want to, I cannot make any money. A fortnight ago I sent round a list, and the only name on it is Swieten's!' (This, of course, was a subscription list for a projected series of concerts. Five years previously a similar list had brought 176 subscribers.) This letter was neither the first nor the last that Mozart sent to Puchberg. Between June 1788 and June 1791 he wrote twenty letters asking for loans, each of them worded more urgently than the last. Mozart would have preferred to have Puchberg lend him a larger amount – he proposed one or two thousand gulden (17 June 1788) – which, he claimed, probably deceiving himself, would free him from his desperate plight. Puchberg did in fact come to his aid, but only with smaller sums amounting over these three years to a total of 1,415 gulden (Konstanze paid them back after her husband's death). Mozart also turned at least three times to other people for loans, including two larger sums.

The great expectations that had accompanied Mozart to Vienna remained, in the long run, unfulfilled, and he was unable to maintain the comfortable life his family had enjoyed from 1784 to 1787. His plans to fetch his father and sister to Vienna so as to improve and safeguard their living conditions seem to have been silently buried. Nor, apparently, could he keep his promise to help pay off the debts his father had incurred from the Paris journey. On the contrary, when his father died in Salzburg on 28 May 1787 Mozart was only too happy to accept a thousand gulden from the sale of his effects.

'He betrays pain at his loss but at the same time takes pleasure in his inheritance.' These macabre words were spoken, if not by Mozart himself, at least by Herr Stachelschwein in the draft playlet *Der Salzburger Lump in Wien* (*Briefe* IV, p. 167). Mozart's calculations were no less doomed to failure than his father's much earlier plans to secure the family's livelihood by putting his children on display. Wolfgang Amadé's quip, 'splendid in point of honour, meagre in point of money' (15 October 1790), might have served as the Mozart family motto. And he had many an occasion to write down these or similar words.

It has been calculated that at no time in his life did Mozart actually face starvation. In the critical year of 1787, for instance, he had an income 'more than triple the salary of a head physician at a Viennese hospital' (Kraemer 1976, p. 207). The arithmetic is doubtless correct: in addition to the 800 gulden Mozart received annually from the imperial coffers beginning in 1787, he always had various other irregular sources of income that also brought in some large amounts, even during the bitter years of 1790 to 1791. At times he could maintain a horse, and he never in his life went without a servant, or Konstanze without household help. (The story of the 'six little Polish ponies' in Mozart's possession, however, is most likely spurious.) It does not seem to have caused him any financial problem to send for an extra portion of sturgeon when his 'appetite today was rather voracious' (8–9 October 1791). True, when Mozart resolved in 1790 to travel to Frankfurt at his own expense and in his own carriage to attend the emperor's coronation, he had to pawn a set of silver tableware to cover the costs of the journey. But in any event he had a set of silver tableware. The final quarters of the Mozart family, in the Rauhensteingasse, had less light and air and were less spacious than those in the Domgasse (Landon 1988, Appendix A). But they were nevertheless situated in Vienna's best district, far better than were his previous lodgings in the Landstrasse or the Alsergrund. Nor were they by any means substandard: there were four rooms with ample space not only for a desk, piano and marital bed but also a billiard table and plenty of furniture for receiving visitors.

As a rule, calculations of Mozart's income are usually accompanied by moralizing and implicit criticism. I would like to avoid both. If only – so the argument goes – Mozart or Konstanze had been better able to budget their household, if only they had been willing to settle for a lifestyle appropriate to musicians at the time, except for castratos or prima donnas with their 'agile throats' and correspondingly sharp elbows, then they would not have had to beg for loans. This is correct, as far as it goes. But who can say whether Mozart would have been able to compose under more modest circumstances? And he would never have been able to maintain relations with influential and well-to-do families – then as now known as 'protection' – while living beneath the standard which everyone, including himself, considered appropriate to his station in life.

No, there is a deeper explanation for Mozart's lifestyle. From childhood on he had been accustomed to lead a life which, though fraught with hard work and exertion, was not without its comforts and even certain luxuries: servants, expensive clothing, hair styling, jewelry. He saw no reason to dispense with these or similar perquisites now that his genius had flowered and his reputation and fame had grown. He had to have a 'certain red tail-coat' on which 'to put on the buttons' that he had long been 'dreaming of' – so reads a letter of 28 September 1782. He had spent many a morning 'in champagne' with Schikaneder, Nissen reports (1828, p. 570), and many a half-night 'in punch'. Konstanze loved 'fancy goods' and was 100 gulden in debt to 'the haberdasher at Stock im Eisen' (early May 1790). Among these goods was presumably that 'ribbon' (*Bandel*) to whose existence we owe the charming Terzetto, K441. Least of all did Mozart want to keep his wife from 'taking the waters' as, by the standards of the time, she was entitled to do, evidently being seriously ill. He was no doubt telling the truth when he wrote about the 'appalling expenses in connection with my wife's cure' (17 July 1789). These expenses resulted not only from doctors' fees, medicine and so forth, but also from the fact that he had at times to maintain two households.

The people in Mozart's circles often calculated expenses in a manner completely alien to frugal puritans:

> The sinecures of the canons in Würzburg and Bamberg are among the best in Germany. In good years they bring in 3,500 gulden and more. To be sure, one seldom finds a canon with only one sinecure. Many have four to five in an equal number of abbeys, and arrive in this way at their eight, ten or twelve thousand gulden each year. The prelates in these abbeys probably receive twenty to thirty thousand gulden annually, and the labour of a German canon consists entirely in appearing one particular month of the year at the performance of the choir of his collegiate church. He needs no talents other than an ability to read Latin and his matrilineal descent from a canoness, for the nobility of his father can, in the strict sense, never be proved.

Thus reads a passage from Risbeck's *Briefe eines reisenden Franzosen* (II, p. 259). Johann Pezzl, in his *Skizze von Wien* (I, p. 97), draws comparisons

> between the prince who, in one year, consumes half a million, and the invalid day-labourer who lives from twenty-five gulden; between the countess who has one thousand gulden to spend

daily and the little embroidery girl in the suburbs who, for her long day's toil, earns three-and-a-half kreuzer.

In Born's *Neueste Naturgeschichte des Mönchthums* we read: 'The caterpillar devours only leaves; the monk, a kingdom. The bedbug drains a tiny capillary; the monk, entire Christian congregations to the last drop' (Preface, 3v.). The Masons in Mozart's lodge did more than simply engross themselves in what Emperor Joseph called 'conjurings'; their regularly held lectures must surely have dealt with these larger issues as well. And Mozart frequented circles of people who resolutely demanded their rights rather than piously making do with what they had.

There is no reason to accept the views given by Uwe Kraemer in the aforementioned article, or any similar allegations, that Mozart squandered vast sums in gambling. Joseph Heinz Eibl, the author of the uncommonly detailed commentary and index to the complete edition of the Mozart family correspondence, likewise refused to believe in the existence of these gambling debts (1976). But some explanation must be forthcoming for the Mozarts' shortage of money. After all, only two years previously they could still afford all of their comforts, though admittedly without Konstanze's expensive cures.

There are two theories about Mozart's straitened finances that must be taken seriously. One of them derives from Joseph's luckless campaign against the Turks, the so-called Little Turkish War of 1787 to 1791, with its disastrous results. Many aristocratic families left the capital, thereby causing its theatre and music life to suffer. The Kärntnertor Theatre shut its doors for three-and-a-half years. But others, including the Burgtheater, remained open, and a new one, the Freihaus or Wiedner Theatre, was built and inaugurated during this period of crisis. Even the balls at the Hofburg went on without interruption. Another theory claims that Mozart was abandoned by the aristocracy, who never forgave him for *Figaro*. The two theories are not mutually exclusive. As yet, according to information kindly supplied by Adelbert Schusser of the Vienna Historical Museum, no special studies have been made of Viennese music life during the Little Turkish War. Research based on diaries, letters and newspaper articles is required. We know that at least one concert series continued unabated: van Swieten's performances of the works of Bach and Handel, for which Mozart made arrangements of the scores and conducted the performances. At least five are known to have taken place during these critical years (*NMA* X/28/1, p. xii). Mozart would not have neglected the opportunity to circulate a subscription list for his proposed academies among the audience. But apart from van Swieten, no one else subscribed.

No less striking is the fact that many of the high-placed persons with whom Mozart was in good standing during his early years in Vienna, including Countess Thun, Count Cobenzl and Baroness Waldstätten, seem to have vanished from his circle of acquaintances, as did the Jacquin brothers. Indeed, we sense a sort of alienation from his early Viennese friends and protectors, and it is not far-fetched to assume that ever since *Figaro* Mozart had become too radical for many of his former acquaintances. It should also be said that the Emperor, whose policies envisioned the curtailing of aristocratic privileges, had less to say against the opera, particularly as it was in Italian, than many a nobleman closer to the rank of Count Almaviva. Nonetheless, although two German translations were obtainable at Vienna's book-shops, the Emperor did have reservations against the performance of the original play in German. As a result of the Emperor's concern, though not directly at his bidding, a performance of the play by Schikaneder's troupe was banned at the last moment.

From earliest childhood Mozart was accustomed to step into his carriage and travel to wherever music could be converted into money. This being so, there was nothing unusual about his sixteenth journey, which took him to Frankfurt-am-Main for the coronation of the Emperor. Nothing unusual, that is, apart from the extraordinary fact that Mozart was not one of the four elect composers (Salieri, Wranitzky, Righini and Vogler) whose works were chosen to grace the celebrations. Nor was he among the fifteen chamber musicians who, under the direction of Salieri and Umlauff, travelled to Frankfurt at the Emperor's expense as part of his retinue. What was unusual, however, were the surrounding circumstances.

Let us take a closer look at one of Mozart's letters. Attention was drawn to it as early as 1959 by Jean and Brigitte Massin in their Mozart book, though their interpretation, as far as I know, has yet to be so much as noticed in the German-language literature on Mozart. On his return journey from Frankfurt Mozart, writing from Munich (before 4 November 1790), sent one of his many letters to Konstanze. In it he discloses plans to 'take this very same journey with you'. This letter offers evidence, both intrinsic and extrinsic, that it is one of those which he considered 'oracular'. 'Schumbla! That is a word to ponder.' Thus Mozart wrote to his wife on 11 June 1791, and the letter we are looking at likewise contains words to be pondered. Something lies enciphered beneath its overt wording.

Let me begin with the extrinsic evidence. It resides in an obvious incongruity. Mozart writes that he wants to take the tour with Konstanze so that she can 'try another spa'. But that is precisely what she would *not* have been able to do on such a tour, as both the author of the letter and its recipient knew full well. A short while previously (12 June 1790 or earlier) Mozart had written to Puchberg that Konstanze would have to 'take the baths sixty times'. He was constantly urging her not to overtax herself with her baths, to take them at long intervals and to sleep long at night. She would never have found the time or the leisure to do this on a concert tour. On this one, too, as with Mozart's other concert tours (and unlike his journeys to rehearse an opera or to await a decision on an application), Mozart did not remain long in any one town. Only in Frankfurt did he stay eighteen days; his stay in Mainz lasted five days, and in the other towns only one or two. And in which place, or places, was she supposed to take her cure? In those days one could not simply step into any random bathtub. In Vienna, for example, there were no medicinal waters to be found, and one was forced to travel to Baden. (This is, incidentally, no different today.) It is unthinkable that Mozart and Konstanze reckoned with finding several spas on their intended tour.

In short, the tour and 'the waters' were incompatible. Mozart did not advise Konstanze to try a different spa but rather to try a different *kind* of spa, and he went on to itemize its ingredients: 'company, activity [*motion*, in the French], change of air'. This regimen, Mozart claimed, 'has done wonders for me' – and we can be sure he did not follow it in a bathtub.

Now let us turn to the letter's intrinsic evidence. Mozart's journey took place during the initial phase of the French Revolution, which had undergone one of its first turning points on 24 January 1789 with the summoning of the States-General and witnessed a series of climaxes in rapid succession: the fall of the Bastille on 14 July 1789, the Declaration of the Rights of Man on 26 August, the forced return of the king from Versailles to Paris on 6 October, the dissolution of monasteries on 13 February 1790, the abolition of the nobility on 19 June, and the Festival of Federation on the first anniversary of the storming of the Bastille. 'Not until the upheavals of 1789', writes Manfred Kossok (1986, p. 9),

> did the central power of the ancien régime fall. The bourgeois revolutionary cycle went beyond the borders of France and entered the phase of its universalization and globalization. A new age dawned in the history of mankind: the advancing bourgeoisie transformed the face of the earth according to its own notions.

These objective facts coincided with a subjective feeling on the part of countless observers that they were witnessing something epochal and earth-shattering. The events in France echoed in the lands of Germany and Austria with a force that was new in the history of the world.

'Had I an hundred voices I should sing the liberty of Gaul'. Thus reads the opening of Klopstock's ode of 24 May 1790, *Sie und nicht wir* ('They, and Not We'). Less passionately, but no less impressively, Immanuel Kant wrote in his *Critique of Judgement* of 1790 of 'a total restructuring, recently undertaken, of a mighty nation into a state' (§ 65, footnote). In May 1790 Wieland wrote his *Unparteiische Betrachtungen über die Staatsrevolution in Frankreich* ('Impartial Observations on the State Revolution in France'), in which we can read:

> No wonder, then, that from the first moment of a revolution so great, so unheard-of, so patently impossible ... the general attention of Europe should be riveted to this astonishing spectacle, [and] that among so many millions of foreign spectators there were few who, in its first days, were not filled with an almost involuntary instinct to take part in it, to applaud those noble men who had been placed by their character, their fortitude and their admirable powers of intellect at the vanguard of a great, noble, enlightened, spirited and courageous nation driven to extremes by insufferable despotism, and who, with unwonted restlessness and greater or lesser feelings of passion, hoped for its victory.

Or, take a letter of 26 September 1791 by Johann Heinrich Voss: 'What times we are witnessing, friend! what vistas into the near future!' Or another, written from Paris on 26 August 1789 by Johann Heinrich Campe (an educationalist, writer and tutor to the Humboldt brothers) and published in Brunswick in 1790: 'And what hopes, what expectations, what inexorable prophesies they give us! My heart warms and swells at the contemplation of these magnificent prospects!' As late as 1796–7 Goethe, in *Hermann und Dorothea* (*Clio*, v. 6ff.), could still write:

> For who would dare deny that his heart beat faster,
> That his breast did swell to the throb of a purer pulse,
> As the new sun arose in its pristine majesty,
> As he heard of the Rights of Man that were common to all,
> Of Liberty's thrill and the merits of Equality!
> In those days all did hope to live their lives themselves,
> The bond that fettered the many countries held in thrall
> To idleness and self-interest, did seem to be untied.
> Did not all the nations in those days of urgency
> Look toward the Capital of the World, a name so long
> Deserved, and yet now more than e'er before?
> Were not those men, who first did trump the glad tidings,
> Names like unto the greatest ever known under the sun?
> Did not courage, spirit and voice swell in every man?
> And we, its neighbours, at first did share the ardour.

(The 'capital of the world' is, of course, Paris.) And here is Hegel, writing about the French Revolution from a distance of three or four decades in his *Vorlesungen über die Philosophie der Weltgeschichte* (IV, p. 936):

> As long as the sun remained implanted in the firmament and the planets circled about it, it had not been noticed that Man stands on his head, that is, on his thought, and creates reality in accordance with his thought. Anaxagoras was the first to say that the world is ruled by *nous* [the Greek word for reason or intellect]. Now, for the first time, Man had come to realize that spiritual reality should be ruled by thought. It was, therefore, a magnificent sunrise! A sublime feeling reigned in those days, an enthusiasm of the spirit transfixed the world, as though for the first time there had been a true reconciliation between the Divinity and the world.

It is not among musicology's most glorious achievements that it should so stubbornly cling to the belief that the greatest composer of the age was one of the few who did not await the success of the Revolution with 'feelings of passion', that so astute and sensitive an observer as Mozart, of all people, should feel nothing of this 'sublime feeling' or 'enthusiasm of the spirit', that the composer of *Figaro* and *Don Giovanni* should not have noticed that the nobility had been abolished in France, the same nobility that he had looked upon with derision and contempt from the day he was capable of critical thought.

What we are discussing, to stress the point once again, is the first phase of the French Revolution. As it progressed, with the execution of Louis XVI in January 1793 and the convening of a Revolutionary Tribunal, many of its former admirers, though by no means all of them, turned away from it in dismay. Mozart did not live to witness this phase, and we have no idea how he might have reacted to it. As for its first phase, however, it remains to be discovered that he was more than a mere contemporary observer, and that he actively took part in it with his music.

Mozart's tour brought him into immediate proximity to the events in France, and this not only in a geographical sense. It led him to the Palatinate, where arbitrary government had raised the exploitation of the population to the level of a fine art. Risbeck had lashed out at this years before in words as notable for their bitterness as for their finely-honed irony (1784, p. 333):

> Yet nothing gave me such a vivid conception of the subserviency of this country as did the list of an electoral tax collector regarding the duties to be levied on its subjects in relation to their prosperity. For my part, it would put me in an insoluble

quandary to devise an item that did not already appear on this list, unless it be an excise on the air inhaled by those residing on Palatinate soil.

In a monumental study of the Mainz Republic (1975, 1981, 1989) Heinrich Scheel has presented a masterfully researched, documented and annotated body of material to show how it came about that the first bourgeois democratic republic on German soil should have arisen precisely within the borders of this ravished country.

In October 1792 the Palatinate towns of Speyer, Worms and Mainz were occupied by an army from revolutionary France. The lines immediately following those quoted above from Goethe's *Hermann und Dorothea* read as follows:

> And then the war began, and files of armèd French
> Drew ever nearer; yet they seemed to bring but friendship.
> And that indeed they brought, for noble were the souls
> Of all; they planted with joy the trees of liberty,
> Promising to each his own, and to each his government.

In Mainz, then, the preconditions had been met for the formation of a 'Society of German Friends of Liberty and Equality' patterned after the Jacobin Clubs in France. Reading the minutes of the club meetings that took place in Mainz between late October 1792 and late May 1793 (Scheel I), one might think that Sarastro, his priests and the Drei Knaben had set about turning into concrete rules their general ideas of the triumph of the wise man who will reward virtue and punish vice. Here the ideas matured that later materialized in the parliament of the Mainz Republic, the Rhenish German National Assembly, which convened on 17 March 1793 (its minutes appear in Scheel II). No fewer than 125 localities sent elected delegates to this assembly, which on the very next day decreed that 'in the stretch of territory from Landau to Bingen all acts of arbitrary power imposed to date shall be rescinded' (III, p. 218). This area of roughly three thousand square kilometres, bounded by the rivers Rhine, Nahe and Queich, had previously consisted of more than two dozen princedoms, earldoms, dukedoms, margraviates, sacerdotal foundations and other suchlike, making it one of the most fragmented regions of Germany.

Mozart did not live to witness the Club or the Assembly. But Scheel's study (III, pp. 15ff.) gives ample proof that even at the time of Mozart's tour the Palatinate towns and regions through which he travelled were in a state of ferment. Demands for the abolition of serfdom were presented to the prince at his residence in Bruchsal; taxes and compulsory labour were withheld in many places; meetings of disgruntled artisans and townsfolk were held which the authorities tried in vain to counter with military force; here a bailiff was transported by peasants over the border, 'bound on a cart', there a senior clerk chose to flee to Mannheim. Occurrences of this sort were reported in newspapers. The Hamburg *Politisches Journal* (1790, I, p. 1157) printed a letter from Mannheim, dated 20 February 1790, in which a body of citizens was said to have formed in Kreuznach, containing three delegates from each guild and chaired by the blacksmiths. Since this time, so the letter continues, 'men, women, children, greybeards, and even persons of authority carry a hammer to signify their patriotism whenever they appear in public' (*ibid.*, p. 18).

In 1791 there appeared, anonymously and without the name of a publisher, an 'original patriotic drama' entitled *Die Rebellion* which, according to its editor Gerhard Steiner, was most likely intended to be set in the town of Speyer. Though by no means a literary masterpiece, it evokes a fascinating picture of the times. As in so many critiques of the day, the author sought corruption not in the 'gracious sovereign' and his ministers but rather among their villainous representatives. When the chief villain, a judicial councillor, questions the ability of the common people even to calculate what they are owed, he is rebuffed by a lawyer who has taken the side of the oppressed and who exclaims, in language foreshadowing Grabbe and Nestroy:

> Every man among the common people understands the princi ples of accounting from their very basis. If he is to pay, something is always added and multiplied; if he is to receive, something is always subtracted and divided. For this reason he must be well apprised of all the operations of arithmetic. When his knowledge of them comes to an end, the remainder is usually nought from nought, and he can no longer apply his acquired art. To pass the time he must then exercise himself in the addition of alms occasionally cast to him by his magnanimous tutors.

Asked who retained him, the lawyer replies: 'Wailing and lamentation have sent me hither... The nation will draw together all its courage to burst the chains of slavery, to shake off the yoke and seize the dog-whip from the hands of its oppressors. Men want to be men, and not the footstools of barbarians.'

The Mainz Republic, then, did not fall from the heavens like a thunderbolt. Even as early as 1790 an observant and sensitive traveller could easily have felt the excitement which had taken hold of the region. One or another incident found its way into newspapers and pamphlets, quite apart from the fact that news naturally travelled by word of mouth, placing it, of course, beyond the reach of documentary evidence.

One point, however, has been documented. Mozart witnessed just how deeply the notions of a bourgeois alternative to aristocratic rule had taken root in the minds of many of his professional colleagues. And he witnessed this in Mainz on his very own terrain: the opera stage. Erich Schenk (1975, p. 630) claims that it was probably music lovers who had attracted Mozart to Mainz,

> perhaps even the accounts of a young musician at court... In the coronation capital he had made the acquaintance of excellent members of the court orchestra not only in Frau Schick, but also in the young violinist and enthusiastic Mozartian Heinrich Anton Hoffmann (1770–1842) ... Just as in Prague, a community of young Mozart devotees seems to have formed in the National Theatre. Of these the two Hoffmanns – the above-mentioned violinist and his elder brother, the pianist Karl Philipp (1769-after 1836) – stood out in particular.

This seems perfectly correct. Since, however, it is considered out of place for musicologists to venture into neighbouring disciplines, the significance of these events for Mozart's thoughts, work, and not least of all his moods, has been as good as ignored. Let us start with the last-named category:

On 30 September 1790 Mozart wrote from Frankfurt:

> To me everything is cold - cold as ice.

and on 8 October, likewise from Frankfurt:

> I am famous, admired and liked here, yet ...

But before 4 November he could advise Konstanze from Munich:

> to try some other spa [which has] done wonders for me.

On 26 June 1784 Friedrich Schiller, who was then not quite twenty-five years of age, some four years younger than Mozart, delivered a speech before the German Society of the Palatinate on the topic, 'What can a good permanent theatre actually accomplish?' Later, in 1802, he included this speech among his published writings under the title 'Die Schaubühne als eine moralische Anstalt betrachtet' ('The Theatre Considered as a Moral Institution'). Even down to its choice of words this essay captures Mozart's ideas in vivid language. In his 'Ankündigung der *Rheinischen Thalia*' of the same year Schiller, in words often reminiscent of *Die Räuber*, plainly states what he wishes to dissociate himself from: the 'shopkeeper's tricks', the 'ringleaders of gangs of playactors', the 'half-starved swarm of theatre-mongers' (1785, pp. 233–4) – these are the things he sought to counter with a theatre that was both good and permanent. In Chapter 10 we saw how, during the eighteenth century, a number of travelling theatrical companies were able to form permanent ensembles in Vienna with premises of their own. We also saw that this process was not a smooth one, because there were outstanding talents working in the travelling companies whereas the 'permanent' court theatres were often provincial and mediocre. Theatre enthusiasts, moreover, regretted that this development undermined the very existence of the art of improvisation and the comedy of the popular stage, both of which were highly appreciated by Mozart. Mozart himself, we saw, wished to have his stage works performed by nothing less than an ensemble of well-trained and experienced singer-actors who, moreover, had a good orchestra at their disposal. Conditions of this sort were simply not available to travelling companies. At the time that Mozart, in his comically touching way, was paternally trying to protect the father of his adored Aloysia, he advised him not to let her fall among the 'players' and the 'companies' with their comedies and singspiels (29 July 1778). The latter, he argued, only served as 'stopgaps' and diversions for the comedies, and Weber should not allow his daughter in this way to land at a station beneath that of the sopranos engaged at court.

Mozart's thoughts and demands exactly parallel those of Lessing and Schiller. Invited to direct the National Theatre in Mannheim, Lessing cordially declined with the remark that the idea of a national theatre in Mannheim was 'so much hot air'. He had no respect for its actors, nor had anyone considered the financial resources required (letter to his brother, Wolfenbüttel, 25 May 1777). Following a brief visit to Mannheim in January 1777 Lessing, with a heavy heart, abandoned any plans to 'bemix' with its theatre. His opportunities would have been no better in Mannheim than they had been in Hamburg or Vienna.

The above-quoted essays by Schiller likewise originated at a time when concrete efforts were being made to establish a national theatre. From 1783 to 1785 Schiller, too, thought primarily in terms of Mannheim, where Mozart, on his return from Paris, had already tried in vain to obtain a commission for an opera or 'monodrama' from the celebrated theatre director Wolfgang Heribert von Dalberg (24 November 1778).

Social security for artists was one prerequisite for the desired moral impact of Schiller's theatre; another was artistic quality. Again and again, at all phases of his career, Mozart returned to this topic. Hardly had he arrived in Vienna than he could write to his sister, an avid theatre-goer (4 July 1781):

> How I wish that you could see a tragedy acted here! Generally speaking, I do not know of any theatre where all kinds of plays are really well performed. But here every part, even the most unimportant and poorest part, is well cast and understudied.

He often had grounds to complain, as for example in Mannheim (4 November 1777), that 'you cannot imagine anything worse than the voices here'. How else than with complete artistic perfection could the theatre, to use Schiller's words (1784, p. 244), become the 'common channel in which the light of wisdom shall radiate from the superior, the thinking part of the nation'. How else could one dream of the 'jurisdiction of the stage' that 'begins where the dominion of worldly laws ends' (*ibid.*, p. 239).

We have, it is true, no direct evidence that Mozart, on his tours or in Vienna, attended a specific performance of Lessing's *Minna von Barnhelm*, *Emilia Galotti* or *Miss Sara Sampson*, of Schiller's *Die Räuber*, *Fiesco* or *Don Carlos*. But neither do we have any reason to doubt that he saw at least one or the other of these frequently performed plays. Nannerl, for instance, saw *Die Räuber* in Salzburg on 19 September 1783, and Konstanze spoke of Lessing as a famous man known to everyone (15 June 1799). Whatever the case, Schiller's impassioned language anticipates not only the figures in his own plays but also those of Mozart's *Don Giovanni* and *Die Zauberflöte*. Take, for example, the following stirring words: 'Bold felons long mouldering in the dust shall now be called forth by the almighty summons of poetry to reenact their shameful lives for the instruction of an awed posterity.' Or these: 'The mists of barbarism and dark superstition shall vanish and night give way to the victorious light.'

It was probably not before he came to Frankfurt that Mozart learnt of the existence of a community of Mozart devotees in Mainz. The Mainz historian Adam B. Gottron reports that Mozart took a fancy to the above-mentioned Hoffmann brothers when he met them in Frankfurt. They had come to the coronation festivities as members of the court orchestra, the violinist being at that time nineteen years of age and the pianist twenty. Here, as Abert testifies (II, p. 690), they apparently often met 'of an evening in Kran's wine locale in the Bleidenstrasse, opposite the little Sandgasse.' The threesome then travelled to Mainz with the market boat, the same means that Mozart had used to leave Mainz twenty-seven years before. The Hoffmann brothers had been to university and presumably belonged to the Amicists, a student organization that propagated the ideas of the Enlightenment. When their father died they took up the profession of music. Heinrich Anton was, or later became, a Freemason, and composed masonic songs. Mozart played music with the brothers in their parents' home, and the Hoffmanns probably took part in his court concert of 20 October 1790 as well. All of this information can be found in Gottron (1952 and 1959, pp. 171–8).

As mentioned above in a different context (see pp. 18–19), Mozart's lodgings in Mainz were opposite the rooms of the reading society. He must have felt what he called a 'change of air' from Vienna in, among other things, the general availability of information. But what must have impressed him most of all was the repertoire of the Mainz Theatre, confirming his claim that fate was hostile to him only in Vienna. Here is what was offered:

24 January 1784:	*Die Entführung aus dem Serail* added to the theatre's repertoire.
31 January 1789:	*La finta giardiniera* in German.
13 March 1789:	*Don Giovanni* likewise in German as *Don Juan*.
25 November 1789:	*Le nozze di Figaro*, again in German.
5 October 1790:	Announcement of a performance of *Don Juan* 'for Mozart's benefit' (the performance never took place).
May 1791:	A performance of *Così fan tutte*, again in German.

The first item is the least striking: *Die Entführung* had been given in thirty towns by 1792 (King 1955, p. 13). But the accumulation of three of his operas in a single year, just one year before his visit, must have convinced Mozart of the extraordinary interest taken in his music, particularly as only one-and-a-half years had passed since the première of the difficult *Don Giovanni*. Nor would it have been kept secret that his most recent opera *Così fan tutte*, then not even a year old, was already planned for the next season. Within a mere seven years, then, the Mainz Theatre had taken no fewer than five of Mozart's operas into its repertoire, where some of them still remained. Italian librettos were translated into German as a matter of course. Mozart immediately accepted at least the title under which one of his works would become known in the German-speaking countries: writing home on 3 October 1790 he reported that 'on Tuesday the theatrical company of the Elector of Mainz are performing my *Don Juan.*'

As we know from Gerhard Steiner's important study of Jacobin theatre (1973), the court theatre in Mainz played an extraordinary part in the history of the German national stage. The owner and financial backer of this theatre was, of course, the Prince-Elector, and his theatre director Karl Theodor von Dalberg – 'a cousin but no spiritual relation of the famous director in Mannheim' (Steiner 1973, p. 35) –

was actively intent on turning it into a bulwark against what he was fond of calling the 'spirit of fraud' (*Schwindelgeist*), by which he meant the movement against absolutist rule. He was opposed by a large part of the Mainz audience, above all by the academic youth and by many of the younger writers. One of them, Aloys Schreiber (1761–1841), edited a theatre journal which appeared in Mainz in 1788 and 1789 and which had carried a 'plan for establishing a permanent theatre in Mainz' along the lines demanded by Lessing, Schiller and Mozart. (One of his demands was for state-supported acting schools.) In a travelogue written in 1791, shortly after Mozart's visit, Schreiber recalls a performance he had attended in the Mainz Theatre: 'The faintest critical allusion to the aristocracy in the play is rewarded with applause from the stalls, even down to the last seats, of a ferocity to make the faces in the boxes turn pale and flushed.' As usual, even in the renovated Mainz Theatre the boxes were reserved for the aristocracy, with less illustrious but favoured guests sitting in the dress circle. The stalls and the middle and topmost balcony ('paradise') were places of congregation for the bourgeoisie. One of the pieces performed was Kotzebue's *Die Sonnenjungfrau*: 'When the High Priest said to his nephew: "Believe me, my son, few men occupy the position that befits them, least of all when it has been assigned to them by birth" – all of those hands that did not belong to the aristocracy or its lackeys were in motion' (Steiner 1973, pp. 34–8).

The Mozart community and rich Mozart repertoire in Mainz should be viewed in this context. The battle between the aristocratic and bourgeois audiences raged to and fro. From 1786 to 1788 the director of the theatre, which then covered both Frankfurt and Mainz, was Siegfried Gotthelf Koch (1754–1831). He, and before him that extraordinary man of the theatre Gustav Friedrich Wilhelm Grossmann (1746–96), had mounted the most significant plays of Lessing, Goethe and Schiller on both stages. From 1788, however, and especially from 1791, when the Mainz director finally withdrew his house from Frankfurt in order to uphold the character of the court theatre and obstruct the trend towards a democratic bourgeois theatre, the repertoire was dominated by superficial drawing-room comedies. Mozart's operas seem to have been included as a compromise between the two camps. The director considered operas in general to be harmless; the adherents of the national theatre knew that Mozart's were not. When *Don Juan* played for the first time the Frankfurt *Dramaturgische Blätter* assessed the subject matter of the opera and its treatment and pronounced the work suitable 'for the general public' but not for its 'educated section' (Deutsch 1965, p. 336). Even the music was felt to be 'grand and harmonious, but difficult and artificial rather than pleasing and popular'. Yet the critic then concedes Mozart this very popularity: 'Another opera that has turned the heads of our public. They were within an inch of storming the theatre because the doors had not been opened three hours before the beginning.'

At the age of thirty-four Mozart must have felt like a father figure within his Mainz community, which was made up largely of young people. But this was a role he liked. The Hoffmann brothers were one-and-a-half decades younger than he; the soprano Margarete Luise Schick, who took the part of the Countess in the Mainz *Figaro* and sang in his Frankfurt concert, was seventeen years old at the time; the theatre's poet-in-residence Heinrich Gottlieb Schmieder, whom Mozart must have met, was about twenty-seven. It was Schmieder who arranged Christian Gottlieb Neefe's German version of *Don Giovanni* for the Mainz stage. (He was not, as Friedrich Dieckmann has shown, the translator.) The German version of *Così fan tutte*, mounted under the title *Liebe und Versuchung* ('Love and Temptation'), was Schmieder's work. He proved to be a valiant champion of the idea of a national theatre. When the Mainz company, with all its singers and orchestra members, disbanded in November 1792 during the French occupation Schmieder was one of the few who remained true to the theatre. In a missive to the president of the provisional administration (apostrophized by Schmieder as 'Citizen President') he announced a plan to establish, together with several like-minded comrades, a 'national citizens' theatre' in lieu of the Elector's theatre. The object of the plan, which he in fact carried out, was to 'kindle the spirit of liberty ... from the stage by an illustrative presentation of great deeds' (Steiner 1973, pp. 51f.).

Mozart may have failed to meet one man in Mainz just as he had missed him six years previously in Vienna: Georg Forster. Since 1788 Forster had been living in Mainz as university librarian, together with his family. Now retiring and withdrawn, he limited his contacts to a small coterie of friends who 'almost daily spent an evening hour at his table for tea'. But his door always remained open for any foreign traveller arriving in Mainz 'from whatever nation, the learned of whom never came to Mainz without paying Forster a visit' (Steiner 1977, p. 49). As Forster also maintained contacts with theatre people and was well aware of Mozart's stature, it is most likely that Mozart, too, took tea at Forster's table. A few weeks after Mozart's visit Forster wrote a letter to Schiller expressly stating that in his tiny circle he enjoyed 'the sole aesthetic pleasure to be had in Mainz'. This letter, however, does not mention Mozart. Knowing that enemies and agents in Vienna would gladly have denounced him as a democrat, Mozart may conceivably have sworn Forster to silence. There is no doubt that had the two met they would have got along famously. Forster had just returned to Mainz a few weeks previously from a long journey that had taken him to highly tumultuous parts of Europe, and he was in the process of writing down his impressions.

Unlike Forster, Mozart had never visited the land of the first successful – if short-lived – bourgeois revolution in Europe, the Republic of the United Netherlands. But he too had witnessed the benefits of (relatively) radical reform, in Bohemia. Forster's proclamation that art is 'the mark of humanity as it lives, works and reshapes' would have won the approval of Mozart, who was well aware of the loving admiration bestowed upon his music by the citizens of Prague, Mannheim and Mainz. Another affinity strikes the eye. On his journey, as Forster wrote in various turns of phrase, he found that diligence and 'laboriousness' (*Arbeitsamkeit*) flourished 'on the soil of true rather than imaginary liberty'. Hardly had a year passed before Mozart, in *Die Zauberflöte*, could have Tamino proclaim the motto 'Labour, Wisdom, Arts' (*Arbeit, Klugheit, Künste*) to be the 'seat of the gods', which he assumed to be located within the precincts of Sarastro's temple. This may well have been the first appearance of the word 'labour' on the operatic stage.

Mozart scholars will not be able for long to stand aloof from the fact that Mozart, like other thinking and feeling men, 'shared the ardour' of the French Revolution. And the notion that his letters 'do not spend so much as a single word on the Revolution' (see p. 33) stands in need of correction. His aforementioned letter to Konstanze from Munich, dated early November 1790, must be read as a metaphorical expression of his high spirits on his travels as he sensed about him the winds of a new era:

> Dearest, most beloved little Wife of my Heart!
> ... I am looking forward to being with you, for I have a great deal to discuss. I am thinking of taking this very same journey with you, my love, at the end of next summer, so that you may try another spa; there the company, activity [*motion*] and change of air will do you good, as it has done wonders for me. I am greatly looking forward to this, and so does everyone else...
>
> Ever, until death, your loving
> Mozart m[anu] p[ropria]

Chapter 24

Mozart in his day and ours

Chrysander's observation about the 'highly unexpected leaps' in Mozart's compositional evolution applies to his intellectual development as well. Both strands are tied together; neither can be reduced to the other.

Mozart's intellectual evolution – or, to use his own vocabulary, the development of his 'thoughts and convictions' – might be summarized as follows. At about the age of twenty Mozart, then living in Salzburg, became acquainted with the ideas of the Illuminati as part of a circle of young people of his own age. These ideas dovetailed perfectly with the religious notions he had acquired in his childhood and youth. The bonds of friendship he formed at that time remained intact throughout his life, and in all likelihood the seeds of his later world-view were also sown at that time.

Mozart himself evidently saw no relation between these youthful experiences and his close contact with Melchior Grimm and Madame d'Epinay in 1778. He did not necessarily realize that both in Salzburg, and now in Paris, he had rubbed elbows with the Enlightenment. All the same, it seems that Mozart learnt from Grimm to be critical of librettists, indeed of the opera business as a whole. In any event, the young composer who produced *Idomeneo* in Munich in 1781, and *Die Entführung* in Vienna in 1782, began to pursue three interlocking motives: his creative impulse, a need to lead his own life, and a critical and 'enlightened' stance toward existing circumstances. At the same time, in his Haydn Quartets, he found novel ways of expressing in instrumental music the ideas which were then taking shape in his operas as composite images of music, poetry and stage action.

In Vienna, after years of vacillation and search, Mozart made two decisions which again were interrelated: in December 1784 he joined a masonic lodge; and with *La villanella rapita* (1785) and *Figaro* (1786) he began to choose opera subjects with a contemporary relevance. His instrumental music now began to centre on symphonies and on piano concertos written for his own use. At the same time, and no doubt in conjunction with his radicalized outlook, he fell out of favour with the

Viennese aristocracy only to be fêted outside Vienna, especially in Prague and Mainz, as the spokesman for a nascent democratic and enlightened world-view. Even when an opera subject was forced upon him, his breadth of mind was such that he found room for that vital empathy which he had conferred on his stage figures ever since *Idomeneo*. We find this same empathy in the ironic detachment with which he benignly chastises human foibles in *Così fan tutte* (1790), or in the stereotype combination of intrigue, assassination and magnanimous forgiveness in *La clemenza di Tito* (1791).

On his journey to Frankfurt in 1790 Mozart benefited from a 'change of air' and sensed that it had come across the Rhine to Germany from revolutionary France. But financial difficulties, increasing solitude and dark moods took hold of him from the moment he returned to Vienna. The playful ease with which Susanna and Figaro attained their goals now belonged to the past. In his masonic music, in *Die Zauberflöte* and the Requiem, and in many of his late instrumental works – string quintets, piano pieces, piano concertos, the Clarinet Concerto – Mozart now directed his musical imagination to techniques (also present in his earlier works) that embody optimistic visions of humanity triumphing over melancholy, danger and adversity. The few performances of *Die Zauberflöte* which Mozart was able to conduct or attend, presented by an ensemble which was devoted to him and respected by him in return, gave him an experience of a new sort: an audience devoid of envy and spite, bestowing upon his work both rousing and 'silent applause' as countless audiences throughout the world have been doing ever since.

The picture of Mozart offered in the pages of this book, and reflected in this brief outline of his life, cannot be reconciled with a different picture which, unfortunately, holds a firm grip even on Wolfgang Hildesheimer. However elegant his demolition of other biographical clichés, Hildesheimer's concept, according to which current events never so much as reached Mozart's 'level of awareness' (1977, p. 23) and Mozart's music 'resists all extra-musical conceptualization' (p. 17), is typical of a view that has dominated Mozart scholarship ever since the nineteenth century. Even today attempts are still being made to shore up this view on three sides: biographical, analytical and philosophical.

Biographically, Mozart scholars have presented a lopsided picture, or no picture at all, of his intellectual surroundings, which I have attempted to bring to life in the preceding pages and the appendix of this book. Admittedly, though, some recent biographies already depart from this practice: the facts of Mozart's life and the books in his library, provided one has the good sense to read them, are all too plain and unambiguous, as are the parallels between Mozart's recorded thoughts and those of the Enlightenment.

The idea of musical autonomy refuses to disappear. There would be no need to contradict this idea if we understood it to mean the peculiarities of music's origins and the uniqueness of its material basis, its mode of application and the manner of its reception. But this is not how the term 'autonomy' is generally understood. Although it presupposes the paradoxical assumption that Mozart banished one half of his gigantic output from his brain when he turned to the other half, the notion still prevails that Mozart's instrumental music bears no relation to anything extra-musical. In fact, though, we have no right even to speak of two 'halves' of his output. No matter how closely he hewed to the specific features of music's various genres and types, no matter how carefully he accommodated the demands of the occasion, for Mozart there was only *one* music.

Turning to the philosophical side of this picture of Mozart, the first thing that strikes the eye is the scant interest and even less sympathy shown in German Mozart scholarship for the music theories of the Enlightenment. Now, as our analyses have repeatedly demonstrated, the cognitive categories of the Enlightenment are not sufficient by themselves to account for Mozart's music. But it cannot be accounted for without them: it is no accident that Mozart made use of them himself.

Yet entire generations of musicians and musicologists in the German-speaking countries have been ignorant or poorly informed of the musical thought of the Enlightenment. Paul Moos's *Philosophie der Musik* (1901, 2nd edition 1922), a highly influential book in its day, was written in deliberate opposition to the Enlightenment. Its main burden is a doctrine which depicts music as non-representational and the emotions it engenders as spurious. 'Metaphysical idealism' is the name that Paul Moos (1863–1952) gave to his doctrine. Awareness of the intellectual achievements of the Enlightenment reached its nadir in Rudolf Schäfke's *Geschichte der Musikästhetik* (1933). Here, to all intents and purposes, the Enlightenment has been made German property. French thinkers appear only in marginal comments; even Hegel receives no more than a few vapid lines in the chapter on German romanticism where he managed to find a niche. And for decades this book was the only history of music aesthetics available in German.

The study of eighteenth-century music aesthetics by Hugo Gold-schmidt (1859–1920), published in 1915, is quite a different matter. He shows some sympathy, after all, for the French adherents of the Enlightenment, even though his book was written at a time when Germany was at war with France. He gives credence to at least some of the thoughts of d'Alembert and Rousseau and calls Diderot a great man. But Goldschmidt's authority on philosophical matters is Paul Moos (p. 11). So secure does he feel in Moos's intellectual edifice that he deigns to maintain of d'Alembert and Rousseau that, though 'on the best path to insight', they were only able to 'see the Promised Land from a distance', while Diderot was under the spell of a 'false doctrine' (pp. 102f.).

Goldschmidt even presumes to teach Mozart how to compose. First, he establishes that Mozart was fond of giving 'melodic shape' to the transition from the first to the second theme of his sonata-allegro movements – a claim which does not hold true at this level of generalization. This has the disadvantage of

> interpolating a new idea between the principal theme and the lyrical theme. And as this new idea itself is laden with emotion, it seems appointed to lessen the effect of the other two. In any event, this practice has no justification in theory. But what are we not willing to forgive Mozart's genius and the triumphant beauty of his music! (p. 18)

To explain where Goldschmidt obtained his authority and derived his theory is to go to right to the crux of musicology.

It is useful to accept Dahlhaus's idea (1967, pp. 954f.) that 'music theory' can have three meanings: 'contemplative observation, pedagogical doctrine and productive reflection'. (By the first he means the process of relating music to universal laws, by the last the study of music's causes, conditions and effects.) We discover that nowadays there is little demand for contemplative observation or productive reflection. Entire generations of music teachers and musicians have understood by 'music theory' nothing more than the rules of musical craftsmanship, and find no need to justify themselves. In the United States, where as we all know trends often appear earlier and more clearly than elsewhere, 'music theory' has for decades meant syntactical analysis, primarily of contemporary music, and nothing more. As Joseph Kerman has aptly criticized in his book *Musicology* (1985), things have reached a point where these theorists pay as little attention to the other branches of musicology as they receive from them in return.

We are now well on the way toward this misguided goal, and Hugo Goldschmidt simply marks one point along the path. The 'theory' which he graciously grants Mozart permission to transgress consisted of nothing but rules derived from descriptions of processes found in musical compositions of Mozart's time. Any theory worthy of the name must ask where these musical processes originated, why compositions were written this way and not otherwise at the time, what lies encoded within them, and how they effect listeners. In the nineteenth century these questions were left to outsiders, although the Enlightenment thinkers of Germany, and above all France, had urgently raised them long before.

Earlier (see p. 43) I had occasion to mention Martin Fontius, a scholar of Romance languages and literature, who recognized that the picture of Melchior Grimm painted by German musicologists was more akin to caricature. Sadly, this same bitter verdict applies to the picture that German musicologists have painted of Enlightenment aesthetics as a whole. Only recently, as already mentioned (see pp. 29-9), has this picture begun to change.

But the reasons for the failings of music theory must also be sought elsewhere. Since 1917, when Russia made its portentous and far-reaching attempt to confront capitalist society with a new social order, the problem of further developing a Marxist aesthetic has been added to the lot. This is not the place to discuss the intellectual achievements that were made in this area. But in a complex interaction with catastrophic political misconceptions and false decisions, aesthetics in the Soviet Union also came increasingly to be dominated by a number of conceptual errors. This was particularly so from the time that A. A. Zhdanov (1896–1948) took Soviet aesthetics in hand and, from 1945, when they were implanted in other countries then attempting to erect socialist societies. Since the material obstacles to mass education had seemingly been removed, the old problem of how to bring together high art and the people was now considered as good as solved. It was overlooked that what had taken millennia to create could not be made to disappear in a matter of decades. Composers and other artists were meant to shoulder the burden of creating works of a kind that would be accessible to the masses of potential art consumers. I am speaking here from my own experience: in the 1950s, basically following Hugo Goldschmidt's approach (though even then I had resolutely begun to distance myself from it), I felt called upon to proclaim what kind of music would be usable in the new world we were trying to build, and what kind would not. Reckoned from the end of the Second World War, it took me about fifteen years fully to realize that this aesthetic and this cultural policy were misconceived, and why this was so. It does not make things any better to add that I was not alone in this matter.

Nor does it make the time-honoured German tradition any better. Weak-minded philosophy, distorted biography and hermetic music analyses threaten once again to obliterate a crucial aspect of Mozart's music: its realism.

To understand what is meant by the word 'realism' we had better not cling to the emasculated and discredited meaning the term possesses today but instead turn to the thoughts and definitions of Mozart's contemporaries. There we can read (Goethe 1801, p. 171) that the poet requires 'a certain kind-hearted narrowness and infatuation with reality, behind which lies concealed the Absolute'. Looking back as an old man to a time when Schiller was still alive and writing his *Wallenstein*, Goethe remarked (1826, p. 161):

> If Schiller had not suffered from an insidious and mortal illness all of this would look quite different. Our correspondence on this topic ... will give all true thinkers occasion for worthwhile reflection, and will bind our aesthetics ever closer to physiology, pathology and physics so as to disclose the conditions that govern individual men no less than entire nations, the general ages of world history no less than the present day.

Schiller too, while still a young man, demanded that 'greater light be shed on the curious contribution of the body to the workings of the mind, on the great and genuine influence of man's animal sensorium on his spiritual life' (1780, p. 104). An essay from his more mature years, 'Über die ästhetische Erziehung des Menschen' ('On the Aesthetic Education of Mankind'), takes the dialectics of body and spirit, unfolding in the dialectics of ego and world, as its underlying idea. One passage (1795, p. 126) puts this idea as follows:

> The more many-sided a man's sensibilities, the more he will grasp of the world and the more capabilities he will develop inside himself. The more powerful and deep his personality and the more unfettered his powers of reasoning, the more he will comprehend of the world and the more form he will create outside himself... Where both qualities are united, there he will be able to combine the greatest amount of independence and liberty with the most bounteous plenitude of existence.

Mozart, in his blunt language, merely hoped that music would soon 'find an arse', for its great misfortune resided precisely in the fact that it already 'had a head' (7 August 1778).

But beyond all of this – beyond the sensualism, the emphasis on worldliness and the desired bond between aesthetics on the one hand and physiology, pathology, physics and the 'animal sensorium' on the other – there was, as we know from our own experience, still room for spirituality, form and the Absolute in the practice of art during those memorable early decades of modern bourgeois society.

Nor do aesthetics today, with their new problems and insights, need to deny the unity of body and spirit or allow the cohesion of artistic creation and reality to fall asunder. In well-put words which we would like to second, Renate Reschke (1989, pp. 46f.) maintains that any history of aesthetics must proceed from the realization that

its empirical basis is not social reality as such, nor the contradictions and conflicts in society and culture, nor the deeds and
interactions of historical persons. Rather, its basis is to be found
in experiences reflected on and in these factors and articulated in
various shapes and forms, whether in concepts, metaphors,
images, or whatever.

We bear on our shoulders the century-old burden of metaphysical
idealism, concocted by minds of a decidedly low calibre. The
objections posed by greater minds – Adorno's, for instance – are
marked by political attitudes we need not share. Moreover, contemporary theorizing about music is still in its infancy. This being so, we
should not dismiss Mozart's concern that music might be too
intellectual, or 'top-heavy', by advancing the contrary thesis that it is
too worldly or 'bottom-heavy'. Let me give a few examples to explain
what I mean.

The Novellos, of whom I spoke on page 16, were told by
Konstanze in 1829 that a quartet Mozart wrote during her first
childbirth on 17 June 1783 – the String Quartet in D minor, K421 –
bore certain traces of this event. Since then all believers in her report,
among them Alfred Einstein (1946, p. 118), are agreed that in the slow
movement of this quartet Mozart set the groans of his wife during
delivery. 'Even for the convoluted brains of those who write history
as romanticized hagiography', remarks Ludwig Finscher of Konstanze's report (1962, p. v), 'the idea of debasing Mozart's pen to the level
of a hospital curve-plotter is unusually silly'. Hildesheimer (1977, p.
173) finds 'the spirit behind [Finscher's] conclusion so correct' that he
too would prefer to discredit Konstanze's remark. Yet he asks us just
this one time to trust her: she could not simply have invented
something of this sort, he argues, pointing to the sudden *fortes* on the
leaps of an octave and a tenth in the Andante movement.

I hold that the spirit that led Ludwig Finscher to his conclusion
deserves also to be criticized. Agreed, Mozart's quill was not a
'hospital curve-plotter', but neither did Konstanze's remarks, as
recorded by the Novellos (1955, p. 112), suggest anything of the sort.
What we read there is that 'the agitation he suffered' and 'her cries' can
be 'traced in several passages'. In other words, we are dealing first of
all with – to use Renate Reschke's above-mentioned definition –
'experiences reflected on and in' his young wife in her confinement.
And these, to use my own terminology (see pp. 172–4), are mirrored
in biogenic musical elements, while Konstanze's cries took the form of
mimeogenic elements. As we saw in Zerlina's aria, the two may very
easily overlap, even fuse. Mozart occasionally did set extra-musical
impressions – waves and wind, footsteps and heartbeats – without
necessarily making them the substance of his music. Why should he

not have opened his music to the agitation he felt at the sufferings of the woman he loved, sufferings of which he himself was the cause? Why should he not have set her cries? Perhaps the biblical passage 'in sorrow shall ye bring forth children' (Genesis 3:16) crossed his mind as he experienced, for the first time, that what had been conceived in pleasure now had to be brought forth with shrieks of pain. Vincent Novello's oft-repeated reference to 'several passages' should be taken literally. The first movement, though not lacking in cheerful episodes, is an extremely agitated piece of music. The second, the Andante, attempts to evoke an idyll which is constantly interrupted by painful darkenings of mood. There is no compelling reason for focusing merely upon bars 31f. and 47f. of the Andante. Nor is Vincent Novello's reference to the Minuet, from which Konstanze sang a passage to her two visitors, necessarily mistaken. With her sixty-six-year-old voice she may very well have ventured to sing:

Example 188

What we need not assume is that the string quartet would have been completely different if Mozart had written it down a day earlier. From all we know about Mozart's habits of work, the piece was already worked out in his head before he put it down on paper. The agitation of the piece is not entirely the product of Konstanze's confinement: we are not dealing with a 'Childbirth Quartet'. Indeed, the first movement may have had to do with a different Konstanze, the one in *Die Entführung*, and more specifically with her 'Traurigkeit' aria (No. 10), whose two introductory measures probably gave the D minor String Quartet its central thematic idea. It is thoroughly in keeping with the nature of music, and with Mozart's own working methods, that he should incorporate new impressions while writing out the finished composition – improvised addenda, as it were, but in this case captured in writing. Konstanze's remarks help us better to understand Mozart's methods.

Constantin Floros, first in a three-volume study of Gustav Mahler (1977–85) and later in his writings on Mozart, attempted to develop a 'new method of musico-semantic analysis' (1979, p. 5). This method consists largely in the assumption that one must explore a composer's 'mental world' in order to prove from there that his music, as Floros claims of Mahler's, is 'beholden to extra-musical *contents*, representations and ideas, whether these be poetic, literary, pictorial or philosophic' (1977, II, p. 9). We need not agree with Floros on every point in order to grant the rightness of his approach. This, however, is exactly what the respected composer Karl Heinz Füssl (1924–92) refuses to do. The arguments are, he claims, 'out of tune with the times': Floros has merely resuscitated the long buried and barren dispute between programme music and absolute music (1987, pp. 11ff.). The main reason for the barrenness of this dispute, however, was that the categories and vocabulary in which it was conducted were unequal to the problem. Even Füssl concedes that a composer can be stimulated by experiences. Today we know that experiences impinge on an unimaginably complex network of neuronal connections – a tight-knit web of the conscious, semiconscious and unconscious, of the analytical and the intuitive, of cognitive and emotional processes, of reactions which are genetically programmed and others acquired by experience. And since we are still leagues away from understanding these connections we should not claim to know exactly what the musical creations initiated by experiences are supposed to be detached from when we say they are 'absolute'. Instead, drawing on the new insights of psychology and neurophysiology, we must readdress the question of how music, in its autonomous way, responds to impressions, events and experiences. Far from offering a 'false perspective', as Füssl claims, Constantin Floros offers us one possible point of access.

The concern not to drag Mozart's music all too close to mundane reality has also left its mark on Stefan Kunze's highly rewarding book on the operas (1984). Discussing the dance scene in *Don Giovanni*, for example, Kunze proceeds on the assumption that the 'ordering properties of metre', and hence 'any force of social cohesion', is suspended by the simultaneous performance of the three dances. This in turn suspends the 'dualism of musical and factual reality', thereby first 'jeopardizing' and then 'obliterating' that unity of apperception which finds an analogy in musical metre. Moreover, this happens at the very moment and 'in the very area that stands, musically, for reality in the most accessible, real, almost naturalistic sense of the term'. Faced with this danger, the orchestra intervenes, literally, to 'save the situation', and 'Anna, Elvira and Ottavio do the same' (Kunze 1984, p. 354). Kunze's analysis of the march scene from Act III of *Figaro* likewise tries to protect Mozart from coming too near to extra-musical reality, precisely in that area where his own argument makes this nearness manifest. In this case, he draws the borderline with the aid of the following mind-boggling pronouncement (p. 261): 'Here Mozart has captured the reality of the march [*Marschwirklichkeit*] without making use of the reality of the march [*Marschrealität*].'

But the rub lies elsewhere. The 'second reality' – namely, that of music – is neither destroyed by the artifice of having three dances sound simultaneously, nor is the march's 'reality' damaged by the effects of alienation imposed upon it. Both levels – the one that Kunze refers to as *Wirklichkeit*, and the other which he tries, not very felicitously, to distinguish from it as *Realität* – are surely in no danger of obliterating each other. Not even the metre is endangered: the 3/4 metre of the minuet remains intact, though held in abeyance by the addition of the two other dances. The sequence of accents within the bar is suspended for the moment. (We can only hope that some day, with a fraction of the technical apparatus available to any rock band, the superimposition of these three dances may become more palpable to the ear than is generally the case on opera stages!) Moreover, the harmonic structure also remains intact, as do the fixed pitch levels and the instrumental sonority. And if, in the march scene from *Figaro*, the woodwind ornaments (discussed on pp. 266–7) clash with the trills in the melody instruments, temporarily bringing the music closer to noise in the same way as Osmin's whip (see pp. 161–2), we are dealing with one of those strokes of genius with which Mozart does, in fact, open up the musical system and its canon of rules to a sudden onrush of impressions from the real acoustical environment. Anyone who sees this as a danger rather than a way of realizing music's 'mimetic impulse' must face the question of why he is afraid of this danger.

Adorno put it in a nutshell. In art, he wrote (1980, pp. 424f.), a 'mimetic impulse' is indeed at work, but great art only becomes autonomous when this impulse is transcended 'through and beyond the level of imitation'. Art, he maintained, 'reaches out gestically toward reality only to recoil from its touch' (p. 425). Wolfgang Heise (1975, pp. 282ff.) has confronted this view in a manner that ought to be considered applicable to parallel questions in music aesthetics. 'Did Homer "recoil"? Did Dante?' he asks. 'Was Goethe out of touch with himself in his "insistent realism"?'

Adorno considers reality to be a 'hostile world of things [*bedrohliche Dinglichkeit*]' (Heise 1975, p. 282). His fear of reality is

> objectified and legitimated within a larger picture of society petrified in universal alienation. Thrust back onto himself and his own intellectual existence, he takes as his absolute the very real experience of helplessness, of depravity, of the objective predicament of the solitary and isolated individual. This absolute is then contrasted with the course of societal events – a course which refuses to bend to the will of the individual – and with the relentless logic of capitalist economy and the preponderance of its governmental and institutional superstructure.

If the relation between reality, society and individual really were as hopeless as all that, Adorno's concept would have to be considered inescapable. In contrast, Heise sees truth in art as residing in its imperviousness to ideologies which, by their very nature, 'celebrate and obscure' social reality. When Heise wrote these words this is exactly what was being done, in different ways, both by the ideology of the East German state and by that of its capitalist counterpart. Artists who allow neither their intuition nor their analytical faculty to be dimmed by ideologies perform nothing less than an act of emancipation.

> Truth in art is not related to a reality that can be reduced to what happens to be the case in the positivist sense. Being part of human existence this reality is itself a process producing human life, containing not only what is finished and complete but also that which is emerging in embryo and still far from being manifest. Reality also contains *possibilities* and the various ways of becoming aware of and realizing them – or, more precisely, of their birth in man's physical and mental activity.

In this way Heise comes to the following conclusion (1975, pp. 293f.):

> It is the movement of emancipation that gives rise to realism. The former is the history of the latter. Brecht once noted in his working journal: 'Realistic art is art that leads reality against the ideologies and makes possible realistic feelings, thoughts and actions.' To view this historically would be to create a guideline to the history and objectives of realism.

Today capitalist conditions have been brutally and cynically imposed on the country in which he wrote those words, and in which the present book was written. The opportunities once given to 'real existing socialism' have been wasted, its possibilities left unrealized. Financial capitalism and property ownership have consolidated their domination; reality has indeed become threatening, and Adorno's scepticism appears justified.

But the same cannot be said of his theorem that great art reaches out gestically towards reality 'only to recoil from its touch'. On the contrary, precisely under today's conditions we can see a tendency towards a renewed alliance between emancipation and art. And it seems to function all over the world. In the novel, in opera and even the concert hall, in lyric poetry and in popular music, the moral impulse to cry out against the rank injustices of our times seems to be gaining strength – an impulse which politicians have done their best to banish to Sunday speeches.

Today, this act of emancipation is brought off under infinitely more difficult conditions than the 'escape from self-imposed immaturity' in Mozart's day. But it is, basically, the same act of emancipation. We will never fully understand how Mozart saw, heard and perceived the world, how he converted aspects of what he saw, heard and experienced into music, and which aspects those were, unless we realize that from the time of his Vienna period he composed his music with a vision of the future. Far from recoiling from reality, he perceived it not only as 'what happens to be the case', but also as what was 'emerging in embryo and still far from being manifest'. Mozart, the realist, set in music the emerging visions of a better world manifest in the ideas of women and men who, like himself, believed in the Enlightenment. But reality proved them wrong: the 'wise man' whose advent was prophesied by the Drei Knaben was not to be victorious.

We have taken no more than the first steps in exploring how Mozart used principles of construction, compositional devices, and relations between separate pieces of music, in order to convert attitudes, convictions, thought processes and actions into music. The connections involved in making music are extremely complex, and especially so when a great composer goes to work at a critical juncture of man's history. But we have at least shown that these steps are possible, and that beyond our immediate questions they point toward a contemporary theory of music.

As we had cause to say earlier (p. 106): 'There is always more at stake than aesthetics.' Nor can we exclude from our musico-aesthetic deliberations the question of how it came about that the relation of music to reality, so self-evident at the dawn of bourgeois society, has since then been repressed, called into question, even regarded with suspicion. It is relevant to ask what has become of that bourgeois society itself, in whose revolutionary beginnings Mozart took part. What has become of its freshly posed realities, its noble intentions, its heroic illusions?

'Egoism has erected its system in the very midst of the most refined conviviality, and without producing a convivial heart we have to suffer all of society's contagions and afflictions.' Thus wrote Friedrich Schiller (1795, p. 320) just four or five years after Mozart's death. And a mere three decades later Franz Schubert (1824, pp. 258f.) could write, 'The age dissipates me, too, with inactivity', a thought as typical of the composer and his music as it is foreign to the phenomenon of Mozart. Thirteen years later Heinrich Heine wrote (1837, pp. 117f.):

> The men of ideas who so tirelessly prepared the Revolution in the eighteenth century would blush to see what sort of people they laboured for, to see how self-interest is raising its wretched hovels on the sites of battered palaces, and how from these hovels is springing forth a new aristocracy even less sufferable than its predecessor, one that does not even attempt to justify itself by an idea or an ideal faith in the propagation of virtue, but finds its ultimate justification solely in acquisitions that are generally

obtained by petty-minded perseverance if not by the most heinous of vices: in the possession of money.

And Heine in turn would blush to see what has become of this new aristocracy that finds its ultimate justification in the possession of money.

The advancement of craft, industry and trade, of science and the arts: that was the goal of the revolutions in America and France. It was also the goal of the Enlightenment, in all countries as also in Germany and Austria. The revolutions succeeded beyond all expectations. The bourgeoisie brought forth the most powerful and productive form of society the world has yet known. The scientific and technological revolution that has begun in the last decades of our century is opening up possibilities of which no one can say whether they will lead humanity to wholesale destruction or, perhaps, bring forth a rational world order where they can be utilized for the happiness of all – and fulfil the dream of the Enlightenment.

To date, however, the most powerful and productive of all known forms of society has fallen short of this goal, and the germ of its aberrant development lay in its beginnings. Many people knew this even at the time. The victor was not the 'wise man' whose advent was prophesied by the Drei Knaben, but rather the monied classes, and the world has most assuredly not been transformed into a paradise under their rule. Four-fifths of humanity live in misery; untold millions are starving in a world of affluence; friendship and harmony are scarcely to be seen. The pious wishes that Mozart set in the final year of his life (K619, bars 92ff.) remain no more than that – pious wishes: 'Into ploughshares turn the iron that has shed the blood of man and brother! ... Burst mountains with the ebon dust that oft hies murd'rous lead through the fraternal breast!' Many of the wise men of today earn billions with this 'iron' and 'ebon dust', now perfected beyond belief, and the planet threatens to perish in the process. It is symptomatic that as early as 1776 all the passages that condemned the enslavement of Black Africans were struck from Jefferson's draft of the Declaration of Independence (see Kossok 1989, pp. 134, 150 and 153). Today's reality makes a mockery of those lines in *Die Zauberflöte* that echo so much of the poetic and legislative writing of the time: *Bald wird der Aberglaube schwinden!* – 'Soon shall superstition vanish'. Any musical culture born under such conditions will, even in its nethermost ramifications, betray symptoms of the state of the world.

In the 1920s my father used to take me to the Grosse Musikvereinssaal in order to hear the subscription concerts of the Vienna Philharmonic – scheduled at 10 o'clock on Sundays so that the music enthusiasts could conveniently breakfast beforehand and return from the concert in good time for the Sunday lunch prepared in the interim by their cooks. To me, the bland elegance of many of Felix Weingartner's performances and the courteous, lukewarm response of the audience were all the more disconcerting as I did not understand their causes. For the bourgeois concert audience as it had emerged in nineteenth-century Europe, the idea that music is non-representational, and that its feelings were sham, was not only plausible but appropriate. The large majority of the audience did not experience genuine feelings at all, that is, impassioned responses of a contemporary relevance. Something of Paul Moos's metaphysical idealism dominated the minds even of those with no knowledge of philosophy. This was the classical age of theories that drew clear lines of demarcation between the practice of art and the reality outside of art.

Nevertheless, there also existed a counter-world to the escapist, complacent musical domain of the bourgeoisie with its sham feelings. At that time many young people discovered this world in Mahler's symphonies, which seemed to burst the bounds of the concert hall and lift the bourgeois world off its hinges. Their readiness to listen to music in this way, in opposition to bourgeois attitudes, was not the result of a particular kind of musicality. What distinguished these young people, including myself, from the majority of bourgeois concert-goers was a political experience that was new in kind. The revolution in Russia, the collapse of the monarchies in Germany, Austria and the Balkans, the upsurge of organized labour, the ferocious response of the reactionary wing of the bourgeoisie – all of this had made us aware of the need for and the possibility of replacing the bourgeois world with another. The degree of this awareness and the complex processes that led to it differed from person to person. What we had in common, however, was a premonition that similar political and moral impulses also lay at the heart of the works of Beethoven and Mahler. The same applied to Mozart as well. In those days the performances of *Figaro* and *Don Giovanni* at the Vienna State Opera – performances that retained something of Mahler's spirit and still used one or another of his original singers – had about them a touch of rebellion. The German playwright Heiner Müller, speaking of ancient Greek tragedy, has captured this sensation: anyone who finds himself at a historical turning point, he claims (1982, pp. 167f.), 'will be able to see old collisions in an entirely new light', and it is important and productive 'to look at the old carousel while standing on the new one.'

The things happening today on our 'carousel' are enough to convince many people that enlightenment and rational world order no longer stand a chance. But we are still in the midst of those processes unleashed by the Enlightenment, processes whose eventual outcome still lies in the hands of human beings.

In the opening scene of Act II of *Die Zauberflöte*, Sarastro calls the assembly of his priests 'one of the most important of our time', and enjoins the Speaker to teach the novices what 'the duty of humanity is'. His words, admittedly, recall the language of children imitating grown-ups. But Mozart took them seriously. We know this from a letter of 9 October 1791 which refers precisely to this scene. In it, Mozart tells Konstanze that he shared a box with an uncouth visitor from Bavaria for one of the first performances of *Die Zauberflöte*. 'Unfortunately', he continues,

> I was there just when the second act began, that is, at the solemn scene. He made fun of everything. At first I was patient enough to try drawing his attention to a few lines. But he laughed at everything. Well, I could stand it no longer. I called him a Papageno and left.

Mozart showed a stronger sense of history than many of his interpreters of today, who wonder whether *Die Zauberflöte* is a shoddy piece of workmanship. In words and concepts appropriate to the audiences of a Viennese suburban theatre, but using the most sublime of musical forms, Mozart and Schikaneder transformed the great ideas of their age into stage scenes. The lines 'one of the most important assemblies of our time' and 'duty of humanity' had a ring of novelty in an age when such assemblies were in fact held and duties of this sort were taken seriously. The term 'history of mankind', indeed, 'mankind' itself, did not begin to take on meaning until the late eighteenth century, when the trade and industry unleashed by its revolutions pulled the remotest corners of the globe into the stream of history. Conventions such as that of 4 July 1776, at which Jefferson's Declaration of Independence was signed and the 'inalienable rights' of all men to 'life, liberty and the pursuit of happiness' were proclaimed to be 'self-evident', were indeed among the most important of the time. Another was the French National Convention of 7 February 1794, which decreed the abolition of slavery and linked Africans in fraternal amity with the white man. This was an occasion at which a black mother could hold up her baby so that the great moment could leave upon him its indelible impression.

Walter Felsenstein took Sarastro's domain seriously in his unforgettable *Zauberflöte* production of 1954. The words were spoken as though written by Lessing, and among the circle of men and women in the realm of the initiated there were black, brown and yellow faces to be seen alongside the white. *Die Zauberflöte* captures the real possibility of human liberation which the American and French revolutions had placed on the agenda of history – where they can be found today, still waiting to be realized.

Although it would be a good beginning, there are more difficult problems awaiting solution than to satisfy the wish:

> Bekämen doch die Lügner alle
> Ein solches Schloss vor ihren Mund!

> (If lying lips could all be fettered
> And made secure with lock and key!)

And the words 'Hass, Verleumdung, schwarze Galle' – 'hatred, falsehood, bitter gall' – are too mild, and the blustering minor seconds of the music Mozart invented for these lines still insufficiently vehement,

Example 189

to portray the 'heinous vices' of those who find their 'ultimate justification in the possession of money'. Thinkers even more politically minded than Mozart and Schikaneder were unable to foresee the extent of infamy made possible by the absence of an 'ideal faith in the propagation of virtue'. The transition from bad to better will not be so gentle that the touching sound of a single unaccompanied oboe will be able to do it justice:

Example 190

And yet! Even two hundred years after Mozart's death, the task still remains of transforming the subjunctive of his vision of the future into the indicative of real human relations:

Example 191

'... there would be love and bonds of brotherhood!'

Appendix

The first five texts, presented here in the order in which they are referred to in the main section of the book, played a role in Mozart's intellectual development. No. 6 sheds light on both the author and the subject of this obituary, both of whom were variously active in Mozart's immediate surroundings. Risbeck's views, style of life and method of writing are typical of the early history of bourgeois literature, indeed probably of its art as a whole. All of this material is presented in new translation. Passages omitted from the excerpts are indicated by ellipses within square brackets [...]. Explanations or other remarks by the author of this book appear in italics or footnotes.

1. Friedrich Melchior Grimm: 'Poème lyrique' ['opera', 'opera libretto'], *Encyclopédie*, XII (Paris, 1765), pp. 823–36

If presented in complete translation, Grimm's article would occupy more than fifty printed pages. We have selected those passages which may well have played a part in his conversations with Mozart.

Page 823 The Italians have given the term 'opera' to the *poème lyrique*, that is, to a stage spectacle set to music, and this term has been adopted in French.

As this opening sentence makes clear, by poème lyrique *Grimm meant nothing less than opera or, alternatively, the poem on which it is based. Accordingly, we have rendered this term either as 'opera' or as 'libretto', depending on the context. Grimm now explains how art was viewed by French spokesmen of the Enlightenment:*

Pages 823 to 824 The entire art of imitation is based upon a lie: this lie is a kind of hypothesis which is permissible and accepted by dint of a tacit agreement between the artist and his judges. Allow me this initial lie, said the artist, and I shall lie to you with so much veracity that though you be fully aware of it you shall nonetheless be deceived. Playwright or painter, sculptor or dancer, pantomime or actor: all have a particular hypothesis that obliges them to lie. They dare not lose sight of it for an instant without robbing us of that illusion which makes our imagination an accomplice in their deceit. For it is not truth which they place before our eyes, but the semblance of truth. And that which constitutes the charm of their accomplishments is by no means Nature, but the imitation of Nature. The closer an artist approaches Nature with his chosen hypothesis, the more talent and genius we attribute to him.

The imitation of Nature by means of song must have been among the first forms of artistic creation. Every sentient being is, at certain moments, stimulated by an awareness of its own vitality to produce more or less melodious sounds in keeping with the constitution of its organs. How could man remain silent amid such a multitude of singers? In all likelihood it was joy that inspired his earliest songs. At first he sang without words; later, he attempted to attach to his singing a few words appropriate to the feeling it was meant to express. In this way, the stanza and the song became the first species of music.

But the man of genius did not limit himself for long to these songs, the creations of unadulterated Nature. Instead, he conceived a much nobler and bolder project, namely, to turn song into an instrument of imitation. He soon noticed that the further our spirit is removed from its customary balance, the louder we raise our voices and the more strength and melody we instil into our discourse. Observing his fellow humans in different situations, he heard them quite literally sing at all important occasions of their lives. He sensed that every passion, every emotion of the soul has its *accent*,[1] its *inflexions*,[2] its melody and its own song.

From this discovery there arose imitative music and the art of singing. The latter became a kind of poetry, a language, an art of imitation, based on the hypothesis that melody, aided by harmony, is capable of expressing any kind of speech, *accent* or passion, and even at times of imitating its physical impact. The union of this art, as sublime as it is near to Nature, with the art of drama gave rise to opera, the noblest and most brilliant of modern theatrical spectacles.

Grimm now discusses the superiority of music to language, from which he concludes:

---

[1] A somewhat imprecisely defined term, here left untranslated, referring both to language and to music. As we know from Rousseau's *Dictionnaire de musique*, it is intended to denote the modification of the voice in accordance with various parameters.

[2] This term, likewise untranslated, is not clearly distinguishable from *accent*. It refers roughly to variations of pitch in the speaking voice.

Pages 824 to 825 Musical drama must perforce make a far stronger impression than tragedy or traditional comedy. It would be useless to employ a highly effective instrument only to achieve mediocre effects. If the tragedy of Merope[3] fills me with compassion, moves me, brings me to tears, then all the fears and dread terrors of this unhappy mother, when presented in an opera, must penetrate the depths of my soul. [...] Any musician to whom I owe no more than a few tears or a fleeting sensation has remained well beneath his art.

The same holds true of comedy. If the comedy of Terence and Molière enchants me, then comedy in music must leave me enraptured. The former shows human beings as they are, the latter gives them, in addition, that grain of vivacity and genius that leads them to the brink of madness. To appreciate the merits of the former all one needs are ears and common sense. Sung comedy, however, would seem to be made for an elite audience with intelligence and taste; music adds to the ridiculous and quotidian a touch of originality, a refinement of expression, which requires not only a precise and delicate sense of tact but also highly trained voices in order to be delivered with conviction.

But passion has its interruptions and moments of repose, and it is the will of the dramatic arts to follow the course of Nature in this regard. In a play, it is no less impossible to laugh ceaselessly at pranks than to dissolve constantly into tears. Orestes is not continually pursued by the Furies; Andromache, amidst her terrors, is comforted by rays of hope. To be sure, it is only one step from this sense of tranquillity to that horrifying moment when she must witness the death of her son; but these two moments differ, and the second is made all the more tragic by the calm that precedes it. [...]

Thus, lyric drama has two different levels: tranquillity and passion. And the composer's foremost concern must be to find two types of declamation essentially different and yet each appropriate: the first to render the quiet dialogue, the second to express the language of passion in all its intensity, variety and excess. This latter type of declamation bears the name *aria*; the former, *recitative*. [...]

When persons reason, deliberate, converse or conduct dialogues, they can do so only in recitative. Nothing could be more wrong-headed than to have them argue in song, or conduct conversations in the form of stanzas in such a way that one stanza is answered by another. Recitative is the only suitable instrument for plot and dialogue; it must not be sung. It must use intervals somewhat more striking and responsive than ordinary declamation in order to express

---

[3] A figure from Greek history whose tragic fate was dramatized by Voltaire and other writers.

the actual *inflexions* of speech. Finally, recitative must preserve within itself both earnestness and impetuosity as well as all other qualities. It must not be performed in strict time, but should be left to the intelligence and temperament of the actor, who must deliver it more quickly or more slowly depending on the spirit of his role and his performance of it. [...]

Aria and song begin with passion; the moment passion appears, the musician must seize control of it with all the resources of his art. [...]

Grimm now provides several detailed examples of how to set aria texts, quoting several of them. Duets and even ensembles are briefly touched upon before the essence of the aria is summarized as follows:

Page 826 to 827 According to a remark made by a celebrated philosopher,[4] the aria is the compendium and climax of a scene. This is why the actor almost invariably leaves the stage once he has finished singing. [...]

One might say, then, that it was the invention and the opposing properties of recitative and aria that created opera. [...]

This economical internal structure of plays set to music, grounded on the one hand in verisimilitude of imitation, and on the other in the nature of our sensory faculties, must serve the librettist [*poète lyrique*] as his fundamental poetics. It is essential, however, that he subordinate himself in all respects to the musician: he can only lay claim to a secondary role, yet he still retains sufficient resources to share the fame of his companion. The choice and presentation of the subject, the sequence and course of the overall drama are the work of the poet. The subject must be stimulating and presented as simply and as interestingly as possible. Everything must be concentrated in action and thrive on grand effects. The poet must never fear to give his composer a task too difficult to accomplish. Just as *rapidité*[5] is a quality indispensable to music and one of the prerequisites for its marvellous effects, so must the pace of the action [*la marche du poème lyrique*] always be *rapide*. Long and superfluous speeches are completely out of place. [...]

Having presented these general observations Grimm now turns to French opera:

Page 828 *Concerning French opera.* According to a definition given by a famous writer,[6] French opera is a heroic poem converted into

---

[4] Diderot.

[5] Literally, rapidity. In this case it means a steady and concise unfolding of the dramatic action. This term, too, has been left untranslated.

[6] Probably also Diderot.

action and spectacle. What the epic poet, in his discretion, merely presents to our imagination, the librettist has undertaken to present before our eyes in France. The tragic poet took his subject from history; the librettist searched for his in epic poetry. Having exhausted the whole of ancient mythology and the entire world of modern sorcery, having placed every conceivable deity on the stage and given him shape and form, he then went on to create beings of his own fantasy. Equipping them with supernatural and magical powers, he then made them the mainspring of his poem.

The soul of French opera, then, is the world of visible marvel. There are gods, goddesses, demigods, shades, genies, fairies, sorcerers, virtues, passions, personifications of abstract ideas and morality, into which the actors transmute themselves. Visible marvels would seem so essential to this species of drama that the poet believes himself unable to handle a historical subject without giving it an admixture of supernatural incidents and fabulous creatures of his own device.

Grimm heaps scorn upon this type of libretto for another two pages and recommends taking opera figures from historical personalities, among whom, in a certain sense, he includes the Greek deities. He then turns to Italian opera, speaking in admiring terms of the famous Pietro Metastasio and of composers such as Leonardo Vinci (1690–1730), Giovanni Battista Pergolesi (1710–36) and Johann Adolf Hasse (1699–1783), only to ask how it happened that Italian opera was nevertheless incapable of bringing forth the shattering effects of ancient tragedy:

Page 830 As a spectacle serves no other purpose than the amusement of an idle public, that is, the elite of a nation, known by the name of 'good society' [*ne sert que d'amusement à un peuple oisif, c'est-à-dire à cette élite d'une nation, qu'on appelle la bonne compagnie*], it is impossible that it should ever attain real significance; and whatever genius you might wish to ascribe to the poet, the rendition of his work on stage and a thousand details of his libretto can only suffer from the frivolity of its destination. Sophocles, when he wrote his tragedies, laboured for his fatherland, for religion, for the most august solemnities of the republic. Of all our modern poets, Metastasio, perhaps, has enjoyed the gentlest and happiest of fates. Safeguarded from envy and persecution (all too often the rewards of genius today, as indeed they were, at times, among the ancients), the talents of this foremost poet of Italy were constantly honoured by the protection of the house of Austria; how different, though, is his role in Vienna from that of Sophocles in Athens! Among the ancients, theatre was an affair of state; for us, when the police deign to notice it, they do so in order to burden it with a thousand niggardly harassments, to place it at the mercy of a thousand bizarre constraints. The audience, the singers, the impresario, a ludicrous empire: all have usurped opera. Its creators – the poet and the musician, themselves victims of this tyranny – are the last whose counsel is sought for the performance.

Grimm now illustrates in detail how a fancy for beautiful voices led to the neglect of everything relating to opera as drama, not only among audiences but among singers as well. It is more than likely that Grimm discussed this point, the core of his notion of opera, during his conversations with Mozart, who had probably never before heard such a telling and polished critique of the operatic 'empire', particularly as regards the impresario:

Page 831 Ultimately, the opera impresario became the most unjust and absurd of all the poet's tyrants. Having studied the taste of his audience, its passion for singing and its indifference to the demands and ensemble of drama, he proposed to the librettist the following contract on the basis of his discoveries:

'You are the man I need least of all in the whole world for the success of my play, and after you comes the composer. Essential are one or two persons idolized by the public; there is no bad opera with a Caffarelli or a Gabrielli.⁷ My business is to make money. As I am obligated to give generous amounts of it to my singers, you will understand that very little will be left for the composer and still less for you. Dream of the fame that will be your portion.

'Here are a few elementary conditions under which I will agree to venture my fortune with your libretto and engage to have it set to music and performed by my singers:

'1. Your libretto must have three acts, and these three acts, all told, must last at least five hours, together with a few ballets that I can have performed during the entr'actes.'

There then follow, neatly listed under seven further items, several rules governing the number and sequence of arias, the only duet permitted to occur, the number of roles and their distribution among the various types of voices, the structure of the plot, and so forth – all rules which were, in fact, valid at the time. Grimm sums them up as follows:

Page 832 These are the principles that underlie the poetics of Italian opera. The librettist is treated almost like a tightrope walker whose feet are fettered so as to make his craft seem the more arduous and his efforts the more brilliant.

If Metastasio, despite these fetters, is able to retain a modicum of nature and truth in his plays, one is justifiably astonished. [...]

---

⁷ Caffarelli (1703–83), a famous Italian castrato; Cattarina Gabrielli (1730–96), a famous Italian coloratura soprano.

In conclusion, skipping Grimm's thoughts on the use of dance and chorus in opera, we quote his boldest idea, which he elaborates at length:

Page 835   Singing is a supremely difficult art requiring so much dedication and practice that one cannot hope to find a great singer who is at the same time a great actor. This combination, at least, is too rare not to be considered exceptional. The execution of a vocal number and its requisite expression already tax the singer to such an extent as to prevent him from devoting the same care to the action. The movements demanded by a situation are very often so violent as to prevent the performer from singing either with grace or with the required strength. I consider it impossible for the same actor, at the pinnacle of passion, to sing with the necessary warmth and enthusiasm and, at the same time, to yield to the delirium and uttermost excesses of passion without causing the accuracy of his singing to suffer in consequence. [...]

Grimm now records an event from ancient Rome, at times quoting an unspecified Latin author. A famous actor, Andronicus, once lost his voice. Since the audience still insisted on seeing him, at subsequent performances he let a boy sing his part in the orchestra while he mimed the role on stage. Grimm, perhaps not without irony, recommends adopting this method and promises in return an operatic renaissance:

Page 836   In this way our castratos, who are normally such excellent singers and such mediocre actors, would become nothing more than vocally gifted instruments situated in the orchestra, as close to the stage as possible. They would execute the vocal parts with a superiority from which nothing could distract them, while an agile pantomime could present the action with equal ardour and expression.

The more one penetrates the spirit of opera, the more one will be attracted to this idea. An opera performed in this manner would no longer merely enchant that small number of overly fine-nerved persons who understand the language of music. Even the most ignorant of the populace would understand it no less than the greatest connoisseur, for the pantomimes would translate the music for them word by word, rendering intelligible to their eyes what they are unable to perceive with their ears. [...]

Grimm then concludes his essay with a few words on the oratorio.

2 Giovanni Battista Casti: Introduction to the libretto of his opera *Il re Teodoro in Venezia* (Vienna, 1784)

This bilingual libretto, which, as always, could be purchased in the theatre, was doubtless known to Mozart. The Italian introduction is entitled Argomento, *the German translation* Stoff *(material). The 'celebrated writer' mentioned in the final section is Voltaire, who incorporated this affair in his novel* Candide.

Theodore, Baron of Neuhoff, is one of the strangest phenomena to have graced the political history of our century. Born in Westphalia, he was possessed of a fiery, adventurous and enthusiastic temperament. After experiencing many an adventure in Germany, France, Sweden and Spain, he embarked for Tunis, where he was able through the intercession of a friend, the famous Baron of Riperda (who, having been relieved of a ministerial office in Spain, had settled in Africa with great wealth), to obtain considerable amounts of money and articles of war from the local Bey and merchants. Using these means he undertook a landing in Corsica, where he was received with all due honours by the discontented population, who were then still under the yoke of Genoa.

Theodore's flattering promises to procure fleets and other aids for the Corsicans from various European courts eventually led to his election and coronation as King of Corsica.

Only, as neither fleet nor support arrived, his subjects revoked their fealty, compelling him to abandon the island and to remove to Holland and England.

In these countries he again had the good fortune to amass a fortune, which encouraged him to reappear in Corsica. This time, however, he was neither accepted by the population nor recognized as king. This circumstance, and the bounty placed upon his head by the Republic of Genoa, forced his return to Holland, where he was imprisoned for debt. On his release he travelled to London, where he was again placed under arrest at the instigation of his creditors, but was soon set at liberty. These untoward coincidences and his thoughts, continually fixed on the execution of clever schemes, softened his brain to such an extent that he fell into a state of lunacy and died shortly thereafter. A few lovers of the outlandish had a funeral monument erected to his memory, on which were described his life and deeds.

This peculiar man constitutes the subject of the present opera, which places Theodore in Venice, under the very aspect in which he appears in a charming sketch that emanated from the pen of a celebrated writer in one of his most ingenious and widely read creations. All of the circumstances are invented, and the meeting of Achmet and Belisa should merely be regarded as an episode. The liberties of the music, the nonsensical customs adopted for the Italian stage, and the brevity to which the performance of such a spectacle must be limited, have rendered impossible that expansiveness of treatment which the subject of this play would otherwise merit.

3 Pierre-Augustin Caron de Beaumarchais (1732–99): *Préface du Mariage de Figaro*, 1784

By 1785 Beaumarchais's celebrated play La Folle Journée, ou le Mariage de Figaro *was already available at Viennese bookdealers in two German translations. In the preface, presented here in excerpt, Beaumarchais sarcastically defends himself against accusations that his earlier plays had presented figures and events which were immoral and harmful to good breeding. His object, he claimed, was merely to depict human beings as they really are. The reception given to his* Barbier de Séville *of 1775, he continued, had been no better. Nonetheless, he had been persuaded to write a sequel, and although actors in particular had urged him to release his new play for performance it had remained locked in his desk drawer for five full years:*

Thanks to the exaggerated encomiums heaped upon my play, every theatre company wanted to become familiar with it; and from that time on, I was forced either to engage in quarrels of every sort or to accede to universal demand. From that time, too, the author's mighty enemies never lost an occasion to announce at court (so rudely insulted in this work) not only that the play was *a tissue of nonsense*, but also that religion, government, every rank of society, good manners, and as the crowning blow, virtue itself were therein confounded and vice triumphant. *As was only to be expected*, they added. If the grave gentlemen who have so often repeated these accusations will do me the honour of reading this preface, they will discover that I, at least, have quoted them accurately; and the bourgeois integrity of my quotations can do no worse than to expose the courtly dissimulation of their own.

In the *Barbier de Séville*, then, I merely shocked the state. In this new play, more infamous and seditious by far, I rocked its very foundations. Nothing would be sacred any longer if the work were to be condoned. The author was abused in the most libellous of reports; plots were hatched in high places; timid ladies took alarm; enemies were made for me on the prayer-benches of oratories. And I, depending upon the man and the occasion, repelled each vile intrigue by excessive patience, by the obduracy of my respect, by the imperturbability of my gentle disposition, and by reason, when anyone would listen to it.

This battle lasted four years. Add the five years that the play languished in my portfolio, and what remains of the allusions one struggles to identify in my work? When it was written, everything that flourishes today – alas! – did not even exist in embryo. It was an entirely different world.

During those four years of debate I asked to be given but one censor. I was accorded five or six. And what did they find in this work, the target of such invective? Only the most frivolous of plots: a Spanish grandee in pursuit of a young girl he wishes to seduce – and the concerted efforts of that bride-to-be, her fiancé and that nobleman's own wife to thwart the schemes of this absolute tyrant, whose rank, fortune and prodigality give him every wherewithal to carry them out. That is all; nothing more. The play lies exposed to view.

Whence, then, these piercing cries? From the fact that instead of hunting down only one vicious character – a gambler, say, or a miser, hypocrite or social striver – and thus throwing himself into the clutches of a single class of enemies, the author dared to use a trifling composition, or rather, fashioned his plot in such a way, as to introduce criticism of a host of abuses that plague society. But since this is insufficient to defile a work of art in the eyes of the enlightened censor, all of them approved it, thereby commending the work to the theatre. The play thus had to be endured; and the mighty of this world were scandalized to witness

> That play, in which an insolent valet is shown
> Shamelessly protecting his wife from his master.
>
> M. Gudin[8]

Oh, how I regret not having turned this moral subject into a bloodthirsty tragedy! Placing a dagger in the hand of the outraged spouse (no longer called Figaro), I would have let him skewer the diabolical tyrant in a seizure of jealousy, avenging his honour in high-flown and orotund verse. And my jealous hero, at the very least a military general, would have been pitted against some monstrous tyrant reigning as wickedly as possible over an impoverished multitude – none of which, I believe, would have offended a soul, being so far removed from our own customs. *Bravo!* they would have cried. *A highly moral work!* And we would have been rescued, my barbarous Figaro and I. But, as my sole desire was to amuse my fellow countrymen, not to draw tears from their wives, I made my guilty

---

[8] A friend of Beaumarchais.

lover a young nobleman of that period – profligate, a little too gallant, even a bit of a libertine, not unlike the other noblemen of his day. Indeed, what can one dare say in the theatre about a single nobleman without giving offence to them all, unless it be to rebuke him for excess of gallantry? After all, is that not the sole defect which they themselves willingly concede? Even now I can see many of them blushing modestly (and a noble effort it is) as they grant that I am right.

Wishing, therefore, to make my nobleman culpable, I nevertheless had the respectful magnanimity not to bestow upon him a single plebeian vice. You say that I could not have done so? that I would have violated every semblance of truth? Pronounce judgement in favour of my play then; for, as you see, I did no such thing.

The very defect of which I accuse him would not have produced the slightest comic effect had I not gleefully pitted him against the nimblest brain in the country, the one and only Figaro, who, while defending Susanne and his rights, mocks his master's schemes and becomes comically indignant when he dares to play tricks on a past master of this type of swordplay.

Thus, there ensues a pleasant game of intrigue, arising out of a quite lively battle between arrogation of power, breach of principle, recklessness, opportunism, and everything else that makes seduction attractive, and the fire, wit and resourcefulness which enable social inferiors goaded into battle to parry these blows. As a result, the *suborning husband* – opposed, provoked, harried, and constantly thwarted in his designs – is obliged on three different occasions during that day to kneel before his wife – virtuous, indulgent, sensitive – who in the end forgives him all, which is what women always do. What, Gentlemen, do you find objectionable in this moral? Perhaps you feel it is a bit lightweight to deserve the serious tone I have adopted? Believe me, the play has a far sterner moral to offend you, although you have failed to look for it. It is this: a nobleman, vicious enough to want to bend his inferiors to his whims in order to take advantage of every young servant girl in his domain, ends by becoming the laughing-stock of his underlings. And the author states this moral in very plain terms when, in the fifth act, the furious *Almaviva*, imagining that he is about to discomfit his unfaithful wife, directs his gardener's attention to a cabinet and cries: *Go in there, Antonio, and bring before her judge the infamous woman who has dishonoured me!* To which the gardener replies: *Crikey, there's a kindly Providence! You've done so much dishonouring yourself in this country that your turn just had to come...*

This deep moral makes itself felt throughout the entire play; and if it pleased the author to show his adversaries that, in the course of his austere lesson, he carried consideration for the dignity of this miscreant further than might have been expected from his unyielding quill, I would remind them that Count *Almaviva*, though frustrated at every turn, is always humbled but never debased.

In fact, if the Countess had tried to blind his jealousy with the intention of betraying him, thereby becoming guilty herself, she could never have driven her husband to his knees without belittling him in our eyes. To show a wife breaking a holy bond with base intent would be indeed to portray corrupt morality, for which the author might justifiably be reprimanded. Our moral verdicts always apply to women; there is not sufficient respect for men to demand so much of them on this delicate issue. But what the play actually establishes is that, far from having any such vile designs, no one wishes to deceive the Count, but only to prevent him from deceiving everyone else. It is the purity of this motive that places the work above reproach; and because the Countess's sole aim is to regain her husband, all the indignities he is made to suffer are indisputably highly moral, and not one of them degrading.

To impress this truth upon you even more forcefully, the author has pitted this rather callous husband against the most virtuous of women, both by nature and by principle.

When is the Countess, abandoned by a husband she has loved too well, first brought to your attention? At that moment when her kindness toward an attractive child, her own godson, threatens to take a dangerous turn if she allows herself to give way to her feelings. It is for the purpose of emphasizing true love of duty that the author places her, briefly, under the spell of an incipient romance which places her in conflict with duty. Oh, how often this trifling dramatic touch has been invoked to accuse us of indecency! In tragedy, every queen or princess is allowed her fiery passion, which she more or less holds at bay. But in comedy, no ordinary female is allowed to struggle against even the mildest of frailties! Oh, the *power of a label!* Oh, sound and rational judgement! By a simple change of genre, what is condemned in comedy is applauded in tragedy. Even so, in both cases, the principle remains the same: no virtue without sacrifice. [...]

In the work I am defending, then, our most genuine concern is for the Countess; and we sympathize with the other characters in the same way.

Why does Susanne, that witty, clever and high-spirited chambermaid, also command our attention? Because, pursued by a mighty seducer equipped with far more power than necessary to seduce a girl in her position, she immediately confides the Count's intentions to the two people most concerned with overseeing her conduct – her mistress and her fiancé – and because in her whole role, almost the longest in the play, she utters not a word nor a phrase which does not exude wisdom and devotion to duty. The sole duplicity she allows herself is for the sake of her mistress, to whom she is affectionately devoted, and whose wishes are never anything less than honest.

Why, when he takes liberties with his master, does Figaro amuse rather than outrage me? Because, unlike all other valets, he is not, as you well know, the villain of the piece. In seeing him forced by his position to parry insults with stratagems, we forgive him everything, for we know he is deceiving his master only to guard the woman he loves and to secure what belongs to him. [...]

Is it my Page, then, who scandalizes you? Is the immorality thought fundamental to this play to be found in a subordinate character? [...] Be fair, for once, instead of trying to stretch a point. A child of thirteen, exploring all and discovering nothing; a child who responds to the first stirrings of his heart, as one is wont to do at that joyous age, by idolizing a divine creature who happens, by chance, to be his godmother – could such a child be food for scandal? Liked by everybody in the palace, lively, mischievous, hot-headed, as are all intelligent children, in his extreme agitation he unwittingly upsets the Count's reprehensible schemes on ten separate occasions. Child of nature that he is, everything he sees ruffles his composure. Perhaps he is no longer a child, but neither is he yet a man; and that is the time of life I chose for him, so that he might be interesting without bringing a blush to anyone's cheek. Whatever he innocently feels he instils with that same innocence. [...]

But hold! you cry, your *Figaro* is a fiery and encircling sun who scorches everyone's cuffs. 'Everyone' is an exaggeration: at least give me credit that he does not even burn the fingers of those who see themselves reflected in my play, for nowadays playwrights have much sport with such mirror-images. Am I supposed to write like an author fresh from school, who can be counted upon to make children laugh but who has nothing to say to adults? And will you not grant me a bit of morality for my good humour, as one grants Frenchmen a little madness for their good sense? [...]

Beaumarchais, having rationalized the character of Marcelline and portrayed himself as a protector of the aristocracy, now takes up the subject of the style of Figaro:

But let us return to *La Folle Journée*. A gentleman of considerable wit, although a bit frugal with it, said to me one evening at the play: 'Please tell me, pray, why your play has so many slipshod phrases that are not at all in your style?' – In my style, Sir? if by some misfortune I possess such a thing, I should force myself to forget it when writing a comedy. I know of nothing more insipid in the theatre than those monotonous cameos where everything is blue, or everything is pink, or everything is author, whoever he may be. When my subject seizes me I summon my characters and put them into a situation: Take heed, Figaro, your master is about to find you out! flee for your life, Chérubin, the Count is at your heels! ah, Countess, how imprudent of you with such a violent spouse! I have no idea what they will say; what concerns me is what they will do. Once they have come to life, I write from their swift dictation, certain that they will not lead me astray. [...]

As you can see, I am by no means the enemy of my enemies. Although they have spoken very badly of me, they have done no harm to my play. And if they have taken as much pleasure in tearing it to shreds as I took in writing it, no one will be the worse off. The great pity is that they never laugh; and the reason they do not laugh at my work is because no one laughs at theirs. I know of several dilettantes who have even lost a good deal of weight since the success of *Le Mariage*; we must, therefore, excuse the consequences of their rage.

In conclusion, and in sum, Beaumarchais represents his play as follows:

In general, its chief defect is *that I neglected to observe the world when I wrote it: it does not depict things as they exist, nor does it suggest the society in which we live today. Its morals, however base and corrupt, do not even possess the merit of being true to life.* These criticisms were recently offered in a splendid essay, composed and published by a man of means, who lacks only a modicum of wit to be a mediocre writer. But mediocre or not, I, who have never employed the oblique and mincing gait of the hired literary assassin who, apparently without deigning to notice you, will suddenly plunge a stiletto in your side – I too am of that gentleman's opinion. I quite agree that what was true a generation ago bears a close resemblance to much of my play, and that the next generation will closely resemble it too. But as for the present generation, there is no resemblance whatsoever; I have never chanced to meet a suborning husband, a licentious nobleman, an avaricious courtier, an ignorant or prejudiced judge, an injurious lawyer, mediocre persons in high places, nor basely jealous persons who drag one from court to court: and if those pure souls who in no way see themselves reflected in my play are still incensed at it and relentlessly demolish it, they do so only out of respect for their grandfathers and deference to their grandchildren. I hope, after this declaration, that I shall be left in peace. AND I HAVE DONE.

4   Johann Pezzl: *Faustin, oder das philosophische Jahrhundert* ['Faustin, or The Philosophical Century'] (Zurich, 1783).

Translated from the revised and enlarged third edition of 1785

Page 5   An outline of the final convulsive death-throes of Superstition, Fanaticism, Clerical Deceit, Despotic Exigency and Lust for Persecution, during which these besetting vices, aided by foes great and small of Tolerance and Enlightenment, of Human Rationality and Common Sympathy, show their waning ire, and spew out the dregs of their despicable poison, before handing the crown of victory to Philosophy and the Rights of Mankind.

This sentence, the first in the book, is a declaration of intention that opens an account in sixty-four chapters and 360 pages of the experiences of Faustin, a young man living in the duchy of Bavaria 'not far from the overstuffed Abbey of "Wansthausen" – or, roughly, 'Paunchville'. Faustin is the illegitimate son of a young washer-woman and the abbot of Wansthausen, who has entrusted his education to a monk by the name of Boniface:

Pages 10 to 14   This was a man like unto none other of all those who stalk the banks of Danube, Lech and Inn in cloak and cowl. He had founded a village school, read more German and French than Latin, subscribed to the latest weekly and monthly periodicals, nay, even sent essays of his own authorship from time to time to the Bavarian *Sammlungen zum Unterricht und Vergnügen* ['Anthologies for Instruction and Pleasure'] under a *nom de plume*, for which his fellow friars only mocked him with the name Pater Belletristicus. He instructed Faustin in geography, history and the natural sciences. His favourite study, however, was philosophy, and his favourite notion all the beneficent effects that follow upon true wisdom: enlightenment, the illumination of the human species, tolerance, political activity, and brilliant philosophical discourse.

II.
A Sketch of Our Century

So greatly has general enlightenment progressed – spake Boniface – that it is a palpable blessing to have been born in this century. We have country schools and academies; journals and magazines; bookshops and learned papers; newspapers of politics and economics, medicine and theatricals; almanacs and pocketbooks; encyclopedias and dictionaries, annals and lexica; philanthropic and theological seminaries; Latin, grammar, trade and mercantile schools; museums and popular educationalists; primers and propaedeutica; economic and patriotic societies; reading cabinets and public libraries. [...] We have a philosophy of nature, a philosophy of history, a philosophy of religion, a philosophy of Christianity, a philosophy of bucolics, a philosophy in graceful apparel, a philosophy of ordinary life, a philosophy for each and every estate. [...] Verily, we have the Philosophical Century. [...]

And who – Faustin ventured to ask – was the first fortunate magician to have frightened the vapours away from Europe? It was, Boniface stammered, a blush on his cheek, it was – to the shame of our nation I must confess it – it was actually not a German. It was a Frenchman, the great Voltaire, the greatest philosopher since philosophers e'er walked the earth. He cried: Let there be light! and there was light. More fortunate than Orpheus, he transformed intolerant, fanatical and murderous beasts of prey into human beings, transfigured the mighty of the earth and opened their hearts to the philanthropic impress of benign philosophy: sovereigns, majesties and excellencies thought themselves fortunate to call him their friend and councillor. [...]

Faustin, who was possessed of an open mind, and indeed was as good-natured and gullible as any genuine Bavarian, listened with rapt attention and credulity when Father Boniface praised the Enlightenment and the Philosophical Century. He attached full credence to all the assurances of his mentor, and had no deeper desire than to make the personal acquaintance of Voltaire, to adopt the latter's principles as his own, and in this manner to contribute his own ha'penny-worth to the progress of tolerance and enlightenment.

Faustin now attempts to convince the peasantry to abolish feast days as a step toward enlightenment – for which he and his father are brutally thrashed:

Pages 18 to 20 How am I to reconcile this abundance of sorrow with the Philosophical Century? asked Faustin of Father Boniface, his eyes welling with tears: Myself nearly beaten to death, my father even dead! Is this your much-lauded tolerance, your much-lauded enlightenment? Indeed it is, replied Boniface: Granted, had the Catholic princes not been so enlightened as to demand the abolition of feast days from the Holy Father, your father would still be alive and you would not have suffered the pummellings of the peasants' fists; but idle superstition would have rested far deeper in the hearts of our people. A victory of such magnitude in the field of philosophy is doubtless worth the slight discomfort endured in its achievement. You should rather thank the philosophy of our century that you were so fortunate as to be its martyr.

To comfort themselves over this incident they now read, without interruption, the writings of the greatest of philosophers. Yet scarcely had they opened the pages of his *Essai sur l'histoire générale* than they were set upon by the abbot and two seminarians. The book was confiscated, and a court of inquisition held regarding Father Boniface's library. To the great scandal of the two seminarians, many books were discovered, both great and small, whose title pages bore in large print the names of Voltaire, Helvétius, Bayle and Montesquieu. Admittedly, they understood nothing of what they read, but the execrable names were sufficient to condemn the contents. They were especially outraged by the *Questions sur l'Encyclopédie*, for they had [...] been taught that the entire lot of the Encyclopedists were apostles of the Devil, and the Encyclopedia itself the Holy Writ of Beelzebub. Zeal for the House of the Lord consumed them utterly as they discovered, before their very eyes, the *Letters on Monasticism*, Haller's poem, the works of the philosopher of Sans Souci [...], and all of these in plain and unadorned German. To make the story short, the entire library was consigned to the flames; Father Boniface was proclaimed incompetent to hold the honours of public office and cast into a dark dungeon, to be nourished on bread and water until further instruction; and his pupil Faustin was banished on the spot, forever, beyond the lower and higher jurisdiction of the Abbey.

Faustin's luck fails to improve. Making his way to Munich, he seeks lodging from a peasant, who soon discovers his true identity:

Page 21   Art thou not the knave who tried to seduce us to work on our last feast day? asked the peasant. I am he, replied Faustin. Thou art he! cried the peasant, his face aflame: Thou art he, and durst appear before my eyes! Away with thee, out of my house, I shall not spend the night under the same roof with a Freethinker! Faustin begged for his indulgence; the good-natured peasant woman herself pleaded on his behalf, and proposed to her husband that the fugitive be allowed to sleep in the hayloft. Not in the shade of any of my trees shall he rest, swore the peasant, and booted Faustin out of doors.

Having arrived in Munich, Faustin enters a coffee house:

Pages 42 to 44   To divert himself, he took in hand the *Kurfürstlich privilegierte Intelligenzblatt* in the hope of discovering one provision or another that might do honour to the Philosophical Century. Ye Heavens! what a shudder passed over him as he read, in a documentary essay by a highly esteemed courtier, that in the years from 1748 to 1776 a total of 1,100 persons in the circuit of Burghausen alone had been dispatched by the public executioner 'in the name of justice'. He recalled that the year 1748 marked the onset of the Philosophical Century. To illuminate further the benign influence of the Goddess Justitia he performed the following calculations. If, in

Burghausen, 1,100 persons had been properly and lawfully throttled within twenty-eight years, then during the same period, in proportion to their populations, at least 1,200 malefactors must be reckoned for Straubingen, 1,200 for Landshut, 1,500 for Munich, and 1,000 for the Upper Palatinate, yielding a tidy sum-total of 6,000 judicial murders within a period of twenty-eight years.

Assuming that these sacrifices to the blind goddess would continue unabated for the remaining two-thirds of the century, he arrived at the handsome figure of 22,000 persons, all of them beheaded, garotted, broken on the wheel, burnt at the stake, drawn and quartered, torn apart by horses, and so on, and so forth, and all within a patch of land 729 square miles in area and a time span from 1748 to 1848, the full duration of the Philosophical Century. And this figure excluded all of those confined to dank prisons who perished of hunger, were devoured by vermin, suffocated in the poisoned air, rotted in their own filth, or were tortured to death under the most grisly of torments ... This, then, was the triumph of reason, the triumph of humanity! – Yet there is comfort: As a substitute for these human beings we have a grand total of 28,709 churches in which it is the simplest of matters to utter 22,000 De Profundis for all the butchered victims.

Faustin had written a small book against this 'legalized depopulation of his Fatherland'. A friend named Traubach warns him that 'men of the cloth and ladies at court are the most ferocious of all the dangerous species to walk the face of God's earth'. On the very same evening the two set out by post-chaise for Italy, experiencing new adventures on the way. Having arrived, they make the acquaintance of a painter:

Pages 68 to 70 This unending cycle of murders is one of Italy's national plagues, the painter explained. It is equally dangerous to be a man of wealth, an accomplished artist or a great savant: in every case one attracts enviers willing for a few groats to hire a scoundrel who plies the trade of poison and dagger. Such a knave will murder without a second thought, even in broad daylight and in an open street. Then he will flee to a church or monastery, these being, especially here in the Papal States, holy sanctuaries of assassination and hence the consecrated dens of cutthroats. To fetch the murderer one must first apply to the priest and bishop for authority to do so, by which time the clerics and monks will have found ten ways to obstruct justice and to remove the culprit, to whom, for a few *scudi*, they will even dispense complete absolution *a culpa et poena*... Triumph of humanity! Faustin again muttered.

At this point they arrived at the palace of Duca di Farinelli. His Excellency had just departed for Madrid to collect the customary 18,000 piasters from his Catholic Majesty for singing six arias. 18,000 piasters for six trills! cried Faustin. A pretty outlet for the treasures of Peru and Chile! ... Shall we proceed to the Duca di Santo Dorata? suggested the painter: His duchy lies not far away. But neither was His Excellency at home. The prior of a nearby Dominican monastery had invited His Transparency to sing a litany... Another duke, said Faustin, who sings litanies to the mendicant friars! It's the gelding Caffarello, the painter whispered in his ear: Just like his neighbour he has warbled his way to a duchy, but will still sing for money. His Excellency arrived, the painter began his work, and Faustin continued his journey to Naples.

XI.
Enlightenment in Naples. – Faustin flees from *aqua tophana*.[9]

The first thing that Faustin encountered was a herald, flanked by two trumpeters and a cavalry guard. In every square our herald read a royal edict which poured anathema on the Freemasons and their followers, helpers, patrons, conspirators and advocates, proclaiming them incompetent to hold the honours of office, divesting them of the rights of citizenship, banishing them from the country, and threatening them with incarceration, trenchwork or the galleys should they be discovered. It concluded by renewing the grim bull in which the wise and omniscient Benedict Lambertini cast a ban of excommunication on the entire Masonic Order, thereby consigning its members body and soul to the Devil. Faustin's senses reeled as these sacred and profane curses fell upon his ear. It was inconceivable to him how anyone could fulminate against the Masons so fanatically, given that even the greatest princes and the most learned savants in Germany belonged to the order. He now presented his letters of recommendation, [...] through which he was granted entrance into a good commercial establishment and was accorded a reception so friendly as to exceed his every expectation. Here he made the acquaintance of a learned man of the town, and soon entered into conversation [...] with him on his favourite subjects: tolerance, enlightenment, and philosophical discourse... Enlightenment! Philosophy! said the sage: How can you expect to find these in a country which has, in addition to a myriad host of arrogant and voluptuous divines of every shade and hue, more than 900 mendicant orders that provide nourishment to some 18,000 holy beggars ...?

A 'miracle' is to be enacted in a church; the statue of a saint is about to bleed:

---

[9] A poison widely known at the time. According to the Novellos, Mozart himself believed that he had been administered *aqua tophana*.

Pages 78 to 79 Yet the clerics were not yet ready to have the blood appear. There must be heretics in our midst, grumbled several of them. Who cares about heretics! cried a few from the throng: Is the town not full of Freemasons, a brood more vicious still than all heretics? It is the Freemasons, this scourge of Hell, who heap misfortune upon us; as long as these blasphemers are about, the blood will never appear. This is precisely what the clerics had expected to hear. With visages of pious rage they signalled their approval; and immediately a band of zealots fell upon any who had not grimaced with sufficient enthusiasm, beating them with their fists, tearing their clothes from their bodies and throwing them more dead than alive out of the church. Faustin, having shown his disapproval, was given a blow to his face so vicious as to dislodge both front teeth from his upper jaw. Nor would he have been dealt with more gently than the others if the savant and several of his friends had not removed him in all haste. Mouth bleeding, he arrived home.

Chapters 20 to 24 depict Faustin's experiences in France. In Paris he makes the acquaintance of a fellow countryman by the name of Brückner, who makes his way as an adventurer and a teacher of German:

Pages 146 to 151 The first place they visited was the Comédie Française as Faustin, while still in the company of Father Boniface, had read much in Voltaire's writings in praise of the masterpieces of Corneille [and] the plays of Voltaire himself [...]. The play being performed, like most of France's theatrical fare, was full of high-flown declamation and maxims, well presented in dialogue, but poor and deficient in action. Faustin, who had already attended plays by Lessing, Goethe and Weisse,[10] soon tired of the cold and arid French declamation and repaired to the Opéra. This, to be sure, was splendid and brilliant enough: yet, he soon drew involuntary parallels between the shepherds cavorting on the wooden scaffolding and genuine peasants from the provinces, and enquired how much it cost annually to maintain these thighs and larynxes. The entire expenditure of the royal spectacle runs to 700,000 livres annually, answered Brückner. A horrifying total for a stage farce, replied Faustin, which probably consumes the revenues of an entire minor province ... Indeed it does, was the language master's response. [...]

A few days later a fire broke out at the Comédie, during which an *actrice* lost her life in the commotion. A pity that the poor maiden must go to the Devil! cried the theatrophiles in a single voice. But surely they say that in jest? asked Faustin. Not at all, replied

---

[10] Christian Felix Weisse (1726–1804), an author of enlightened bourgeois dramas.

Brückner: You realize, of course, that each and every actor in the whole territory of France, from the Rhine to the Pyrenees, has been excommunicated? ... 'Excommunicated? [...] But even His Most Supreme Christian Majesty amuses himself at the spectacle, year in, year out, as do the entire court and even the most distinguished prelates, who, after all, possess the key to power.' ... 'Satan doesn't mind in the slightest: the *excommunicatio major*, *excommunicatio ipso facto* and *excommunicatio latae sententiae* have been imposed on the theatre altogether, and anyone who dances a step or sings a note on the boards [...] is damned body and soul to the Devil' ... 'And can no amount of talent provide protection?' ... 'None at all [...].'

Do the people of Paris also believe that we are witnessing the Enlightened Century and the general triumph of reason? asked Faustin, interrupting Brückner... Indeed, was his reply. They believe it, continued Faustin, and yet they are mad enough to endure this monument to fanatical papistry from the darkest age of superstition without cringing in shame? How is this possible? The excommunicated are condemned to Hell: How can one maintain this as a clergyman and yet spend money to be entertained by the very people who must forfeit paradise in the process? What a disgraceful contradiction for our Illuminated Century! And this from the *église gallicane libre*! Has that national masterwork, the *Encyclopédie*, so little influence on the French spirit that it cannot expunge at least the most grievous of such follies? ... The *Encyclopédie*? queried Brückner. What influence should it have? It is locked in the Bastille. ... The *Encyclopédie* in the Bastille? ... Yes, my dear fellow countryman, the *Encyclopédie* is very palpably locked in the Bastille, from head to toe and from alpha to omega. Louis XV did it long ago, and the *Encyclopédie* has been rotting there ever since... The *Encyclopédie* in the Bastille! Farewell, enlightenment! Farewell, triumph of reason!

Sickened by his experiences, Faustin tries to recover by following a suggestion from Brückner:

Pages 160 to 163 Faustin agreed, and they set out on a short pleasure trip to Chanteloup, the splendid palace of the Duc de Choiseul, partly to see this noble edifice and partly to visit the great ex-minister, Voltaire. For several days they had taken delight in viewing the tasteful gardens, paintings and other treasures of this location when Faustin heard the dreadful grating of a weathercock, twisting in the breeze above the palace gate. Looking up in simple curiosity, he noticed something akin to a human visage, which only pricked his curiosity the more. Imagine his astonishment as he peered more closely through his lorgnette and discovered an exact likeness of the great philosopher Voltaire as a weathercock, turning hither and thither in the wind on the roof!... By all the Nine Muses! he cried: What sort of prank is the Duke about, placing the greatest philosopher since e'er philosophers walked the earth, on the top of his roof as a weathercock! Is this not the most heinous of insults to noble philosophy? How should anyone take pleasure in the business of enlightenment when he sees himself demoted to a weathercock? The Duke had his good reasons, remarked Brückner. Impossible, replied Faustin, whose boundless enthusiasm for Voltaire revived at this sight: It's impossible that he could have good reasons for such a farce ... At least it is claimed, Brückner continued, that the philosopher, who owes to the Duke his country seat at Ferney, played a less than honourable role against his benefactor. As long as the Duke was still in power, Voltaire bowed and scraped like all the other professional insects of the antechamber. But the moment that the minister fell Voltaire pilloried him with relish, just like the other weathercocks at court. The Duke has now installed him in the position he himself assumed. [...] What must I hear! But to judge from many passages in his writings it might well be possible. So, let us make it our axiom: Voltaire's writings are estimable, the man himself of no further account. I will not press further for an audience, Faustin concluded.

Having returned to Germany, Faustin pays a visit to Mannheim:

Pages 181 to 185   In Mannheim they attended the final performance at the opera before the bulk of the company departed for Munich. They were told that all of this twittering and doodling and prancing cost a good 200,000 gulden annually, and this in a state whose revenues amount to no more than a few million thalers, and thousands of whose subjects emigrate every few months. When the King of France squanders 700,000 of his annual 400 million livres on the opera, one laughs, explained Brückner; but when a count palatine spends over 100,000 of his two million thalers on such frivolities, one cries...

In a small town south of Mannheim a man in a grey threadbare cloak sat down beside them in the boat. Faustin sounded him out, and discovering him to belong to the order of divines, he immediately drew him out on the matters dearest to his heart: tolerance and enlightenment. Tolerance! Enlightenment! sighed the man in the grey cloak: Let us not desecrate these sacred words as long as we continue to reside in a land where they merely serve as catchphrases for persecution and oppression. In me you see a veritable martyr of those sacred rights: I am the seminarist Hunteln who wrote a small book on and against the most recent plight of the Palatine Calvinists... My compliments to you for doing so, said Faustin... Ah, if only there were grounds for the compliment, dear sir! You should rather pity me as an exile who must wander this world without a crumb... How can that be? exclaimed Faustin: Or are things really so dreadful in our paradisiacal Germany as one hears rumoured? And the seminarist explained the matter to him as follows: The court, blinded by the endless intrigues of a few ex-Jesuits and non-ex-Jesuits, seems to have taken upon itself fully to suppress the constitutionally safeguarded denomination of the Calvinists. The government loyally second the court on this point, and are unashamed to perform the basest of subterfuges. Indeed, so thick-skinned have they become that they no longer blush to hear the many lamentations and well-warranted reproaches. All posts, livings, offices and graces are conferred without exception upon the most wretched applicants, so long as they profess themselves to be Catholic. The Protestants are pressed and harassed by the most cunning and disgraceful of deceits: many are only allowed to marry if they swear to raise their children in the Catholic faith. – Most of the so-called ecclesiastical councillors, spiritual administrators, inspectors, and so forth, are creatures of the court, voracious flatterers, cringing coxcombs, who will pull the wool over the eyes of their charges for the few thalers that the court is willing to cast their way, so long as they do not protest its scheme of intolerance. And if a righteous German stands up in dignity to censure this mischief, he is soon silenced by threats and extortion. It is this religious oppression, along with the equally severe political suppression at the hands of monopolies and other institutions of Asian fashion, that continually and quite understandably force so many thousands of our conscientious citizens to emigrate, to abandon their Fatherland in cold blood and seek more tolerant climes.

'But if this continues the country will be depopulated within a matter of years!'... Nothing less than that: and there is no more honourable, no more noble means of doing so than by zealous proselytizing. A horde of highwaymen, vagabonds, cutpurses and bankrotteurs on both banks of the Rhine, men with bounties on their heads and branded in public newspapers as rogues, rush to the Palatinate, turn Catholic, and are now offered protection, accommodation and public office. Even miscreants from our penitentiaries can put an end to their trials and transform themselves once again into honest men by becoming proselytes.

And this is what I call the triumph of reason and humanity! the century of illumination and tolerance! Faustin interposed with a bitter laugh. And what does the ruler of the land say about this? ... He occasionally has a decree issued that bears his signature and condemns these goings-on as mischievous; yet none of the higher or lower judicial authorities prosecute these decrees. On the contrary, they are violated in a trice and with full confidence, so that all can see that they are nothing more than paper ordinances used by the honourable lackeys at court to deceive their neighbours.

Chapter 28 ends with a characterization of aristocrats that recalls Mozart's own language twice on a single page. First, anticipating a well-known passage in Die Zauberflöte, *certain forms of behaviour are recommended when confronting an 'overlord' who 'has ordered a padlock placed on the lips of Truth'. The chapter's final sentence invokes the artistically ignorant King Midas of Greek legend, to whom Mozart compared the Archbishop of Salzburg:*

Page 199   King Midas has – what does he have?

> piano   p.p.
>   donkey's ears.
>   pianissimo

Our selection from Pezzl's novel concludes with lengthy extracts from the two final chapters. It need only be remarked that, in his later writings, Pezzl was somewhat more circumspect in his admiration for Joseph II.

Pages 332 to 348

LXIII.
Philosophy Enthroned

After all this reading, admiration and praise they finally arrived in Vienna. Of the ill-starred visit of the Bishop of Rome[11] the only remaining evidence they saw were the few inscriptions of this strange occurrence, inscriptions which shall impress eternally upon our neighbours that under the reign of Joseph II the Roman Catholic usurpations had come to an end in the largest part of Germany. [...] Their first walk took them to the grounds of the Augarten. Faustin read the inscription which Joseph had placed over the entrance:

> *Allen Menschen gewidmeter Belustigungsort*
> *von ihrem Schätzer.*
> *(A place of diversion dedicated to all people*
> *from one who holds them in esteem.)*

O, sacred grove! he cried at the sight of this motto: O, blessed monument to philosophy enthroned! Happy we who are allowed to wander in thy shadows, near to humanity's sublime esteemer! – This motto was dearer to him than than any ever brought forth by an academy of inscriptions [...]. Traubach's chest swelled with patriotic delight at the prospect of praising to his friend the sage institutions

---

[11] The Pope.

now radiating light and life beyond our horizon. He proffered the following philosophical sketch of some of the many things that Joseph had already accomplished for the good of enlightenment, the advancement of tolerance, and the reconstitution of the national cast of thought.

> Abolition of those sacred farces known by the name of processions, of ridiculous formulae in prayer, and of nightly devotionals, where more is sacrificed to Aphrodite than to any of the saints.
>
> Purification of literary censorship according to superior principles. Private libraries to be taken intact into the monarchy without prior examination.
>
> All monastic orders are liberated from their generals in Rome and made subservient to the nation's bishops, thereby blocking the first channel of revenue to Rome.
>
> Dispensations in matters of marriage are referred to the bishops. Ban on obtaining dispensations from Rome, thereby blocking the second channel of revenue to the papal coffers.
>
> Abolition of papal donations, the dispensation of benefits, etc., thereby blocking the third channel of revenue to Rome.
>
> Protection of Blarer[12] against Migazzi's[13] intrigues.
>
> Removal of the nonsensical bulls *In coena Domini* and *Unigenitus*[14] from all rituals.
>
> Proclamation of edicts of tolerance throughout the monarchy.
>
> Abolition of the sanctimonious idleness of the contemplative monks and nuns.
>
> Conferral of human rights upon Jews.
>
> Abolition of serfdom throughout the monarchy.
>
> Monks are enjoined to perform labours of ministry, thereby reaffirming their duties to humanity.
>
> Annulment of the offensive episcopal oath to the Bishop of Rome.

---

[12] Balthasar Blarer, a Swiss priest and a member of the radical wing among Catholic reformers.

[13] Christoph Anton, Count Migazzi (1714–1803), cardinal archbishop of Vienna, a bitter foe of the Enlightenment.

[14] Two papal bulls directed against the Enlightenment.

The fantastical oath of the immaculateness of the Virgin Mary is prohibited for all times.

Casus reservati and similar cutpurse tactics of the Roman Church are abolished for all times.

Introduction of Protestant houses of worship as a solemn demonstration of tolerance. [...]

Cleansing of churches from all the usual ornaments of fanaticism, theatricality, superstition-mongering, nonsense and bric-a-brac.

Addition and improvement of schools in town and country-side.

The riches of the church are to be employed in support of those in poverty and ill-health.

Contredanses prohibited at church; German hymns introduced.

The judiciary purged and perfected.

etc. etc. etc.

At this point he added a brief commentary to each article in order to impress upon his friend the full value of these and all other decrees enacted at the pleasure of the Philosopher and Philanthropist since the end of the year 1780. Faustin, however, began to sing the lines of Klopstock:

—— Who e'er hath ended
As Thou hast begun?

He praised his much-beloved Joseph in the fulness of his heart, from the depths of his soul, and to the utmost of his powers. All the hardships he had endured from Wansthausen to London were now forgot, as were all those foes of tolerance and enlightenment, of human reason and common sense, who had caused him so many hours of bitterness and rancour.

Looking at the court church, with its noble religious simplicity and its single crucifix, they recalled the church in Ferney; from which Faustin concluded that the Emperor was not entirely predisposed against the precepts of the greatest of philosophers. [...]

Thus they passed the first few days. The longer they remained, the more evidence they discovered of a resurgence of creativity in the once dark and limited minds of the Viennese public. Faustin proposed to Traubach that in their correspondence with their friends they should proclaim a new age – the Age of Enlightenment in the Southern Germanies, the Josephine Era – and define 1780 as the year of its inception.

Traubach agreed to the proposal, and wished that this chronology, redounding to Germany's honour, be introduced in the country as a whole, though he feared that it would not. But in the hope that our fatherland would nonetheless raise this monument to its greatest benefactor – the primogenitor of freedom of thought and purified religion; of the rights of the throne against Roman incursions; of the rights of reason against pedantry, ossified scholasticism and the apostles of superstition; of the rights of mankind against the harassment and oppression of gluttonous subtyrants – they proclaimed among themselves that the year 1780 was now to be known as the

Year of Salvation

and the outset of the illuminated Philosophical Century, that it be celebrated with jubilation by future generations and enter the annals of mankind alongside the reigns of Sesostris, Fohi, Orpheus, Antoninus and Marcus Aurelius. [...]

XLIV.
Conclusion

The two friends have resolved to spend their remaining days within the agreeable confines of the imperial capital. They find that Mercier speaks the truth when he maintains that great cities are the only fitting abode of the true philosopher: it is here that his powers of observation are given new nourishment daily by a thousandfold variety of events; it is here, lost in the throng, that he can live in greater freedom from duress; it is here, in the endless interminglings of the estates, that he discovers a greater degree of equality; it is here that he can choose his own companions and escape the gazes of the buffoons and dunderheads who are unavoidable in lesser places. [...]

Faustin enjoys the pleasant advantages of this capital of Germany, so envied and abused by small-town burghers. Unnoticed by the buffoons and dunderheads, he lives in philosophical independence in a circle of confrères with Johann Physiophilus [i.e. Ignaz von Born], with Blumauer, Haschka and Ratschky. The nobler and more enlightened part of Vienna has bestowed its friendship upon him, while a few aristocratic Tartuffes and a horde of loutish clerics leer at him in silence. [...]

The Court Library and the National Theatre are the places he visits most often for his instruction and pleasure. He often enjoys the Augarten in the company of his friends; even more often they wander in the Prater under the hospitable shade of thousand-year-old oaks, exulting in their existence and imploring Heaven to preserve

Joseph,
Mankind's Delight,
the German Titus.

With hearts full of hope they look upon his magnificent reign, the longevity of which holds out to fortunate Germany the full measure of its bliss; and with each new step Joseph takes in his glorious career, they clasp his portrait with overflowing hearts and cry out at the top of their voices:

Under Joseph's reign
shall reason and humanity triumph
and the Philosophical Century begin!

5 Joseph Franz Ratschky: 'Über die Wohltätigkeit des Maurers: eine Rede von Br. R***' ['Concerning the Philanthropy of the Mason: an Address by Brother R***'], *Journal für Freymaurer*, Volume 1, First Quarter (Vienna, 1784)

The following brief extract from this address illustrates the good intentions of the Freemasons as well as the limited options available to them:

Pages 173 to 177   Lest I be misunderstood – Lest philanthropy be limited to the dispensation of alms – an often undeserved merit in which the hand is usually more at work than the heart – Lest one think I had nothing more noble to praise than that manner of philanthropy which is often the handmaid of timidity; in which the benefactor, moved by soft-heartedness, seeks to rid himself of a sufferer's groans and lamentations by extending a paltry gift, the more quickly the better, for fear of being distracted from his pleasures by disagreeable thoughts; or which consists in deeds without reflection – Lest I be thus misunderstood, I find myself enjoined to explain myself at greater length. Permit me, then, my dearest brethren, to present an outline of genuine philanthropy that adheres to those notions which every Freemason conscious of his duty should make of it.

Philanthropy, as widely conceived, is an inner compulsion, an active desire either to establish or to consolidate the happiness of one's fellow creatures. It is the property of only a small number of noble spirits, and is expressed in manifold ways. Sometimes it assumes the office of teacher, supporting those in need of advice with healing counsels, providing the wherewithal to pilot them clear and unscathed past the shoals of approaching danger, warning against the coils and snares of temptation, pointing out the path of virtue, unveiling the treasures of its insight, and enriching the needy with teachings so as to bring both their cast of thought and their physical well-being to the uttermost degree of perfection. At other times it assumes the role of a friend, applying itself ceaselessly and tirelessly to the welfare of a deserving confrère, offering, when unable to be of immediate benefit, to draw on its supply of eloquence so as to improve the external fortunes of a friend through earnest intercession; seeking wherever necessary to benefit him also in a moral sense; and pointing out to him, with fraternal moderation, the faults and blemishes which might cast a false light upon his character, and whose discovery is welcome only from the lips of a friend, being but unsought importunity from any other. At still other times it assumes the sublime garb of philanthropy in the actual sense of the term, opening its willing hands and emptying its cornucopia of kindnesses onto the lap of a less fortunate and unhappy soul languishing in unwarranted need, his mouth stilled by an insurmountable sense of honour and silent shame.

My brethren! The true philanthropist, the man fully deserving of this honourable epithet, is not satisfied to sense in his heart the virtues of another man, but will seek to broadcast them to the world. He is not content merely to observe merits, but will search for them. Not only does he allow noble actions and exceptional talents to receive their just rewards, he takes upon himself the duty of becoming their zealous advocate at every opportunity. He will show concern for the good reputation of his fellows, concealing their faults and foibles unless compelled by greater duties to expose them, and resisting the public and treacherous deceit of slandering the innocent with the same firmness, and the same efficacy, as if his own good name were at stake. These, in outline, are the qualities of a truly philanthropic man, a man whose natural kindness is set in motion by more than a fleeting upsurge of emotion, being directed by well-reasoned wisdom and mature contemplation, a man convinced in his inmost being that each hand must aid and support the other. [...]

6 Anonymous [Johann Pezzl]: *Biographisches Denkmal Risbeck's, Verfasser der Briefe eines reisenden Franzosen und anderer Schriften* ['Biographical Monument to Risbeck, the Author of the "Letters of a French Traveller" and Other Writings'] (Kempten, 1786)

This fifty-four-page pamphlet, published in the year of Risbeck's death, presents a lively but by no means uncritical view of a writer whom Pezzl had met on many occasions. It is highly likely that Mozart, Pezzl and Risbeck were acquainted with each other in Salzburg during the late 1770s. Risbeck was born in 1749 or 1750 (according to Pezzl) in the town of Höchst, where his father owned a small handkerchief factory. He studied at Mainz University, at first with the intention of joining the ministry, but soon abandoned these plans for the study of law and undertook lengthy journeys. At this point in his life an episode occurred which Pezzl describes as follows:

Pages 9 to 11 Toward the end of Risbeck's years at university Germany was seized by the Age of Genius – by those unruly, unkempt, impulsive Calibans who crushed the iron fetters of rule and paid court to Mother Nature alone, forging in the heat of their ferment those monstrosities, fortunately for the most part now forgotten, which once haunted our stages and bookshops under the names of *Götz von Berlichingen*,[15] *Der Hofmeister*,[16] *Sturm und Drang*,[17] *Die Kindermörderin*[18] and *Prometheus, Deukalion und seine Rezensenten*.[19] Chance had placed the fathers of these works of genius in the vicinity of Höchst; and thus Risbeck made the personal acquaintance of Wolfgang Goethe, Max Klinger, Johann [*sic*] Michael Lenz and Heinrich Leopold Wagner. His receptive brain, unable to withstand these nearby flames, likewise caught fire, and for a while he could be found enthusing in Frankfurt, Hanau, Darmstadt and elsewhere, writing ballads, tales of murder and ghosts, and plying the genius's trade.

As we know, one of the first articles of faith in the creed of these geniuses was to foreswear all bourgeois and social amenities and every manner of regular occupation and office. Their vigour would bear no political fetters, no duties of office, no unfeeling and mechanical service which might provide honourable and legal nourishment to its

---

[15] The well-known early play by Goethe.

[16] A play of 1774 by Jakob Michael Reinhold Lenz (1751–92).

[17] A play of 1776 by Friedrich Maximilian Klinger (1752–1831).

[18] A play of 1776 by Heinrich Leopold Wagner (1747–79).

[19] A play of 1775 by H. L. Wagner.

practitioner. They fled and vilified such habits. In a man such as Risbeck this high art of paroxysm could not remain at full strength for very long, although it left upon him an imprint which he was never to eradicate as long as he lived.

A disagreement with a clergyman forced Risbeck to leave Mainz. He then travelled, probably around 1775, to Vienna, where he applied for a post in the civil service:

Pages 14 to 15 I am unable to say with certainty whether this enterprise miscarried or whether he gave up the idea himself. The latter is more probable, for he was still sufficiently beholden to the Age of Genius to avoid as far as possible any walk of life connected with a modicum of compulsion or routine labour.

Risbeck then became an actor at the Kärntnertor Theatre in Vienna, where he took both tragic and comic parts. By 1777, however, he had already left for Prague. After staying in Linz for half a year he arrived in December 1777 in Salzburg, where he settled for a lengthy stay:

Pages 19 to 20 Avoiding any particular occupation, Risbeck lived for himself, refreshing his earlier knowledge of the beaux arts, reading assiduously the latest publications, and setting out with greater alacrity to study statistics, politics and history.

At the death of his father, who had provided him with financial assistance, Risbeck was forced to earn his own livelihood as a writer. His very first book, Briefe über das Mönchswesen *(Letters on Monasticism, 1780), was a resounding success, earning Pezzl's high esteem and spawning numerous imitations and sequels. In 1779 Risbeck left Salzburg for Zurich, where he soon adopted a critical attitude toward Switzerland as well:*

Page 38 During his lengthy sojourn he developed quite different notions of those Swiss deities which have been lauded so highly in recent years – freedom, open-mindedness, moral innocence, equality of the estates, selflessness, forthrightness, and so on and so forth – and opinions quite different from those one ordinarily encounters in travelogues of this country.

In 1783, after a few years of travel, Risbeck settled in the town of Arau in the Swiss canton of Berne, where he completed his Briefe eines reisenden Franzosen *(Letters of a French Traveller). Pezzl concludes his booklet with the following description of this unusual man:*

Pages 50 to 54 Risbeck was of medium height, slight build and strong constitution. He had an open and winning expression, a lofty brow, indeed, a somewhat romantic physiognomy, together with an agile frame, easy manners and model deportment. [...]

Risbeck had a thorough command of his studies, spoke French, and could understand English and Italian. He had a solid knowledge of statistics, geography and politics, and was a connoisseur of writings in the beaux arts, which, however, he tended in his final six years to neglect.

In his social intercourse he was extraordinarily animated, talkative and witty. He was capable of entertaining an entire gathering and keeping it in high spirits. I have known few men more sociable than he. He loved jokes, banqueting and pleasure; and like all men of spirit he was an ardent admirer of the fair sex. A strong dose of light-headedness remained with him until the end, at times causing great confusion in his economic affairs. He would then return to work, and this with astonishing ease and rapidity. I myself witnessed how he wrote his *Briefe über das Mönchswesen* on single sheets of paper and handed them sheet by sheet to the printers. Indeed, he would often merely jot down the final phrase of the last page on a scrap of paper and resume writing a few days later without a break in thought, as though he had the entire manuscript before him.

Even the *Briefe eines reisenden Franzosen*, in which, admittedly, a goodly portion of haste was at times noticeable to all, were produced with a lightness of touch as if he were writing a newspaper.

He was, incidentally, a kindly, philanthropic and peaceable man, offensive to none, at home in any company, and capable of taking part in anything that might serve to enliven his circle. A pity that he led so excessively profligate a life, thereby shortening his days.

From the time he left Mainz Risbeck never again applied energetically for an ordinary office. His independence became a daily necessity: and when he worked, he did so in order to enjoy the fruits of his labour to the fullest and to his own taste.

Select bibliography

Source references in the text of this book are keyed to the following bibliography. The name of the author and the year of publication refer to the items in this list. Page references are not necessarily taken from the first edition but rather from the edition actually consulted, likewise listed here. A list of abbreviations and sigla can be found on page xvii.

Abert, Hermann (*1919–21*): *W. A. Mozart*, revised and enlarged fifth edition of Jahn (1856–9) (Leipzig). Quoted from 6th edn., 1923–4.

Adorno, Theodor W. (*1982*): 'Huldigung an Zerlina' [1952–3], *Gesammelte Schriften*, XVII (Frankfurt am Main).

(*1980*) *Ästhetische Theorie* (Frankfurt am Main).

Allanbrook, Wye Jamison (*1983*): *Rhythmic Gesture in Mozart: 'Le nozze di Figaro' and 'Don Giovanni'* (Chicago and London).

angebote: Organ für Ästhetik, ed. J. Petruschat and A. Trebess, no.1 (Berlin, GDR, 1988); no. 2 (Berlin, GDR, 1989).

Autexier, Philippe A. (*1984*): *Mozart et Liszt sub rosa* (Poitiers).

(*1986*) 'Wann wurde die Maurerische Trauermusik uraufgeführt?', *Mozart-Jahrbuch 1984–5* (Kassel).

(*1987*) 'La musique maçonnique', *Dix-huitième siècle* 19 (Paris).

Balázs, Eva N., L. Hammermayer, Hans Wagner, J. Wojtovic, eds. (*1979*): *Beförderer der Aufklärung in Mittel- und Osteuropa* (Berlin).

Bemetzrieder, Anton (*1771*): *Leçons de clavecin et principes d'harmonie* (Paris).

Benary, Peter (*1961*): *Die deutsche Kompositionslehre des 18. Jahrhunderts* (Leipzig). With appendix: Johann Adolph Scheibe: *Compendium Musices,* 1728–36.

Berlyne, D. E. (*1965*): *Measures of Aesthetic Preference,* Proceedings of the First International Colloquium on Experimental Aesthetics (Paris).

(*1973*) *Pleasure, Reward, Preference* (New York and London).

(*1974*) *Studies in the New Experimental Aesthetics* (New York, London, Sydney and Toronto).

Bertalanffy, Ludwig von (*1968*): *General System Theory* (New York).

Besseler, Heinrich (*1951*): 'Bach und das Mittelalter', *Bericht über die Wissenschaftliche Bachtagung Leipzig 1950* (Leipzig). Quoted from Besseler 1978.

(*1954*) 'Singstil und Instrumentalstil in der europäischen Musik', *Bericht über den Kongress der Gesellschaft für Musikforschung Bamberg 1953* (Kassel). Quoted from Besseler 1978.

(*1955*) 'Bach als Wegbereiter', *Archiv für Musikwissenschaft* 12. Quoted from Besseler 1978.

(*1958*) 'Mozart und die "Deutsche Klassik"', *Kongressbericht Mozartjahr 1956* (Graz and Cologne). Quoted from Besseler 1978.

(*1978*) *Aufsätze zur Musikästhetik und Musikgeschichte,* ed. Peter Gülke (Leipzig).

Bierwisch, Manfred (*1979*): 'Sprache und Musik', *Jahrbuch Peters 1977* (Leipzig).

(*1989*) 'Vergangenheit und Zukunft der kognitiven Linguistik'. Unpubd. typescript.

Blumauer, Aloys (*1782*): *Beobachtungen über Österreichs Aufklärung und Literatur* (Vienna). Quoted from Rosenstrauch-Königsberg 1988.

Blümml, Emil Karl, and **G. Gugitz (*1925*):** *Alt-Wiener Thespiskarren: die Frühzeit der Wiener Vorstadtbühnen* (Vienna).

Born, Gunthard (*1985*): *Mozarts Musiksprache* (Munich).

Bibliography

Born, Ignaz von (*1783–8*): *Physikalische Arbeiten der einträchtigen Freunde in Wien, aufgesammelt von Ignaz Edler von Born,* 4 vols. (Vienna).

(1783a) Joannis Physiophilii Specimen Monachologiae Linnaeana (n.p.).

(1783b) Neueste Naturgeschichte des Mönchthums (n.p.).

(1788) Über das Anquicken der gold- und silberhaltigen Erze (n.p.).

Braunbehrens, Volkmar (*1986*): *Mozart in Wien* (Munich).

Chladni, Ernst Florens Friedrich (*1980*): *Entdeckungen über die Theorie des Klanges* (Leipzig; 1787 repr.).

Chomsky, Noam (*1980*): *Rules and Representations* (Oxford).

Chrysander, Friedrich: 'Mozarts Werke', *Allgemeine musikalische Zeitung,* 16 (1881), cols. 65, 641, 657, 673, 689, 705, 721, 739, 785, 801, 817; and 17 (1882), cols. 8, 25, 36, 54, 70, 85, 103, 122, 893.

Dahlhaus, Carl (*1967*): 'Theorie der Musik', *Riemann Musiklexikon* (Mainz).

(1978) Die Idee der absoluten Musik (Kassel).

(1978) 'Musikalische Prosa', *Neue Zeitschrift für Musik,* 125 (1964). Also in Dahlhaus.

(1978) Schönberg und andere (Mainz).

Dahlhaus, Carl and M. Zimmermann (*1984*): *Musik zur Sprache gebracht* (Kassel).

Danuser, Hermann (*1978*): 'Musikalische Prosa', *Handwörterbuch der musikalischen Terminologie* (Wiesbaden).

Da Ponte, Lorenzo (*1924*): *Denkwürdigkeiten des Venezianers Lorenzo da Ponte* [1823–7], ed. G. Gugitz, 3 vols. (Dresden).

de la Motte, Helga (*1985*): *Handbuch der Musikpsychologie* (Laaber).

Dennerlein, Hanns (*1955*): *Der unbekannte Mozart: die Welt seiner Klavierwerke,* 2nd edn. (Leipzig).

Deutsch, O. E. (*1932*): *Mozart und die Wiener Logen* (Vienna).

(1965) Mozart: a Documentary Biography (Stanford).

Bibliography

Devrient, Eduard (*1967*): *Geschichte der deutschen Schauspielkunst* [1848], ed. R. Kabel and C. Trilse (Berlin, GDR).

Diderot, Denis (*1755*): 'Encyclopédie', *Encyclopédie*, V (Paris). Quoted from Diderot 1961.

(*1961*) *Philosophische Schrifte*, 2 vols. (Berlin, GDR).

(*1968*) *Ästhetische Schriften*, 2 vols. (Berlin, GDR).

Dieckmann, Friedrich (*1981*): 'Gespaltene Welt und ein liebendes Paar: Aspekte der Zauberflöte', *Oper heute* 4 (Berlin, GDR).

(*1984*) *Die Zauberflöte: Max Slevogts Randzeichnungen zu Mozarts Handschrift, mit dem Text von E. Schikaneder* (Berlin, GDR).

Dies, Albert Christoph (*1959*): *Biographische Nachrichten von Joseph Haydn* [1810], ed. H. Seeger (Berlin, GDR).

Dietze, Walter (*1985*): *Poesie der Humanität: Anspruch und Leistung im lyrischen Werk Johann Wolfgang Goethes* (Berlin and Weimar).

Eibl, Joseph Heinz (*1965*): *Wolfgang Amadeus Mozart: Chronik eines Lebens* (Kassel).

(*1971*) *Briefe: Kommentar*, V-VI (Kassel).

(*1976*) 'W. A. Mozart – ein Spieler? Bemerkungen zu Uwe Kraemers Untersuchung', *Musica* 30.

(*1980*) *Mozart: die Dokumente seines Lebens. Addenda und Corrigenda* (Leipzig).

Einstein, Alfred (*1946*): *Mozart: his Character, his Work* (London; repr. 1973).

(*1969*) *Köchelverzeichnis* 6th edn. (Leipzig).

Engel, Hans (*1954*): 'Die Finali der Mozartschen Opern', *Mozart-Jahrbuch*.

Fellerer, K. G. (*1985*) *Die Kirchenmusik W. A. Mozarts* (Laaber).

Finscher, Ludwig (*1962*): 'Vorwort', *W. A. Mozart: Haydn-Quartette*, study score (Kassel)

(*1988*) 'Don Giovanni', *Mozart-Jahrbuch 1987–8* (Kassel).

Fischer, Kurt von (*1986*): 'Das Dramatische in Mozarts Klavierkonzerten 1784', *Mozart-Jahrbuch* (Kassel).

Floros, Constantin (*1977–1985*): *Gustav Mahler*, I: *Die geistige Welt Gustav Mahlers* (Wiesbaden); II: *Mahler und die Symphonie des 19. Jahrhunderts* (Wiesbaden); III: *Die Symphonien* (Wiesbaden).

(*1979*) *Mozart-Studien* I (Wiesbaden).

Fontius, Martin (*1989*): 'Mozart im Hause Grimm', *Mozart und die Ästhetik der Aufklärung*, Sitzungsberichte der Akademie der Wissenschaften der DDR, no. 11/G (Berlin, GDR).

Forster, Georg (*1958–*): *Werke: Sämtliche Schriften, Tagebücher, Briefe in 18 Bänden*, ed. Gerhard Steiner, Horst Fiedler, Klaus Georg Popp, Siegfried Scheibe (Berlin, GDR).

Füssl, Karl Heinz (*1987*): 'Das Mahler-Bild von Constantin Floros', *Nachrichten zur Mahler-Forschung* 17 (Vienna).

Gemmingen, Otto (*1782–3*) *Der Weltmann: eine Wochenschrift* (Vienna).

(*1783*) *Der deutsche Hausvater oder Die Familie: ein Schauspiel in fünf Akten*, Theater der Deutschen, no. 19 (Königsberg and Leipzig).

(*1784–5*) *Magazin für Wissenschaft und Litteratur*.

(*1786–7*) *Wiener Ephemeriden* (Vienna).

Gerber, Ernst Ludwig (*1790*): *Lexikon der Tonkünstler* (Leipzig).

Giese, Alexander(*1988*): *Freimaurerisches Geistesleben im Zeitalter der Spätaufklärung am Beispiel des Journals für Freimaurer* (Graz). Commentary to reprint.

Goethe, Johann Wolfgang (*1988*): Letter to Schiller of 3–4 April 1801. Quoted from Heise.

'Naturformen der Dichtung', *Noten und Abhandlungen zu besserem Verständnis des West-östlichen Divans*. Quoted from *BA* III.

'Ludwig Tiecks "Dramaturgische Blätter"'. 1826. Quoted from *BA* XVII.

(*1968*) Conversation with Eckermann, 13 February 1829. Quoted from J. P. Eckermann: *Gespräche mit Goethe*, ed. F. Bergemann (Leipzig).

Goldschmidt, Harry (*1985*): 'Motivvariation und Gestaltmetamorphose', *Die Erscheinung Beethoven* (Leipzig).

Goldschmidt, Hugo (*1915*): *Die Musikästhetik des 18. Jahrhunderts und ihre Beziehung zu seinem Kunstschaffen* (Zurich and Leipzig).

Gottron, Adam B. (*1952*): *Mozart und Mainz* (Mainz).

(*1959*) *Mainzer Musikgeschichte von 1500 bis 1800* (Mainz).

Grimm, Friedrich Melchior (*1753*): *Le Petit Prophète de Boemisch Broda* (Paris).

(*1765*) 'Motif', *Encyclopédie*, X (Paris).

(*1765*) 'Poème lyrique', *Encyclopédie*, XII (Paris).

Gruber, Gernot (*1985*): *Mozart und die Nachwelt* (Salzburg and Vienna).

Gülke, Peter, ed. (*1984a*): *J. J. Rousseau: Musik und Sprache* (Wilhelmshaven).

(*1984b*) *Rousseau und die Musik oder Von der Zuständigkeit des Dilettanten* (Wilhelmshaven).

Hammermayer, Ludwig (*1979*): 'Zur Geschichte der europäischen Freimaurerei und der Geheimgesellschaften im 18. Jahrhundert', in Balázs.

Hammerstein, Reinhold (*1956*): 'Der Gesang der geharnischten Männer', *Archiv für Musikwissenschaft* 13.

Harnoncourt, Nicolaus (*1984*): *Der musikalische Dialog: Gedanken zu Monteverdi, Bach und Mozart* (Salzburg and Vienna). Quoted from 2nd edn., 1988.

Hawkins, John (*1776*): *A General History of the Science and Practice of Music* (London). Quoted from 3rd edn., 1875.

Hegel, G. W. F. (*1955*): *Ästhetik 1817–1829*, ed. G. Lukács (Berlin, GDR).

(*1955*) *Vorlesungen über die Philosophie der Weltgeschichte* [1822–

3], IV: *Die germanische Welt* (Hamburg). Quoted from GDR edn. (Berlin, GDR, 1970).

Heine, Heinrich (*1925*): 'Über die französische Bühne: vierter Brief, 1837', *Sämtliche Werke*, VI (Munich).

Heise, Wolfgang (*1976*): 'Probleme der Kunsttheorie Kants: ein Vortrag', *BzMw* 18.

(*1975*) 'Zehn Paraphrasen zu "Wandrers Nachtlied"', J. Kuczynski and W. Heise: *Bild und Begriff* (Berlin, GDR).

(*1988*) *Hölderlin: Schönheit und Geschichte* (Berlin and Weimar).

Heister, Hanns-Werner (*1983*): *Das Konzert: Theorie einer Kulturform*, 2 vols. (Wilhelmshaven).

Helmholtz, Hermann von (*1863*): *Die Lehre von den Tonempfindungen*. Brunswick, 6th edn., 1913.

Hildesheimer, Wolfgang (*1977*): *Mozart* (Munich).

Hoffmann, E. T. A. (*1900*): 'Beethovens Instrumentalmusik', *Fantasiestücke in Callot's Manier*, III: *Kreisleriana*, no. 4. Quoted from *Sämtliche Werke*, I (Leipzig).

Hoke, Hans-Gunter (*1962*): 'Programmmusik', *MGG* X (Kassel).

Holbach, Paul-Henri Dietrich, Baron d' (*1770*): *Essai sur les Préjugés* (London). Quoted from the German translation by W. Blochwitz: *Essay über die Vorurteile* (Leipzig, 1972).

Irmen, Hans-Josef (*1988*): *Mozart – Mitglied geheimer Gesellschaften* (Neustadt an der Aisch).

Jahn, Otto (*1856–9*): *W. A. Mozart*, 4 vols. (Leipzig).

Kaden, Christian (*1984*): *Musiksoziologie* (Berlin, GDR).

Kann, Robert A. (*1960*): *A Study in Austrian Intellectual History* (New York).

Kant, Immanuel (*1790*): *Kritik der Urteilskraft* (Berlin and Libau).

Kerman, Joseph W. (*1985*): *Musicology* (London).

King, Alexander Hyatt (*1955*): *Mozart in Retrospect: Studies in Criticism and Bibliography* (London).

Klaus, Georg (*1965*): *Die Macht des Wortes: ein erkenntnistheoretisch-pragmatischer Traktat* (Berlin, GDR).

Klenner, Hermann (*1984*): *Vom Recht der Natur zur Natur des Rechtes* (Berlin, GDR).

Knepler, Georg (*1976*): 'Ein Instrumentalthema Mozarts', *BzMw* 18, no. 2.

(*1980*) 'Versuch einer historischen Grundlegung der Musikästhetik', *Gedanken über Musik* (Berlin, GDR).

(*1988*) 'Die Rolle des Ästhetischen in der Menschwerdung', *Weimarer Beiträge* 34, no. 3.

Koch, Heinrich Christoph (1782, 1787–93): *Versuch einer Anleitung zur Composition*, I (Rudolstadt), II-III (Leipzig).

Koch, Richard (*1911*): *Mozart: Freimaurer und Illuminat* (Bad Reichenhall).

Komponisten, auf Werk und Leben befragt: ein Kolloquium, ed. Harry Goldschmidt, Georg Knepler and Konrad Niemann (Leipzig, 1985).

Kossok, Manfred (*1986*): 'Frankreichs Grosse Revolution', *Spectrum* 17, no. 9.

(*1989*) *In Tyrannos: Revolutionen der Weltgeschichte von den Hussiten zur Commune* (Leipzig).

Kraemer, Uwe (*1976*): 'Wer hat Mozart verhungern lassen?', *Musica* 30.

Krauss, Werner (*1963*): *Die französische Literatur im Spiegel der deutschen Literatur des 18. Jahrhunderts* (Berlin, GDR).

(*1987*) 'Einführung in das Studium der französischen Aufklärung' [1952], *Das wissenschaftliche Werk, Aufklärung*, II: *Frankreich* (Berlin and Weimar).

Kretzschmar, Hermann (*1911*): 'Anregungen zur Förderung musikalischer Hermeneutik' [1902], *Gesammelte Aufsätze*, II (Leipzig).

(*1911*) 'Die Correspondance littéraire als musikgeschichtliche Quelle' [1903], *Gesammelte Aufsätze*, II (Leipzig).

(*1911*) 'Neue Anregungen zur Förderung musikalischer Hermeneutik' [1905], *Gesammelte Aufsätze*, II (Leipzig).

Kühne, Lothar (*1985*): *Haus und Landschaft* (Dresden).

Kunze, Stefan (*1984*): *Mozarts Opern* (Stuttgart).

Landon, H. C. Robbins (*1988*): *Mozart's Last Year* (London).

(*1989*) *Mozart: the Golden Years* (London).

Lange, Joseph (*1808*): *Erinnerungen* (Vienna).

Lenin, W. I. (*1963 ff.*): *Werke* (Berlin).

Lessing, Gotthold Ephraim (*1875*): *Hamburgische Dramaturgie*
[1766–8]. Quoted from *Werke in acht Bänden*, ed. R. Gosche,
VIII (Berlin).

(*1875*) *Ernst und Falk: Gespräche für Freimäurer* [1778–9]. Quoted
from *Werke in acht Bänden*, ed. R. Gosche, VI (Berlin).

Lewandowski, Theodor, ed. (*1980*): *Linguistisches Wörterbuch*, 3rd
edn. (Heidelberg).

Lichtenberg, Georg Christoph (*1975*): *Aphorismen*. Quoted from
Die französische Revolution im Spiegel der deutschen Literatur,
ed. C. Träger (Leipzig).

Mahling, Christoph-Helmut (*1970*): 'Zum vorliegenden Band',
NMA, IV/11/6 (Kassel).

Mann, Thomas (*1978*): *Der Zauberberg* [1924] (Frankfurt).

Massin, Jean and Brigitte (*1959*): *Wolfgang Amadeus Mozart* (Paris).

Mendelssohn, Moses (*1978*): *Kleine philosophische Schriften* (Berlin,
GDR).

Moos, Paul (*1901*): *Die Philosophie der Musik von Kant bis Eduard
von Hartmann* (Leipzig, 2nd edn., 1922).

Mozart, Leopold (*1756*): *Gründliche Violinschule* (Augsburg, 3rd
edn., 1787, rept. Leipzig 1956).

Mozart, Wolfgang Amadé (*1955–91*): *Neue Ausgabe sämtlicher
Werke* (Kassel and Basle).

Bibliography

(1962–3) *Briefe und Aufzeichnungen*, ed. Wilhelm A. Bauer and Otto Erich Deutsch (Kassel).

Müller, Heiner (*1986*): 'Gespräch mit Sylvère Lotringer' [1982], *Gesammelte Irrtümer: Interviews und Gespräche* (Frankfurt am Main).

Nagel, Ivan (*1985*): *Autonomie und Gnade: über Mozarts Opern* (Munich and Vienna).

Nettl, Paul (*1955*): 'Freiermusik', *Die Musik in Geschichte und Gegenwart, Allgemeine Enzyklopädie der Musik*, ed. Friedrich Blume, IV (Kassel).

Niemetschek, Franz X. (*1798*): *Leben des K. K. Kapellmeisters Wolfgang Gottlieb Mozart* (Prague).

Nissen, Georg Nikolaus von (*1828*): *Biographie W. A. Mozart's, nach dessen Tode herausgegeben von Constanze, Wittwe von Nissen, früher Wittwe Mozart* (Leipzig).

Noske, Frits (*1977*): *The Signifier and the Signified* (The Hague).

Novello, Vincent and Mary (*1955*): *A Mozart Pilgrimage*, ed. R. Hughes (London).

Pahlen, Kurt (*1979*): *Einführung und Kommentar zu W. A. Mozart, Le nozze di Figaro, Textbuch* (Mainz and Munich, 4th edn., 1988).

Pezzl, Johann (*1783*): *Faustin oder das philosophische Jahrhundert* (Zurich).

(*1784*) *Reise durch den Baiernschen Kreis* (Salzburg).

(*1784*) *Marokkanische Briefe* (Frankfurt and Leipzig).

(*1786*) *Biographisches Denkmal Risbeck's* (Kempten).

(*1786–90*) *Skizze von Wien* (Vienna and Leipzig).

(*1787*) *Vertraute Briefe über Katholiken und Protestanten* (Strassburg).

(*1790*) *Charakteristik Joseph II* (Vienna, 3rd edn., 1803).

(*1792*) 'Lebensbeschreibung des Hofrats Ignaz von Born', *Österreichische Biographien*, IV (Vienna).

Bibliography

Pirker, Max, ed. (*1927*): *Teutsche Arien* (Vienna).

Plath, Wolfgang (*1982*): 'Vorwort', *Einzelstücke für Klavier, NMA* IX/27/2 (Kassel).

Prüsener (*1972*): 'Lesegesellschaften', *Börsenblatt für den deutschen Buchhandel* 28.

Redlich, Hans F. (*1957*): *Alban Berg* (Vienna).

Reschke, Renate (*1989*): 'Geschichte denken', *angebote* 2 (Berlin, GDR).

Risbeck, Johann Kaspar (*1784*): *Briefe über das Mönchswesen von einem catholischen Pfarrer an einen Freund*, 2nd edn. (n.p.).

(*1780*) *Briefe eines reisenden Franzosen über Deutschland an seinen Bruder zu Paris*, 3rd edn. (n.p.).

(*1788–90*) *Geschichte der Deutschen* (Zurich).

Rommel, Otto (*1952*): *Die Alt-Wiener Volkskomödie* (Vienna).

Rosen, Charles (*1971*): *The Classical Style: Haydn, Mozart, Beethoven* (London).

(*1980*) *Sonata Forms* (London).

Rosenstrauch-Königsberg, Edith (*1979*): 'Ausstrahlung des "Journals für Freimaurer"', in Balázs.

(*1988*) ed.: *Literatur der Aufklärung 1765–1800*, (Berlin, GDR).

Rousseau, Jean Jacques (*1767*): *Dictionnaire de musique* (Geneva).

(*1965*) *Confessions* [1770]. Quoted from the German edn. (Leipzig).

(*1984*) *Musik und Sprache: Ausgewählte Schriften*, translated by Dorothea and Peter Gülke (Wilhelmshaven).

Ruf, Wolfgang (*1977*): *Die Rezeption von Mozarts 'Le nozze di Figaro' bei den Zeitgenossen* (Wiesbaden).

Scheel, Heinrich (*1975, 1981, 1989*): *Die Mainzer Republik*, I: *Protokolle des Jakobinerklubs*; II: *Protokolle des Rheinisch-deutschen Nationalkonvents mit Quellen zu seiner Vorgeschichte*; III: *Die erste bürgerlich-demokratische Republik auf deutschem Boden: Eine Darstellung* (Berlin, GDR).

Bibliography

Scheibe, Johann Adolph (*1961*): *Compendium musices* [c.1730]. Quoted from Benary.

Scheit, Gerhard (*1988*): *Am Beispiel von Brecht und Bronnen: Krise und Kritik des modernen Dramas* (Vienna, Cologne and Graz).

Schenk, Erich (*1975*): *Mozart: sein Leben, seine Welt*, 2nd edn. (Munich).

Schering, Arnold (*1934*): *Beethoven in neuer Deutung* (Leipzig).

(*1936*) *Beethoven und die Dichtung* (Berlin).

Schiller, Friedrich (*1988*): 'Über den Zusammenhang der tierischen Natur des Menschen mit seiner geistigen' [1780]. Quoted from Heise.

(*1967*) 'Die Schaubühne als eine moralische Anstalt betrachtet' [1784], *Schillers Werke in fünf Bänden*, 1 (Berlin and Weimar).

(*1988*) 'Über die ästhetische Erziehung des Menschen' [1795]. Quoted from Heise.

(*1988*) Letter to Goethe, 27 March 1801. Quoted from Heise.

Schindler, Otto G. (*1976*): *Das Publikum des Burgtheaters in der josephinischen Ära* (Vienna).

Schmid, Ernst Fritz (*1953*): 'Der Mozartfreund J. Bullinger', *Mozart-Jahrbuch* (Salzburg).

(*1955*) *W. A. Mozart: Werke für zwei Klaviere, Kritischer Bericht, NMA* (Kassel).

Schoenberg, Arnold (*1975*): 'Brahms the Progressive' [1933], *Style and Idea* (London).

(*1989*) *Stil und Gedanke*, ed. Frank Schneider (Leipzig).

Schubart, Christian Friedrich Daniel (*1774–7, 1787–91*): *Deutsche Chronik*.

Schubert, Franz (*1964*): 'Klage an das Volk' [1824], *Schubert: die Dokumente seines Lebens*, ed. O. E. Deutsch (Leipzig).

Schumann, Robert (*1988*): 'Kulenkamp, Caprice (D moll)' [c.1834], *Schriften über Musik und Musiker*, ed. H. Simon (Leipzig).

Bibliography

Seume, Johann Gottfried (*1806*): *Mein Sommer im Jahr 1805* (Leipzig).

Siegmund-Schultze, Walther (*1939*): 'Mozarts Vokal- und Instrumentalmusik in ihren motivisch-thematischen Beziehungen'. Typescript.

Spiel, Hilde (*1962*): *Fanny von Arnstein oder Die Emanzipation: ein Frauenleben an der Zeitenwende 1758–1818* (Frankfurt am Main).

Steiner, Gerhard (*1973*): *Jakobinerschauspiel und Jakobinertheater* (Stuttgart).

 (*1977*) *Georg Forster* (Stuttgart).

 (*1985*) *Freimaurer und Rosenkreuzer: Georg Forsters Weg durch Geheimbünde* (Berlin, GDR).

Steiner, Gerhard et al., eds. (*1968–*): *Georg Forsters Werke*, 18 vols. (Berlin, GDR).

Tembrock, Günter (*1980*): *Grundriss der Verhaltensforschung* (Jena).

 (*1983*) 'Interdisziplinäre Probleme zwischen Musikwissenschaft und Bioakustik: Protokoll eines Gesprächs zwischen Doris Stockmann und Günter Tembrock', *BzMw*, 25, 3–4.

Thomson, Katharine (*1977*): *The Masonic Thread in Mozart* (London).

Till, Nicholas (*1992*): *Mozart and the Enlightenment: Truth, Virtue and Beauty in Mozart's Operas*, (London).

Tyson, Alan (*1987*): *Mozart: Studies of the Autograph Scores* (Cambridge, Mass., and London).

Valjavec, Fritz (*1944*): *Der Josephinismus* (Brno, Munich and Vienna).

Wagner, Hans (*1979*): 'Die politische und kulturelle Bedeutung der Freimaurer im 18. Jahrhundert', in Balász.

Wagner, Richard: '"Zukunftsmusik": an einen französischen Freund', *Gesammelte Schriften und Dichtungen*, third edn., VII (Leipzig, n.d.).

Wallin, Nils L. (*1992*): *Biomusicology: Neurophysiological, Neuro-*

psychological and Evolutionary Perspectives on the Origins and Purposes of Music (New York).

Wangermann, Ernst (*1959*): *From Joseph II to the Jacobin Trials* (London).

(*1989*) 'Das österreichische Echo auf die französische Revolution', *Tagebuch*, III (Vienna).

Weimann, Robert (*1967*): *Shakespeare und die Tradition des Volkstheaters* (Berlin, GDR).

(*1982*) *Kunstensemble und Öffentlichkeit* (Halle and Leipzig).

(*1988*) *Shakespeare und die Macht der Mimesis: Autorität und Repräsentation im elisabethanischen Theater* (Berlin, GDR).

Wieland, Christoph Martin (*1826*): *Versuch über das deutsche Singspiel* [1775], *Sämmtliche Werke*, XLV (Leipzig).

Winter, Eduard (*1962*): *Der Josefinismus: die Geschichte des österreichischen Reformkatholizismus 1740–1848* (Brno, 1943); revised edition (Berlin, GDR).

Wiora, Walter (*1949*): 'Absolute Musik', *MGG*, I (Kassel), cols. 46–56.

Wurzbach, Constantin von (*1856–91*): *Biographisches Lexikon des Kaiserthums Österreich* (Vienna).

Wyzewa, Théodore de, and **G. de Saint-Foix** (*1911–46*): *Mozart: sa vie musicale de l'enfance à la pleine maturité* (Paris).

Zelter, Karl Friedrich, and **Johann Wolfgang Goethe** (*1987*): *Briefwechsel: eine Auswahl*, ed. H.-G. Ottenburg (Leipzig).

Index

Index